TECHNOLOGY, INNOVATION, and POLICY 3

Series of the Fraunhofer Institute
for Systems and Innovation Research (ISI)

Guido Reger · Ulrich Schmoch (Eds.)

Organisation of Science and Technology at the Watershed

The Academic and Industrial Perspective

With 82 Figures
and 16 Tables

Physica-Verlag

A Springer-Verlag Company

658.57
O 68

Guido Reger and Dr. Ulrich Schmoch
Fraunhofer Institute for
Systems and Innovation Research
Breslauer Str. 48
D-76139 Karlsruhe, Germany

ISBN 3-7908-0910-1 Physica-Verlag Heidelberg

JR Die Deutsche Bibliothek – CIP-Einheitsaufnahme

Organisation of science and technology at the watershed: th
academic and industrial perspective; with 16 tables / Guido
Reger; Ulrich Schmoch (ed.). – Heidelberg: Physica-Verl.,
1996
   (Technology, innovation, and policy; 3)
   ISBN 3-7908-0910-1
NE: Reger, Guido [Hrsg.]; GT

SPIN: 105 331 28   88/2202-5 4 3 2 1 0 - Printed on acid-free paper

Foreword

A modern system of production and dissemination of research, technology and development (RTD) results is characterized by a high push/pull interaction and close linkages within the research system, as well as between the research system and industry/public demand. This is contrary to the traditional understanding of technology transfer. Partly the European Union also used this traditional concept in promoting technology transfer and innovation. For example, the mandate of the former European VALUE Programme was the exploitation and dissemination of *existing* results of RTD of the framework programme.

The specific ways of producing RTD results have a decisive influence on the dissemination and exploitability for the ultimate clients of this dissemination process, industry and society. Modern systems of knowledge production will be transdisciplinary, application-oriented and network-dominated in contrast to discipline-based, internally driven and individually dominated traditional systems. Within the new dynamic systems, public bodies like national governments or the European Commission increasingly have to play the role of a mediator between disciplines, institutions and nations. One major aim is the creation of stronger linkages between basic and applied research, for which new ways in the management of R&D systems are required. This dynamic interaction between science and technology is the main focus of this book. Therefore it emphasizes a highly relevant policy issue.

From the perspective of firms and their technology management, as well as from the viewpoint of research systems, the studies in this book show in an exemplary manner how the evolution of concepts of innovation, empirical evidence of modern research systems and firms' technology management lead to new insights. They are the basis for highly relevant policy conclusions and the development of a new integrated policy approach promoting dissemination and exploitation.

Frieder Meyer-Krahmer
Director of Fraunhofer Institute for Systems and Innovation Research, Karlsruhe, Germany

Table of Contents

Introduction: the rationale behind this book

The economic development of the 20th century is characterised by an increasing significance of science-based technology. At the beginning of the 21st century the impact of science and technology will become even more important, and the limits between pure basic research, oriented basic research and applied research will become blurred. Against this background, a more detailed understanding of the interaction between science and technology is necessary, in order to develop appropriate tools for future R&D management and technology policy.

In 1992, the General Directorate XIII of the European Commission launched a new research programme called VALUE II which aims at an improved dissemination and exploitation of European research activities. Within this programme, the sub-section Interface II concerns the examination of the interface between European activities and the scientific community. According to the recommendations of the Think-Tank group of VALUE II, Interface II should analyse new ways of diffusing already existing results of research supported by the Commission as well as a better integration of scientific institutions in the conception of new European research programmes. Therefore, the aims of VALUE II, Interface II, largely meet the above formulated need of a better understanding of the interaction between science and technology.

The present book consists of three research projects which the Fraunhofer Institute for Systems and Innovation Research (ISI) in Karlsruhe carried out within the framework of VALUE II, Interface II[1]. Each of the three parts of the book represents a revised version of a separate final report to the European Commission and can be read independently of the other parts of the book. In consequence, each part has its own introduction and executive summary; furthermore, specific conclusions for the work of the European Commission are drawn. Due to the common context of these projects, the three parts have certain overlaps; but at the same time, a variety of interesting cross references appear.

The first part describes the structure of the science/technology interface on different levels of aggregation and with different approaches. A major concern of this part is to analyse the role of science for the generation of new technologies and to examine

---

[1] Schmoch et al. (1993b), Reger et al. (1994), Schmoch et al. (1994).

the respective organisational and institutional problems. Within these considerations, special emphasis is placed on the view-point of academic institutions. By contrast, the second part analyses the challenges of R&D management from the perspective of industrial enterprises, where-by scientific research and the collaboration with academic institution appear to be only one of many other requirements. Despite the different approaches, both parts show many linkages, for example concerning the internationalisation of R&D, the growing need for interdisciplinarity or the role of R&D networks. At the same time, many statements are relativised by the comparison of both parts; for example, the specific context of models of the innovation process becomes obvious: the models presented in the first part aim primarily at the description of the interaction between academic and industrial institutions whereas the models of the second part chiefly describe the organisation of R&D within companies. Parts I and II are chiefly based on a literature survey; in addition, part II contains a variety of illustrative examples based on company interviews.

Part III documents the results of two field studies in the science-intensive areas of medical lasers and neural networks. The field analysis includes interviews with companies, non-industrial research centres and universities, thus part III can be seen as an illustration of the theoretical conclusions of part I and part II. As an example, the communication and division of labour between different types of research institutions in the area of neural networks gives an idea of the implementation of the interaction model of part I in the real world.

The literature surveys on different topics given in each part of the book are far from being complete. The major aim of the book is to bring together the variety of different approaches for describing the challenges of modern R&D management from an academic and industrial perspective. Therefore, only some representative works of literature were chosen for the introduction of each sub-topic. The authors want to demonstrate that the R&D management in science-based fields of technology cannot be tackled by a one-dimensional approach, but has a variety of facets. Therefore, only a realistic multi-dimensional approach can lead to an adequate picture and to appropriate recommendations for research and technology policy.

Karlsruhe, December 1995

Guido Reger   Ulrich Schmoch

PART I

U. Schmoch, S. Hinze, G. Jäckel, N. Kirsch, F. Meyer-Krahmer, G. Münt

The Role of the Scientific Community
in the Generation of Technology

Executive summary of part I

Part I describes constraints and opportunities for the dissemination and exploitation of research and development (R&D) results, particularily those of European research programmes. The related study was performed within the framework of the VALUE II programme in the sub-section Interface II, which is focussed on the situation of the scientific community. Against this background, the aim of part I is to get a better insight into the factors which determine the structure and the effectiveness of the interface between science and technology (S&T interface), with a special focus on the perspective of the scientific community. The study largely took the form of a survey of already existing publications in order to determine the state of the art and to identify promising areas for future investigations. As to the special needs of the European Commission (EC), the general findings on the characteristics of the S&T interface can be largely transferred to the interface between EC research and the scientific community. On this basis, some recommendations on the ex-post exploitation and dissemination of results of EC research and technical development (RTD) can be elaborated. It is, however, more important to work out structures for future EC RTD programmes wherein an optimal participation of the European scientific community can be realized. As an important result, the study underlines that, apart from "management of R&D", the "management of R&D systems" - instead of the general context of R&D - will be highly influential for the exploitation process.

The scientific community being the focal area of this study, it is necessary to have an adequate definition of science. Generally, there exist two different approaches to definition: an institutional approach and a cognitive approach. The institutional approach differentiates between "scientific institutions" on the one hand and "industry" on the other hand. This definition can be helpful for a pragmatic distinction between the industrial and the non-industrial research sector and a description of the different behaviours of academic and industrial researchers.

Cognitive definitions of science chiefly emphasise the systematic production of new knowledge, and in consequence there exists a broad similarity to definitions of different types of R&D and of technology. A detailed comparison of general definitions of science and types of R&D according to the Frascati Manual shows that scientific activities are not limited to basic research, but include applied R&D as well. In consequence, a large proportion of scientific activity is performed in industry. Even if the definition is restricted to basic research, industrial researchers largely perform scientific research, and they participate in scientific discussions by contributing articles to scientific journals or attending scientific conferences. It is important to recognise the involvement of industrial researchers in the scientific community is important, because this group determines the co-operation between industrial laboratories and non-industrial research institutions. This also applies to the special co-operation within EC RTD programmes. As a consequence for the dissemination of results of EC research programmes, any information to the scientific community should be circulated not only among non-industrial institutions, but sent to industrial researchers as well. Furthermore, the stimulation of publishing the outcome of EC programmes in scientific journals is helpful to address all relevant actors of the scientific community.

A comparison of the R&D systems in Germany, Great Britain, and Greece reveals that the institutional structures on the national level differ widely. There are, of course, enormous differences between advanced and less-favoured countries: In advanced countries, the largest part of R&D is performed and financed by industry, whereas in less-favoured countries public institutions dominate the R&D system. Empirical studies show that in the latter countries basic R&D has no measurable impact on their international competitiveness, in contrast to advanced countries. Therefore, the initiation and promotion of R&D within industry and the establishment of effective transfer mechanisms between the public and the private sector are major aims for less-favoured countries.

In advanced countries, the quantitative volume of research by universities is considerable, but the amount of formal co-operation between university and industry is relatively low. Between universities and industry, there exists a more or less differentiated landscape of *intermediate research institutions*. In the United Kingdom, these institutions are mainly organized according to technical areas, whereas in Germany they are often brought together within associations with special missions such as basic research, contract research, or co-operative research. In any case, these intermediate institutions play an important role for the knowledge transfer from (basic) science to (applied) technology. Any activity which aims at the scientific community must include these intermediate research institutions, a statement which applies to advanced as well as less-favoured countries.

A review of literature shows that it is very difficult to evaluate the impact of basic science on technology in an exact quantitative way. In any case, the contribution of science to the development of technology is higher than is reflected in the general figures of formal co-operation between non-industrial institutes and industry. A major obstacle to making an appropriate assessment is the large time-lag which can often be observed between a scientific discovery and its introduction into technical applications. Furthermore, a characteristic of many radical innovations is the combination of scientific knowledge of different areas; thus interdisciplinarity is a main feature of leading-edge innovations. Therefore, the transfer path of basic scientific knowledge is mostly obscured and traditional cost-benefit approaches are not appropriate. New information-theoretic descriptions of basic research seem to be more prosperous.

The science intensity of technology is not homogeneous, but varies widely among technical areas. Therefore, it is possible to distinguish science-intensive and less science-intensive areas. Science-based firms have a key function for the whole economy, because they give decisive input to other types of companies such as supplier-dominated firms, scale-intensive firms, or specialized equipment suppliers. On the basis of a patent analysis, it is possible to distinguish science-intensive areas and to operationalize the element of science intensity for a variety of analyses. These investigations confirm the role of science as a driving force for technological innovations and for economic growth.

The most appropriate way to describe the knowledge transfer between non-industrial institutions and industry is the so-called network approach. It describes the co-operation of different actors in developing, manufacturing, and selling products and processes and also in combining their respective resources. The latter can be subdivided into tangible resources (e.g. machines, natural resources and other equipment), human capital (e.g., work-force, know-how, connections), and financial assets. In the co-operation between industry and non-industrial institutions, human capital is the most important factor. The other resources, however, have to be taken into account as well.

The main channels of transfer can be subdivided into:

- information transfer
- research contacts
- transfer of personnel
- scientific training

The most widely used channel is the direct or indirect information transfer between universities, other non-industrial research institutions and industry. A successful transfer, however, is possible only if a sufficient absorptive capacity on the side of industry exists. Therefore, industry must perform a certain level of internal research for an effective use of scientific advances.

Direct research contacts and the transfer of personnel are the most effective transfer channels; but especially in the interaction of universities and industry, many barriers exist. In the case of personnel transfer, the main barriers are organizational problems, career incentives, and limitations on social mobility. In the case of direct research co-operation, e.g., contract research, a variety of factors is crucial for the success:

- match of interest
- bridging different structures
- sufficient potentials
- maturity of results
- free information exchange
- confidence
- appropriate transfer level

Especially broad structural differences between universities and industry hamper an efficient knowledge transfer. The situation in universities is characterized, among other points, by a long-term orientation and, consequently, a sluggish re-orientation and resource allocation to upcoming fields of research. Furthermore, academic scientists have a vital interest in publishing their results, because it is crucial for their academic career. In contrast, companies are short-term and application-oriented and have a vital interest in immediate reaction to emerging market requirements. They have less interest in publishing their results because they want to maintain their lead in knowledge and not transfer their research results to their competitors. Nevertheless, research contacts between universities and industry do take place, because universities are interested in new results of applied research and need additional funding for their activities, whereas industry is interested in getting new scientific results with limited costs.

In science-intensive areas, the strong interest in common research fields increasingly leads to the emergence of techno-scientific communities comprising academic and industrial researchers. This common interest stimulates the members of these communities to overcome the above-mentioned barriers.

Research on the economic structures of regions has revealed that the local proximity of different partners can be stimulating for the creation of R&D networks and helps to reduce transfer costs. Therefore, the focus of the Commission on international co-operation can only be viewed as an addition to national and regional R&D programmes. With its growing role, the Commission will have to persue regional approaches not only in less-favoured countries, but in advanced countries as well.

Because of the strategic role of science-based technologies, the promotion of co-operation between non-industrial research institutions and industry will become a crucial element of R&D policy. For that purpose, a variety of instruments, which originally were conceived to aid co-operation among firms, are available:

- new media of S&T information
- contract research institutions
- co-operative research institutions
- transfer units, innovation consultancies
- network approach
- exchange of persons
- tax reduction, subsidies for extramural R&D
- subsidies for selected R&D co-operation projects

The Commission already applies most of the above-mentioned instruments for the promotion of R&D co-operation. Up to now, it has not used institutional arrangements as a major instrument for the improvement of links between universities, research institutions and industries. In the framework of RTD activities of the EC, the establishment of temporary networks consisting of various types of existing institutions seems to be appropriate for the achievement of strategic goals. This present lack of institutional arrangements can be regarded as a real deficit, because this approach has proved to be very successful in areas of leading-edge technology. In contrast to the generally quite short-termed RTD programmes, these networks should have a longer perspective and the freedom to adjust research aims according to intermediate results. Of course, experiences at the national level cannot be directly applied to the transnational level. Nevertheless, it seems to be promising to consider this institutional approach in more detail.

In the sixties, the knowledge transfer from science to technology was generally discussed in a linear perspective. According to this view, basic research is, first of all, performed by universities and other non-industrial research institutions, applied research and experimental development by industries. In this model, the knowledge transfer is limited to a short period when the results of academic research have reached a sufficient maturity. In contrast to that, recent models state a continuous interaction betweeen industries and non-industrial institutions during the whole innovation process. Even after the first introduction of a new product or process into the market, there is still a continuous improvement in the form of incremental innovations or micro-radical innovations. The research in this phase is also demanding and not simple routine and therefore still interesting for non-industrial researchers.

As a further finding of new models, the different types of R&D activity, i.e., basic research, applied research, and experimental development, do not follow each other in a sequential way, but generally happen in parallel at different stages of the innovation process. Even the stages of innovation do not always have a strict sequence. Thus, in some cases the technical design takes place before the development of the related theory.

In any case, the promotion of co-operation between academic institutions and industry should aim at the whole cycle of innovation and not only at its early stages. The experiences in later application-oriented stages can be a fruitful stimulation for transforming pure basic research into oriented basic research. Furthermore, the decisive bridging function of intermediate institutions between universities and industries has to be taken into account.

All in all, national systems of innovation consist of a variety of elements, all of them very complex and largely intertwined. The most important elements are the firms and their R&D activity; the structure of industry; the governmental policy in the area of science, technology and economy; the education and training system; and non-industrial R&D institutions. The effectiveness of a national system of innovation is largely determined by a close, effective interaction of these elements, so a steady process of interactive learning is necessary.

Because of the variety of constituting elements, national systems of innovation differ considerably and one can draw the conclusion that it is almost impossible to find an optimal structure. As all elements of national systems of innovations are closely intertwined in a complex balance, specific national patterns and long-standing traditions predominante and cannot be changed overnight. A radical intervention at one point can, therefore, cause unforeseeable effects in other areas. Hence, every change has to be planned with care. Furthermore, the modification of existing systems should not rely on pure copying of other national systems which are esteemed as being more efficient. Each nation should shape its own system according to its unique framework conditions, because the competitiveness of the various nations is largely based upon differences, not similarities.

As to the specific situation of universities, the academic system is based on historical developments and traditions, too. A nation's academic structure depends heavily on a two-fold influential structure which might be attributed on the one hand to academic tradition and on the other hand to the impact of industry. Industrial efforts to create science-intensive goods often affect the direction and contents of education and research at universities. Especially the structures of contract research largely depend on academic traditions, the general social background, and the legal framework. In consequence, the role of universities within national systems of innovation differs widely.

All in all, a broad range of publications on the position of the scientific community in national systems of innovation, especially on a general descriptive level, already exists. There are, however, some open research questions which - building on this state of the art - should be examined in further detail:

1. The distinction between academic and industrial research is not as clear-cut as often assumed. Against the background of the emergence of science-based technologies, a deeper analysis of structural similarities and convergences is necessary.

2. The institutional and legal framework of the different research institutions have to be examined in a more detailed way, because they largely determine the constraints and opportunities of the dissemination and exploitation of RTD results.

3. As to national innovation systems, further detailed comparisons of strategic elements are more promising than analyses on a general level.

Figure A: Main elements of the RTD dissemination policies of the European Commission

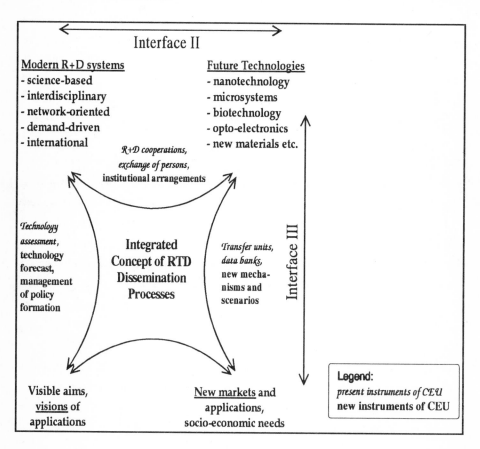

4. The interaction of different institutions being a key element of the innovation process, further research on the co-operation intensity and the change of roles during the technology life cycle is needed.
5. As to the role of basic research, further work based on an information-theoretic concept is more promosing than traditional cost-benefit approaches.
6. Information-theoretic approaches will be also helpful for the analysis of innovation networks.

As to the dissemination of RTD, the basic lesson of this study leads to an integrated approach in several dimensions instead of a uni-directional supply of science/technology results. The main dimensions of future activities should be future technologies, modern R&D systems, new markets and socio-economic needs, and visions of new applications of technology (cf. figure A). In consequence, the dissemination policy should not be limited to offering existing RTD results, but already intervene at the stage of programme design as the conditions of RTD production are decisive for the efficiency of dissemination. This approach can be called "integrated dissemination policy".

As to the elements of an integrated dissemination policy, the present study provides a variety of indications:

The programme design should take the structures of modern R&D systems into account. These systems are characterized by the growing importance of science-based technologies and interdisciplinary research topics. The RTD activities should be network-oriented and international; thus the programme design should not only aim at technological areas, but at the integration of relevant institutions as well. Finally, modern R&D systems are not only built on technological potentials, but are increasingly demand-driven.

Forecast studies have identified areas such as nanotechnology, microsystems, biotechnology, opto-electronics, photonics, new materials, and advanced information technology as technologies of the future. These strategic areas appear only to a limited extent in existing EC programmes. These topics are science-intensive and hold good prospects of integrating different research institutions. Furthermore, the Commission should be active in emerging areas where well-established national

R&D systems do not yet exist; so the potential for the Commission to play an active role is quite large.

Besides the already existing instruments of international R&D co-operation and exchange of persons, the use of institutional arrangements should be taken into account as already discussed above in the context of instruments for the promotion of university-industry co-operation.

Most present activities of technological forecast do not yet sufficiently look at the transformation of functional technology options into marketable products or processes. The market success of innovations, however, largely depends on market demand and socio-economic needs. This linkage of research and society is the major area of the Interface III activities. In addition to the existing dissemination instruments such as transfer units and data banks - which, once again, are based on a technology/science push approach - new instruments have to be found which actively involve the society in the process of RTD planning as early as possible. Potential instruments can be the organization of awareness workshops or the elaboration and public discussion of scenarios. In this area - which was not in the focus of this study - further new instruments have to be looked for.

The fourth dimension of the RTD dissemination policy is the elaboration of major goals which can be guideposts commonly accepted by society, industry, and the scientific community. For the elaboration of such goals, several instruments exist. These include technology assessment, technology forecast, and the management and moderation of strategic dialogs and policy formation processes.

The following theses on the role of the Commission have to be seen against the background of such a broadened approach:

1. The mandate of the the Commission is the exploitation and dissemination of existing results of RTD. This study, however, shows that the specific means of the production of RTD results already have a decisive influence on the dissemination and exploitation process.
2. Decisive determinants of the dissemination and exploitation process are the legal and financial requirements, the "division of labour", and the linkages between research institutions. This aspects have to be taken into account in the planning of

new RTD programmes as well as for the dissemination of already existing results in the member countries.

3. Modern systems of knowledge production will be transdisciplinary, application-oriented and network-dominated in contrast to discipline-based, internally driven and individually dominated traditional systems. Within the new dynamic systems, public bodies like national governments or the Commission increasingly have to play the role of a mediator between disciplines, institutions, and nations. In this context, a major aim is the creation of stronger linkages between basic and applied research for which new ways of managing of research systems are required.

4. New challenges result from the increasing importance of science-based industries and the increasing importance of basic research for industrial applications. This implies closer linkages between academic research and the industrial part of the scientific community as well as new types of transferring RTD results. The transfer from basic to applied industrial R&D becomes more complex, and the flow of knowledge in the opposite direction also becomes more important. Applied research organizations have to translate complex application problems into an agenda of (oriented) basic research.

5. The guideline of the research policy of the Commission should not be the creation of a unique EU-wide innovation structure, as the variety of national systems of innovation within the EU has many advantages. Furthermore, intervention in existing structures is quite difficult and can induce only minor effects because of strong mechanisms of persistence. In this situation, the present policy of the Commission of bringing together researchers and scientists of different nationalities is adequate: it initiates processes of mutual learning and helps to overcome specific intranational inefficiencies.

6. In the area of new, emerging technologies, the potential for the Commission to play an active role is much greater than in well-established fields, because new R&D structures are needed which do not yet exist on the national level or which exist only in a rudimentary form. For that purpose, the Commission can use traditional instruments such as R&D subsidies in strategic areas, or the new instrument of institutional arrangements.

7. In recent years, national governments have become increasingly involved in an active development of S&T policy. Many national activities are concentrated on the recognition of long-term trends and the identification of strategic goals. In this context, the Commission should develop its own forecast activities in order to

identify strategic goals beyond national borders and potentials for strategic EU-wide co-operation.

8. The early identification of socio-economic needs is an essential precondition of the efficient use and transfer of RTD results. Projected future applications of new technologies are needed as visible aims and goals of a European RTD policy. Consequently, the distinction between Interface II (research/scientific community) and Interface III (research/society) increasingly becomes artificial. A modern system of production and dissemination of RTD results is characterized by a high push/pull interaction and close linkages within the research system as well as between the research system and public and private demand and needs.

To sum up, the present study describes the role of the scientific community within innovation systems from different perspectives: the institutional organization of R&D systems, taking selected European countries as example; the knowledge transfer from non-industrial research institutions to industry; the role of science within models and theories of the innovation process; and the role of scientific institutions within national systems of innovation. These different approaches lead to the common conclusion that science already has a decisive impact on the development of technology and that its significance will even grow. The beginning of the next century will be characterized by science-based technologies playing a key role. This clear trend poses a challenge to all actors in innovation systems to find new ways of producing scientific and technological knowledge.

1.   Introduction to part I

The study on which part I is based was performed within the framework of the VALUE II programme of the European Commission (EC). The activities of VALUE II aim at promoting the dissemination and exploitation of the results of (EC) research and technical development (RTD). The measures of the programme are grouped within 3 areas:

- research/industry interface (Interface I)
- research/scientific community interface (Interface II)
- research/society interface (Interface III)

The present study was made in the second group, the research/scientific community interface (Interface II): Thus, the general focus of the activities within this area is the dissemination of knowledge achieved in EC research programmes to the European scientific community.

The advisory committee (think tank group) of VALUE II, Interface II, suggested an initial "diagnosis" phase before the launch of specific actions of dissemination and exploitation. On this background, the main purpose of this study is to analyse the target group of Interface II, the *scientific community*. In the present context, the study does not give a general description of academic institutions, but focuses on *their role in processes of technological innovation*. Hence, the aim is to get a better insight into the factors which determine the structure and the effectiveness of the science/technology interface (S&T interface) from the perspective of the scientific community and to draw conclusions on possible improvement of the dissemination and exploitation process.

The S&T interface has been a major topic of the economic debate in recent years. On this background, the study analyses the broad existing literature in a systematic way and puts forward the most important results. By a comparison and integration of the different sources, new insights into the structure and mechanisms of the S&T interface can be achieved. The study did not undertake its own empirical investigations in order to avoid duplication of already existing studies. Therefore, one target of this study was the identification of areas where additional empirical work is needed.

The general findings on the characteristics of the S&T interface can be largely transferred to the EU research/scientific community interface, the focus of Interface II, and are important for the description of the general context of research. On this basis, some recommendations on the exploitation and dissemination of already existing results of EU RTD can be elaborated. It is more important, however, to work out structures for future programmes, which allow an optimal participation of the European scientific community. This will lead to the conclusion that, apart from the general context of research, the "management of the research system" will become an increasingly important issue.

In the literature, the role of the scientific community in technological innovation is discussed from a variety of viewpoints of which this study introduces the main approaches in separate chapters. Of course, overlaps cannot always be avoided nor can certain inconsistencies. All in all, the study has a generally inductive structure; it starts with specific points and ends on a general level. Specifically chapter 2 discusses the definitions of science, research, and development and their mutual relation in order to establish a clear starting point for the further analysis. Chapter 3, then, describes the R&D landscape for three selected countries, i.e., Germany, Great Britain, and Greece, in order to give a first empirical impression of the role of institutional structures for innovation. A further purpose of this chapter is to show the differences and the large variety of organisations and institutions among different countries.

The specific transfer mechanisms between basic science and technology are examined in more detail in chapter 4. Beside a discussion of the related theoretical approaches, the main goal is to identify factors hampering an efficient knowledge transfer and means of improving such transfer.

The embedding of this specific discussion into broader models of innovation is introduced in chapter 5. The review of the literature brings up a large number of different approaches. In recent years, however, the approaches have begun to converge somewhat, and at the end of the chapter a new model is introduced which integrates the major elements of current approaches.

As a last step of the literature analysis, chapter 6 summarizes the recent debate on national systems of innovation, thus integrating the different elements of the previous chapters. At the same time, the empirical findings of chapter 3 on the innovation landscape in three selected countries are put into a broader theoretical framework.

Chapter 7 gives a résumé of major results of our survey of the literature. On this basis, conclusions concerning open research questions and concerning future actions of the Commission are drawn.

2. Relation of science to research and development - definition of concepts

The present study examines the role of the scientific community within the innovation system. Before a detailed discussion of this subject, a definition of the concepts used is necessary, because in the literature there exists considerable confusion concerning appropriate terms and categories. Within this study, unified concepts will be used as far as possible, and the attempt will be made to relate the categories of the different examined sources to the unified terminology suggested in this section.

As to research and development (R&D), the definitions of this study will be based on the international standardized categories of the Frascati Manual (OECD 1980 and 1994). Although these definitions are well known, they will be explicitly quoted in the section in order to achieve clear references for the further discussion. Furthermore, a new version of the Frascati Manual was recently published, wherein the definitions of R&D are modified.

The Frascati Manual in both its old and new versions defines research and development in the following way:

"Research and experimental development (R&D) comprise creative work undertaken on a systematic basis in order to increase the stock of knowledge, including knowledge of man, culture and society, and the use of this stock of knowledge to devise new applications." (OECD 1994, 29)

This definition is very broad and comprises all areas of innovation, including economic or social innovations as well. This study is, of course, focused on the technological part of R&D. In this context, the European Commission often uses the concept of "Research and Technological Development (RTD)" which does not point to a different definition from that of Frascati version, but to a focus of the European research programmes on technology.

The Frascati Manual distinguishes between basic research, applied research, and experimental development. In the new version of the Frascati Manual, basic research is further sub-divided into two types so that the following pattern results:

- basic research
- - pure basic research
- - oriented basic research
- applied research
- experimental development

Basic research is defined by the Frascati Manual in the following way:

"Basic research is experimental or theoretical work undertaken primarily to acquire new knowledge of the underlying foundation of phenomena and observable facts, without any particular application or use in view." (OECD 1994, 29)

Recent results of studies on the R&D process showed that basic research has an important function for the progress of technology and that many results of basic research are transferred into technological applications. The sub-division of basic research into pure research and oriented basic research is a reaction to these findings. The following new definitions have been introduced:

"Pure research which is carried out for the advancement of knowledge without working for long-term economic or social benefits and with no positive efforts being made to apply the results to practical problems or to transfer the results to sectors responsible for its applications.
Oriented basic research which is carried out with the expectation that it will produce a broad base of knowledge likely to form the background of the solution of recognised or expected current or future problems or possibilities." (OECD 1994, 69)

In the literature, the terms "curiosity-oriented", "pure", or "fundamental" are often used as equivalent to "basic" (Irvine/Martin 1984, 2-5). The Frascati concept of "oriented basic research" is a good description of its general, loose orientation on application. In this context, some authors use the terms "strategic" (Irvine/Martin, 1984) or "long-term application-oriented" (Krupp 1984).

The sub-division of basic research into two types is helpful for future statistical analyses. Up to now, all data were compiled on the basis of the old Frascati version so that a further differentiation of basic research was not possible. This shortcoming also concerns the analysis in section 3 of the institutional structure of scientific activities in selected countries.

Sometimes, the concept of "strategic" research is used to denote R&D activities required to achieve national strategic objectives (Irvine/Martin 1984, 3). As for the new version of the Frascati Manual, the experts discussed the inclusion of strategic research with the meaning described. They agreed that international comparability could not be achieved and therefore decided not to include a definition of this concept into the new Frascati Manual (OECD 1992).

In the new Frascati Manual the definition of "applied research" did not change compared to the old version:

"Applied research is also original investigation undertaken in order to acquire new knowledge. It is, however, directed primarily towards specific practical aim or objective." (OECD 1994, 69)

The original suggestion of a further subdivision into "generally directed applied research" and "specific applied research" was not introduced in the latest version, because a clear distinction between "generally directed applied research" and "oriented basic research" would be quite difficult to make (OECD 1992).

As for experimental research, the definition in the new version was only slightly expanded:

"Experimental development is systematic work, drawing on existing knowledge gained from research and practical experience, that is directed towards producing new materials, products and devices; to installing new processes, systems and services; or to improving substantially those already produced or installed." (OECD 1994, 70)

The adjective "experimental" chiefly points to a distinction between development activities and pure engineering. It is, however, difficult to define precisely the cut-off point between experimental development and production in such a way that it is applicable to all situations. However, the basic rules laid down by the National Science Foundation provide a practical basis for the exercise of judgement in difficult cases:

"If the primary objective is to make further technical improvements on the product or process, then the work comes within the definition of R&D. If, on the other hand, the product, process or approach is substantially set and the primary objective is to develop markets, to do pre-production planning, or to get a production or control system working smoothly, then the work is no longer R&D" (cited according to OECD 1992).

In addition to this general rule, the Frascati Manual enumerates and explains in more detail a variety of activities to be excluded from R&D. The main items of this list are

- education and training,
- scientific and technical information services,
- general purpose data collection,
- testing and standardisation,
- feasibility studies,
- specialised medical care,
- patent and licence work,
- policy related studies,
- routine software development, and
- other industrial activities.

The last item generally refers to other scientific, technical, commercial, and financial steps for the successful development and marketing of a manufactured product and the commercial use of the processes and equipment which are not covered by the above definitions of R&D.

The Frascati definitions may have many shortcomings, especially because they are often explained using negative statements (exclusions) (Majer 1978, 12-20). Nevertheless, the activities in the context of R&D are so complex and so diversified that it will never be possible to achieve clear delimitations. In any case, the Frascati definitions represent a valuable pragmatic basis which describes at least the decisive elements of R&D in an appropriate way.

The use of the concept "science" in the literature is even more confusing than that of R&D, because many authors introduce the term without any definition or only with an implicit definition. Generally, there exist two different approaches to definition: an institutional approach and a cognitive one. The institutional approach differentiates between "scientific institutions" on the one hand and "industry" on the other hand. According to this definition, science is represented by universities and non-industrial research institutions, thus chiefly the public research sector or the academic research sector. In many articles, a very simplistic association of these scientific institutions with basic research or even pure basic research is made. If this institutional definition is explicitly introduced, it can be helpful for a pragmatic distinction between the industrial and the non-industrial research sector.

Dasgupta/David (1992) emphasise the different social organisations of industrial and academic research, leading to different incentive systems and mechanisms of knowledge production. "As to the goals differentiating Science from Technology, ...the community of Science is concerned with additions to the stock of public knowledge, whereas the community of Technology is concerned with adding to the stream of rents that may be derived from possession of (rights of use) private knowledge" (ibid., see also the similar reasoning of Weingart 1976).

In the case of the European work programme for VALUE II, the three areas of activities are described as the interfaces of European research to industry, the scientific community, and society (cf. chapter 1). Hence, the definition of the scientific community is an institutional one.

The cognitive approach tries to define science itself without a specific linkage to institutions. For example, the Academic Press Dictionary of Science and Technology gives the following definition of science:

"1. The systematic observation of natural events and conditions in order to discover facts about them and to formulate laws and principles based on these facts,
2. *the organised body of knowledge that is derived from such observations and that can be verified or tested by further investigation,*

3. any specific branch of this general body of knowledge, such as biology, physics, geology, or astronomy." (Morris 1992, 1926)

According to this concept, science is closely related to *knowledge* so that terms such as "knowledge-oriented" are often used as equivalents for "science-oriented". (Grupp/Schmoch 1992c, 2). Kline/Rosenberg (1986) suggest a special definition of science in the context of innovation theory:

"We can take science to be the creation, discovery, verification, collation, reorganisation, and dissemination of knowledge about physical, biological, and social nature" (Kline/Rosenberg 1986, 287).

According to them, "the two main components of science that affect innovation are (1) the current totality of stored human knowledge about nature and (2) the processes by which we correct and add to that knowledge".

As to the generation and storage of knowledge, all available definitions of science emphasise the *systematic approach*. The terms "systematic" or "organised" implicitly point to a certain level of *complexity* of scientific activities (as to different types of knowledge see Machlup 1962, 21-22).

If these definitions of science are compared to the above definitions of basic research, applied research, and experimental development, the similarity is striking. According to the Frascati Manual, basic and applied research is carried out "with the aim of acquiring new knowledge", and experimental development "is systematic work drawing on existing knowledge". In consequence, most R&D activities qualify as scientific (see also Hughes 1986). In this context, the above-mentioned dictionary defines the term "scientific" - besides other characteristics - in the following way:

"...of technical or practical activities, carried out in a manner that it is thought of being comparable to science, as by being systematic, highly accurate, painstaking, and so on." (Morris 1992, 1926)

As for basic and applied research, the close relation to science is obvious. But not all activities of development are so systematic and complex that they can be described as scientific. A certain part of development, however, has to be considered to be scientific as well.

Nevertheless, *R&D and science are not equivalents.* On the one hand, R&D includes many scientific activities but also comprises other things, such as the construction of industrial prototypes or of test equipment (Grupp/Schmoch 1992c, 2-3). On the other hand, many statistical studies include education and training as scientific activities which are explicitly excluded from the definition of R&D according to the Frascati Manual.

Figure 2-1:   Qualitative illustration of the "location" of science in R&D performing institutions

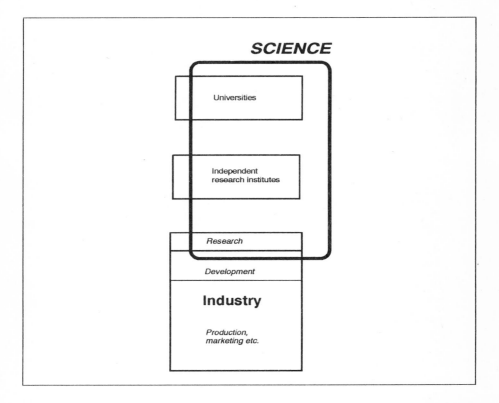

As a major inference arising out of the cognitive definition, a large share of scientific activities is performed in industry. This situation is an important reason for the introduction of the new concept of oriented basic research into the Frascati Manual. Furthermore, not all activities in universities and non-industrial research institutions can be described as scientific. For example, non-industrial institutions often perform standard tests and analyses (Mowery 1983) and academic people perform consulting not related to R&D. The resulting "location" of science in institutions according to the cognitive approach is illustrated in figure 2-1.

Although the scope of VALUE II, Interface II, is limited to the non-industrial part of the scientific community, the present study starts with a broader definition in this first, "diagnostic" phase of the programme. The activities of non-industrial institutions which are linked to technological innovation can only be understood against the background of scientific activities in the industry. Furthermore, the knowledge transfer between the industrial and the non-industrial sector largely depends on the behaviour of the scientists within industrial enterprises. Therefore, the isolated examination of scientists in academic institutions would result in a very limited perception of the role of science within the innovation process. Only a broad approach can lead to a complete picture of the scientific community in the non-industrial sector.

As this study analyses the role of the scientific community for technological innovation, it is, furthermore, necessary to have an appropriate definition of "technology" to compare with "science". The knowledge transfer from non-industrial research institutions, especially universities, is often described as a transfer from science to technology. This simplified concept might be useful as a reductionist form, but it conceals some of the underlying definitions. According to Morris (1992, 2176), "technology" encompasses technical embodiments and the related processes as well as "the application of scientific knowledge for practical purposes", thus also comprises applied science (see also Freeman 1982, 4, for a similar definition). Therefore, "technology" and "science" are largely overlapping domains so that, strictly speaking, a transfer is impossible in the narrow sense of the definition. Even if science is defined as basic research and technology as applied research and development, the concept of transfer will not be clear cut due to the growing importance of basic science in industrial research. (On the similarities and differences in the concepts of science and technology see also Rammert 1993, 74-78; Mittelstraß 1994; Spinner 1994, 53-56.)

Therefore, this report largely avoids the simplified concept of "knowledge transfer from science to technology". In cases where we cannot evade it an institutional definition is adopted, so that "science" refers to "basic science" in non-industrial institutions and "technology" to "applied research and development" in industry.

The problems of definition discussed above illustrate that the institutional as well as the cognitive approach has advantages and shortcomings. Whereas the institutional approach emphasises the social differences of academic and industrial organisations, the cognitive approach aims at demonstrating structural similarities. Both perspectives will be discussed in further detail in section 4.3.

3. R&D systems in selected countries

After the theoretical discussion of the position of the scientific community within R&D systems, the following chapter will give a more concrete idea by describing the R&D landscape of three selected countries. For that purpose, the examples of Germany, Great Britain, and Greece were chosen. At the beginning of each country section, some general R&D indicators are given. In the next step, the main R&D-financing and -performing institutions are described. On this basis, conclusions on the main characteristics of each national R&D system are brought out. At the end of this chapter, some general structures of R&D systems in Europe are discussed.

3.1 Germany

In absolute terms, Germany spent about $ 32 bn (in purchasing power parities) on research and development (R&D) in 1990 (OECD 1993). With this Gross Domestic Expenditure on R&D (GERD), Germany had the highest R&D level in Europe; compared to the United States, it amounted to about 23 per cent, compared to Japan to about 49 per cent. In any case, Germany is one of the leading countries in the R&D area.

To understand the R&D structures of a country, it is more interesting not to look at absolute figures, but at relative indicators. The most common relative indicator for the innovation activity of a national economy is the expenditure on R&D in relation to the Gross Domestic Product (GDP); this indicator is called GERD factor. In Germany, the GERD factor started at the beginning of the eighties at a level of 2.45 per cent and at the end of the eighties reached a level of nearly 2.9 per cent. Until 1991, a decline back to 2.6 per cent can be observed (cf. figure 3.1-1). This GERD factor represents a top position in comparison to other European countries and about the same level as the United States and Japan. Since 1989 an increase of the Japanese R&D activities has led to an index of nearly 3.1 per cent. Nevertheless, the German activities are high in absolute as well as in relative terms.

The second comonly used indicator is the so-called BERD factor, which is the R&D expenditure of business enterprises in relation to the GDP. Thus, the BERD factor describes the privately financed R&D within a national economy. The BERD factor shows, of course on a lower level, the same trend as the GERD factor. In consequence, the decline in the total relative R&D activities at the beginning of the nineties is mainly caused by a decline in the privately financed R&D expenditures.

A third interesting indicator is the average R&D intensity of a country's industry, calculated as the total industrial R&D in relation to the Domestic Product of Industry (DPI), i. e., the producing part of business enterprises. In the case of Germany, the trends of the BERD factor and of the industrial R&D intensity are very similar, thus showing the high share of industrial R&D within the total volume of privately financed R&D.

Figure 3.1-1:   GERD factor, BERD factor, and industrial BERD per DPI for Germany

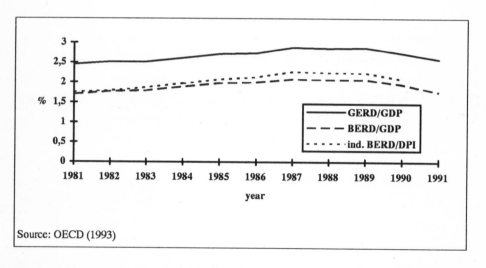

Source: OECD (1993)

In Germany, about one third of all R&D expenditures (33 per cent) are financed by public bodies. Within the EC, only Belgium has a lower share. With about 48 per cent, the respective value for the United States is distinctly higher due to a high amount of defence-related R&D. In contrast, the share of Japan with about 17 per cent is distinctly lower (eurostat 1992).

Figure 3.1-2: Organisation chart of the German R&D system

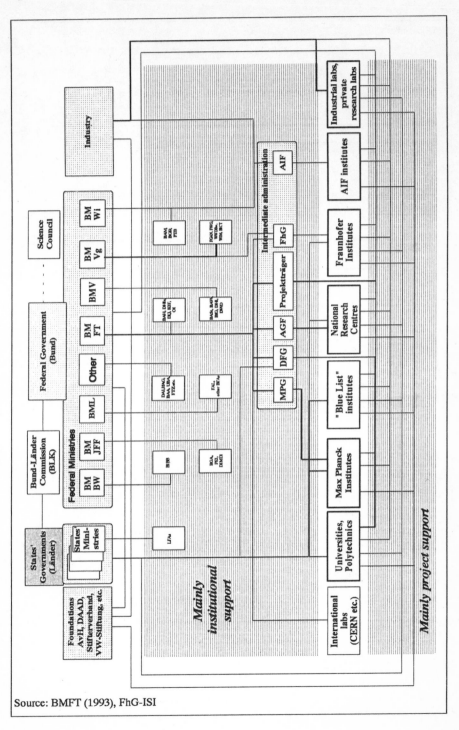

Source: BMFT (1993), FhG-ISI

Figure 3.1-3: Main R&D-performing institutions in Germany, 1989

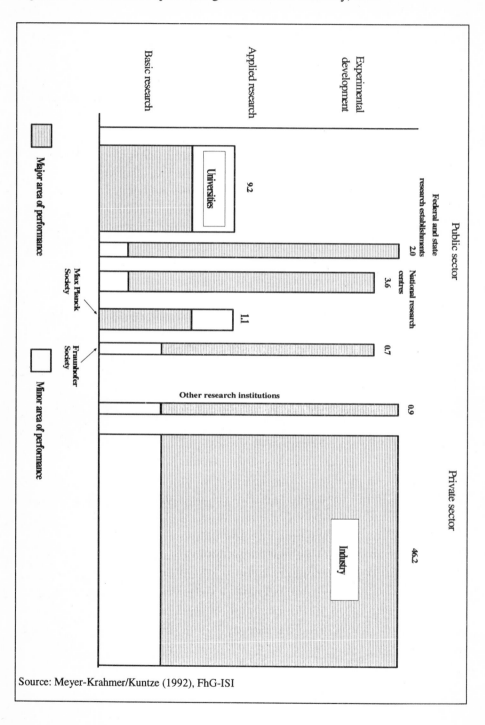

Source: Meyer-Krahmer/Kuntze (1992), FhG-ISI

To sum up, the general indicators show a leading position of Germany in the R&D sector within the EU. But in comparison to Japan and the United States, structural differences and some shortcomings become visible. In particular, the very high share of privately financed R&D in Japan is remarkable.

The general R&D indicators can give only a rough picture of national R&D structures. Therefore, the institutional organisation of R&D is described in more detail. The description for Germany is largely based on Meyer-Krahmer (1990). In Germany, the organisation of R&D is largely determined by the federal system in which the political responsibilities are divided between the central government and the states (*Länder*). The states are responsible for the educational sector, and as a major consequence they finance the largest part of the university budgets. This situation is depicted in the organisation chart in figure 3.1-2 by a bold line between the state ministries and the universities. These lines between related institutions represent financial flows (Döge 1992). The line from the state ministries to the universities comes from the upper part of the diagram because the support is mainly of an institutional nature. Nevertheless, a small part of the funding of the states is linked to projects indicated on the chart by a thin line coming from below.

Apart from the universities, there are further institutions which are partly supported by the states and can be easily found in figure 3.1-2. They comprise the institutes of the Max Planck Society for the Promotion of Sciences, the national research centres (*Großforschungseinrichtungen*, GFE), the institutes of the Fraunhofer Society, and the so-called "Blue List" institutes, a variety of independent research establishments which are active in different areas such as social sciences, economics, biology, or other natural sciences.

In the context of the universities, a further typical feature of the German R&D landscape, the balance between institutional and project funding has already been mentioned. As to institutional support, several institutions are directly connected to specific ministries, especially those of the federal government, which work generally in the respective areas, not only in the field of R&D. Nevertheless, they often play an important role in the R&D landscape; some of them are actually leading in special R&D sectors. The R&D activities of these institutions are called departmental R&D.

In the federal government, the most important ministry for the distribution of R&D funds is the Ministry for Research and Technology (BMFT, since October 1994 Ministry for Education, Science, Research, and Technology, BMBF). The direct influence of the BMFT, however, on the R&D-performing institutions is less important than in the case of the departmental R&D. There exists a variety of intermediate institutions leading to quite differentiated decision-making procedures and a complex distribution system for R&D funds. The BMFT is chiefly responsible for budgets and long-term programmes on a general level. The specific decisions are generally made by intermediate management institutions, administrating institutional as well as project R&D. Typical institutions in this system are the so-called *Projektträger* which are responsible for the details of management of nearly all R&D fields supported by the BMFT. In figure 3.1-2, the Projektträger are located in a special highlighted area reserved for institutions which are responsible for the intermediate management of R&D funds. A further important institution in this field is the German Research Society (DFG), which is mainly responsible for projects in basic research, especially that of universities. Thus, there is a complementary support of the universities from the states and from the federal government.

Other institutions of intermediate R&D management are the Max Planck Society (MPG), the Fraunhofer Society (FhG), the Industrial Research Association (AiF) and the Association of National Research Centres (AGF). These bodies will be described below in further detail. At first sight, this variety of decision-making institutions seems to indicate high flexibility in the German public funding of R&D. In reality, a large portion of the public funds are earmarked for long-term commitments, and in consequence only about 10 per cent of the BMFT budget is available for new tasks (Meyer-Krahmer 1990).

In figure 3.1-2, the institutions with a high level of basic research are located on the left side, the more applied institutions on the right side. A typical institution in the area of fundamental research with a high reputation is the **Max Planck Society**. In particular, it takes up new areas of research not yet sufficiently developed or, because of their scope or administrative structure, less suitable for university research. The basic units of the Max Planck Society are the Max Planck institutes (MPI). The research is actually conducted in approximately 60 institutes, three clinical research units and 2 independent research groups. The Society has a permanent staff of nearly 9,000 people, more than 2,500 of them being scientists and engineers. In addition, there are some 4,000 graduate students, fellows, and visiting scientists. The Max Planck Society is financed largely by public funds made available jointly by the federal and the state governments. However, bigger and more specialised research projects are in general managed by the aforementioned German Research Society (DFG).

The **National Research Centres** (*Großforschungseinrichtungen*, GFE, literal translation: big research institutions) employ their multidisciplinary research and development capacities for the solution of long-term problems entailing economic risks, in what are considered strategic areas. They are engaged in scientific and technical R&D projects whose execution requires special man-power, funding, and equipment. All centres carry out fundamental research in their specific fields. Usually this is long-term application-oriented research.

The National Research Centres were created chiefly within the framework of government-funded programmes for nuclear research and nuclear technology, aerospace research, data processing, and, increasingly in recent years, biomedical research, polar research, environmental research, and non-nuclear energy technology. All in all, there exist 16 National Research Centres with some 16,000 employees, among them 8,500 scientists and engineers, thus the personnel capacity of the National Research Centres is distinctly higher than that of the Max Planck Society.

The **Fraunhofer Society** (FhG) is a very characteristic element of the German R&D landscape. It earns its money through contract research for industry and for the public sector. Since the inclusion of additional institutes in the new federal states, the Fraunhofer Society now comprises 45 institutes. Due to their special character, the Fraunhofer institutes perform first of all application-oriented research. The main fields are:

- microelectronics,
- information technology, production automation,
- production technologies, materials, and components,
- process engineering, energy technology, and construction engineering,
- environmental and health research, and
- studies and technical information exchange.

The Society has some 7,600 employees, one third being scientists and engineers. Thus it has nearly the size of the Max Planck Society.

The FhG has to pursue a convincing demand-oriented strategy to attract the attention of prospective partners who will commission research projects. This necessitates research in selected research fields on a long-term basis in order to obtain scientific and organisational competence and market experience. At the same time, scientific, organisational, and personnel-related flexibility are vital to meet the specific requirements of projects and contract partners. Research focuses are continually reviewed against market developments and demand. This practise enables the institutes to concentrate on the effective transformation of research findings into economic processes and marketable products. Public funding provides the infrastructure which is necessary to carry out a certain level of self-defined R&D. It amounts to about 20 per cent of the total turnover. The Fraunhofer Society is organised as a non-profit organisation, with the charges for contract research being limited to the actual costs incurred.

The **Federation of Industrial Research Associations** (AiF) was set up by private-sector industry to sponsor application-oriented research and development. The AiF serves the interest of industry in obtaining public support for collective research efforts, and the federal interest in channelling public funds through one efficient and mediating umbrella organisation to the various industrial research associations. Collective industrial research within AiF is performed by more than 90 industrial research associations in various sectors of industry. In this context, the term "collective" refers to the collective definition of research projects by several companies and associations. The research projects are carried out by single institutes. All in all, the associations run 63 research institutes. The major aims of the AiF are to finance research projects conceived by the member associations and to co-ordinate projects. AiF supervises the responsible use of funds and assists the transfer of research results into industrial application.

Figure 3.1-3 shows, from a more general perspective, the structure of R&D-performing institutions in Germany. Along the horizontal axis, the institutions are classified according to their main sources of funding, namely public or private (Wissenschaftsrat 1993, Krupp 1984, Meyer-Krahmer/Kuntze 1992). The private institutions are mainly industrial research laboratories. There is an intermediate class of institutions, especially the Fraunhofer Society and the institutes of the AiF, which receive joint government and industry funding. Along the vertical axis, the type of R&D activity is indicated: basic research, applied research, and experimental development. The difference between the type of R&D activity and the stage within an innovation cycle is discussed in more detail in chapter 5. The hatching indicates the major and minor areas of performance of the respective institutions. Thus, as extreme examples, the Max Planck Society concentrates on basic research, whereas research in industry is mostly short-term application-oriented with time horizons on the order of three to five years. The areas of the rectangles in figure 3.1-3 indicate the annual budgets of the respective institutions. For the universities, only research activities are covered, education being excluded.

The greater orientation towards basic research on the left side of the diagram is linked to a larger share of "non-economic" (in the broader sense), society-related targets. The depiction shows that the government tends to support earlier stages of the innovation cycle, whereas industry concentrates on later phases. Therefore, technology transfer from the left to the right side is important for the efficiency of the total system.

Figures 3.1-2 and 3.1-3 show that R&D in a national economy is performed by many different actors in a network of interrelations and co-operations. Therefore, it is not surprising that, deviating from the general structures, industrial laboratories perform some basic research and public research institutes and universities some applied R&D. It is important to know in which fields the different actors or groups are working in order to achieve an optimal allocation of capital and manpower.

As to the position of the scientific community within the R&D system, it is interesting to compare the overall R&D funds at the participating institutions. For Germany, the relation of the universities to other research institutes and to industry is 1 : 0.86 : 5.0. Thus, the German R&D landscape is characterised by intermediate research institutions between universities and industry which, in total, have at their disposal nearly the same budget as the universities. If the definition of the scientific community is an institutional one, thus non-industrial versus industrial R&D, the relation science to industry is 1 : 2.7.

If scientific activities are defined as basic research, it is not possible to get reliable figures for the whole R&D system due to the broad variety of participating institutions. As already mentioned, not all research activities of the universities and the Max Planck Society are in basic research, and many applied institutions perform a certain amount of basic research as well. As to industrial R&D, Grenzmann et al. (1991) relate nearly 6 per cent of the internal R&D activities to basic research, although they use a quite narrow definition. In absolute terms, basic research is performed by industrial laboratories at a volume of about DM 2.8 bn which is equivalent to about one third of the total budget of the universities. This figure shows that even by a very strict definition the scientific activities of industry are not inconsiderable.

It is quite difficult to estimate the amount of transfer between the main R&D sectors in an appropriate way. As to the formal co-operation between universities and industry, DM 0.65 bn of the R&D by universities, in 1989, was financed by the business sector (BMFT 1993). Large parts thereof, however, are linked to private foundations which mainly fund projects of basic research, not contract research. DM 0.4 bn can be qualified as direct contract research, which is equivalent to about 0.9 per cent of all industrial R&D or 4.4 per cent of the universities' R&D budget (Wissenschaftsrat 1993). According to Grenzmann et al. (1991), more than 9 per cent of the industrial R&D activities, equivalent to about DM 4.2 bn, are performed by external institutions. Thus, barely 10 per cent of the external industrial R&D budget is commissioned to universities. All in all, the amount of formal co-operation between universities and industries is quite limited.

In 1989, the volume of publicly performed R&D financed by industry was very low, corresponding to DM 0.085 bn. This is due to the fact that most publicly supported R&D institutions legally have private status. The share of R&D at these institutions which is not publicly financed (a further differentiation is not available) amounts to about DM 0.26 bn. In any case, the amount of public and semi-public R&D for industry is lower than that done by universities. The Fraunhofer Society is included in these figures, so that the transfer volume seems surprisingly modest. This can be explained by a relatively large share of (contract) research at the Fraunhofer institutes for public clients such as BMFT or the European Commission.

To sum up, the institutional landscape in a well-developed R&D system such as the German one is so complex that it is not possible to describe the relation of science and the scientific community to institutions in a clear and unambiguous way.

Therefore, the relations between science and technology cannot be described by simplistic schemata, but a variety of different aspects and dimensions have to be taken into consideration.

3.2 Great Britain

In 1990 the British expenditure on R&D amounted in total to about $ 20 bn (in purchasing power parities), which is equivalent to about two thirds of the German spending. Nevertheless, Great Britain is among the countries with the highest R&D budgets in the world and is, behind the United States, Japan, Germany, and France, in fifth position.

Figure 3.2-1:   GERD factor, BERD factor, and industrial BERD per DPI, for Great Britain

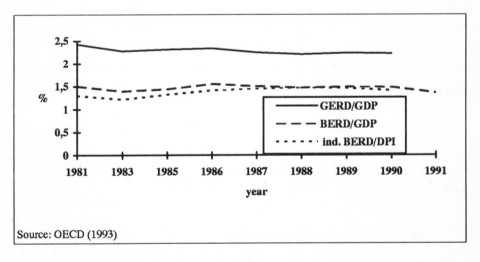

Source: OECD (1993)

The R&D expenditures in relation to the Gross Domestic Product, the GERD factor, started at the beginning of the eighties at about 2.4 per cent, thus at the same level as Germany (cf. figure 3.2-1). But after that time the GERD factor continuously decreased and reached a level of 2.2 per cent in 1990. Thus, the R&D intensity of the British economy decreased in the course of the eighties, whereas in other leading industrial countries such as Japan, the United States, Germany, France, or Italy the GERD factor generally increased. During the same period, the share of privately financed R&D in comparison to the GDP, the BERD factor, stagnated, and the R&D intensity of the industry (industrial BERD/DPI) even increased slightly. As a conclusion, the decrease of the R&D intensity of the British economy is, above all, due to a reduction of public R&D. Nevertheless, the share of publicly financed R&D in 1989 came to 36.5 per cent and was still a little higher than the respective German share.

In Great Britain the public R&D policy of the last decades is characterised by a division of responsibility among a variety of ministries of the central government. Thus, the responsibility was less focused than in the German system; a real equivalent to the German BMFT does not exist. In the mid sixties, a Ministry for Technology was established, but it was merged with other ministries and finally incorporated into the Department of Trade and Industry (DTI). After the seventies, the main competencies were re-delegated to other ministries, but the DTI played still an important role. A certain centralisation of the R&D policy was achieved by the establishment of the Advisory Board for the Research Councils (ABRC) and the Advisory Council on the Application of Research and Development (ACARD) in the mid seventies, later on called the Advisory Council on Science and Technology (ACOST). A new step in the direction of centralisation was reached in April 1982, when the responsibility for co-ordinating science and technology issues across government was brought together under the Office of Science and Technology (OST). It was created within the Cabinet Office, incorporating the former science branch of the Department of Education and Science and the Office of the Chief Scientific Advisor of the Cabinet Office. The new office will have responsibility for the ACOST and the ABRC. This new structure is depicted in the organisation chart of the British R&D landscape in figure 3.2-2.

The organisation chart for Great Britain has a comparable structure to that for Germany (figure 3.1-2). In the upper part, one can find the central government and its different ministries and advisory bodies. In the middle of the diagram, the institutions for the intermediate administration of R&D funds, the intermediate funders, are found in a special highlighted area. In the lower part, the R&D performing institutions are located. In contrast to the German diagram, the differentiation between basic and applied institutions from the left to the right is less clear; and the lines for the budget flows cannot be clearly linked to institutional or project support.

Figure 3.2-2: Organisation chart of the British R&D system

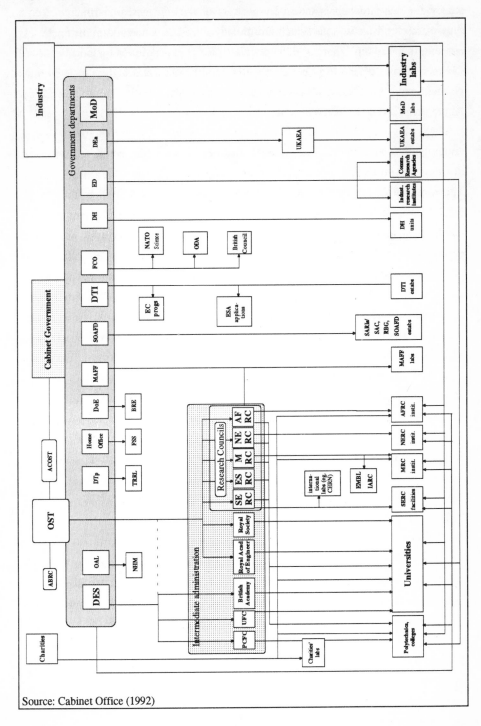

Source: Cabinet Office (1992)

The British R&D system is characterised by a chiefly institutional R&D funding. One reason for this situation is the important role of the so-called departmental R&D, thus of research institutions which are directly linked to a specific ministry. In this context, the very high share of defence-related R&D expenditures by the Ministry of Defence (MoD) of about 44 per cent of the total public R&D budget in 1989 must be mentioned. Of course, defence-related research is not only performed by MoD laboratories, but by industry as well.

Although the establishment of the OST indicates a centralisation of the R&D system, the situation on the level of intermediate funders did not change in a decisive way. The most important bodies are the five Research Councils SERC, ESRC, MRC, NERC, and ARC. Additionally, the OST is responsible for the Government grants to the Royal Society and the Royal Academy of Engineering, whereas the British Academy, the Universities Funding Council (UFC), and the Polyclinics and Colleagues Funding Council (PCFC) remained within the competence of the Department of Education and Science (DES). The funding channelled through the intermediate funders is mainly institutional as well. Individual projects are funded only on a small scale as for example within the scope of the LINK programme, which had a relatively small budget of about £ 30 m p.a. in 1991. The LINK programme is mainly supported by the DTI. LINK aims to encourage strategic collaborative research of medium-term industrial significance and, by strengthening the link between industry and the public research base, improve the transfer of new technology into UK industry. It operates by supporting collaborative research projects, with up to 50 per cent of the project costs being met by the government.

Because of their key function, the Research Councils and the UFC merit description in further detail:

The principal objective of the **Agricultural and Food Research Council** (AFRC) is to support multidisciplinary and training research programmes with an emphasis on biological sciences, biotechnology, and engineering designed to provide options that are useful in the development of sustainable and diversified agriculture. The AFRC receives funds from the science budget of the DES, through commissions from the Ministry of Agriculture, Fisheries and Food (MAFF), and from industry and other bodies. The funds are distributed to special AFRC institutes and universities. The research of AFRC does not aim primarily at the development of specific products or processes for short-term purposes, but supports areas of basic and strategic research.

The objective of the **Medical Research Council** (MRC) is the promotion of research for the maintenance and improvement of human health. The MRC has a duty to protect and strengthen the research infrastructure through training programmes, the provision of career structures, and the establishment of major facilities, and hence to fund research on a long-term basis. The MRC has a special responsibility to work closely with other government departments, especially the Health Department (DH). Within this co-operation, the MRC institutes perform mostly basic research; the DH unit applied research.

The **Natural Environment Research Council** (NERC) is the only body in the UK that supports the whole spectrum of research on the natural environment. It contributes to the generation of the science base needed for the development of environmental policy. NERC plans, encourages and supports basic and strategic research in its own institutes and in institutions of higher education. The results of this research are disseminated to a broad public and provide a basis for impartial advice to government and others on environmental issues. Commissioned research is a major instrument by which the results and benefits of NERC research are transferred to a broader public. In 1991, the commissioned research receipts amounted to about 25 per cent of the whole expenditures of NERC.

The objectives of the **Science and Engineering Research Council** (SERC) are to encourage and support research in various branches of science and engineering and to support education and training of qualified manpower in these areas. The Council tries to achieve these objectives by awarding research grants to universities, polytechnics, and independent research centres, or providing research facilities in its own institutions. The SERC maintains a minimum share of 40 per cent of its total expenditures for basic research.

The main objective of the **Economic and Social Research Council** (ESRC) is to support high-quality social science research in universities, polytechnics, and independent research centres. It especially promotes interdisciplinary and inter-council research.

The **Universities Funding Council** (UFC) allocates resources to universities in the form of grants for both teaching and research. The universities are the major national providers of basic research in all areas of science, ranging from the social sciences and the humanities to natural science, technology, and medicine. While much of their research can be classified as basic research, they also carry out a substantial and growing amount of strategic and applied research.

The main structures of the research-performing institutions are depicted in figure 3.2-3 in a similar way as in figure 3.1-3 for Germany. Here, the low internal differentiation of non-industrial research institutions outside universities is obvious. The situation is characterised by a relation of 1 : 1.2 : 4.2 between universities, other non-industrial institutes, and industry. Compared to the structure in Germany, the higher weight of the other non-industrial institutions is remarkable, partly reflecting the considerable involvement of governmental laboratories in the area of defence. Furthermore, the relative share of industry-performed R&D is lower than in Germany, although the publicly financed R&D budget is only slightly higher than in the German case. As a conclusion, in Great Britain a higher share of publicly financed R&D is performed in governmental laboratories and not by industry.

Although there exist no task-oriented research associations such as the Max Planck Society or the Fraunhofer Society in Germany, it is possible to bring out some major structures concerning dominant types of R&D. First of all, the non-defence R&D budget can be divided into a "science base" and a "civil departments" part. The science base part comprises the funds for the Research Councils, the UFC and PCFC and amounted to £ 1.6 bn in 1989/90; of this £ 745 m are administered by the Research Councils, the rest mainly by the UFC. About 73 per cent of the science base R&D is basic research according to the Frascati definitions, a further 22 per cent qualify as strategic R&D, a category between basic and applied R&D. Thus the funds of the Research Councils are primarily devoted to basic research, although detailed figures are not given in the official statistics.

The Civil Departments' R&D amounted to £ 1.0 bn in 1989/90; thus the relative weight of departmental R&D is still higher than that of the Research Councils. These relations show that the influence of OST will always be limited, if the system is not completely revised in the area of departmental research. The Civil Departments' R&D includes a large portion of specific applied research (48 per cent) and experimental development (16 per cent). Thus, a division of labour between basic research by the Research Councils and applied R&D by the Civil Departments is obvious. For the exact interpretation of these figures, it has to be taken into account that the financing side, not the performing side is considered. Nevertheless, the main activities of the performing institutions are reflected by these budget structures closely.

There is a remainder of R&D institutions not clearly identified in figure 3.2-3 which are assumed to perform fundamental and applied research equally (Cheese 1991). Private laboratories working in close relation to industry are included in this block.

In 1989, the higher education sector received £ 132 m from industry for R&D, and it can be assumed that the largest part was contract research. If this assumption holds, about 1.7 per cent of the total industrial R&D budget is performed by universities, or 27 per cent of the external R&D of industry. The activities on behalf of industry comprise 7.4 per cent of all research by universities. These figures show that the research linkages between universities and industry are obviously much stronger than in Germany.

In 1989, an even higher sum of £ 157 m of the industrial R&D budget was granted to governmental research institutes. In consequence, the co-operation of industries with public centres is also higher than in Germany, although a special group of contract research institutes like the Fraunhofer institutes does not exist.

All in all, the R&D landscapes in Germany and Great Britain are quite different, although the general R&D indicators seem to be quite similar. Nevertheless, the creation of the OST as a more centralised institution and the suggestion of the establishment of Faraday centres, as a copy of the Fraunhofer institutes, indicates a trend towards German structures (House of Lords 1993).

Figure 3.2-3: Main R&D-performing institutions in Great Britain, 1989

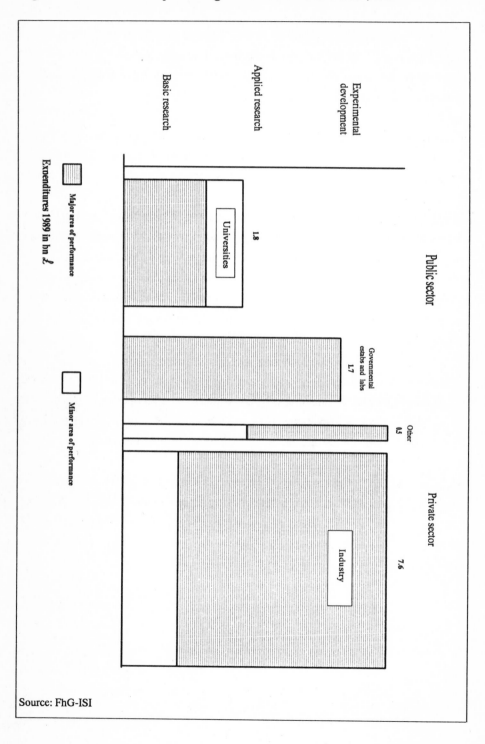

Source: FhG-ISI

3.3   Greece

In 1989, the total R&D expenditures of Greece amounted to $ 336 m (in purchasing power parities). Within the European Union, this is one of the lowest R&D budgets, and only the expenditures of Portugal and Ireland have about the same order of magnitude. The absolute Greek budget represents about 1 per cent of the German one, the exact figures largely depending on the unit of comparison (ECU or dollar in purchasing power parities). This relatively low budget is, of course, largely due to the small size of the Greek economy. Nevertheless, the share of R&D expenditures in relation to the gross domestic product, the GERD factor, is quite low as well, with a value of 0.47 per cent at the end of the eighties. Within the EU, only Portugal has a comparably low share. The GERD factor, however, steadily increased during the eighties so that there is a clearly positive trend (cf. figure 3.3-1).

Figure 3.3-1:   GERD factor, BERD factor and industrial BERD per DPI for Greece

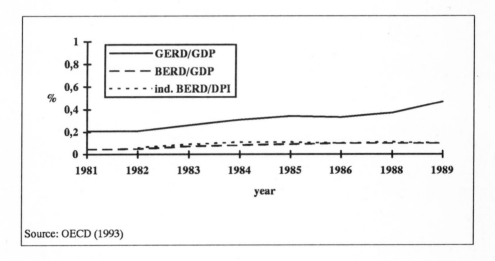

Source: OECD (1993)

The growth of the R&D activities in the eighties is above all due to increased public activities. Thus, in 1989, 69 per cent of the total R&D was publicly financed. Within the EU, this high share is, once again, only comparable to the situation of Portugal. Nevertheless, the two industry-related R&D indicators show a distinct growth during the eighties as well. The following description of the institutional structure of the R&D system is largely based on Kuhlmann (1992).

The organisation of the R&D system in Greece is characterised by a very centralised administration concentrated in the Athens area. The general framework of centralised structures has largely affected the conception and implementation of R&D policy. The most important actor within the government is the General Secretariat of Research and Technology (GSRT), which belongs to the Ministry of Industry, Energy, and Technology. It is responsible for 43 per cent of the public R&D funds (cf. figure 3.3-2).

GSRT supervises the National Research Centres, a category of institutions comprising 6 centres created in the fifties and the sixties. Among them are the biggest Greek research centre Demokritos (700 employees); the National Research Foundation (200 employees); and the Hellenic Pasteur Institute. After the early eighties, the GSRT created the "academic research centres and institutes" near the universities with the mission of undertaking research related to technological and societal applications. Today they form the Foundation of Research and Technology Hellas (FORTH). These centres are located in Crete, Patras and Thessaloniki.

Figure 3.3-2:   Organisation chart of the Greek R&D system

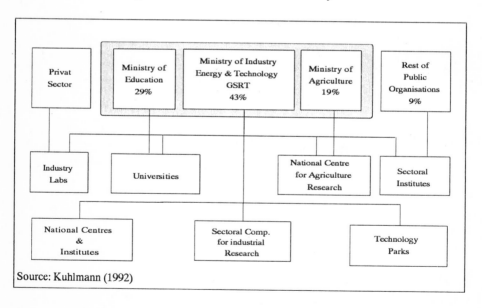

Source: Kuhlmann (1992)

In the middle of the last decade, GSRT started to create "sectoral R&D companies". These companies have a clear industrial orientation, and their mission is the dissemination of new technology and know-how to companies of a specific sector and the exploitation of research results. Until today, a certain reluctance has remained on the part of private entrepreneurs to co-operate actively with these companies. Their distrust in the operation is justified by the low effectiveness of the public sector. In figure 3.2-2 the sectoral companies are listed under the heading "technological centres".

It was only at the end of the seventies that modern policies for science and technology were initiated. Within this context, the following programmes were supported by GSRT:
• Programme for the Advancement of Industrial Research,
• Co-financing research projects in public institutions and business enterprises,
• Co-ordinated or Concerted Programmes, and
• Programme for the Reinforcement of the Research Potential.

Figure 3.3-3:   Research institutes and sectoral companies under supervision of GSRT

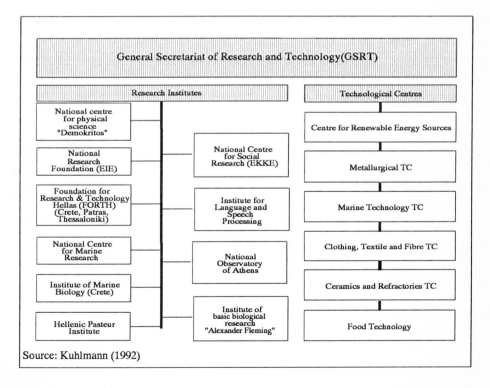

Source: Kuhlmann (1992)

Beyond GRST's institutional and programme-driven efforts to support R&D in Greece, the Organisation for Small and Medium-sized Enterprises and Handicraft (EOMMEX) has to be mentioned. With the OECD's Technical Co-operation Programme, EOMMEX created 5 innovation offices and introduced funding for inventors. Moreover, it carries out specific programmes for the production and sale of Greek industrial products, technical assistance to small and medium-sized enterprises, execution of technological research for the improvement of products, and valorisation of inventions and patents.

The European Union contributes to Greek R&D activities in the Community Support Frameworks (CSFs), agreed upon in 1988. One of the main aims of the CSFs was to foster R&D. In Greece, the most important programmes launched in this context are
- The Integrated Mediterranean Programmes for Information Technology (IMP IT), and
- the Operational Programme for Science and Technology (EPET).

In late 1991, the EU additionally supported the implementation of STRIDE Hellas. It is quite difficult to estimate the total annual support of the EU, because the flow of funds per year is not regular and projects may not be realised as planned. In 1989, the contribution of the EU to the total Greek R&D budget amounted to about 6 to 9 per cent.

Within the government, the Ministry of Agriculture has the oldest and most intensive research network. It manages about 19 per cent of the public budget and has some 75 centres, institutes and laboratories with about 400 researchers. These institutions are supervised by four ministry divisions for plant research, forest research, veterinary research, and fishing.

The last important public actor is the Ministry of Education which is responsible for general universities, technical universities, technical colleges, and other institutes of higher education. Its R&D-related budget amounts to 29 per cent of all public R&D expenditures. The universities are furthermore supported by GSRT, but the available statistics do not record the respective amount in detail. Therefore, it is not possible to calculate the relation between the research activities in universities, public research institutes, and industry as was done for Germany and Great Britain. A rough estimate, however, can be obtained, if only the funds of the Ministry of Education are taken into consideration. Based on that, the relation of universities, public research institutes, and industry is 1 : 2.5 : 1.6. In these figures, the activities of the universities are underestimated, those of the public research centres overestimated. Consequently, the activities of the universities in Greece have the same order of magnitude as those of industry; hence the situation is completely different from that in Great Britain or Germany, where the industrial R&D activities largely dominate.

A more detailed description of Greek R&D institutions and programmes, especially those with involvement of the European Commission, is given by Kuhlmann (1992).

All in all, the situation in Greece is hardly comparable to that in more advanced countries like Great Britain and Germany. As a major difference, the role of the state is much more important and a significant factor. In consequence, the creation of an effective knowledge transfer from public research to industry is more decisive than in larger countries. Furthermore, the stimulation of R&D by industry itself is a major task for the future.

3.4   General conclusions

The three case studies of Germany, Great Britain, and Greece show that national R&D systems may have quite different structures. Because of complex institutional structures, it is difficult to exactly determine the position of the scientific community and to evaluate its share within the total R&D activities of a country. Especially if science is defined as basic research, only rough estimates can be given. In any case, a not inconsiderable portion of basic research is performed by industry, at least in advanced R&D systems. The available figures point to a quite low level of formal co-operation between universities and public research centres on the one side and industry on the other side. Nevertheless, there is a growing trend towards such co-operation: in Germany, a publicly supported organisation for industry-oriented contract research, the Fraunhofer Society, has already been established; the same is intended for Great Britain in the form of the so-called Faraday Centres. In smaller countries, effective knowledge transfer must be a major task of the future.

In 1989, the R&D expenditures of the European Union as a whole amounted, to ECU 19 bn compared to ECU 73 bn for Japan and ECU 132 bn for the United States (calculated on the basis of eurostat 1992). The BERD factor was 2.04 per cent, reflecting the fact that the EU consists of a variety of countries with more and less advanced R&D systems. The average share of publicly financed R&D had a level of 40 per cent. Within that system, the European Commission spent ECU 1.3 bn for R&D purposes, equivalent to nearly 1.5 per cent of the whole expenditures of all R&D expenditures of EU countries. In relation to publicly funded R&D, the share of the EC-funded R&D was 3.6 per cent. This share is low in general, but in focal areas like information technology or agriculture, the impact of the support by the Commission is more important. Furthermore, the Commission plays a decisive, very stimulating role in smaller countries such as Portugal or Greece. These general figures, however, show that it is actually all but impossible to evaluate the quantitative impact of EC RTD programmes on the R&D landscape of the member countries, i. e., to show statistically significant trend changes. Therefore, quantitative assessments should only be used in the context of other qualitative evaluations.

The findings of this chapter may be used as a general background for the next chapters on knowledge transfer from non-industrial institutions to industry, innovation models, and national systems of innovation.

3.5   Abbreviations of chapter 3

Germany

AA	Auswärtiges Amt, Bonn
AGF	Arbeitsgemeinschaft der Großforschungseinrichtungen, Bonn
AIF	Arbeitsgemeinschaft Industrieller Forschungsvereinigungen e. V., Köln
AvH	Alexander von Humboldt-Stiftung, Bonn
AWI	Stiftung Alfred-Wegener-Institut für Polarforschung, Bremerhaven
BAA	Bundesanstalt für Arbeitsschutz, Dortmund
BAH	Biologische Anstalt Helgoland, Hamburg
BAM	Bundesanstalt für Materialprüfung, Berlin
BASt	Bundesanstalt für Straßenwesen, Bergisch-Gladbach
BAW	Bundesanstalt für Wasserbau, Karlsruhe
BIBB	Bundesinstitut für Berufsbildungsforschung, Berlin
BICT	Bundesinstitut für chemisch-technische Untersuchungen, Swisttal
BFA	Bundesforschungsanstalt
BfG	Bundesanstalt für Gewässerkunde, Koblenz
BGA	Bundesgesundheitsamt, Berlin
BGR	Bundesanstalt für Geowissenschaften und Rohstoffe, Hannover
BLK	Bund-Länder-Kommission für Bildungsplanung und Forschungsförderung, Bonn
BMA	Bundesminister für Arbeit und Sozialordnung, Bonn (Federal Ministry for Labour and Social Affairs)
BMBau	Bundesminister für Raumordnung, Bauwesen und Städtebau, Bonn (Federal Ministry for Regional Planning, Building, and Urban Development)
BMBW	Bundesminister für Bildung, Forschung und Technologie, Bonn (Federal Ministry of Education, Science and Technology)
BMFT	Bundesminister für Forschung und Technologie, Bonn (Federal Ministry for Research and Technology)
BMI	Bundesminister des Inneren, Bonn (Federal Ministry of the Interior)
BMJFFG	Bundesminister für Jugend, Familie, Frauen und Gesundheit, Bonn (Federal Ministry for Youth, Family, Women and Health)
BML	Bundesminister für Ernährung, Landwirtschaft und Forsten, Bonn (Federal Ministry of Food, Agriculture, and Forestry)
BMPT	Bundesminister für Post und Telekommunikation, Bonn (Federal Ministry for Post and Telecommunications)
BMU	Bundesminister für Umwelt, Naturschutz und Reaktorsicherheit, Bonn (Federal Ministry of the Environment, Nature Conservation and Reactor Safety)
BMV	Bundesminister für Verkehr, Bonn (Federal Ministry of Transport)

BMVg	Bundesminister für Verteidigung, Bonn (Federal Ministry of Defence)
BMWi	Bundesminister für Wirtschaft, Bonn (Federal Ministry of Economics)
BMZ	Bundesminister für wirtschaftliche Zusammenarbeit, Bonn (Federal Ministry of Economic Cooperation)
CERN	Conseil Européen pour la Recherche Nucléaire, Genf
DAAD	Deutscher Akademischer Austauschdienst e. V., Bonn
DAI	Deutsches Archäologisches Institut, Berlin
DESY	Deutsches Elektronen-Synchrotron, Hamburg
DFG	Deutsche Forschungsgemeinschaft e. V., Bonn
DHIs	Deutsches Historisches Institut, Paris, Rom, London, Washington
DHI	Deutsches Hydrographisches Institut, Hamburg
DIJ	Deutsches Institut für Japanstudien, Tokio
DIMDI	Deutsches Institut für medizinische Dokumentation und Information, Köln
DKFZ	Stiftung Deutsches Krebsforschungszentrum, Heidelberg
DLR	Deutsche Forschungsanstalt für Luft- und Raumfahrt e. V., Köln
DWD	Deutscher Wetterdienst, Offenbach
FAL	Bundesforschungsanstalt für Landwirtschaft, Braunschweig
FGAN	Forschungsgesellschaft für Angewandte Naturwissenschaften, Wachtberg
FhG	Fraunhofer-Gesellschaft zur Förderung der angewandten Forschung e. V., München (Fraunhofer Society for the Promotion of Applied Research)
FhI	Fraunhofer-Institut
FTZ	Forschungsinstitut der Deutschen Bundespost beim Fernmeldetechnischen Zentralamt, Darmstadt
FWG	Forschungsanstalt der Bundeswehr für Wasserschall und Geophysik, Kiel
GBF	Gesellschaft für Biotechnologische Forschung mbH, Braunschweig
GFE	Großforschungseinrichtung (National Research Centre)
GFZ	Geo-Forschungszentrum, Potsdam
GKSS	GKSS-Forschungszentrum Geesthacht GmbH, Geesthacht
GMD	Gesellschaft für Mathematik und Datenverarbeitung mbH, St. Augustin
GSF	Gesellschaft für Strahlen- und Umweltforschung mbH, Neuherberg
GSI	Gesellschaft für Schwerionenforschung mbH, Darmstadt
IfAG	Institut für Angewandte Geodäsie, Frankfurt/Main
IPP	Max-Planck-Institut für Plasmaphysik, Garching
KFA	Forschungszentrum Jülich GmbH, Jülich
KfK	Kernforschungszentrum Karlsruhe GmbH, Karlsruhe
KIF	Kunsthistorisches Institut Florenz
LFA	Landesforschungsanstalt
MDC	Max-Delbrück-Centrum, Berlin

MPG	Max-Planck-Gesellschaft zur Förderung der Wissenschaften e. V., München (Max Planck Society for the Promotion of the Sciences)
MPI	Max-Planck-Institut
OI	Orient-Institut Beirut
PEI	Paul-Ehrlich-Institut, Frankfurt/Main
PTB	Physikalisch-Technische Bundesanstalt, Braunschweig
UBA	Umweltbundesamt, Berlin
UFZ	Umweltforschungszentrum Leipzig-Halle
WIM	Wehrwissenschaftliches Institut für Materialuntersuchungen, Erding
WWDBw	Wehrwissenschaftliche Dienststelle der Bundeswehr, Munster

Great Britain

ABRC	Advisory Board for the Research Councils
ACOST	Advisory Committee on Science and Technology
AFRC	Agriculture and Food Research council
BJAB	Biotechnology Joint Advisory Board
BRE	Building Research Establishment
CERN	European Organisation for Nuclear Research
DEn	Department of Energy
DES	Department of Education and Science
DH	Department of Health
DoE	Department of Environment
DTI	Department of Trade and Industry
DTp	Department of Transport
EC	European Commission
ED	Employment Department
EMBL	European Molecular Biology Laboratory
ESA	European Space Agency
ESRC	Economic and Social Research Council
FCO	Foreign and Commenwealth Office
FSS	Forensic Science Service
ICBT	Interdepartmental Commission of Biotechnology
ILL	Institute Laue-Langevin
IARC	International Agency for Research on Cancer
MAFF	Ministry of Agriculture Fisheries and Food
MoD	Ministry of Defence
MRC	Medical Research Council
NATO	North Atlantic Treaty Organisation
NERC	Natural Environment Research Council
NHM	National History Museum
OAR	Office of Arts and Libraries
ODA	Overseas Development Administration
OST	Office of Science and Technology
PCFC	Polyclinics and Colleges Funding Council
RBC	Royal Botanic Gardens

RTO	Research and Technology Organisations
SAC	Scottish Agricultural Colleges
SARIs	Scottish Agricultural Research Institutes
SERC	Science and Engineering Research Council
SOAFD	Scottish Office Agriculture and Fisheries Department
TRRL	Transport and Road Research Laboratory
UFC	Universities Funding Council
UKAEA	United Kingdom Atomic Energy Authority

Greece

EIE	National Research Foundation
ELKEPA	Greek Productivity Centre
ELOT	Hellenic Organization for Standardization
EKKE	National Centre for Social Research
EOMMEX	Organization for Small and Medium-sized Enterprises and Handicrafts
FORTH	Foundation for Research and Technology Hellas
GSRT	General Secretariat of Research and Technology
KEDE	The Public Works Laboratory
KEPE	Centre for Planning and Economic Research
PERPA	Programme for Monitoring the Pollution in the Athens Area

4.   Knowledge transfer from non-industrial research institutions to industry

Basically the relationship between non-industrial research institutions and industry may be described as "interaction". In contrast to the concept of "transfer", this characterisation puts emphasis on the fact that knowledge is not only transferred, one-way, from research institutions to industry but that there also exist flows of know-how in the opposite direction. The main subject of part I of this book, however, is the role of the scientific community in technological innovation; thus it focusses primarily on the industrial use of scientific knowledge (for the definition of "technology" as compared with "science" see chapter 2). In part II of this book, the industrial perspective of this interaction is described. In the case studies of part III, the mutual exchange of knowledge between academic and industrial institutions is a major topic of the analysis.

During the past decades, the initiation of innovations has moved to the centre of interest in industrial policy, following the recognition of the crucial impact of innovations on national competitiveness. In this context, many authors, e.g., Gibbons (1992) or Freeman (1982), outline the dependence of national competitiveness on the efficient linking of non-industrial research institutions and industries in the national innovation system. In their view, a closer linkage between science and technology generates a decisive shift to more efficient, dynamic systems.

This chapter is arranged in five sections. The first one examines the quantitative and qualitative importance of basic scientific knowledge for innovations on a general basis. In the second section, a differentiation according to industrial sectors, company types, and technical areas is made. Third, we focus on the transfer mechanisms between non-industrial institutions and industry. Fourth, we describe the conditions for success of transfer, and, finally, we conclude this chapter with a list of instruments for improving the transfer of knowledge.

4.1   The contribution of basic science to technology

In this section we examine the contribution of advances in basic science to the development of new technologies, without, however, looking at the underlying mechanisms of knowledge transfer in more detail. The discussion of the relevant studies will show how complex the evaluation of this problem is. The description of the following two studies draws on Irvine/Martin (1984).

Starting in the sixties there has been a growing number of retrospective studies that try to evaluate the dependence of past innovations on scientific work. The first of these large-scale studies was the so-called Project Hindsight, carried out by the U.S. Department of Defense (DoD). The study assessed the relative contributions of science and technology to the development of 20 weapon systems. Among the issues considered were the optimum balance between basic and applied research, and whether R&D was carried out more effectively by DoD laboratories, industry, or universities. For analytical purposes, each discrete contribution was termed an event. These events were classified as either "science events" or "technology events". As a result only 8 per cent of these events were found to be scientific compared with 92 per cent "technology events". Furthermore, only 4 per cent of the scientific events were the result of pure basic research. As regards the institutional sources of all science or technology events, about 9 per cent arose from the university sector. Summarizing these results, basic research seems to be relatively unimportant whereas applied research and experimental development show the highest pay-back (cf. Sherwin/Isenson 1966, 11-15)

The findings of Project Hindsight almost immediately had a considerable impact on R&D policies. However, the study was open to at least two major criticisms. First, an arbitrary cut-off of twenty years was used in tracing back the science and technology events, thereby excluding from consideration any significant basic research arising before this time. Second, there was widespread suspicion that the sample was biased in favour of in-house applied research.

As a reaction to the negative findings of the Project Hindsight study, the National Science Foundation launched a second study named with the acronym TRACES. The TRACES findings provided evidence to support the science-push model of innovation. The results, however, are mostly dependent on the choice of five radical innovations in the case studies (magnetic ferrites, video-tape recorder, oral contraceptive pill, electron microscope, and matrix isolation). Therefore, the study is not representative of all types of innovation. The methodological approach was comparable to that used in Project Hindsight; as a main difference, however, TRACES employed to a historical cut-off of 50 years. In order to classify the research events, three categories of non-mission research, of mission-oriented research, and of development and application work were established. As a result, all five innovations originated in basic research. In total, 70 per cent of the events were found to have been the product of non-mission research, while mission-oriented research accounted for only 20 per cent, and development and application work under 10 per cent. Furthermore, universities appeared to have played a very important role, having been responsible for three quarters of the non-mission and a third of the mission-oriented research events. The significant differences between the TRACES and the Project Hindsight findings are largely due to the longer observation period. According to the TRACES findings the non-mission research events peaked some 20 to 30 years before each innovation, precisely the period excluded in the DoD study. These very long time-lags between scientific discoveries and their technical realisation are confirmed by other retrospective case studies of Schneider (1991). Gibbons/Johnston (1974), however, detected an average time-lag of 12 years examining innovations in the British industry. The age distribution of scientific papers referenced by patents peaks within 2 to 5 years for science-intensive areas, and, thus, also hints at shorter time-lags, (cf. Collins/Wyatt 1987, Schmoch et al. 1993c, Van Vianen et al. 1990). The large delay observed in the TRACES study may be a characteristic feature of radical innovations drawing on basic findings of pure research, whereas patents already cite more elaborated outcomes.

A further important finding of TRACES is the clear recognition that important innovations often stem from the interaction of several previously unconnected streams of scientific and technological activity. For example, the research paths of the video-tape recorder reveal that this particular innovation depended on the merging of several streams of scientific and technological activity, including control theory, magnetic and recording materials, magnetic theory, magnetic recording, electronics, and frequency modulation. On this background, the authors of TRACES come to the conclusion: "Another important factor ... was that of interaction between scientific disciplines and/or highly effective personal communication ....

Organisations which support and guide research must increase their emphasis on communication particularly among disciplines and between non-mission and mission-oriented research .... The continued involvement of a variety of institutions would appear to be a worthwhile objective to help the need for diversity of research" (ITT Research Institute 1968, 22-23, as cited by Irvine/Martin 1984, 20).

Two other studies examined the British industry with the same objective as the aforementioned studies. Townsend et al. (1981) analysed more than 2,000 important innovations in British industry. Their results show that universities supplied important knowledge input to less than 2 per cent of the innovations studied. Military or non-military public institutions provided the knowledge input for 5.9 per cent of the innovations, whereas 2.7 per cent of the innovations studied received knowledge from research associations. Taken together, less than 11 per cent of the innovations draw on knowledge from non-industrial institutions. These results, however, should be interpreted carefully. Presumably, the impact of universities is underestimated, because the survey answers are themselves biased in favour of recent events, whereas the importance of basic research increases with the distance of time. Consequently, the importance of in-house and industrial knowledge is overestimated.

Gibbons/Johnston (1974) examined the knowledge inputs to innovations in British industry between 1945 and 1979. They found that about 12 per cent of the knowledge input came from non-industrial sources, thus, confirming the findings of Townsend et al. (1981).

Mansfield (1990) tried to measure the contribution of science to technology in a survey of 76 large U.S. companies. He found out that, on average, 11 per cent of the product innovations and 9 per cent of the process innovations could not have been developed at such an early date without academic research. The inputs non-industrial institutes provided to the different industrial sectors, however, fluctuate heavily. The time-lag between the publication of the scientific results and their introduction into the market was 7 years.

Further similar studies on the impact of science on technology are reviewed and discussed in Irvine/Martin (1984).

All of the above studies, however, fail to give clear estimates on the (monetary) value of scientific research for technology, and therefore can only be interpreted as qualitative indications. David et al. (1993) show that "basic research results rarely lead directly to new processes or products without substantial modifications". Furthermore, as the TRACES results reveal, technological innovations are often based on the integration of results of different scientific disciplines. Therefore "the path from basic research to technological development is mostly obscured and it is rarely possible to isolate 'key' contributions of basic research to commercial applications" (David et al., op. cit). In consequence, strict cost-benefit analyses of basic research cannot be performed. In view of this situation, David et al. suggest an information-theoretic approach. Within this analytical framework, basic research generates general orientation knowledge which helps to identify promising areas for applied research and, also important, less fruitful areas. Applied research provides information on potential products or processes, and development selects and realises those products with the highest economic benefit. In any case, this approach seems to be very helpful for analysing the impact of basic research, e.g., for evaluation purposes.

To sum up, basic science contributes to the progress of technology in a decisive way. It is, however, difficult to measure this impact precisely. The results of such investigations largely depend on the definition of science versus technology and its specific introduction into questionnaires. Furthermore, it is necessary to provide a sufficiently long observation period, because in many cases there is a large time-lag between scientific discoveries and their introduction into technology. Finally, the impact of scientific input into innovations heavily depends on the industrial sector and the technical area considered. Due to these complex problems, a careful methodological approach is crucial for this type of studies.

4.2 Impact of science according to industrial sectors, company types, and technical areas

The above review of different studies revealed a close link between the industrial sector or the selected technical area and the relevance of scientific input. In this context, Pavitt (1984) presented an analysis based on a study of Townsend et al. (1981) on industrial sectors. Therein Pavitt identified four main types of firms: supplier-dominated firms, scale-intensive firms, specialised equipment suppliers, and science-based firms.

Figure 4.2-1:   Main technological linkages amongst different categories of firms

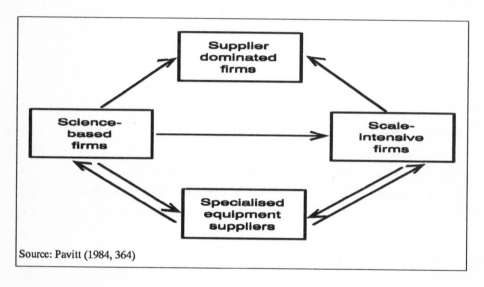

Source: Pavitt (1984, 364)

Supplier-dominated firms mainly belong to the traditional (industrial) sectors of manufacturing such as textiles, leather and foot wear, house building, etc. Scale-intensive firms, or production-intensive firms, are concentrated in the sectors of food, metal manufacturing, ship building, motor vehicles, or glass and cement. Specialised equipment suppliers are mainly found in the sectors of mechanical engineering and instrumental engineering. Science-based firms, the most interesting type in the context of this study, are located in the sectors of chemicals and electrical and electronic engineering. These science-based industries rely heavily on the R&D activities of firms in the same sectors. These R&D activities, in turn, are largely based on the rapid development of the underlying sciences in universities and elsewhere (ibid., 362). The science-based firms develop a high percentage of process technology in their own laboratories. In science-based sectors, the share of large companies is relatively high, a finding corresponding with that of Mowery (1974) and Freeman (1982) who found a minimum level or a threshold size to be relevant for performing in-house R&D.

A further important feature of science-based firms is the high proportion of product innovations which are used in other sectors. Based on the empirical findings, Pavitt describes the main technological flows between the four categories of firms. As a major conclusion, it comes out that the economy as a whole relies heavily on the innovations of the science-based sectors, although this effect is often not tangible in the final products (cf. figure 4.2-1).

Industrial sectors are not homogenous in their structure: They include companies which produce a broad variety of products, each of them relying more or less on science. Thus, the sectoral approach which is the basis of Pavitt's approach only gives a rough idea of the underlying patterns. That is why Grupp (1991b, 1993a) characterised different product groups according to their R&D intensity. The area of R&D-intensive products is subdivided into leading-edge technology and high-level technology. R&D expenditure for leading-edge technology exceeds 8.5 per cent of turnover, for high-level technology the same figure ranges between 3.5 and 8.5 per cent. Table 4.2-1 provides a list of the R&D-intensive product groups. As may be seen, product groups in the fields of chemicals and electronics prevail, a finding that corresponds to that of Pavitt. Some R&D-intensive groups, however, such as motors, aircraft, machine-tools and the like do not belong to Pavitt's science-based sector.

A further approach to defining the area of science-based products is that of Grupp/Schmoch (1992b). They analyse 28 areas of technology by means of patent indicators and use the average number of references to non-patent literature in patent search reports as a measure for science intensity. This implicit definition of science, based on scientific publications, is not limited to the academic sector, but encompasses scientific activities in industry as well, because scientists in industry

Table 4.2-1:   List of R&D-intensive product groups based on SITC Rev. III

h:	SITC III	Product group (non-official terms)
	Leading-edge technology:	
1	516	Advanced organic chemicals
2	525	Radio-active materials
3	541	Pharmaceutical products
4	575	Advanced plastics
5	591	Agricultural chemicals
6	714	Turbines and reaction engines
7	718	Nuclear,water,wind power generators
8	752	Automatic data processing machines
9	764	Telecommunications equipment
10	774	Medical electronics
11	776	Semi-conductor devices
12	778	Advanced electrical machinery
13	792	Aircraft and spacecraft
14	871	Advanced optical instruments
15	874	Advanced measuring instruments
16	891	Arms and ammunition
	High-level technology:	
17	266	Synthetic fibres
18	277	Advanced industrial abrasives
19	515	Heterocyclic chemistry
20	522	Rare inorganic chemicals
21	524	Other precious chemicals
22	531	Synthetic colouring matter
23	533	Pigments, paints, varnishes
24	542	Medicaments
25	551	Essential oils, perfume, flavour
26	574	Polyethers and resins
27	598	Advanced chemical products
28	663	Mineral manufactures, fine ceramics
29	689	Precious non-ferrous base metals
30	724	Textile and leather machinery
31	725	Paper and pulp machinery
32	726	Printing and bookbinding machinery
33	727	Industrial food-processing machines
34	728	Advanced machine-tools
35	731	Machine-tools working by removing
36	733	Machine-tools without removing
37	735	Parts for machine-tools
38	737	Advanced metalworking equipment
39	741	Industrial heating and cooling goods
40	744	Mechanical handling equipment
41	745	Other non-electrical machinery
42	746	Ball and roller bearings
43	751	Office machines, word-processing
44	759	Advanced parts for computers
45	761	Television and video equipment
46	762	Radio-broadcast,radiotelephony goods
47	763	Sound and video recorders
48	772	Traditional electronics
49	773	Optical fibre and other cables
50	781	Motor vehicles for persons
51	782	Motor vehicles for good transport
52	791	Railway vehicles
53	872	Medical instruments and appliances
54	873	Traditional measuring equipment
55	881	Photographic apparatus and equipment
56	882	Photo- and cinematographic supplies
57	884	Optical fibres,contact,other lenses

Source: Grupp (1993a)

also publish articles in scientific journals. The result of the study is illustrated in figure 4.2-2 in the form of a cartographic depiction. There, not only the relation of the different areas to science but also their mutual technological proximity is visually represented. As in the studies mentioned above, the most science-based areas are located in chemistry and electronics. On the basis of a scale with 4 levels, however, a further differentiation becomes obvious. As a major advantage, this approach can be operationalised for the examination of other aspects. For example, Schmoch/Grupp found out that the technical sub-areas with the greatest growth in patent activities in the eighties are more science-dependent than others (ibid., 100). A cross-country comparison shows Japan and the United States to be more active than European countries in science-intensive technologies. According to an institutional analysis for West Germany, universities take out more than 4 per cent of all West German national patents. This figure chiefly reflects the direct contribution of universities to technology, because broad areas of basic research are not patentable. The authors conclude that "West German universities are important centres for technology production" (ibid., 110). All in all, patent analysis proves to be an important tool for the analysis of science involvement in technology.

As scientific activities are performed in non-industrial research institutions as well as in industry, the notion of science-linkage does not necessarily imply that an intensive flow of knowledge from academic circles exists. For example, in the case of the British industry Pavitt reveals that the public research infrastructure heavily supports the development and manufacturing of electronic components, computers and electronic capital goods. In contrast to this, the public contribution to the area of chemicals is quite low, thus reflecting the fact that firms in this area rely more on their own scientific in-house research (Pavitt 1984, 346-348).

In Germany, however, Grupp/Schmoch (1992c, 96-97) observe a high contribution of universities to chemistry and a much weaker reliance on the public research infrastructure in electronics. Obviously, the actual patterns of knowledge transfer largely depend on the national academic and industrial traditions that have evolved over time and shaped the different systems of innovation (see also chapter 6). Apart from these national characteristics, Grupp/Schmoch find out a significant correlation between the science-intensity of technical areas and the technology-oriented activities of German universities.

The same generally applies for other public research centres, but often a distinct focus on selected strategic areas of technology is revealed. For example, in the seventies and eighties, public research centres in Germany concentrated a large part of their activities on the nuclear sector (Grupp/Schmoch 1992c, 99-109). In the period of 1945 to 1979, the British public research centres made enormous contributions to the areas of iron and steel or coal mining (Townsend et al. 1991). These national topics of public research are often linked to large prestige projects or the requirements of sectoral or local pressure groups and are, therefore, not necessarily science-intensive; they are examined in more detail by Bräunling/Allesch (1982).

Figure 4.2-2:   Cartographic depiction of the structure of technology in 28 areas and their linkage to science

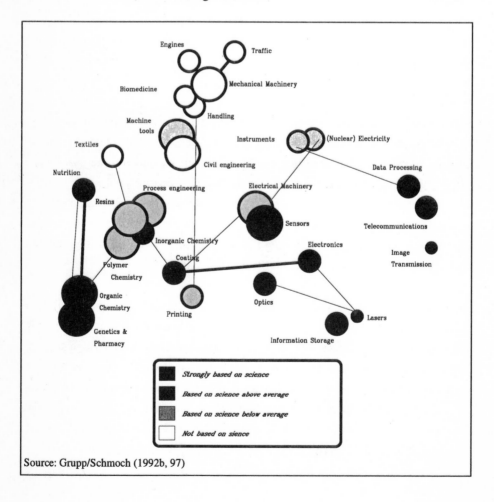

Source: Grupp/Schmoch (1992b, 97)

4.3   Types and mechanisms of knowledge transfer

In the previous sections, the impact of basic science on technology was described in a general way without looking at the underlying mechanisms of knowledge transfer. As to this question, the economic literature offers a large variety of - sometimes contradictory - theories of the interaction between different industrial and non-industrial institutions. In this context, we can only refer to some of the most important points.

The institutional branch of economic theory has developed three concepts of interaction, each tied to characteristic institutions (Powell 1990): markets, hierarchies, or networks. According to the first approach, markets serve as the main mechanism for organising interactions and are flexible in adapting to a dynamic environment. This theory, however, assumes that prices reflect all relevant costs in a correct way. In reality, only a part of all costs are included in prices and so-called external effects play a decisive role.

Within firms, hierarchies seem to efficiently co-ordinate all kinds of interactions. They are, however, highly inflexible in coping with new upcoming organisational demands and innovative technologies. Thus, this concept cannot explain the phenomenon of adaptation to new situations as it is constantly happening in real life.

Against this background, during the past decade the concept of networks has emerged as a theoretical and a practical guideline. It takes into account the changing relationship between companies in managing upcoming changes.

The network approach is one of the suitable theoretical models that describe the information transfer between institutions. The version we are referring to has been developed by Scandinavian authors and is just one type of the various forms of network models. This approach proposes a concept in which knowledge transfer cannot be regarded as a single and isolated activity but emerges as a result of a web of connections evolved over time.

In Hakansson's (1989) view, companies keep up connections with other institutions, thus creating a network. The relation between non-industrial institutions and companies is just one of these (cf. figure 4.3-1). The actors work together in developing, manufacturing, and selling different products and processes or in combining their respective resources. These co-operations may occur once, continuously, in different periods of time or in parallel. The network may be described as an arena companies and other institutions are operating in. The more a company communicates with another institution, the more this relationship becomes established, and the more both partners rely on each other in solving future problems together. The idea behind this is that the more institutions become accustomed to each other, the more the risk of failure in problem-solving decreases, thus lowering costs. The concept of transaction-cost reductions (Williamson 1979) in acquiring new, strategic knowledge is illustrated by the case of a company that has established regular contacts with well-known suppliers, customers, other companies doing business in related areas, public research institutions, and universities.

Figure 4.3-1:   Potential partners of a firm within an innovation-oriented network

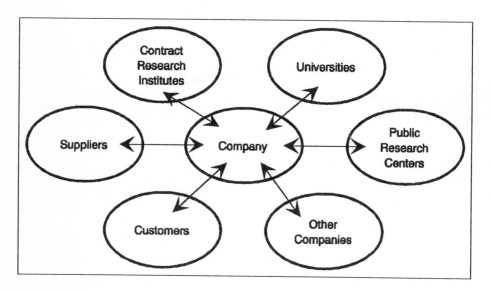

The network connects not only different institutions but also different *types of resources*. These are subdivided into 3 groups: tangible resources (e.g., natural resources, machines, and other equipment), human capital (work-force, know-how, connections), and financial assets. They constitute preconditions for each industrial activity. Activities comprise combination, exchange, transformation or creation of resources within the network. The type of relationship may be either technical, time-related, knowledge-related, social, or economic/legal (Hakansson 1989). A technical relationship will emerge if, for example, two companies share their knowledge on the use of a special machine. Experience and daily routines may result from connections which are often renewed and may be described as time-related bonds between partners. Knowledge-related ties are usually formed when two parties gradually acquire knowledge about each other's knowledge pool. This type of relationship becomes more important, if companies try to keep up with the frontiers of knowledge in many areas. The exchanged knowledge is then integrated into each one's own knowledge pool. Social and economic/legal ties may be considered together, because they are characterised by similar features. Social as well as legal relations are mainly based on confidence between the two partners; contracts cannot substitute for confidence (Kuhlmann/Kuntze 1991).

An important aspect of co-operation related to the concept of networks is geographic proximity. Although experts are not homogeneous in their opinion of whether local distances determine the quality of network contacts, there seems to be an increasing number of authors who argue that proximity matters. Findings in regional studies show that companies are embedded in a regional infrastructure ranging from public services and existence of suppliers to research institutions (Kulicke 1988; Hassink 1992, Rothwell/Dodgson 1992). Within a region, contacts and co-operations may be more easily established, because transaction costs are lower, and thus co-operations are more intensive. The same applies to the problem of knowledge transfer. As far as R&D co-operations are concerned, however, the relevance of regional networks mainly depends on the complexity of the knowledge to be transferred (Wolff et al. 1993). Tassey (1992) describes how nationwide or even global networks are necessary in order to profit from new, complex technologies. Therefore companies have to rely on contacts beyond regional borders, if they are dealing with very sophisticated technology. In this case, local proximity does not matter.

In order to fill this quite abstract description with facts of real life, we will take a closer look at some studies which try to evaluate the different types of interaction between institutions. From the above description it has become obvious that the network approach is suitable for modelling R&D co-operations and the process of knowledge transfer. The following examples examine the knowledge transfer between non-industrial institutions and companies in a broad sense. As firms usually take advantage of new scientific knowledge, universities and other non-industrial institutions normally become members of innovation networks (cf. figure 4.3-1).

The most simple and least expensive type of knowledge transfer for companies seems to be the regular reading of all relevant publications dealing with the findings in basic science. According to Freeman (1982), however, this type of transfer is in no way sufficient. Consequently, companies have to rely on other sources of information and types of co-operation as well. Walter (1992, referring to Kayser 1987) divides these alternative transfer channels into:

- information transfer,
- research contacts,
- transfer of personnel, and
- scientific training.

The above list of transfer channels draws heavily on an institutional definition and, therefore, fits quite well into the network approach. As an alternative classification of transfer mechanisms, Bräunling/Maas (1988), who examine innovation networks with respect to the possibility of public support, differentiate among several forms of knowledge transfer:

- direct research contacts: the partners are searching for a direct engagement in R&D co-operations in order to create or exchange knowledge
- companies adaptation: internal or external R&D results for their own products without considerable additional spending
- secondary use: companies happen to use R&D results destined originally for other applications

A fourth category which does not fit exactly into the scheme discussed in this section is indirect knowledge transfer, e.g., by publications. This aspect will be examined in more detail in the last section. The most relevant type of knowledge transfer considered here is, however, direct research contacts. As we have seen, there are several facets of knowledge transfer which complicate an unambiguous classification scheme for the transfer channels.

Table 4.3-1:   Types of know-how transfer from academic institutions to industry
in the context of innovation. Results of a questionnaire to German
small and medium-sized firms (1340 firms surveyed)

Question asked: Have you directly received technical knowledge from research
institutions and/or universities during the last five years ?

yes: 24.5 %   *not yet but planning to: 8.4 %*   *no: 67.1%*

Transfer of technical knowledge through the following channels:
(Multiple selection possible)

Information about the market potential of new products:	17.7%
Consultation on problem solution:	69.8%
Licensing:	9.1%
Laboratory and equipment sharing:	24.1%
Joint implementation of R&D projects:	33.5%
Subcontracting of R&D projects:	25.9%
Directed search for R&D personnel:	17.4%
Directed search for young graduates (non-R&D personnel):	14.6%
Short-term assignment of R&D personnel to universities:	5.2%
Training of qualified personnel at universities:	45.4%

Source: Herden (1992, 152)

Now we will focus on two studies, one examining the frequency of usage of specific
transfer channels, the other concentrating on the outcome of the different transfer
channels. As illustrated in table 4.3-1, Herden (1992) surveyed 1340 German small
and medium-sized firms, asking them about the type and frequency of their contacts
with universities and other research institutions during the last five years without
specific reference to successful innovations.

The findings do not exactly fit into the above-mentioned pattern of transfer channels. However, we can extract from table 4.3-1 the main conclusions as follows: Less than a quarter of the surveyed companies have had research contacts. Concentrating on this small group of firms, it becomes obvious, first, that the channel of information transfer is relied upon most frequently. As the questionnaire used in the survey allows for multiple answers, we cannot simply add up the figures in different categories. However, we can make statements about individual channels and their relative ranking: consultations on problem solutions were used by nearly 70 per cent of the companies. Licensing, which may also be added to the channel of information transfer, was of minor importance. Ranking second, nearly one half relied on scientific training such as the training of qualified R&D personnel at universities. Third, more than 30 per cent engaged in research contacts such as the joint implementation of R&D projects. Unfortunately, the questionnaire did not ask companies about their use of personnel transfer, that is the temporal assignment of university personnel to industry. Consequently, quantification of this type of knowledge transfer is almost impossible, although some of the questions concerning scientific training slightly overlap with the transfer of personnel.

What is really remarkable about Herden's findings is the fact that only the relatively low share of one third of the companies with research contacts, that is, approximately 8 per cent of all companies surveyed, co-operated in joint R&D projects with academic institutions. This finding must, however, be interpreted with the fact in mind that Herden examined only small and medium-sized enterprises. The share would be higher for larger companies.

Gibbons/Johnston (1974) focused on the impact of different types of knowledge transfer in the context of 30 successful innovations. As we are interested only in the knowledge transferred from non-industrial research institutions to industry, we will concentrate on the contribution of that 11 per cent of all information coming from external sources and being scientific in character. Although Gibbons/Johnston have examined only information units, they roughly divided their data into two separate transfer channels, one relying on knowledge transfer via scientific literature and textbooks, the other on research contacts between academic personnel from non-industrial research institutions and industry. Almost one half of the relevant information was transferred via scientific literature, the other half via research contacts, thus, making up 5 per cent of the total information used. The exchange of personnel and scientific training, however, were not explicitly examined.

Figure 4.3-2:   Preferred partners of small and medium-sized enterprises for R&D co-operations or other forms of technology-related co-operation

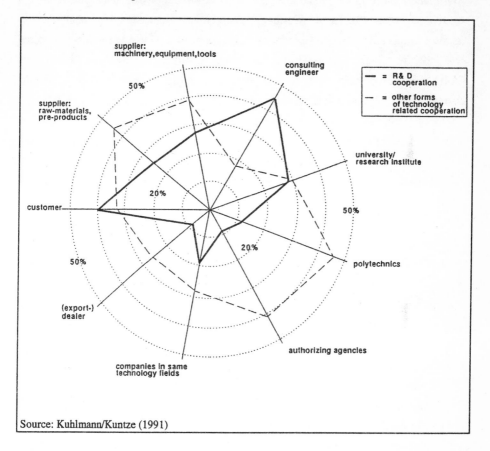

Source: Kuhlmann/Kuntze (1991)

Because of the different methodological approaches pursued, the results of the two studies cannot be compared without interpretation. Gibbons/Johnston (1974) filtered out 30 innovations and searched for the relevant underlying information sources. So it comes as no surprise that their findings are biased in favour of the information transfer channel. Presumably, the importance of scientific literature is overemphasised. Herden (1992), on the other hand, surveyed a large variety of possibilities of co-operation without referring to specific innovations, thus, it is natural that the importance of any single source of knowledge transfer decreases.

However, what both studies have in common is the finding that less than 10 per cent of all companies engage in direct research contacts, a figure that is surprisingly low in light of the potential impact of new scientific knowledge created and transferred via direct R&D co-operations on new products and processes.

Kuhlmann/Kuntze (1991) examined the R&D co-operations of small and medium-sized enterprises (SMEs) in Germany. As a major outcome, they analysed the relative importance of co-operations with universities and research institutes compared to other partners; furthermore they distinguished between "hard" and "soft" forms of co-operation. According to their results, consulting engineers and customers are the most frequent partners in "hard" co-operation, i.e., R&D co-operation; universities and research institutes, however, occupy an average position. Also in "soft" co-operation, the latter hold an average level. All in all, universities and research institutes are not the most important R&D partners of SMEs, but their contribution to industrial R&D is not inconsiderable.

As shown above, certain areas of technology are more science-intensive than others. In such areas, close networks between academic and industrial researchers can emerge which Rappa/Debackere (1992) call "technological communities". They define these as a "group of scientists and engineers, who are working on an interrelated set of technological problems and who may be organisationally and geographically dispersed but who nevertheless communicate with each other". For the example of area of neural networks, they show striking similarities in the communication structures used by academic and industrial researchers. Thus they identify conferences, publications, and direct personal contacts as the - still - most frequently employed media of scientific communication and observe that these are intensively used by industrial researchers as well. These findings support the view of a broad overlap of science and technology according to a cognitive definition of science (see section 2). In any case, industrial researchers as members of a technological community - and less the industrial management - play an important role for establishing ties to academic institutions. By the way, it seems to be more appropriate to call these networks "techno-scientific communities" instead of "technological communities" as the specific channels of communication are largely determined by the scientific character of the examined area.

4.4 Conditions for success of efficient knowledge transfer

From a theoretical perspective, knowledge transfer from non-industrial institutions to industry is highly profitable to both partners. The development and implementation of new technological knowledge swallow large sums of money and success cannot be guaranteed. R&D co-operation with universities, however, offers the opportunity to tap already existing knowledge pools or to take advantage of publicly subsidised research at universities and thus to get research input at low costs. On the other hand, non-industrial institutions are interested in getting access to new sources of knowledge from the side of industrial research, too. Furthermore, a joint R&D project with companies is a highly welcome possibility to finance badly needed new equipment and additional staff and, thus, to get rid of the notorious money shortage at public research institutions. However, as we have seen from the last section, empirical evidence does not corroborate this hypothesis. Consequently, we have to look in more detail at the underlying barriers to and conditions for success.

The following list of seven crucial success factors is taken from Puck (1987) who reviews them against the background of the above-mentioned direct channels of knowledge transfer:

- match of interest,
- bridging of different structures,
- sufficient potentials,
- free information exchange,
- confidence,
- maturity of results, and
- appropriate transfer level.

Every type of professional interaction between individuals as well as between institutions is based on mutual interests. While the range of interests, the respective partners are searching for, does not necessarily have to correspond in total, both are looking for gains. In the case of knowledge transfer from non-industrial institutions, especially universities, to companies, the **match of interest** cannot be taken for granted.

Bräunling/Allesch (1982) are sceptical about the motivation of university researchers concerning technology transfer. In their view, the career system within the scientific community and public financial subsidies for scientific research tend to reduce the scientists' interests in transfering their new knowledge. Comparison of the U.S. academic system, which relies more on grants and research contracts from business, and German universities, financed almost completely from public sources, underlines this argument.

Apart from the question of financial constraints, other areas of conflict emerge. First of all, university researchers in general focus primarily on basic knowledge with long-term effects and little impact on direct applications. Furthermore, universities are interested in early publication of their results, even if they are rather incomplete. Companies, on the other hand, are keen on an immediate application of new knowledge to their products and processes. In order to extract the highest possible profits from new products, companies are eager to avoid any kind of publication and prefer secrecy. If this is not guaranteed, they will apply for protection under the existing patent laws to prevent competitors from copying. These diverging interests concerning the publication of research results and their impact on the behaviour of the scientists are discussed in more detail by Dasgupta/David (1992).

The above cited example of neural networks shows that a strong common interest in specific techno-scientific areas is a key element of linking universities and industry, stimulating them to overcome existing barriers (cf. Rappa/Debackere 1992).

Beyond these problems of diverging interests and motivation, there exist broad structural differences between universities and industry which might hamper an efficient knowledge transfer. For successful co-operation a **bridging of different structures** is necessary. In the view of Puck (1987), universities are characterised by notorious scarcity of equipment and personnel. Their research activities suffer from sluggish reorientation and resource allocation to upcoming fields of research. In general, universities lack the flexibility to quickly found new research groups and to dissolve them when their task has become obsolete. On the other hand, companies have vital interest in reacting immediately to emerging market requirements and to make use of newly created knowledge in many areas of research. Thus, they establish project groups which consist of personnel from different sections and dissolve them when their task is completed.

There is a controversy about research organised in single disciplines. Some argue that it is just the discipline-bound organisation of research at universities that hinders flexibility and instant co-operation between different research fields. Stankiewicz (1986), however, takes the opposite standpoint in arguing that discipline-bound structures still are the basis for efficient academic research. In his view, organisation into discrete disciplines serves as an appropriate tool for socialising the academic community, for supervising research quality and for controlling future developments.

As a result of his analysis of the structural relationship between universities and industry he enumerates three cases of university-industry co-operation that probably will not fail:

- consultancies requiring a relatively limited amount of time on the part of the academics involved. This implies that the advice sought should be technical and highly specific
- research projects which are long-term in character, capable of being handled by a single discipline and which, preferably, pose a genuine intellectual challenge in terms of criteria of the field
- research projects which are relatively free of secrecy and in which no serious problems regarding proprietary rights are likely to emerge

Stankiewicz proposes maintaining the discipline-bound, traditional organisation structure of universities. Interdisciplinarity, however, has become a characteristic feature of modern technology. This is why universities have to contemplate how to engage in interdisciplinary projects, because the interdisciplinary organisation of research will be the only way to cope with the future development of technology.

Matching interest and corresponding structures for a specific R&D project are not enough to guarantee the success of technology transfer. Each of the partners involved has to have sufficient equipment (e.g., laboratories) and qualified personnel, i. e., **sufficient potentials**.

Technology transfer, as one form of knowledge transfer, is based on an intensive participation of staff and material: "Knowledge and technology transfer are themselves knowledge-intensive processes" (Mowery 1983, 363). Only firms with their own research centres can master this. Two characteristic problems are inseparably tied to the process of knowledge transfer. First, problems do not resemble each other and, thus, each time require new solutions. Second, new knowledge and its means of implementation are distinct from each other. That means, e.g., that a technical solution translated into verbal language often loses some facets of its meaning (Poser 1990, 16). Taking these difficulties into account, Cohen/Levinthal (1989) established a theory of learning proposing a company's absorption capacity to be the decisive factor for a successful adaptation of academic knowledge. Furthermore, Mowery (1983) and Kuhlmann/Kuntze (1991) point to the fact that the potential technological competence decides whether external know-how can be absorbed. Following Rotering (1990), they listed three factors for success they regard as crucial: first, a corporate management that is highly willing to make changes and engage in innovation; second, similar qualifications of both partners and a similar understanding of problems, thus, common perceptions and attitudes: and third, a transparent organisation of joint R&D projects. Seaton/Cordey-Hayes (1993) also emphasise the ability to relate to and act effectively on this knowledge (receptivity). This prerequisite for technology transfer was often ignored, and many studies put one-sided focus on the accessibility of new ideas and technology.

In any case, researchers at universities have to actively transfer their knowledge and should help to adapt and implement this knowledge in industry, too. The burden on the scientists involved is often enormous, because this type of activity exceeds their normal research work. Consequently it becomes obvious that both management and technological factors influence the success of co-operative R&D projects.

In this context, a further factor for a successful co-operation is the size of the company. There are a number of studies which show that, in general, large firms co-operate more often with universities. Link/Rees (1990, 27) conclude in their study examining 209 U.S. companies that just over 50 per cent of the smallest firms (with fewer than 250 employees) were active in at least one research relationship with a university, whereas about 90 per cent of the firms with more than 1000 employees were involved in such a co-operation. In their study on technology transfer, Böhler et al. (1989) came to nearly the same findings: the smaller the company, the smaller the number of potential co-operation partners, and the smaller the number of external knowledge sources used, and the smaller the number of subcontracting in specific R&D projects. This is, however, only a general rule. According to Wolff et al. (1993, 84), companies with 100 to 500 employees are very active in external

R&D co-operation and even exceed the co-operation level of companies of all other sizes.

As a further important point, **free information exchange** may be reduced, if the need for secrecy in industry is overemphasised. Universities especially depend on an intensive return flow of information from industry. E.g., the success of further research work will be seriously damaged, if university researchers are not freely allowed to test results. Still, industry has to make sure that crucial findings do not leak to competitors.

The relationship between industry and university is often traditionally clouded. Mistrust and prejudices may be rooted in former co-operations which failed. Thus, the creation of **confidence** and the establishment of regular contacts, as propounded in the above-discussed network approach, is one of the prerequisites for success, because contracts often do not lead to a balance of interests, but favour one party and thus cannot rule out conflicts. Unfortunately, Hakansson's theory remains conspicuously vague on this subject. Walter (1992), however, emphasises the outstanding importance of creating social relations, confidence, and a feeling of mutual reliability for developing innovations (see also Kuhlmann/Kuntze 1991).

The persistent conflict between basic science at universities and application-oriented research in industry will be aggravated, if the **maturity of results** in the technological fields is not guaranteed. Although early research contacts between university and industry on newly emerging technologies are useful, the early adaptation of premature technology in industry will stir up a large number of problems. Basic research may be hampered if industry interests interfere too early with the interest of scientists. Then scientists at universities are no longer free to direct research to unknown paths, because they have to produce applicable results. On the other hand, industry expectations are often deflated when early research findings do not prove to be applicable.

Research partners have to choose the **appropriate transfer level** that fits their respective potentials and needs. In principle, R&D co-operations and knowledge transfer may use different channels, each of them requiring that both partners possess of the necessary resources. As Puck (1987) emphasises, the exchange of personnel proves to be the most efficient transfer channel. Therefore, he recommends that each type of knowledge transfer should be supported by the exchange of qualified R&D personnel. This type of transfer channel is, however, the most complicated one and relies on a high level of organisational flexibility.

4.5   Instruments for promoting knowledge transfer

The last sections have shown that the co-operation between non-industrial research institutions and industry is an important element of modern innovation systems. However, many areas of potential conflict between the partners exist which can hinder or even prevent co-operation. Against this background, a number of decisive preconditions for successful co-operations was given. In this chapter, we want to discuss how much policy measures can improve the knowledge transfer from science to technology.

Before we look at the instruments of public support in more detail, it is necessary to emphasise the broad scope of already existing knowledge transfer managed by the partners involved without external assistance. Above all large companies with huge R&D resources of their own are capable of establishing and keeping up relations with non-industrial research institutions without any public support. The same applies to many small and medium-sized enterprises (SMEs). Wolff et al. (1993) show for the case of Germany that the extent of R&D co-operation of SMEs is increasing. Nevertheless, the contacts between large enterprises and academic institutions often can be intensified, and primarily SMEs have problems establishing research linkages to universities and other research institutions. Against this background, a variety of policy measures for the promotion of knowledge transfer from science to technology has emerged over the last several years. Meyer-Krahmer (1990) gives a comprehensive overview of the available measures. He mainly differntiates institutional arrangements, financial support, transfer agencies, and exchange of personnel. Table 4.5-1 summarises the main aims and effects as well as selected problems of the different instruments.

Table 4.5-1:   Instruments for the promotion of research co-operations

Instruments	Aims, effects	Selected problems
new media of S&T information	accessibility, transparency of information	acceptance
contract research institutes	high degree of user-orientation	time horizon of research may be too short-term
co-operative research institutes	high participation of SMEs	mainly for sector-specific problems
transfer units, innovation consultancies	high participation of SMEs; initiating R&D co-operation and start-ups	low acceptance of newly established agencies by industry and host institutions
network approach	establishment of effective national or international R&D networks	precondition: a well developed private and public R&D base
exchange of persons	increasing mobility of R&D personnel	different carrier structure in universities and firms
tax reduction, subsidies for extramural R&D	enforcing of existing intramural or extramural R&D	only small effects on initiating R&D co-operation
subsidies for selected R&D co-operation projects	establishment of strategic technology fields	diverging interests of research and business systems

Source: Meyer-Krahmer (1990), FhG-ISI

During the last few years, many industrial countries have introduced **new media of S&T information** in order to improve accessibility and transparency. For that purpose the public library systems have been improved, for example, by the establishment of special libraries, or journals on knowledge transfer have begun to be published. A major instrument in this context is the setting up of S&T-related

databases in off-line or on-line versions. Furthermore, special information services have been introduced (Schmidt 1992). All these measures can be classified as indirect means of knowledge transfer. A major problem is the relatively poor acceptance by industry, because these indirect channels are - as already mentioned above - less effective than direct research contacts. Furthermore, in many cases, different problems arise when using the mentioned sources in practice. For example, the use of on-line databases is not as simple as often assumed and requires sufficient experience on the part of the user or external assistance.

As to **institutional arrangements**, the establishment of **contract research institutions** - in general outside of universities - plays a major role. Contract research institutions generally rely on funds that come from public bodies as well as from industry. Their research interests are medium-term in character and focuse on the application of knowledge. In addition, there is a less strong need for the early publication of results; the organisation is more flexible than at universities. An important advantage is that these institutions can better adapt their internal structures to the needs of industry, because they are not directly linked to the university system. Therefore, many of the problems discussed above do not arise. Nevertheless, contract research institutions must have close contact to academic institutions in order to get access to new scientific knowledge. But their activities are not just a simple knowledge transfer from academia to industry. They have to engage in their own research activities in order to achieve a sufficient maturity of the basic scientific knowledge for technical realisations. Examples of contract research institutions are the semi-public Fraunhofer Society in Germany or the projected Faraday Centres in Great Britain (cf. the more detailed description in chapter 3 and Traill/Miège 1989). Of course, other organisational forms are possible, for example with a closer legal binding to universities or as privately run research institutes. The borders between contract research institutes and consultancies are not always clear-cut.

Co-operative research institutes are chiefly industry-financed with limited public support. Their main purpose is to bring together different industrial partners in a research project of common interest; they solve sector-specific problems which exceed the capacity of single companies. In Germany, a high participation of SMEs has been observed (Meyer-Krahmer 1990). The R&D aims and target areas are generally collectively determined by a majority vote of a board representing the relevant companies. The results and findings are instantly transferred into the participating companies. As a major problem of this approach, it is often difficult and time-consuming to reach an agreement on common R&D projects. Furthermore, this institutional arrangement can, in general, only be used for specific problems of quite homogeneous sectors. Up to now, co-operative research institutes have been established only in Germany (cf. section 3.1); their clear success should stimulate other countries to use this instrument, too.

Transfer units and **innovation consultancies** should not be subsumed under the heading of institutional arrangements, because as a decisive difference to contract research institutes and co-operative research institutes, they do not perform their own R&D activities at a significant level. The main purpose of transfer units and innovation consultancies is the knowledge transfer from universities to industry and the initiation of respective R&D co-operations. The investigations of Kuhlmann et al. (1991) on Industry Liaison Officers (ILO) and ILO-units in 11 European countries showed that the liaison units have a broad variety of activities which largely depend on the specific local situation and the respective national innovation system. According to these results, most university ILOs spend a great deal of their time on marketing activities (the "window" function), whereas the contracting function in which the ILOs negotiate research contracts on behalf of the university is less important (ibid., 18). Furthermore, the authors conclude: "Generally it is assumed that there is a need (for ILO-units) but there is hardly any empirical evidence of this ..." (ibid., 19). In any case, transfer units can promote knowledge transfer from universities to industry, especially to SMEs, and they can initiate R&D co-operations and start-ups of new science-based companies. But their role is often overestimated, and especially newly established agencies suffer from a low acceptance by industry as well as the host institutions. Nevertheless, their impact is relatively important in countries where universities form the main basis of non-industrial R&D and where contacts between academically oriented institutions and industry have yet to be developed.

The establishment of **R&D networks** by participation at conferences, the initiation of specific R&D co-operations, or other instruments is a quite difficult and time-consuming task. A decisive precondition is a well-developed private and public R&D base so that every partner can profit from joining the network. As discussed above in more detail, a successfully established R&D network is a major advantage for international competitiveness. Looking at the EU, the promotion of intra-European transborder co-operation is considered to be increasingly important (cf. Tsipouri et al. 1992).

A further very effective instrument of knowledge transfer is the promotion of the **exchange of persons** by special grants or subsidies. Because of different career structures in universities and firms and the social problems of mobility, the transfer of personnel will always be limited compared to other measures.

Financial incentives for extramural R&D or R&D co-operations in specific fields are widely used instruments of technology policy. A major problem are free-rider effects; furthermore, the financial incentives can bring inappropriate partners together who would not co-operate within other circumstances. Because financial incentives are the most commonly used instrument for the stimulation of R&D co-operations, they are also the best known. Therefore, they will not be discussed in this study in further detail. Examples for recent discussions, e.g., on direct or indirect means of support or on R&D tax credit, can be found in Meyer-Krahmer (1989) or Leyden/Link (1993).

In research programmes of the European Commission, many of the instruments discussed are already used. The main instruments are financial incentives for R&D co-operations in selected areas whereby a major condition is the co-operation of partners of different nationality. This approach is very useful for achieving a mutual understanding of national innovation systems and for learning from the respective advantages and deficits. Nevertheless, one has to be aware that this specific type of support of international co-operations can only be made in addition to already existing national R&D programmes. The grater the role the Commission plays in public European research activities, the more regional approaches will become necessary. Regional R&D networks are very important because of limited transaction costs and cannot be replaced by international R&D networks. Therefore, regional initiatives are not only important for less-favoured regions but for all other regions of the EU as well. In this context, it must be pointed out that the Commission already supports regional approaches: Since 1989, the Community Support Framework (CSF) as part of the Structural Funds, accompanied by initiatives like STRIDE, has particularly been helping to develop the R&D base of least favoured regions (objective No. 1 regions). Thus, the above comments are mainly aimed at international R&D co-operations in leading-edge technologies chiefly engaged in by advanced countries.

The research activities of the Commission are supplemented by the organisation of international meetings and conferences. Furthermore, it promotes the international exchange of research personnel. Thus, the network approach and the exchange of persons are well-known instruments of European R&D policy, too. The same applies to transfer units, which have been established at different national and international levels.

Up to now, the Commission has not used institutional arrangements as a major instrument for the improvement of links between universities, research institutes and industries. This lack of institutional arrangements can be regarded as a real deficit, because this approach has proved to be very successful in the area of leading-edge technologies. Of course, the national experiences with research institutions such as the Fraunhofer Society in Germany cannot be directly transferred to the transnational level. Nevertheless it seems to be promising to think in more detail about possible institutional arrangements by the Commission. Its initiative for a European Association of Contract Research Organisations is a first step in this direction (Traill/Miège 1989). Further steps for specific European institutional approaches should follow (cf. also chapter 7.2 and chapter 3.4.5 of part III).

5. The role of science within models and theories of the innovation process

"When you adopt a new systematic model of economic principles you comprehend reality in a new and different way."
Samuelson (1967, 10)

Models are generally used for the description of complex systems. Models emphasise those features or elements of the system which are considered to be important; they ignore aspects which seem to have only minor effects. Thus, models are only a proxy or a "limited abstraction" of reality (Ferrata et al. 1992, 17). Models can only describe a certain aspect of the reality, and their design largely depends on the intentions and special problems addressed by their authors.

In the next section, different models of the innovation process are described and critically discussed. By a systematic comparison of the models presented, the special perspective of their authors can be described. Furthermore, the history of thinking about the innovation process can be portrayed. All models focus on industrial innovation, and it is interesting to see the specific role of science within these models. At the end of this section a new model of innovation is suggested which integrates the most important elements of the examined models and theories. Innovation models which emphasise the internal R&D management of companies are discussed in more detail in chapter 2.3 of part II.

5.1 Innovation theories of Schumpeter

In the most general sense, economists have always recognised the central importance of technological innovation for economic progress. The theories of Adam Smith, David Ricardo, and Karl Marx are famous examples. Nevertheless, Schumpeter was the first who gave innovation an explicit function within economic theory. Schumpeter made the extremely important distinction between inventions and innovations, which is still valid and generally used in the current discussion on innovation processes. According to the definition of Schumpeter, "an *invention* is an idea, a sketch or a model for a new or improved device, product, process or system ... an *innovation* in the economic sense is accomplished only with the first *commercial* transaction involving the new product, process, system or device" (Freeman 1982, 7). Thus, innovation is the event of the first introduction of a new product or process into the market; the activities leading to this event constitute the innovation process. Furthermore, Schumpeter introduced the concept of diffusion, designating the phase of the propagation of a new technology in different fields of application.

Phillips (1971) pointed out that there is not one Schumpeterian model but two. Figures 5.1-1 and 5.1-2 are schematic representations of these two models. They are based essentially on diagrams used by Phillips with minor modifications by Freeman (1982, 212-213). In the first model, which traces back to Schumpeter (1912), the entrepreneur has a key function for the economic process and especially for the initiation of innovation. The entrepreneur realises the future potential of inventions, which are seen as exogenous to industrial enterprises. The model is generally a linear one with successive phases, but there already exists a strong positive feedback loop from successful innovation to increased R&D activities depicted by a linkage from "profits from innovation" to "entrepreneurial activities" and "innovative investment". This feedback has to be interpreted above all as an incentive to use R&D as a tool for economic success, not as a flow of ideas for the improvement of innovations.

Figure 5.1-1:   Schematic representation of Schumpeter's model of entrepreneurial innovation (Mark I)

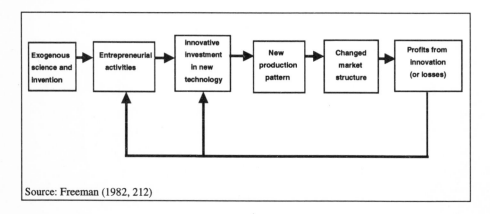

Source: Freeman (1982, 212)

Figure 5.1-2:   Schematic representation of Schumper's model of large-firm managed innovation (Mark II)

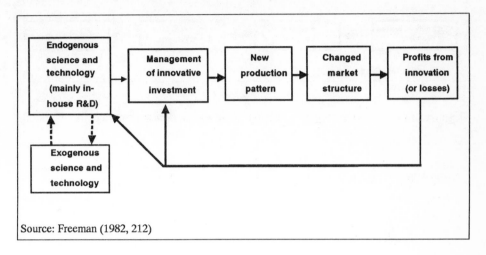

Source: Freeman (1982, 212)

In the second model, based on Schumpeter (1942), large firms have taken the place of the entrepreneur and the R&D activities are mainly performed in-house. Nevertheless, exogenous science and technology still exist with a coupling to endogenous science and technology. The change of models reflects the increased use of in-house research by large companies in the twentieth century, a trend discussed in more detail by Freeman (1982) and Mowery (1983). Freeman describes this increasing role of research for technology as the "rise of science-related technology" (see the definitions of research and science in chapter 2).

5.2   Linear models

The discussion on innovation after the Second World War until the late seventies was largely dominated by linear models of the innovation process which Schmidt-Tiedemann (1982) calls "pipeline models" (see, e.g., Price/Bass 1969, Henfling 1981, or Merrifield 1979). These models assume a simple sequence of the phases research, development, production, and marketing with no or only a slight overlap; they are also called "sequential" models. Even today, these models are often used because of their quite convincing simplicity and utility for unreflected technology push policy.

Figure 5.2-1: Schematic representation of the science-push model

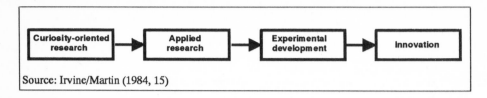

Source: Irvine/Martin (1984, 15)

Figure 5.2-2: Schematic representation of the market-pull model

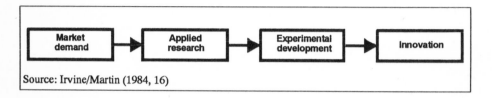

Source: Irvine/Martin (1984, 16)

The use of linear models is closely linked to the intensive debate of the sixties and seventies over whether innovation is generated by new scientific ideas or by new or changed market demands. The science-push and market-pull models are depicted in figures 5.2-1 and 5.2-2. According to the science-push model, the innovation process starts with curiosity-oriented research which is equivalent to pure basic research according to the definitions of chapter 2. The ideas generated by basic research induce the target-oriented part of the innovation process with applied research and experimental development, finally leading to innovation. The idea of science-push traces back to Bush (1945), according to whom "new products and processes are founded on new principles and conceptions which, in turn, are developed by research in the purist realms of science." (ibid., 19). In contrast to that, the market-pull model assumes market demand as the origin of innovations, whereas basic research does not play any important role. A prominent representative for the latter position is Schmoockler (1966), whose broad empirical work, based on patent statistics, led to a stronger influence of market-pull compared to science- and technology-push on patterns of innovative activity, both across industry and over time.

The discussion of the two models was largely influenced by the outcome of different retrospective studies on the impact of basic science on technical innovations. The most important ones are presented in further detail in chapter 4. At this point, only some important results of the debate regarding innovation models are recapitulated.

It is possible to demonstrate a clear impact of basic science on technological innovation. But in many cases, a long delay between a scientific discovery and its introduction into a technical application can be observed. Science is seldom, if ever, the sole driving force for innovations, and generally plays a dominant role only for radical innovations. Furthermore, such breakthroughs mostly do not trace back to only one scientific discovery, but are related to many different scientific areas which have to be integrated for the generation of a new technical product or process. Finally, the linkage of technological areas to science varies considerably in strength; hence it is possible to distinguish between science-intensive and less science-intensive areas.

Most studies show a dominant influence of the market on innovation compared to the role of science. This nonetheless does not prove the validity of the market-pull model, because the economic forces can only operate within a framework of scientific and technical constraints (Blume 1992, 40; Rosenberg 1976). According to Dosi (1988, 1142), "market conditions exert a powerful influence on the conduct of technological search, but they do so primarily by stimulating, hindering, and focusing the search for new technological paradigms. When established, however, each paradigm ... remains quite 'sticky' in its basic technical imperatives". Therefore, Irvine/Martin (1984, 24) conclude: "While the picture that emerges from retrospective studies of innovation is exceedingly complex, one conclusion that stands out clearly is that neither the 'science-push' nor the 'demand-pull' model provides an adequate description of the innovation process."

In a review of the recent innovation debate, Dosi (1988, 1140-1142) calls linear models of the innovation process into question as well. Nevertheless, a further, quite recent linear model shall be described which was suggested by **Rothwell/Gardiner** (1988). This special model, which represents a bridge between linear and complex models, is illustrated in figure 5.2-3. The first phases are quite similar to those of other models, starting with basic ideas leading to invention and then innovation. The new element of the model is the phase of re-design with the result of a re-innovation. The authors put the focus on the re-design stage, because according to their estimates only about 10 per cent of all innovations can be characterised as larger design steps (i.e., landmark innovations, radical innovations, major innovations) whereas bulk rest concerns smaller design steps (i.e., incremental innovations, generational innovations, new mark numbers, improvement innovations, minor detailed innovations). Against this background, they see the necessity of a more systematic management of the re-design phase. In this context they underline the need for an interaction of producers and users, thus "a technology/market coupling ... especially in the area of re-innovation which dominates much of the contemporary 'real' industrial world" (ibid., 386).

Figure 5.2-3:   Schematic representation of the model of Rothwell/Gardiner

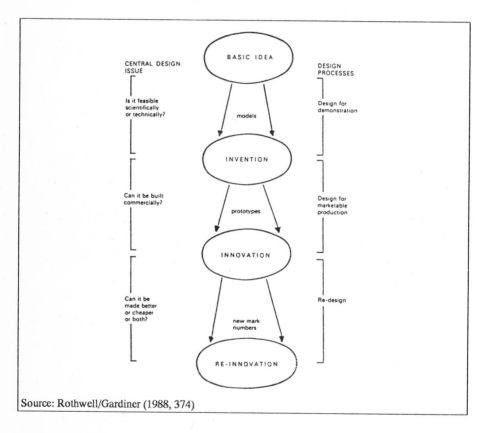

Source: Rothwell/Gardiner (1988, 374)

The focus of Rothwell/Gardiner on re-design accords well with findings of Enos (1958) on the petroleum-refining industry. The author distinguishes between an "alpha phase" (i.e., cost reductions due to the first introduction of a new process) and a "beta phase" (i.e., cost reductions from subsequent improvements of the new process). Enos found that the average annual cost reduction generated by the beta phase exceeded three times that generated by the alpha phase. On this basis he concluded: "The evidence from the petroleum-refining industry indicates that improving a process contributes even more to technological progress than does its initial development" (ibid., 180, cited according to Kline/Rosenberg 1986, 283).

5.3   Feedback and parallel models of the innovation process

In view of the obvious shortcomings of linear models, different attempts to improve them were made in the seventies and eighties. A major aim of these new models was the combination of science- and technology-push and market-pull aspects. For that purpose, many models use feedback loops which are derived from control theory. In order to illustrate the underlying ideas, figure 5.3-1 shows a block diagram of a negative feedback control system. A component or process of the system is represented by a block. In the given example, the input signal is transformed by the forward element F into an output signal. Then, the output signal is fed into the backward element B, the output of which is added, in a negative way, to the input signal. Hence the input signal of F and consequently the output signal is changed. The characteristics of such a feedback loop largely depend on the transfer characteristics of the blocks F and B, which are often not explicit ("black box"). But as a general rule, negative feedback loops lead to stable output signals, whereas positive feedback loops induce a steadily increasing output. To sum up, the feedback does not represent a return to a former state of the system, but a special combination of control signals to achieve a desired output.

Ropohl (1989) - based on Ropohl (1979) - suggests, from a sociological perspective, a system of action for the development of technology. He divides the system into the three main blocks "production of knowledge", "production of goods" and "utilisation of goods" (see figure 5.3-2). A main characteristic of this system model are feedback loops from the utilisation of goods, i.e., the market, to the production of goods and the production of knowledge. In terms of control theory, there are two forward elements (knowledge, production) and a positive feedback

Figure 5.3-1: Block diagram of a negative feedback loop system

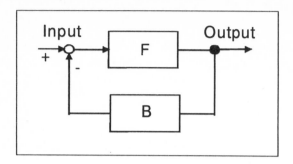

Figure 5.3-2: Socio-technical systems and their impact on technical change according to Ropohl (Abbreviations: BD = needs, TM = technical potentials, PI = product information, P = products, ZS = target system, IS = information system, AS = execution system) (English translation by the present authors)

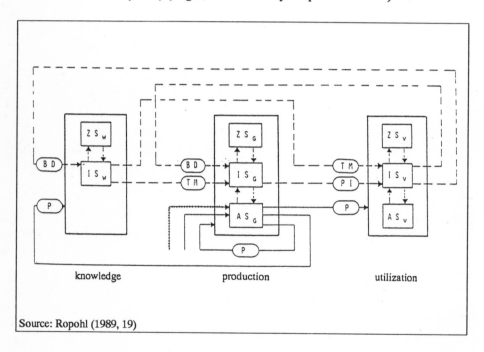

Source: Ropohl (1989, 19)

loop with one backward element (utilisation). Further feedback loops connect the output of the goods production block to its input and to the input side of knowledge production. Additionally, the output of knowledge production is directly linked to the input of the utilisation of goods. According to this model, the production of goods depends on signals (needs) of the markets and inputs of the knowledge production system as well; a strict distinction of science-push and market-pull is no longer possible. A shortcoming of Ropohl's model is the strict distinction between knowledge production and goods production wherein the position of industrial research is not clear. But the author states that in the case of science-based enterprises the systems of knowledge and goods production are integrated (ibid., 20). The depiction of figure 5.3-2 refers to a meso-level of the innovation system. In a further, more complex graph the author combines the micro-, meso-, and macro-level, thus additionally introduces on the one hand the individual level of scientists, inventors, and engineers and on the other hand the super-ordinate level of the state and the society. Further sociology-oriented theories of technical charge are discussed in Rammert (1992).

Figure 5.3-3:   Model of the evolution of a successful innovation according to Roy/Cross

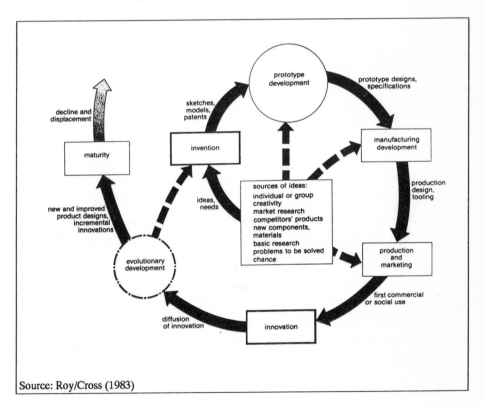

Source: Roy/Cross (1983)

Roy/Cross (1983) look at innovation as a cyclic process where technical possibilities are linked to market needs (figure 5.3-3). According to them, the creation of ideas occupies a central block which comprises not only basic research but, e.g. market research as well. The main path of innovation leads from the central idea block through invention, prototype development, manufacturing development, and production and marketing to innovation. At the same time the knowledge generation block is directly linked to prototype development, manufacturing development, and production and marketing so that the strict sequential mode of the main path is broken up. Like Ropohl, the authors propose a feedback path from the market (diffusion of innovation) to knowledge production (invention). This feedback once again follows the main path through development and marketing leading to new and improved products. The model additionally refers to theories of the product cycle, which will be discussed later on in more detail. According to this cycle, the product will reach a state of maturity, followed by decline and displacement of the product. The model of Roy/Cross uses common concepts such as invention, development, and innovation so that it can be directly linked to the general discussion on innovation. Compared to the model of Ropohl, a clear disadvantage are the missing links from elements of the central path, e.g., manufacturing development, to the central block of idea generation. Interestingly, the above-discussed linear model of Rothwell/Gardiner (1988) with the focus on re-design is largely based on the cyclic model of Roy/Cross (see Rothwell/Gardiner 1985). Whereas Roy/Cross emphasise the cyclic flow of knowledge through the industrial innovation system, Rothwell/Gardiner want to preserve the sequential ordering of innovative actions, and thus the time axis.

Kline suggested an improved model (Kline 1985, Kline/Rosenberg 1986) which broadly influenced the discussion on the structure of innovation processes (for example, the Oslo Manual of the OECD refers to this model). The depiction of this so-called chain-linked model is shown in figure 5.3-4. The model consists of several elements which are linked to each other in different ways. Within this complex structure, Kline sees five major paths of innovation. The first central path begins with the stage of invention and analytic design and continues through detailed design and test and afterwards re-design and production to distribution and market (Kline/Rosenberg 1986, 289). The stages of detailed design and re-design can be regarded as equivalents to the more common term of development.

The second path is a series of feedback links from the market to the other stages of the central path. Of particular note is that the main feedback connects the market to a block called potential market, which is located before the block of invention and analytic design. Thus, Kline sees the market as a major source of innovation.

Figure 5.3-4:   Chain-linked model of Kline with original explanations by the cited authors

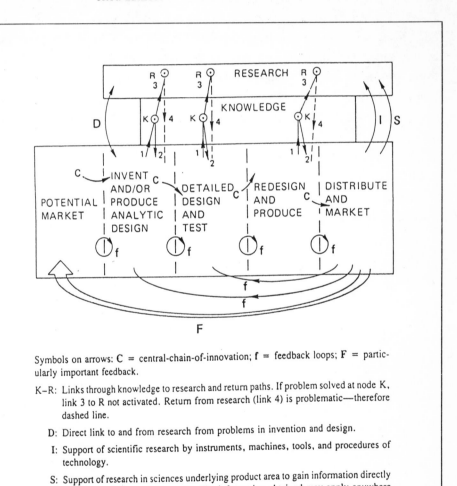

Symbols on arrows: C = central-chain-of-innovation; f = feedback loops; F = partic-ularly important feedback.

K–R: Links through knowledge to research and return paths. If problem solved at node K, link 3 to R not activated. Return from research (link 4) is problematic—therefore dashed line.

D: Direct link to and from research from problems in invention and design.

I: Support of scientific research by instruments, machines, tools, and procedures of technology.

S: Support of research in sciences underlying product area to gain information directly and by monitoring outside work. The information obtained may apply anywhere along the chain.

Source: Kline/Rosenberg (1986, 290)

The third path links science, divided into research and knowledge, to all steps of the central path. In the diagram, science is not located at the beginning of the main path but alongside the development process. Kline/Rosenberg emphasise that experts try first of all to find a solution for their problems on the basis of existing knowledge. Only if they fail to provide an answer on this basis, do they initiate research for the creation of new knowledge, illustrated by a direct arrow between research and invention, which is the fourth path of the model. The fifth path is the feedback from innovation, or more precisely from the products of innovation, to science, for example in the form of new or improved analytic instruments.

For Kline/Rosenberg, the main consequence of their model is the greater emphasis on the market as an initiating factor of the innovation process; therefore, the main path begins and ends with the market. Hence, their ideas are very similar to those of Rothwell/Gardiner (1988) with their focus on re-design after the first introduction of a product into the market. In this context, Kline/Rosenberg underline the less visible or invisible, often small changes of design for technological change (ibid., 282). Within this context, they point out the special role of process innovation and the related great impact of scientific research. All in all, Kline/Rosenberg put their focus on re-design; but for them the impact of science is not negligible: "New science does sometimes make possible radical innovations ... these occurrences are rare, but often mark major changes that create whole new industries, and they should therefore not be left from consideration" (ibid., 293).

A shortcoming of the chain-linked model is the sometimes unconventional terminology otherwise not used in the general debate on innovation. For example, the distinction between invention and analytic design does not lead to new insights into the innovation process. Kline/Rosenberg define analytic design as new arrangements or modifications of designs already within the state of the art to accomplish new tasks or to accomplish old tasks more effectively or at lower costs (ibid., 292). In practice, few innovations consist of radical new features, whereas most are based on new arrangements of already known elements. Therefore, the latter type of innovations can generally be patented. Besides, the multiple use of the term "design" with its multiple meanings (such as concept, construction, or preparation of drawings) can lead to confusion with other stages of the innovation processes. Furthermore, the analytic categories of the model are not very clear. The elements of the central chain of innovation are obviously partial steps of the innovation process, whereas research and knowledge are cognitive or partially institutional categories. The block of the potential market seems to represent perceived market needs, which should already be sufficiently depicted by the big feedback arrow from market to invention.

Figure 5.3-5:   Schematic representation of the model developed by Grupp and Albrecht

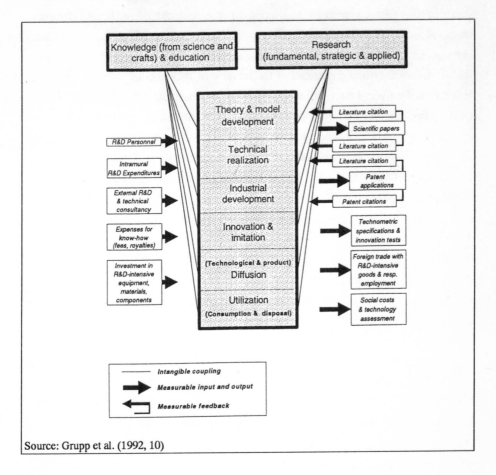

Source: Grupp et al. (1992, 10)

Grupp and Albrecht, independently of each other, developed a function-oriented model of the innovation process which chiefly aims at a connection of input and output indicators of research and development to stages of the innovation process (Grupp et al. 1992, 8-12). At the same time, the model itself introduces new elements not present in approaches discussed above. The authors differentiate six types of innovation-related functions, not assuming that these are clearly distinct and nonopverlapping or sequential (see figure 5.3-5). One function is "theory and model development", which is chiefly linked to basic scientific approaches. Another function of technical realisation comprises the transformation of basic ideas into technical concepts up to the realisation of prototypes. Grupp/Schmoch (1992a, 277) mention historic cases where realisation *preceded* the theory function. A further function is industrial development, where the technical concepts are transformed into marketable products. For Grupp/Albrecht, another function is innovation itself, in the sense of the first commercial realisation of a new technology. In this function, imitation is included, because "imitations may be as painful and difficult as pioneer innovations" (ibid., 9). One may add, from the viewpoint of business administration, that imitators are often convinced of the novelty of their innovation until they learn that a rival firm was first, e. g., when a related patent application is rejected for lack of novelty. The further functions of diffusion and utilisation comprise adaptations, incremental innovations, and product improvements (as for product differentiation see Grupp 1994b), thus re-design in the sense of Rothwell/Gardiner (1988). The distinction between diffusion and utilisation is made, because different output indicators can be used for their representation. Thus, the functions implicitly include cyclic effects, but the depiction of the model illustrates this aspect less clearly than models with explicit feedback paths.

As the described elements are interpreted as functions of the innovation process, Grupp/Albrecht can introduce knowledge, education, and research as new, separate categories. These knowledge-generating elements may be coupled to each function of the innovation process. The similarity to the model of Kline/Rosenberg is obvious. Nevertheless, the clear distinction between science ("stock" knowledge and research) and the functions of the innovation process is analytically clearer.

Already at the beginning of the eighties, **Schmidt-Tiedemann** (1982) introduced a functional model of the innovation process which seems not to have received sufficient attention up to now. His "concomitance" model is closely linked to innovation procedures within an enterprise and thus to business management. The model distinguishes "three functions: the research function (basic and applied, corporate or decentralised); the technical function (development, production, etc.), and the commercial function (marketing, sales, distribution, and service)" (ibid., 18). The three functions can be directly associated with departments of (big) industrial enterprises. The model describes the three functions as simultaneous activities and explicitly depicts the temporal sequence of the tasks. It takes into account the interactions among the functions during the lifetime of the innovation process.

Beside the activities within the functions, Schmidt-Tiedemann introduces key decisions and milestones as additional elements.

Figure 5.3-6:   Schmidt-Tiedemann's concomitance model of an industrial product innovation

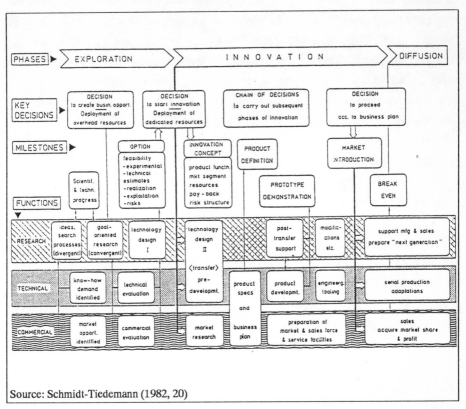

Source: Schmidt-Tiedemann (1982, 20)

The main difference to the previously discussed models is the two-dimensional representation. The first dimension is the time sequence with the sub-phases of exploration, innovation, and diffusion. The second axis represents the differentiation according to the three functions. On this basis, the various (knowledge/co-operation) feedback paths of the innovation process can be drawn as lateral linkages between the research, technical, and commercial functions, and the progress of innovation in the course of the time can also be shown. This illustration of the parallel activities of the three functions (industrial departments) is the main advantage of the model and justifies the name concomitance model. For example, a qualified knowledge transfer from the research to the technical function has to be organised during predevelopment and product development, and even in the engineering stage, the research function can introduce "modifications in essential (i.e., science-based) parameters. If the technology transferred is very 'new' to development, it might be dangerous to leave development alone with problems in a field where there is no adequate expertise available" (ibid., 21). All in all, the concomitance model represents real progress in the discussion on innovation. The functional categories influenced the Grupp/Albrecht model; however, the latter authors did not want to establish an identification of functions with business organisation structures, as these may be subject to change and differ between firms. A minor criticism of the concomitance model concerns the definition of the end of the innovation phase by the break-even point, thus the time when the capital laid out is paid back and the new product contributes to profit (ibid., 20). The break-even point is, of course, very interesting from the perspective of enterprises. Nevertheless, the widely accepted definition by Schumpeter as the first introduction into the market should be used in order to avoid confusion.

Interestingly, Schmidt-Tiedemann emphasises the importance of research especially in the exploration phase. As he sees it, basic and applied research are the origin of many products, but he also recognises the role of the technical and commercial functions in this initial phase (ibid., 19). The differences between the positions of Schmidt-Tiedemann and Kline concerning the role of science can be largely explained by their different background of experience. Kline mainly worked as a consultant in the area of mechanics, whereas Schmidt-Tiedemann is director of the Phillips research laboratory in Hamburg, thus the laboratory of an electronics enterprise. These differences between technical areas are discussed in further detail in section 4.

In this context, **Majer** (1978) introduces a further interesting aspect. This author describes the structure of science, defined as in chapter 2 with the inclusion of industrial research, by a vertical and a horizontal dimension leading to the model of a "cone of research" (*Forschungskegel*, cf. figure 5.3-7). The vertical dimension illustrates the hierarchical structure within the different disciplines from basic research to intermediate application steps and finally to end products. The horizontal dimension symbolises the variety of disciplines. Against this background, scientific activities are characterised by vertical relations within one area of science, horizontal relations between different areas, and feedback paths within and between areas.

These complex interactions lead to chains of intermediate results, often structured like a tree with many branchings. The model illustrates the importance of different types of interaction within the innovation process, in particular the interdependence of different product and technology developments. The reduction of most other innovation models to single products or product families proves to be a quite simplifying abstraction.

Figure 5.3-7:   Depiction of the research cone of Majer (English translation by the present authors)

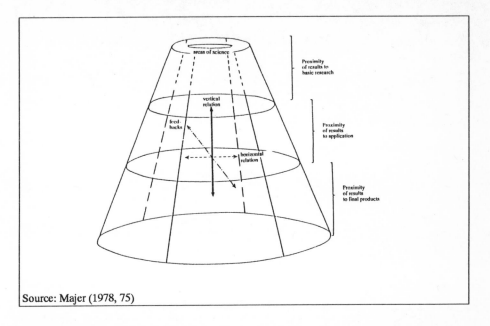

Source: Majer (1978, 75)

Meyer-Krahmer (1989, 38-41) extends Majer's model by the addition of an innovation/diffusion phase, thus transforming the research cone into an innovation cone (cf. figure 5.3-8). Furthermore, he uses not only the outer surface of the cone, but introduces a supplementary radial dimension. On this basis, he distinguishes

- a central technology core with a high level of innovation,
- an inner mantle of technology with chiefly incremental innovations, and
- an outer mantle of technology with pure adoption of innovations.

With this model, the author can describe different types of innovation within a selected field and the related division of labour between companies. For example, semiconductor technology can be located in the core where chiefly large companies are active. The inner mantle, then, represents improvements and adaptations of semiconductors for special applications; here, many small and medium-sized companies are active. Companies of traditional sectors chiefly innovate by buying new products or processes; they are positioned in the outer mantle.

Figure 5.3-8:   Innovation cone according to Meyer-Krahmer

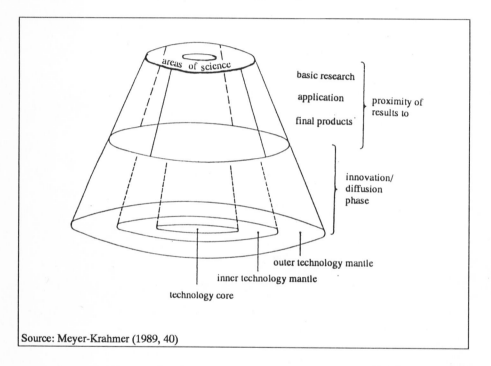

Source: Meyer-Krahmer (1989, 40)

All in all, a major advantage of cone models is the possibility of depicting complex interconnections by the introduction of a third dimension. As a shortcoming, the innovation cone does not describe the continuing role of scientific research during the innovation/diffusion phase in a satisfying way.

The above discussed models of the innovation process represent only a selection of some important examples. Höft (1992, 56-66) gives an overview of about 20 different models, chiefly of German origin. Among the models surveyed, really new ideas compared to the models presented above do not appear.

5.4   Embedding of innovation models into broader conceptions

The models discussed above are focused on product innovation as an early period of the product cycle. The later stages after the innovation are mentioned in the form of re-design, incremental innovations, or diffusion, but not examined in the context of broader economic theories. Therefore, the connection of the discussed models to enlarged models of product life cycle can give deeper insight into the environment of R&D processes. Most models of product life cycles start with the introduction of a product on the market, i.e., the innovation. But, in enlarged integrated concepts the innovation process is included as well. As an example, a diagram of **Pfeiffer/Bischof** (1982, 136) is reproduced (cf. figure 5.4-1). The model was developed in the context of business management, especially strategic marketing and technology management; thus it is made from the perspective of a business enterprise. The authors distinguish three main cycles: the observation cycle, the generation cycle and the market cycle wherein the generation cycle is equivalent to the period of applied industrial research and development. The observation cycle comprises activities of market and technology observation, and it is the main area of industrial and non-industrial basic research. This early cycle is the central subject of the retrospective studies of innovation which are discussed in section 4 in the context of the impact of science on technology. As these precursory scientific activities can not yet be clearly linked to special products, it is difficult to represent them in a quantitative way on the firm level. But a realistic approach for their description can be performed on a more aggregate level, as in section 3 of this report. As to the market cycle, Pfeiffer/Bischof give only a general graph of the turnover or profit, but not of the development activities. But in view of the above-discussed importance of re-design, it would be extremely interesting to examine the relation of the market cycle and the related R&D. This is, of course, a very difficult task, because Pfeiffer/Bischof depict only an ideal market cycle, whereas in reality many different types of life cycles exist (cf. Höft 1992, 22-26).

Utterback/Abernathy (1975) systematically analysed models of process and product development and suggested a model with a combination of both aspects. The main result is depicted in figure 5.4-2, where graphs for product and process

Figure 5.4-1: Schematic representation of the integrated product life cycle concept of Pfeiffer/Bischof (English translation by the present authors)

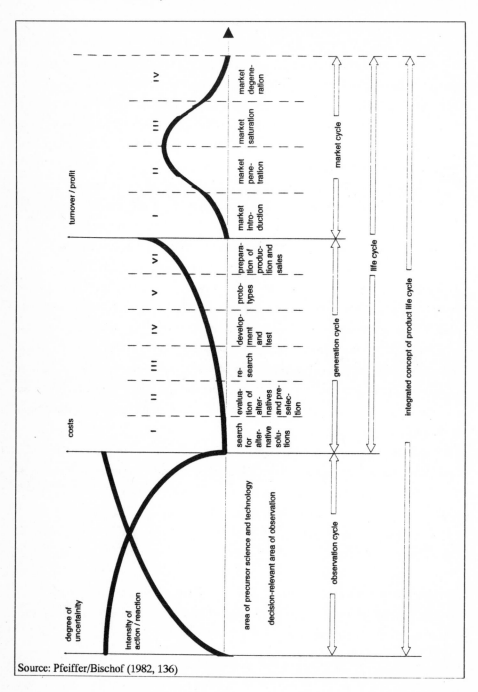

Source: Pfeiffer/Bischof (1982, 136)

innovation are shown in one diagram. As for process development, the authors distinguish an uncoordinated, a segmental, and a systemic stage. The uncoordinated stage is linked to the early life stage of a product where production processes are developed with a great diversity among competitors; the processes are composed largely of unstandardised and manual operations. In the segmental stage, the product line is mature, and price competition becomes more intense. Therefore, production must become more effective and the process-related innovation activities increase. This stage is called segmental, because some parts of the production processes are highly automated while others remain essentially manual or rely upon general-purpose equipment. In the systemic stage, further improvements of the product are not possible, but a further reduction of cost by complete automatisation of processes

Figure 5.4-2:   Innovation and stage of development according to Utterback/Abernathy

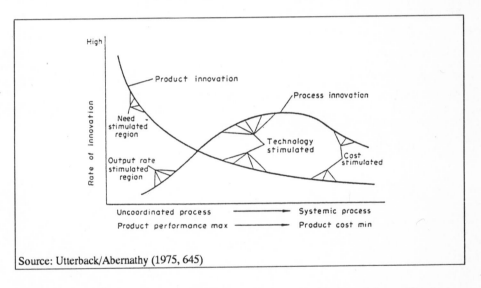

Source: Utterback/Abernathy (1975, 645)

is. As to the product life cycle, the early phases are dominated by performance-maximising so that the rate of innovation is high. The next stage is characterised by the appearance of dominant product designs and by sales-maximising. At the end of the product life cycle cost-minimising is the major aim. As a major consequence, the locus of innovation shifts with the stage of development from product innovation to process innovation. There are different criticisms concerning the general validity of the model (Höft 1992, 119):

- Some products cannot be standardised which is a precondition for the emergence of dominant designs.
- Mass production cannot be used for all products, because the market potential may be too low or the products are too complex.
- Discontinuities such as change of demand, introduction of substitute products, or change in the price level of substitute products are not taken into account.

Furthermore, the starting point of the model with reference to enlarged product life cycle models is not really clear. Obviously, the time axis begins with the innovation, thus the first introduction of the product into the market. Therefore, innovation according to this model means incremental or improvement innovations. When the generation cycle of the product is included, the graphs of product and process innovation of **Teece** (1986, 289) seem to be more realistic (see figure 5.4-3). It is interesting to note that Teece distinguishes between a preparadigmatic and a paradigmatic design phase. Indeed, the conception of the emergence of standardised designs is very near to the ideas of Dosi (1982) on the emergence of technological paradigms and technological trajectories.

Figure 5.4-3:   Innovation over the product life cycle according to Teece

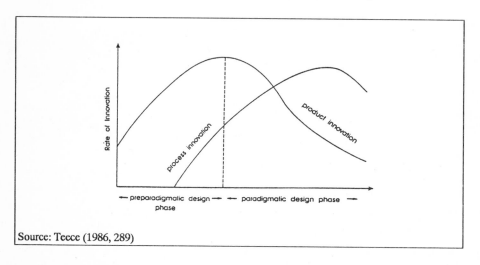

Source: Teece (1986, 289)

In Utterback/Abernathy and Teece models, the early stage of innovation is dominated by product innovation. In many industries, such as the chemical or the electronics industry, however, the development of new products is closely related to the introduction of new processes. Freeman (1982) illustrates this important impact of processes by the example of oil refining (ibid., 33-47). Schmoch et al. (1993a) show the close relationships of products and processes for the cases of flat panel displays, optical storage, and chemical vapor deposition in micro-electronics which clearly disproves the general applicability of Teece's picture. For this type of industry, the relative locus of product and process innovation shown in figure 5.4-4 seems to be more realistic. At the beginning, the dynamics of process and product innovation are quite similar, and it is only in later stages, that process innovations dominate.

Figure 5.4-4:   Innovation over the product life cycle for areas of close linkage of product and process innovation according to findings of Schmoch et al.

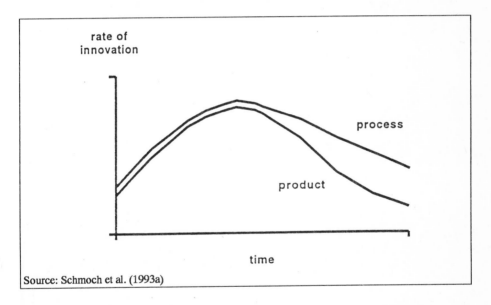

Source: Schmoch et al. (1993a)

The theories of **Lundvall** (1988) on innovation as an interactive process shed a new light on the model of Utterback/Abernathy. Lundvall attributes a key function for innovation to the interaction of users and producers. The relation of users and producers is focused primarily on process innovations; hence "producers" are producers of investment goods and "users" are producers of consumer goods. A close relation between user and producer is necessary, because the producer must have sufficient information on the needs of the user, and the user himself often generates process innovations. Therefore, direct co-operation at different stages is necessary to develop complex and specialised process equipment. The perspective of user-producer interaction can be transferred to the relations of producers of consumer goods and final consumers, and to the relationship of the academic community as producer and industry as user. Lundvall emphasises that even pure science has its users (ibid., 364). All in all, the theory of Lundvall describes innovation as a chain of dynamic user-producer interactions, from pure science up to the final users.

Blume (1992) describes the different types of user-producer relations as a variety of markets inducing a variety of innovations. From this perspective, producers and users are buyers and sellers. Therefore innovation is determined by the preferences of many groups, but "they do not all have identical possibilities of expressing these preferences (for example through purchasing power)" (ibid., 54).

Figure 5.4-5:   Long-term trends of patent applications for laser beam sources and of laser sales

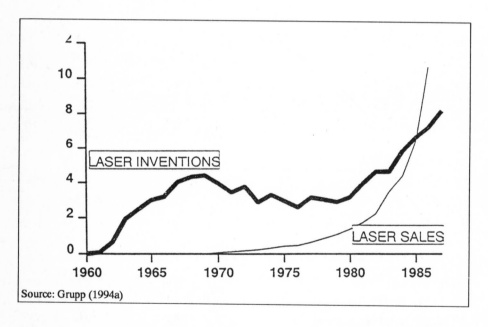

Source: Grupp (1994a)

The discussed models of product life cycle give only a general insight into characteristics of R&D processes. For a more detailed analysis, it is necessary to examine the situation for each product, product line, or product family. Patent statistics have proven to be a valuable tool for the analysis of R&D cycles, because patents are taken out for the first raw inventions as well as later fully developed inventions (Freeman 1982, 8-9). They do not only concern improvements of technical performance but of cost reduction as well. Thus, patents are taken out repeatedly during a long period within the life cycle, from basic inventions to incremental inventions. Merkle (1985) demonstrates for different examples such as magnetic stores, optical stores, or catalysts for exhaust gases that patents reflect phases of increase, maturity and degeneration of the product life cycle.

Grupp (1994a) shows for the example of laser beam sources a very interesting realisationship between the number of patent application and sales (see figure 5.4-5). In laser technology, a steady increase of patents can be observed until the end of the sixties, which is followed by a decline until the middle of the seventies. Afterwards, the registered laser inventions increase again together with the growth of sales. The first cycle can be described as a technology appropriation cycle, whereas the second cycle is related to innovations and improvements concerning specific areas of use. Schmoch (1993) found the same characteristics for polyimides. Rickerby/Matthews (1991) show a similar graph for coating technology, whereby they label the first peak as "promise" and the trough before the second increase as "problems". These examples cannot be generalised to all areas, but it seems to be at least a characteristic type of development in science-intensive technologies. Hence, Grupp (1993b) suggest a standardised scheme of innovation stages for science-based technologies (cf. figure 5.4-6).

Within the same context of work, Meyer-Krahmer (in Meyer-Krahmer/Kuntze 1992) has developed a generalised scheme, showing the linkage of the technological life cycle (generation of new technology) and the product life cycle (market cycle). In contrast to the above discussed scheme of Pfeiffer/Bischof, there is an explicit, broad overlap of the technology cycle and the product cycle (cf. figure 5.4-7).

Figure 5.4-6:   Standardised scheme of innovation stages in science-based areas
                 of technology (English translation by Grupp)

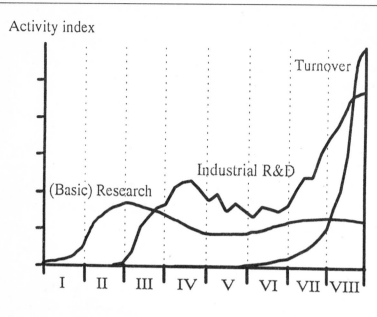

- phase I: First exploratory research in scientific institutions
- phase II: Well established strategic research with perspectives for
              further extensions
- phase III: Fully developed research with first technical realisations
              and prototypes
- phase IV: Difficulties in transforming scientific and technical achievements
              into economic opportunities becoming apparent
- phase V: Temporary stagnation in science and technology
              and reorientations
- phase VI: Industrial R&D recognises new opportunities and
              perspectives for further applications
- phase VII: First commercial applications; industrial R&D
              and economic development safely established
- phase VIII: Diffusion into and penetration of many markets; industrial
              R&D intensity in relation to turnover loses importance.

Source: Grupp (1993b)

Figure 5.4-7:   Generalised scheme of technology and product life cycles according to Meyer-Krahmer/Kuntze

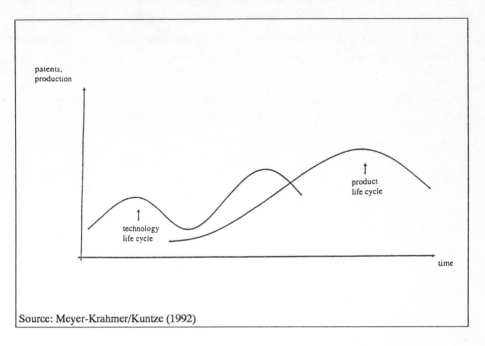

Source: Meyer-Krahmer/Kuntze (1992)

As a last point of this section, the problem of an adequate delimitation of (integrated) product life cycles shall be addressed. The basic question is to what extent improvement innovations should be included in the life cycle or constitute a new cycle, and whether parallel, related developments should be included. In this context, the reflections and findings of **Durand** (1992) can give a helpful orientation. First, the author suggests the introduction of "micro-radical" innovations between the generally used concepts of incremental and radical innovations. According to this model, the start of a new life cycle is defined by a radical innovation, whereas micro-radical innovations still belong to the re-design phase. Second, Durand emphasises the close relationship of product and process which he calls product/process duality. On this basis, he elaborates "Dual Technology Trees" (DTT) depicting the development paths. Horizontal branches represent product designs, while vertical branches show process technologies (cf. figure 5.4-8). Bold lines stand for dominant paths or trajectories. The general representation shows a first innovation cycle with a variety of micro-radical and incremental innovations linked to a first dominant trajectory. When the related technology reaches its limits in terms of performance and/or costs, it is replaced by an alternative technology represented by another

114

parallel branch of development. All in all, technological change is described as a "discrete continuum". The proximity of the tree representation to the research cone of Majer is obvious. Durand demonstrates the utility of his model for the analysis of real cases by the examples of insulin production and public switching (in telecommunications).

Figure 5.4-8:   Innovation cycles represented as cost/performance graphs and Dual Technology Trees according to Durand

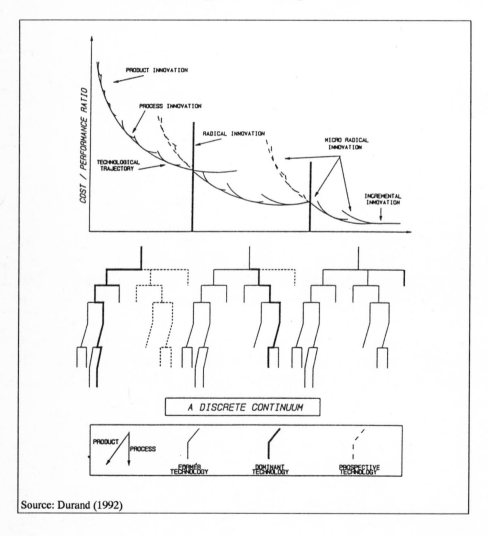

5.5 Interaction model of innovation

Based on the above discussed models and theories, we have developed a new model of the innovation process. In keeping with the subject of the present study, it is focused on the main actors of R&D systems and especially stresses the division of labour between industrial and non-industrial institutions. On the side of the non-industrial institutions, universities/basic research institutions and applied research institutions are introduced. On the side of industry a distinction is made between the research and the technical function, following Schmidt-Tiedemann, is made. Furthermore, the market appears as an independent actor (cf. figure 5.5-1).

As a further decisive feature of the model, it explicitly describes the temporal sequence, once again following the ideas of Schmidt-Tiedemann. The different stages of the innovation process are chiefly derived from Grupp, Schmidt-Tiedemann, and Blume. The first step of "ideas, theories, and exploration" includes basic research as well as the observation of market needs so that the model can be applied to areas of low or of high science linkage. Before the phase of "industrial design", the intermediate stage of "technical concept" - the technical realisation of ideas or the first design - is introduced in agreement with Grupp et al. The model does not end with innovation, i.e., the *first* introduction of a product or process into the market, but continues with "diffusion/utilisation" (of new products/processes). "Invention" and "innovation" are single events within the temporal sequence, whereas "imitation/improvement" is a steady process with several incremental or micro-radical innovations.

Throughout the innovation cycle, there is steady interaction between the different institutional actors and the research and technical function within industry. This interaction is symbolised by lateral arrows. Because of the explicit time sequence, there are no feedback paths. If ideas or suggestions for new products or processes are generated, they are introduced into improvement innovations, or, if a completely new product line or product family is concerned, there are lateral linkages to parallel innovation paths (cf. also Durand 1992).

Figure 5.5-1:   Interaction model of the innovation process

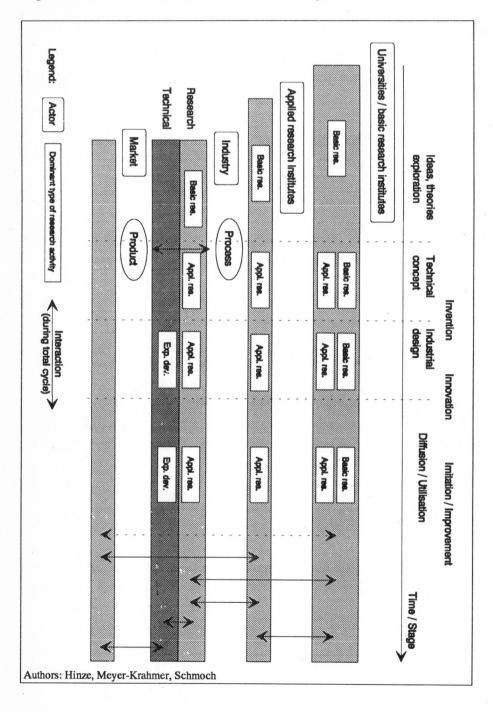

Authors: Hinze, Meyer-Krahmer, Schmoch

As the above discussion reveals, the innovation process is largely determined by an interaction of product and process innovations. This interaction may happen within an enterprise or between different enterprises, i.e., producers of investment goods and producers of consumer goods. This important feature of product/process interaction is explicitly highlighted by labels next to the bar for industry. It is, however, important for all stages of innovation and all interactions between institutions. Following Utterback/Abernathy, it can be assumed that in the last phase of the innovation process, i.e. the phase of declining prices, process innovation is more important than product innovation.

In addition to the stages of innovation, the dominant types of R&D activity according to the Frascati definitions are introduced. This form of representation illustrates that the different types of R&D can be performed in parallel. In this context, it is important to clearly distinguish the innovation stage "industrial design" and the type of R&D activity "experimental development". Against this background, a major shortcoming of many linear innovation models becomes visible since these view the different types of R&D activities as subsequent stages of the innovation process. For a realistic model, a clear distinction between innovation stages on the one hand and types of R&D on the other hand is necessary. Both categories are helpful for the description of innovation, but they represent different perspectives or levels of description.

As for the role of universities and basic research institutions, the first exploration phase is characterised by a focus on basic research, and it often starts, as discussed above, long before related research activities on the side of industry. When the first possibilities for application emerge, the applied research institutes take these ideas over and perform their own oriented basic research. After this early phase, the first product/process ideas are generated on the side of industry. This phase is characterised by an exchange of ideas between universities/basic research institutions, applied research institutions and industry, but the needs of the market have to be taken into consideration as well. Therefore, it is essential to integrate market needs on the one hand with scientific and technical opportunities on the other hand.

The market perspective can be introduced into industry - as in the model of Schmidt-Tiedemann - through a special market function (marketing department) or by direct market contacts of the research or technical function, e.g., contacts between industrial clients and research engineers. Furthermore, the applied research institutions always plan their activities against the background of market needs, and even universities and basic research institutions react, on a lower level, to developments of the market.

Figure 5.5-2:   Association of S&T indicators with stages of innovation and R&D types

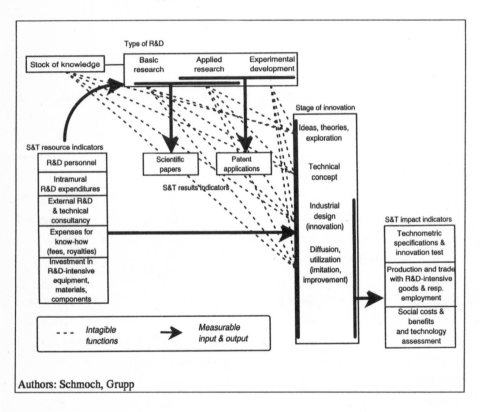

In the following stages, when the concept of the product (process) is defined in a clearer way, the R&D activities in non-industrial institutions will have to become applied, if they want to participate in the innovation process. An important part of this research is performed as contract research. In universities and basic research institutions, the ongoing work in basic research is stimulated and influenced by applied activities; a change from pure basic to oriented basic research may take place. In any case, the activities of universities and basic research institutions do not stop with the early stages of innovation, but continue during the whole innovation process. It is important to acknowledge that the later phases of innovation during the market cycle are important as well and can be quite demanding as to the level of research.

The role of non-industrial research institutions can, of course, vary considerably, according to the technical area. Thus, in many cases, the role of non-industrial institutions may be less important or even negligible in the early phases in comparison to the market impact. Nevertheless, the suggested model does not have special bars for non-industrial institutions only because the study focuses on the scientific community. Whereas in older studies of the sixties and seventies the role of basic research was disputed, most recent authors agree on its increasing importance for modern technology. As an illustrative example, Stankiewicz (1990) sees a growing dependence of technological innovation on scientific advances, because the complexity of technical systems grows. Therefore, he introduces a "parallel development model" of the relations between science and technology, wherein science is largely associated with non-industrial institutions. All in all, the interaction between non-industrial institutions and industry is crucial for the future development of technology.

The finding of the suggested interaction model that a clear distinction must be made between innovation stages and R&D type leads to a new association of S&T indicators similar to that in the model of Grupp/Albrecht (cf. figure 5.3-5). It has been shown above that patents are generated during the whole cycle of a product (process) or a technology and, therefore, cannot be associated with a special stage of innovation. The same observation applies to scientific publications and to most other indicators. As a result of these considerations, a further model was developed which, for reasons of illustration, presents major elements of the interaction model in a different way. The different stages of innovation are depicted in a vertical block and the different types of R&D, and additionally knowledge, are drawn as a separate, horizontal block (cf. figure 5.5-2). As each type of R&D can take place in each stage of innovation, there are multiple intangible linkages between the two blocks. The different input or S&T resource indicators shown on the left side of the diagram are not associated with specific innovation stages or R&D types. Patents are not linked to special stages of R&D, but to applied research and experimental development, sometimes to basic research. Publications have stronger connections to basic and applied research, and thus in comparison to patents, to more basic types of R&D.

The different S&T impact indicators - the terminology follows a recommendation of the OECD (see Sirilli 1992) - can be observed only if a product or process has been introduced into the market; they are associated with the diffusion/utilisation stage. All in all, reflection on appropriate models for the innovation process also helps to better understand which "objects" are measured by indicators.

As a general conclusion, improved models of innovation should not be called "non-linear", as this term could be associated with set-backs or irregularities of R&D activities. Concepts like "parallel", "co-operative" or "interaction-oriented" are more appropriate, because steady interaction in all stages of innovation is a crucial feature of new models. In addition, the role of non-industrial research centres is increasingly important for the genesis of modern technologies.

6. The role of scientific institutions within national systems of innovation

At present, competitiveness and economic growth are national goals of first priority. It is widely acknowledged that innovations are a key factor in reaching these goals. As nations differ in their ability to innovate, different national patterns of innovation are assumed to exist. These different patterns might be attributed to the existence of different national systems of innovation (NSI). Thus, the identification of major elements of NSIs and their mechanisms of interaction have emerged as central topics of economic research. Especially the question of how the existing systems have to be changed in order to increase national competitive strength is of outstanding interest.

In this chapter, the main lines of the discussion on NSIs will be described, with a focus on the specific results for non-industrial research institutions. Within this study, the analysis of NSIs represents the most general level, and it puts the more detailed aspects of the preceding chapters into a broader framework.

6.1 Theories on national systems of innovation

To date, a consistent theory of NSIs does not exist. What all of the available approaches have in common is their endeavour to analyse innovativeness in a socio-economic context (McKelvey 1992). Nonetheless, different approaches to analysing NSIs may be found. Therefore we begin with a short description of some of these approaches. Frequently, as in the case of Nelson (1988) and Freeman (1988), an institutional approach is chosen. They analysed the U.S. and the Japanese system, respectively. In their studies the existence of different systems of innovation is taken for granted. **Freeman** defined an NSI as a "network of institutions in the public and private sectors whose activities and interactions initiate, import, modify and diffuse new technologies" (Freeman 1987, cited according to McKelvey 1991, 11). He pays special attention to four elements: the role of government policy, the role of firms and their R&D efforts, the role of education and training, and the structure of industry (Freeman 1988). Furthermore, Freeman especially stresses the necessity, in the case of radical technological changes, of combining technical with organisational and social innovations. Success and failure depend on a nation's ability to adjust its socio-institutional paradigms to the requirements and possibilities of the techno-economic paradigms.

Figure 6.1-1: Main elements of national systems of innovation according to the theories of Freeman and Nelson

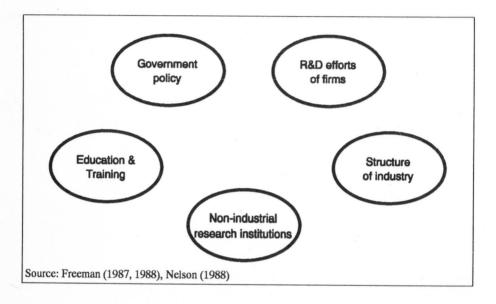

Source: Freeman (1987, 1988), Nelson (1988)

Nelson's (1988) analysis takes as a starting point the existence of technical change and its evolutionary character. As in the case of Freeman, he puts emphasis on the necessity of change and adaptation of institutional structures, because the nature of science and technology in general is constantly changing and varies among technical areas (ibid, 325). Nelson furthermore stresses the uncertainty of scientific and technological development, thus offering a variety of possible strategies. Therefore it is almost impossible to decide ex ante which one would be the best, because the market will answer that question ex post by selection (ibid., 313). Thus, Nelson argues, the main task is to ensure a "pluralistic context for technology" (cited in to McKelvey 1991, 20). That means that institutional richness as a whole, mechanisms of sharing technological knowledge and co-operation of the respective institutions and organisations are interdependant phenomena (ibid., 315). According to Nelson, the differences in the "mix of industries" between nations "strongly influence the shapes of the national systems of innovation". Each nation has its own "composition and structure of institutions other than companies. These institutions differ in the role they play; their organisation and problem-orientation; how much they help national firms; as well as whether funding is public or private. These national characteristics of the R&D system have their implications for how well science and technology is integrated into the activities of industry and therefore how easy/difficult it is for innovation to occur in a country" (cited according to McKelvey 1991, 20). The main structures of NSIs according to Freeman and Nelson are summarised in figure 6.1-1.

According to **Gibbons** (1993), differences in NSIs begin with the chosen type of industrial capitalism. He differentiates among three idealised types: Anglo-Saxon market capitalism, German social market capitalism, and Japanese bureaucratic capitalism. In reality there exist only mixtures of features of these ideal types. The interplay between these real features determines the patterns of action within individual systems and their accompanying value system. Gibbons defines two types of NSIs: the technologically dynamic and the technologically myopic. They are used to characterise the differences in the ability of nations to compete or, in this context, to innovate, referring to their differences in assessing innovations. Gibbons stresses the following features characterising the differences between dynamic and myopic systems. Typical for dynamic systems is that they rate strategic success higher than short-term profits. Dynamic systems take into account the cumulative character and uncertainty of technological activities, whereas myopic systems consider them normal investments and tend, therefore, to perform R&D only for directly visible needs and not for potential future markets. A higher level of education is typical for dynamic systems. This implies that a higher degree of technological knowledge is accumulated at the management level. Technologies with future market potential are strategically pursued. All in all, companies are more flexible in matching their organisational patterns with quickly emerging technological possibilities. Furthermore, dynamic systems are increasingly specialised in technologies with cross-sectional character which demand higher organisational flexibility. According to Gibbons, there will be a shift from static to dynamic competition, leading to a new role of technological innovation. That means that, in addition to market competition concerning the selection of products and processes, a new competition over "selection among design configurations and technological trajectories" emerges (ibid., 5).

Porter (1990) shifted the analysis from the national to the company level because, in his view, it is actually successful companies that are responsible for national advantages. It is not nations that are competing on the world markets but companies in special branches of industry. The nation features only as the environment for companies, thereby strengthening or weakening their competitiveness. As a consequence, the government may influence the innovation process invarious ways. According to Porter, governments should pursue as a main goal the creation of an appropriate, innovation-stimulating environment for the nation's companies. He elaborates four determinants of national advantage, each subject to governmental influence. These determinants are: first, factor conditions which may be influenced by subsidies, policies affecting capital markets and education, etc.; second, demand conditions which may be modified through product or process standards, e.g. regulations concerning the environmental norms. In addition, the government may stimulate demand by buying advanced products, especially in those sectors which affect the infrastructure of a country. Third, related and supporting industries may be influenced by a countless number of means, e. g., the "control of advertising media or regulation of supportive services". Fourth, the structure of the companies' strategy and rivalry is an important determinant which may be affected by different governmental policies, e. g., by capital market regulations, tax policy, and antitrust laws (Porter 1990, 126-128). The modification of existing systems, however, should not rely on pure copying of other national systems which are deemed better according to individual opinions. Each nation should shape its own system depending on the unique relevant conditions. Porter (1990, 623) described the situation as follows: "Nations gain advantage because of differences, not similarities".

Lundvall (1988, 1992) interprets innovation as an interactive process between user and producer which may be understood as a mutual process of interactive learning. These interactions are of special importance for innovations. Lundvall differentiates between the national system of innovation in a narrow sense, thus including "organisations and institutions involved in searching and exploring - such as R&D departments, technological institutes and universities, and in a broader sense, whereby it includes "all parts and aspects of the economic structure and the institutional set-up affecting learning as well as searching and exploring - the production system, the marketing system and system of finance present themselves as sub-systems in which learning takes place" (Lundvall 1992, 12). Lundvall's concept is applicable to all stages of the innovation process, even to the interactions between the stages of basic and applied research. The type and level of organisation of these interactions depend on the complexity of the intended innovations. The flow of information in the user-producer interactions, reflecting user needs and technical opportunities, is of special importance for the innovation process. Matching the needs of user and producer presupposes an efficient information flow, including the existence or the establishment of efficient information channels and information codes. As a consequence of these communication needs, Lundvall emphasises the positive influence of geographical and cultural proximity between users and producers on successful innovations. Proximity becomes even more important along with the steadily increasing complexity of innovations (cf. also section 4.5).

To sum up, NSIs consist of different elements, all of them being very complex and largely intertwined. This finding relates to all activities of the innovation process (see chapter 5) and, thus, all institutions performing innovation activities, together with their interactions, have to be considered. Furthermore, governmental policies are a decisive factor influencing the structure and performance of NSIs.

6.2 National patterns of specialisation and their impact on the science system

In general, NSIs encompass the whole process of innovation (see chapter 5). The analysis of differences between NSIs should be based on the analysis of the economic structures which have envolved over time and show different patterns of industrial specialisation. These patterns have to rely on an optimal factor allocation in the national economy, thereby drawing heavily on the nationally abundant but internationally scarce factors of production (Legler et al. 1992). Specialisation applies to special branches of industry as well as to different types of industry.

Pavitt (1984) divided the branches into different types of industry, characterising each one by its mode of generation of new knowledge: supplier dominated, production intensive and science-based, indicating the differences in the extent of reliance upon science in industries (see also section 4.1). This classification is not without drawbacks: "In the science-based industrial sector, innovations are said to be directly linked to technical advances made possible by quantum leaps forward in scientific knowledge.... The trouble is that the typology is oriented to industrial branches... and thus embraces technologically very heterogeneous structures" (Grupp/Schmoch 1992b, 76-77). Furthermore, companies which, according to their main production areas, belong to a defined branch often show activities in fields belonging to other branches (Grupp 1991b). This technological heterogeneity of branches also implies internal differences as to science dependence. The organisation and modification of national systems of innovation consequently has to take into account the existing national specialisation structure of the branches and their heterogeneous reliance on science. The approach of Grupp/Schmoch (1992b), differentiating between technological sectors, subdivided on the basis of the International Patent Classification (IPC), seems to be more suitable. They investigated science-based technologies and drew the conclusion that the "science connection strongly differentiates between technical areas and yet tenuously between countries. It is an internal feature of technology..." (ibid, 90). Differences between nations depend on their different industrial structures, varying in their focus on science-based technologies. Therefore the economic structure, defined in terms of specialisation on technological sectors, proves to be a major determinant of the science orientation of NSIs.

The technological specialisation patterns of nations have grown up over a long period of time; their historical foundations should not be overlooked. This observation implies that patterns of NSIs do not change overnight. As regards their flexibility, other parameters show the same sluggishness, too. Especially a nation's system of values and its cultural background are only very slowly changed by the behaviour of industrial and academic institutions, the government, and social groups. Both the nation's system of values and the cultural background remain stable over a long period of time and, thus, the innovation system is inherently stable, too.

In this context, it has to be mentioned that the current structure of any academic system is based on historical developments and traditions, too. A nation's academic tradition depends heavily on a twofold influence structure which might be described as the pure academic tradition on the one hand and the structure of the national industry on the other hand. Industrial efforts to implement scientific knowledge in products often affect the direction and content of research and education at universities. The example of the U.S. academic tradition compared to the European situation illustrates related differences. Similarly, there exist different solutions as far as the orientation of universities towards science-based technologies is concerned: in principle these technologies require a higher involvement of science, but scientific knowledge can be achieved either through strongly linking companies to academic or non-academic research institutions or through an increase of in-house capacities within companies (cf. section 4.2). In the case of contract research, universities and research institutions are directly responding to the specific national industrial demand, and their structure and orientation is influenced. An increasing number of co-operations between universities and industry generally induces a decline in the proportion of pure basic research in favour of oriented basic and applied research.

6.3 Technological forecast and change in national systems of innovation

In order to maintain national competitiveness permanently, it is important to identify long-term strategic goals and the ways to achieve them. In this context, the availability of qualified information turns out to be crucial. In particular, the availability of information about trends of development plays an increasing role in a nation's becoming and maintaining competitive. As example commendable contrasted with the role European and North American ministries play in forecasting technological developments, Freeman (1988) describes the Japanese technological forecasting system, which concentrates primarily on the recognition of long-term trends and the identification of strategic goals.

Different Japanese ministries and agencies have carried out studies concerning the identification of technologies with future economic potentials. One example illustrating this is the periodically renewed Delphi inquiry "Future Technology in Japan", carried out by the Science and Technology Agency (STA) in order to estimate the best time for the introduction of new technologies into the market. Other recent studies are the "White Paper to Science and Technology", also issued also by the STA, the "Report of the year 2010 Committee", issued by the Economic Planning Agency (EPA), and several other studies dealing with special industrial sectors, carried out by the Ministry of International Trade and Industry (MITI). The broad diffusion of the results of these forecasting efforts makes the respective information available to all companies - one crucial condition for success.

Similar efforts are undertaken by the U.S. departments or public research institutions with different objectives. These studies are either oriented towards special fields of industry, like the report "Micro Tech 2000", issued by the National Advisory Committee on Semiconductors, examining only the semiconductor industry, or towards the goal of maintaining or improving the competitiveness of the economy as a whole, like the report "Emerging technologies", issued by the Department of Commerce (DoC).

In 1992/93, the German Ministry of Science and Technology (BMFT) became increasingly engaged in similar activities. The report "Technology at the Threshold of the 21st Century" (Grupp 1993b) and a Delphi inquiry (BMFT 1993b), comparable to that carried out in Japan, have been initiated on behalf of the BMFT. The former study is of special interest because of the applied methods; all defined technology areas were evaluated according to a set of criteria, taking into account scientific, economic, and social possibilities, as well as necessities and threats. Among other aspects the strength of the national R&D infrastructure, the extent of public funding, and the interest of industry in each technology area were assessed. Thus, the identification of promising future technologies supports the political decisions on which areas research should be pursued in. In this context, the criteria on infrastructure can show whether the existing institutional landscape in the selected areas is appropriate, has to be modified, or whether new capacities have to be created.

The development of a consistent strategy to channel research on future technologies requires both, the identification of long-term strategic goals by governments and companies, and a considerable degree of flexibility to meet the new demands. The differences concerning the assessment of long-term strategic goals vs. the short-term profit-driven orientation is also discussed in Gibbons' above-mentioned differentiation between technologically dynamic and myopic systems.

The increasing forecasting activities of national governments can be taken as an indication of the intention to play a more active role in the shaping of national R&D systems. Yet the effects and consequences of this interference in the R&D systems cannot be exactly predicted. In any case, the governments' role in selecting future high-potential technologies will also strongly affect the landscape of the respective NSIs. The strategies of companies will be greatly influenced, because their representatives are involved in the public forecasting activities either as direct experts or as members of advisory committees, and because public subsidies are focused on strategic areas. The impact on public research institutions, especially universities, however, will be even more important, as they directly depend on public funding. Therefore, the scientific community will have to face enormous challenges. With respect to society, the forecasting procedures can lead to the development of new visions or ideals of technological orientation (e.g., "clean car").

All in all, many experts are now supporting a more active role of governments because the well-known strategies of either "picking the winners" or "laissez faire" are no longer appropriate. The government should act as an "honest broker" (Gibbons 1993, 9) between science and technology. Particularly, those institutional barriers have to be reduced which hinder efficient co-operation activities. Different policy areas like education policy, tax policy, fiscal policy, health care policy, and environmental policy, bear upon the setting a general framework and stimmulation of innovation.

The policy measures have to correspond to the specialisation pattern of the nation, and they have to consider the changing nature of new technologies, which is characterised by an increasing degree of interconnection. The already mentioned study of Grupp (1993b) stresses that technology at the beginning of the next century cannot be classified according to conventional disciplines. As different as the paths of technology might seem, they are all linked together in the end. The high degree of interconnection between science and technology, on the one hand, and between different technological areas, on the other hand, requires new organisational forms; technical innovations will have to be increasingly accompanied by organisational and social innovations. According to Gibbons (1993) "scientific and technological knowledge is coming to be produced in new ways.... The familiar discipline-based, internally driven, individually dominated structures that currently dominate the universities and the public sector laboratories are yielding to practically oriented, transdisciplinary, network-dominated, flexible structures that are characteristic of the mode of organisation of science and technology in the most advanced sectors" (cf. table 6.3-1).

Table 6.3-1: Characteristics of traditional and modern production of scientific and technological knowledge according to Gibbons (1993)

Traditional / myopic systems	-	Modern / dynamic systems
discipline-based	-	transdisciplinary
internally driven	-	practically oriented
individually dominated	-	network dominated

Organisational innovations will be necessary in the arrangement of the system of education and training, too. The government must shape the educational subsystem of the national system of innovation according to the new requirements. The skills and knowledge of students have to be matched to this demand which will be put forward by industry and other institutions from the non-industrial sector. Up to now, these challenges have not been sufficiently reflected by the still traditional, discipline-oriented organisational structures of the existing universities.

6.4   Inferences of the theory of national systems of innovation

Weighing the above-mentioned facts, one can draw the conclusion that it is almost impossible to find an optimal structure for national systems of innovation. As far as the existing systems are concerned, national special feutures and long-standing traditions predominante that cannot be changed overnight. As all elements of NSIs are closely intertwined, a radical intervention at one point can cause unforeseen effects in other areas. Hence, every change has to be planned with care. As a further conclusion, the main target of technology policy should not be a unification of the large variety of NSIs, because the differences are a major driving force for technological change and national peculiarities are important for competitiveness.

Against this background, the guideline for the research policy of the Commission should not be the creation of a unique EU-wide innovation structure, as the variety of NSIs within the EU is a major advantage. Furthermore, the intervention in existing structures of NSIs is quite difficult and can induce only minor effects because of the noted mechanisms of persistence. In this situation, the current policy of the Commission of bringing together researchers and scientists of different nationalities is adequate: It initiates processes of mutual learning and helps to overcome specific international inefficiencies.

In the area of new, emerging technologies, the potential for an active role of the Commission is much greater, because new R&D structures are needed which do not yet exist on the national level or which merely exist in rudimentary form. For that purpose, the Commission can use traditional instruments such as R&D subsidies in strategic areas, or the new instrument of institutional arrangements. For example, the establishment of European research networks with multidisciplinary focus can be important for coping with the challenges of the future.

As future technologies will be a decisive area, the Commission should, furthermore, engage more in forecast studies in order to actively participate in this new trend of technology policy. In this context, a decisive contribution could be the comparative assessment of the research structures of the member countries for integrating their specific strengths in strategic areas.

7.   Conclusions and recommendations

7.1   Open research questions

The literature review performed in this study reveals that there already exists a broad variety of publications on the role of the scientific community in the generation of technology. In this area of research, some problems have been extensively and sufficiently explored, and further studies on these questions would not lead to additional valuable results. Therefore, the review can help to identify research topics which should *not* be repeated. At the same time, open research questions become visible, some of which will be described in further detail:

Many authors analyse the structures of universities and industry and the respective transfer mechanisms in a quite stylised, often simplistic way. The discussion on the definition of science and technology, the description of selected national innovation systems, and that of the emergence of science-based technologies and techno-scientific communities illustrate that the borderlines between universities and industry or between academic and industrial researchers are not as clear-cut as often assumed, and that therefore the situation is quite complex. On the one hand, industrial researchers often have communication behaviours largely comparable to academic scientists, and on the other hand, many academic researchers are engaged in the development of technology and use instruments of private appropriation of knowledge such as patents. Furthermore, the impact of non-university research institutions is not at all negligible: quantitatively, their activities are at nearly the same level as that of universities. In view of the growing importance of science-based technologies, further research on the institutional and social structures at the borderline of science and technology is necessary, aiming at the exploration of causes and framework of "unorthodox" behaviour of academic and industrial researchers. These investigations are important for dissemination policies, because their focus is more on the detection of positive transfer mechanisms, less on structural barriers. In addition, the structures of "other, intermediate" research institutions should be a major topic of future studies.

The chapter on knowledge transfer between non-industrial research institutions and industry documents many research activities in this area. However, further work on a more detailed level on the legal and institutional structures of universities, other research institutions, and industry seems to be necessary in order to describe and explain constraints and opportunities for the dissemination and exploitation of R&D activities. The debate on national systems of innovation (NSIs) has been very helpful for the elaboration of decisive structural elements for R&D policy. Nevertheless, on the present, quite general level it seems to have reached a point of maturity where further work would be less productive. But on a more specific level of branches or technologies, the systematic comparison of strategic elements of NSIs in several countries can still be useful. For example, the quite general figures in the country comparison of chapter 3 already indicate that universities play different roles in different NSIs, and a further examination of the underlying structures would be very revealing.

The discussion and comparison of various innovation models gives broad evidence of a co-operation between universities, other research institutions and industry during nearly the whole life cycle of products, processes, or technology. This finding has led to the development of a new interaction model of the innovation process. But the research on the variations in co-operation intensity and on the change of roles during the life cycle is still at the beginning. In part 3 of this book, the analysis of institutional interaction in the areas medical lasers and neural networks is a first step in this direction. Further investigations, e.g., on the basis of historical case studies, would lead to new decisive insights into the mechanisms of innovation systems.

The considerations of the impact of (basic) science on technology have shown that conventional cost-benefit analyses on the influence of basic research have reached obviously insurmountable limits. In contrast, an information-theoretic approach promises to achieve substantial progress in this field. This latter approach would furthermore be effective for analysing the structures of innovation-oriented networks. It would be possible to describe not only the frequency of external contacts, but the quality of the information transfer and the function of the different partners, as well.

7.2   RTD dissemination policies

As to the current activities within VALUE II, Interface II, i.e., the dissemination of result of European RTD programmes to the scientific community, the literature states that publications and conferences continue to play a dominant role as communication media among scientists. Therefore, the Commission should put even more emphasis than already exists on these information channels. The publication of EC-supported RTD results in journals in addition to the final report is time-consuming and therefore cost-intensive. Particularly publications of academic scientists in industry-oriented journals and of industrial researcher in scientific journals need a well-deliberated strategy. Thus, the costs for dissemination-oriented publications should be explicitly included in the budgets of RTD projects. As to conferences, the present activities of the Commission are generally sufficient. A major challenge will be the achievement of high quality, being attractive for scientists, and of an orientation integrating academic and industrial researchers.

A dissemination policy which is exclusively based on publications, conferences, and similar media will always have clear limitations of impact. The main problem is the restriction on the dissemination of *existing* RTD results, thus on a science/technology push approach, without looking at the demand side. This study leads to the basic conclusion that the RTD dissemination policy of the Commission has to operate in an area of multiple dimensions the main elements of which are depicted in figure 7.2-1. The main dimensions are future technologies, modern R&D systems, visions of application, and new markets and socio-economic needs. If these dimensions are taken into account, the dissemination policy can be improved significantly. In consequence, the dissemination policy should not be limited to the offer of existing RTD results, but already intervene at the stage of programme design as the conditions of RTD production are decisive for the efficiency of dissemination. This broad approach, which includes the early stages of technology generation, can be called "integrated dissemination policy". As to the elements of an integrated dissemination policy, the present study provides a variety of indications:

The programme design should take the structures of modern R&D systems into account. These systems are characterised by the growing importance of science-based technologies and interdisciplinary research topics. The RTD activities should be network-oriented and international; thus the programme design should not only aim at technological areas, but at the integration of relevant institutions as well. Finally, modern R&D systems do not only look at technological potentials, but are increasingly demand-driven.

Figure 7.2-1:   Main elements of an integrated RTD dissemination policy of the European Commission

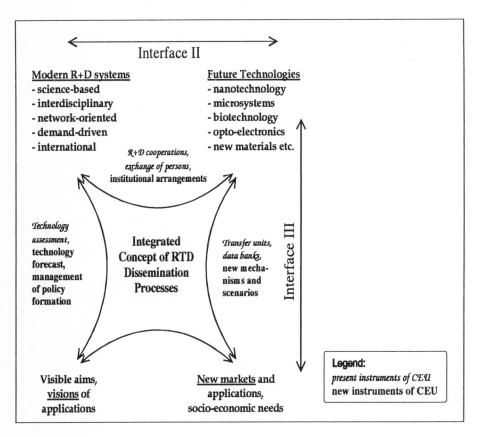

The forecast studies discussed in section 6.3 have identified areas such as nanotechnology, microsystems, biotechnology, opto-electronics, photonics, new materials, or advanced information technology as technologies of the future. These strategic areas only partly appear in existing European RTD programmes. These topics are science-intensive and hold good prospects of integrating different research institutions. Furthermore, the Commission would be active in new emerging areas where well-established national R&D systems do not yet exist, so that the potential for the Commission to play an active role is quite large.

Besides the already existing instruments of international R&D co-operation and exchange of persons, the results of section 4.5 additionally suggest the use of institutional arrangements. This does not necessarily mean the establishment of new large European research institutions which would entail conflicts with national interests. Rather one should aim at the building-up of longer-term institutional - and not only short-term project-specific - networks of existing institutions which are competent in a selected strategic area. In contrast to the generally quite short-termed RTD programmes, these networks should have a temporary, but longer perspective and the liberty to adjust the aims of their research according to intermediate results which generally cannot be exactly predicted in these areas of strategic research. Of course, it will be necessary to elaborate the framework of such institutional arrangements in more detail, e.g., to determine guidelines for the intermediate evaluation of the results and the joining or leaving of institutions. Furthermore, the new establishment of small European institutions with limited R&D of their own activities but the major task of co-ordination should be considered. The new instrument of institutional arrangements will be a "radical innovation" with all implied risks; nevertheless, it seems to be very promising and should be seriously considered.

Most present activities of technological forecast do not yet sufficiently look at the transformation of functional technology options into marketable products or processes. The market success of innovations, however, largely depends on market demand and socio-economic needs, as discussed in section 5 in the context of innovation models. This linkage of research and society is the major area of the Interface III activities. In addition to the existing dissemination instruments such as transfer units and data banks - which, once again, are based on a technology/science push approach - new instruments have to be found which actively involve the society in the process of RTD planning as early as possible. Potential instruments can be the organisation of awareness workshops or the elaboration and public discussion of scenarios. In this area - which was not in the focus of this study - further instruments have to be looked for.

The fourth dimension the RTD dissemination policy is the elaboration of major goals which can be guideposts commonly accepted by society, industry, and the scientific community. An example can be the vision of the "clean car" or more generally a clean environment. The recent Delphi studies in Japan and Germany - mentioned in section 6.3 - have revealed that this aim has high priority in all groups of the respective society, including industrial researchers, and it can therefore be assumed that environmental technology will meet promising markets. For the elaboration of such visions, several instruments exist, including technology assessment, technology forecast and the management and moderation of strategic dialogues and policy formation processes.

To sum up, the study shows that the relation between research and the scientific community is embedded in complex multidimensional structures for which the scope of traditional dissemination instruments is too narrow. There is a strong need for a new integrated concept of dissemination of RTD results which not only contains the main elements of RTD dissemination processes, but also integrates Interfaces II and III of the VALUE II programme in a holistic approach.

PART II

G. Reger, K. Cuhls, D. von Wichert-Nick

Challenges to and Management of R&D Activities

Executive summary of part II

The aim of this part is to describe the main challenges to research and development (R&D) and different models of R&D management and tools which are used by firms to response to these challenges and support the acquisition of scientific and technical knowledge. The investigation should give insights into the linkages between structural aspects and management practices such as the internal/external division of labour, the structural and procedural organisation of R&D activities, the internal generation and external acquisition of knowledge and the ways of bringing together different scientific and technical disciplines. Thus, this part should help R&D managers to recognize new challenges to R&D and give hints to respond to them with appropriate management tools.

Methodologically, the investigation is mainly based on an analysis and evaluation of the relevant literature concerning R&D management and tools. An empirical part aimed at reviewing the theoretical results consists of case studies of European firms which are based on interviews in 20 enterprises.

The frequently used notion of "best practice" suggests that an ideal model for enterprises to manage R&D in the one and only ideal way successfully exists. This assumption can only be followed with strong restrictions because enterprises are acting in different environments (sector, market, competition, technology), having to face different challenges, and are following various strategies. Therefore, the underlying thesis concerning the issue of "best management practices for R&D" is that there is no "best practice", since the use of tools depends on the specific context and situation of the enterprise. However, the challenges, tasks, and approaches to R&D management lead to various "generations of R&D management". Three different models are discussed and presented as guidelines and stimulus for a successful management of R&D.

The three models presented show not only different conceptions of R&D management, but also common trends and problems in the management of R&D and their changes over the past three decades. All three models for a future R&D management have in common, on the one hand, the concept of integrating R&D and businesses. This concerns strategic and organisational features as well as funding and resource allocation. On the other hand, the relationship between long-term, centralized R&D versus short-term, decentralized R&D has to be re-defined. Taking both aspects into account, the significance of coordination and networking inside the corporation for the management of R&D is increasing. R&D management in multi-divisional enterprises has to deal mainly with the coordination of centralized and decentralized R&D, an appropriate mix of corporate and business unit funding, the integration of R&D in corporate and business strategy, the development of long-term visions and the coordination of R&D portfolio and resources between corporate and business level.

The models for a future R&D management are clearly focused on large, multi-divisional enterprises and are hardly appropriate for SMEs. Additionally, a crucial challenge for the management of R&D and an adequate response is missing in the models presented: the growing complexity and the overlapping of technologies and scientific disciplines is a challenge that has to be faced by inter- or transdisciplinary approaches of R&D activities. Knowledge of different scientific and technical disciplines has to be combined by short-term as well as institutional arrangements within the company.

R&D management differs according to the economic, technological, and scientific changes. The main challenges to industrial R&D are the following issues:

- changes of demand and customers' behaviour,
- flexible specialisation and organisational changes,
- shortening of the life cycles of products and industries,
- growing complexity and overlapping of technologies,
- growing significance of science for innovation activities,
- globalisation of markets, competition and R&D activities,
- human resources: higher qualification, new skills, and change of values,
- environmental protection and sustainable development.

Tools for R&D activities are the response of companies to cope with these challenges. The description and discussion of these tools is analytically separated into three interfaces which are crucial to the generation of knowledge and the success of technological development. From the large number of R&D management tools mentioned in the literature, we have concentrated on the following and assigned them to three aspects:

(1) Internal R&D activities:
- corporate culture and significance for R&D,
- organisation of R&D,
- development and renewal of core competences and the role of R&D,
- instruments for technological forecasting.

(2) Acquisition of external scientific and technical know-how:
- cooperation: co-development, strategic alliances, networking.

(3) Scientific, technical, and functional boundaries:
- management of scientific, technical and functional interfaces.

The review of the literature shows that a broad variety of publications exists on challenges to enterprises and the management of R&D in general as well as on single tools for R&D activities. Nevertheless, some important open research questions appeared:

- Most models for R&D management are based upon observations in large international and multi-divisional enterprises; a model regarding changes over time and explicitly created for the management of innovation and R&D in SMEs was not found and, therefore, requires further research.

- Concerning organisational aspects of multi-national enterprises (MNEs), the re-definition and the underlying challenges seem to be identified; further research is required for the creation of modern instruments for coordination and their institutional implementation. Regarding SMEs, and especially new technology-based firms, managing organisational change, as well as maintaining and getting an "innovative, learning organisation" is an important subject of further research.

- The concept of core competences is not sufficiently operationalized, the process of identification within the company as well as the allocation of resources is unclear; further research is necessary to bring this interesting concept to an operational level and to evaluate the impacts on resource allocation and organisation in the company.

- Technology forecasting and its application in R&D management still presents a lot of problems. An interesting, new research question is the institutionalisation of technological forecasting as a process of organisational learning as well as the coordination of technical and market trends. Additionally, the integration of technology forecasting and technology assessment has to be fostered. This can be done by further research dealing with the development of integrated forecasting and assessment systems for use in enterprises.

- Literature about managing interfaces in companies is mainly concerned with functional barriers and less with disciplinary ones. According to the growing importance of overlapping technologies ("technology fusion"), the management of disciplinary interfaces concerning mainly questions of culture, organisational structures and human resources is an important area for further research.

Concerning policy aspects, one main result from this study is that the characterized challenges to the enterprises also present new challenges to the research and technological development policy (RTD) of the European Union (EU). New issues derive from the fusing and overlapping of technology, increasing globalisation and ecological problems. Furthermore, the RTD policy of the EU should not only support the technological competence, but also the entrepreneurial competence and the learning ability of European firms. In order to improve the technological competence of European enterprises the EU could offer programmes or subprogrammes aiming at a better utilisation of technologies from various disciplines, which exceed the classic areas e.g. through linking different technologies such as optics, ceramics, microelectronics, micromechanics, optoelectronics or sensorics. Besides that, the European RTD promotion should boost the entrepreneurial competence and the learning ability of the enterprises with appropriate instruments. A modern European RTD policy should therefore encompass not only the technological areas (what or which technology should be promoted?) but also companies' management of R&D and innovation (how or which instruments, methods or approach should be promoted?). Starting points are developed and described in the end of this part.

1.   Introduction: main issues of part II

The aim of this part is to identify new challenges to R&D and different types of research and development (R&D) management and tools which are used by firms to support the acquisition of scientific and technical knowledge. Insights should be given into the linkages between structural aspects and management practices such as the internal/external division of labour, the structural and procedural organisation of R&D activities, the internal generation and external acquisition of knowledge, and the ways of bringing together different scientific and technical disciplines. The core question of part II is how firms respond to new challenges to R&D and manage the internal and external interfaces to acquire and integrate know-how from various sources into their R&D activities. This part is based on a study (Reger/Cuhls/Nick 1994) which was carried out on behalf of the Commission of the European Communities, General Directorate XIII-D-2, and would not have been possible without the promotion of the Commission.

R&D management differs according to the economic, technological, and scientific, changes. The following main challenges to industrial R&D are described and discussed in chapter 2:

- changes of demand and customers' behaviour,
- flexible specialisation and organisational changes,
- shortening of the life cycles of products and industries,
- growing complexity and overlapping of technologies,
- growing significance of science for innovation activities,
- globalisation of markets, competition and R&D activities,
- human resources: higher qualification, new skills, and change of values,
- environmental protection and sustainable development.

Chapter 3 describes the tasks of R&D management in enterprises and examines the question whether so-called "best management practices for R&D" exist. The underlying core thesis concerning this issue is that there is no "best practice" that all enterprises have to follow, since an appropriate management depends on the specific context and situation of the enterprise. However, the challenges, tasks, and approaches to R&D management lead to various "generations" of R&D

management. These models can serve as guidelines for a successful management of the firm's R&D activities. While the issues mentioned above are the challenges to today's and future R&D management, tools for R&D activities describe how firms can respond to them (see chapter 4). From the large number of R&D management tools mentioned in the literature, we have concentrated on the following:

- corporate culture and the role of R&D (chapter 4.1),
- organisation of R&D: centralisation and decentralisation of R&D (chapter 4.2),
- renewal of core competences through R&D (chapter 4.3),
- instruments and processes for technological forecasting (chapter 4.4),
- cooperation: co-development with clients/users, strategic alliances, networking (chapter 4.5),
- management of scientific, technical and functional interfaces, e.g. with the help of interdisciplinary working groups and the use of simultaneous engineering (chapter 4.6).

Methodologically, the investigation is mainly based on an analysis and evaluation of the relevant literature concerning R&D management and tools. An empirical part aimed at reviewing the theoretical results and presenting different types of managing the acquisition of scientific and technological knowledge; it consists of case studies of 20 European firms which are presented as "illustrative boxes" in the text. The interviews were carried out with support from TNO Centre of Technology and Policy Studies in Apeldoorn, Netherlands.

Chapter 5 provides a resumé of the main results and open research questions. Furthermore, starting points for a modern European research and technological development policy are presented.

2.   Challenges to the management of R&D

In modern economies, market and government are not independent of each other, both have complementary roles. In principle, governments intervene in the case of market failure but do not influence the economic processes in general. Technology is developed primarily in the enterprise as a reaction to a change in the demands of markets and consumers. But the whole process of innovation and technology creation cannot be regarded as a reaction to market forces. Other factors, like scientific knowledge and the circumstances of the technology itself force companies to adapt to technological evolution and changing economic conditions (see OECD 1991).

R&D management practices are developed in response to economic and technological trends. This relation between the organisation and strategies of science and technology on the one hand and market forces on the other is much more direct in private firms than in large universities and government research institutes. These are somewhat insulated from the forces of the market. For an optimisation of the effectiveness of research and technological development policy (RTD policy), it is therefore essential to study changes in R&D management in private firms as well as the forces to which these respond. These forces are in general changes in the economic system and in the technological and scientific development, the trend of internationalisation, and the growing importance of human resources and environmental issues.

Of course, there are more than this small number of challenges mentioned. Regarding innovation, one cannot ignore the complexity, not only of natural sciences and technology itself, but of historical, social, cultural, political and other complex problems and challenges which mark the background of all developments (for an overview see Kennedy 1992). This fact has to be taken into account in order to create new knowledge, to strengthen the progress of technological development and to face the technological and economic challenges of the future.

2.1 Economic challenges

The most important trend of the past 20 years is the emergence of global markets dominated by demand rather than by supply. The balance of power in almost all world markets has shifted from the producer of goods to the buyer, the customer. This development contrasts strongly with the situation in post World War II Europe and in socialist economies, where, due to general scarcity, the power was with the producers. It has led to a multiplication of markets, for example markets for subcontracting of work and components which used to be produced in vertically integrated companies. Also technical information is traded in the market place much more easily than before. This is of some importance for make-or-buy decisions in private firms with respect to appropriate technological knowledge and for both national and European RTD policy.

Customer demands for products with a high quality standard, a greater differentiation and better requirements are increasing steadily and quality standards for products competing in these open world markets have been raised in such a way that companies can no longer afford to be active outside their area of highest competence. As a consequence, quality of products and processes has to be improved continuously as is already being done in Japanese enterprises, which started their success with the incremental improvement of product quality and a consistent "follower" strategy. Nowadays, Japanese companies are the strongest competitors in many high-tech products, using concepts of improvement like the "Kaizen" philosophy (see Imai 1991) or quality circles (see Cuhls 1993) which are often imitated in Western companies.

The shortening of product cycles and higher R&D expenditures for one certain technology are other problems companies have to face (Bleicher 1991, 174; OECD 1991, Gerpott/Wittkemper 1991, pp. 121; Bullinger 1992, 11). Permanent improvement of R&D is necessary but cost-intensive, and the leader in a technological area cannot expect profits and return on investments to be as high and as fast as during the last years (Bleicher 1991, 174). Refusing to improve a new technology because existing products are still in a sufficiently strong economic position leads to a lack of dynamism inside the companies and an increasing inflexibility. It has to be kept in mind that the international competition in most of the markets is still growing.

Companies' practice: reduction of product life cycles

One general trend is the reduction of product life cycles and the reduction of the time to bring a new product to market, or set up a new assembly line. A respondent reported the building of a new assembly line in two months compared to the usual twelve months as the major technical achievement of the year. Computer simulation techniques are often mentioned as an important technical tool for rapid prototyping. Of course management techniques are also an important complementary part of these new technical tools.

Another trend in sectors where products are at a later stage of their life cycle (e.g. automobiles, textiles, watches, calculators, cameras etc.) is the decreasing importance of economies of scale in industrialized nations. Instead, a shift to transplant production of mass products to countries with lower production costs occurred. A study was carried out at MIT in which 10,000 firms were followed between 1975 and 1985 (Brynjolfsson 1992). In that period, the average size of these firms in terms of employment actually decreased by 20%. There are also figures that show a decline of the average size of new plants since the mid 1970s. At the same time, total employment in small firms is growing at the expense of employment in large firms.

In the modern economic environment, flexibility is more important than economies of scale and scope. The Science Policy Research Unit (SPRU) at the University of Sussex has a databank that tracks important innovations (Pavitt et al. 1987). It appears from their research that the share of firms smaller than 500 employees in the total annual number of innovations has been increasing. If we look at Fortune's annual list of the 500 largest firms in the world, it is clear that within branches of industry, the recently most successful firms - in particular the Japanese, but their example is increasing, being followed in the U.S. and Europe - have vastly larger turnovers per employee than the less successful ones. Large firms are rapidly "down-scaling"; examples are Asea Brown Boveri or General Electric. The latter proudly claims in its annual report that in ten years its "down-scaling" has led to a reduction in the number of salary scales from 19 to 5, a decrease of employees from 400,000 to 300,000, a doubling of the sales volume and a tripling of profits. In the

Netherlands, the R&D expenditure of firms with fewer than 500 employees has increased 65% in the past five years, while R&D expenditure of the largest industrial firms has been declining (Kleinknecht 1989).

These tendencies have led to a new global economic system that has aptly been designated as "flexible specialisation" (Ernste/Meier 1992). Current management strategies are a reflection of this new economic system, as enterprises in almost all industrial sectors need to respond to the new and different demands for their survival. Resulting management trends such as "lean management", "organisational learning" and the concept of "core competences" or "core capabilities" are also having a major impact on R&D management practices.

Companies' practice: the concentration on core competences

A crucial aspect of the firms' technology strategies is what could be called incrementalism, or "back to basics". More than in the 1980s it is now considered good business not to venture too far into areas of technological uncertainty, but to orient innovation efforts towards learning from practice in areas of core competence.

This trend is strongly visible in the chemical firms that were interviewed. While they each had invested substantially in the 1980s in major innovation efforts in areas like biotechnology and advanced materials, today they report having ended such efforts because of a lack of economic potential. A number of large-scale attempts at radical, scientific opportunity-driven innovations have been ended and priorities have been shifted to certain core businesses and core technologies.

2.2   Technological developments

The dynamics of technological development are not the same over time. Each technology - for example shipbuilding versus railways, electrification, synthetic fibres or information technology - has its characteristic dynamics. If in a time frame, a particular technology is dominant, as electrification was during the 1920s and information technology is now, those particular dynamics should be taken into consideration in shaping R&D strategies and technology policies. The dynamics of pharmaceuticals and synthetic fibres are characterized by an orientation towards science and research. New products are developed in the research laboratory and find their way to the market in a relatively straightforward manner. Developments in automobiles and aircraft are characterized by a design orientation: available scientific knowledge, often not at all new, is used to create complex products.

Regarding technology, there are some fields which have proved to be more science-based (like e.g. metrology and sensors, genetics and pharmacy, optics, coating, nutrition) than others (like traditional machine tools, mechanical machinery, resins, printing, engines or traffic). Grupp (1993a, 191) also shows an increasing invention activity as a function of science involvement, e.g. in laser technology, data processing or electronic components. These are some typical examples for technologies which are science-based, but will be or are already used in innovative products. Technology fields which are more science-based seem to grow more than others. This effects a shift to more research activities even in enterprises which have to explore their own basic or core technologies and lead them to the application in a product. Enterprises will have to face the challenge to find new ways for gaining knowledge also in basic sciences, e.g. by new requirements of R&D institutes and higher education institutes.

Computer systems, either in administration or in manufacturing, are developed in close interaction with their actual application in offices and factories. Many different types of readily available chip designs work equally well. But economic success depends on the quality of the user-producer relationship. Technology firms get successful information from their customers and from software firms specialized in particular applications. In a recent study of trends in signal processing, TNO found (Schaffers et al. 1992) that success in this rapidly developing field depends on firms developing inter-mediation systems that are able to act as system integrators, combining knowledge of the latest chip designs (e.g. DSP chip) with the area of application. Examples for integration are quality control in cheese making, the geo-physics of oil exploration or heart monitoring in academic hospitals. Some of the first robot makers in the US lost market shares to Japanese and German competitors because they concentrated on perfecting robot design instead of optimizing the robots as regards the application needs. The identification of (future) needs is as important as the technology itself.

Technological challenges in mechanical engineering

The technological challenges presently facing mechanical engineering firms are mainly represented by the four areas microelectronics-based technologies, modular technology, new materials and the so-called cross-point technologies (see Reger/Kungl 1994):

Microelectronics-based technologies are the key technologies of mechanical engineering, both in product and in process innovations; the potential applications of microelectronics in manufacturing ("automated factory", "computer integrated manufacturing (CIM)") and in new products of the sector seem to be innumerable and affect all aspects of the branch. According to the results of our expert interviews these key technologies are crucial for the innovative success of mechanical engineering firms.

The significance of modular technology is increasing due to the growth of price-sensitive markets. This thesis is confirmed by the results of our interviews with European mechanical engineering firms; modular technology is used for the design of new products and the cost reductions of the development and manufacturing process. Modular-based products are very interesting for large mechanical engineering firms in volume markets which have to realize cost advantages and are oriented towards cost leadership.

The application of new materials is limited in mechanical engineering firms compared with other branches, e.g. the automobile or manufacturing industry. This low importance of new materials is also confirmed by the interview results; the lack of internal know-how and the necessarily high investments in new types of machines for shaping new materials mainly hinder broad application.

The fourth area of technological challenge is the overlapping and growing together of different technological areas like e.g. information and communication technologies, software, optics, laser, microsystem technology, nanotechnology. The merging of electro-mechanical with software systems seems to be a very challenging step, since software is not only part of the machinery but rather a conceptual system. The share and significance of these "cross-point technologies" is growing in mechanical engineering and concerns the firms' own manufacturing process and technological opportunities for new products.

Technological challenges the companies conducting R&D will have to face are marked by a growing significance of research and development for products and production processes, an increase in complexity, the overlapping of technologies and new dynamics of science-based innovation (Grupp 1992b). The growing complexity of technology and products leads to higher consumer expectations in quality, requirements and efficiency of a certain product (GWP 1991, 10) forcing the producers to adapt their products rapidly in equipment, quality, capacity, and application possibilities. Some firms faced this challenge by diversifying their range of products or by offering one product in a broadened range of varieties which need more in-house technology. But as there is more than one producer in most of the markets, competition is increasing and high-tech products are getting less different from each other.

Companies' practice: using modularity and systems to deal with growing complexity

---

Examples from the branch of mechanical engineering show that a possible strategy to meet the trend of growing complexity is the production of whole systems based upon modularity. While the business with systems induces a closer relationship between user and producer, modularity enables the producer to build more customized machines.

Examples:
medium-sized french enterprise (heat exchangers and pumps)
Product range of the firm is shifting towards the market for systems while subcontracting some components. In this branch, the competitive strengths of the firm, that is flexibility and fast decision-making, are very important.

Large italian enterprise (machine tools)
Product supply was changed from single machines to flexible manufacturing systems. Implications for technology management resulting from that decision are an extension of the variety of technologies applied and increasing complexity in order to link the various machines to systems. Production of this firm was based on many microelectronic technologies; module technology is applied and cooperations with other related firms to develop modules in the field of mechanical components are realized.

This development forces producers to combine common mechanical knowledge with new developments in materials, textiles, computer technology, communication and other technologies. A single technology does not automatically lead to a single product. At the same time the invention of a basic technology that can be applied to different products is becoming increasingly time-consuming and expensive, as basic research needs better facilities and longer time, resulting in higher R&D expenditure (OECD 1991). New products now and in the future need new ideas, basic (core) technologies, technologies from other fields or a new combination of existing technologies. Examples of these new technologies can be seen in Grupp (1993b) and

BMFT (1993b). As scientists and engineers involved in R&D are used to thinking in the technical terms defined by their own disciplines and the scientific community, they often have difficulties communicating with other scientific communities or R&D departments of companies. As a consequence, personnel educated at the "border lines" between the traditional natural science faculties or those doing interdisciplinary research (as in opto-electronics, laser medicine, bio-electronics etc.) are necessary, in order to cope with the growing significance of science in most of these technologies.

On the other hand, technologies are already overlapping in certain areas (figure 2.2-1). In science, new disciplines which combine the knowledge of different faculties and technologies are founded, like bio-electronics, laser medicine, opto-electronics and many others. Similar trends can be seen in many fields of science and technology. Investigating the structure and development of technology at the threshold of the 21st century, Grupp (1993b) found that emerging technologies no longer correspond to classification schemes based on traditional concepts of technical disciplines. The development of a technology cannot be seen in isolation, but in the context of an early and intensive networking between different areas of science and disciplines. Inter- or multidisciplinary education and research are necessary in the higher education institutes, R&D institutes and in the companies in order to provide the appropriately trained personnel for tomorrow's technologies and products.

2.3   Internationalisation of markets and R&D

From the historical point of view, internationalisation started with trade and the exploration of new export markets. Resources like oil, coal or spices have already been traded internationally for a long time. With better transportation facilities and knowledge about other nations the export of other products began which were, at first, resources or highly standardized, simple goods. Later on the technology-intensity of export products increased. Over the period 1950 to 1975, world trade increased by more than 500 per cent (OECD 1991). Economies of scope, and the

Figure 2.2-1: Interlacing of technology at the threshold of the 21st century

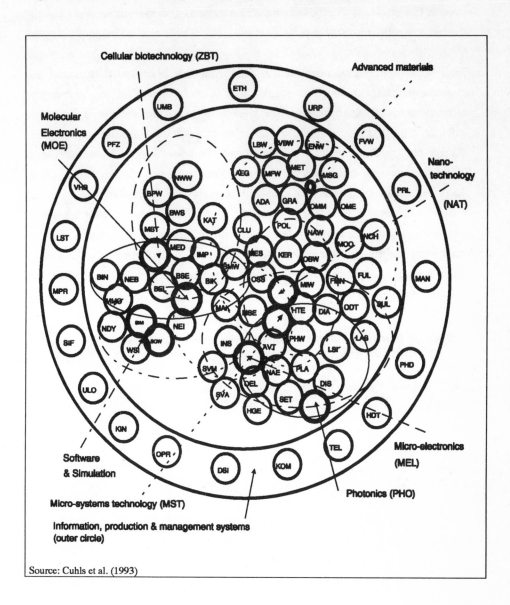

Source: Cuhls et al. (1993)

export of labour-intensive goods in large quantities, were the main factors of success. Companies with efficient production systems and low labour costs had the greatest competitive advantages.

But as trade frictions occurred and in many countries labour costs increased and consumer demands shifted from standardized to more diversified and technology-intensive products, many enterprises started to internationalize their economic activities. The first step was the construction of production facilities in countries offering cheap labour, natural resources and tax advantages. For production in Tayloristic systems, education of the workforce was not the important point. Nevertheless, when international competition grew, the criteria to invest abroad shifted to advantages in other production factors like capital, human resources, infrastructure and, later on, to the access to technological knowledge. Foreign investment was a major internationalisation factor: from 1983 to 1988, the growth rate of foreign direct investment was almost 20 per cent, that means three times that of foreign trade or GDP (OECD 1991, 20).

Companies' practice: European reaction to global competition

The strongest strategic focus of the firms investigated in our sample is on the whole aimed at survival against Japanese and other South East Asian competition. These competitors are setting the pace for the new market place. Cooperation with Japanese firms occurs, for example in the shape of strategic alliances, joint ventures, and supplier relationships, but more than with North American partners there is a hesitancy to create long-term dependencies.

With increasing cooperation and interlinkages among firms at a global level, a large step in technological innovation was possible (Bartlett/Ghoshal 1990). Cost advantages or global sourcing were not the only reasons for that phenomenon, but also protection from or exploitation of market failures and the growing convergence of consumers' preferences and taste. This development started with sectors, in which products are highly standardized and can easily be transferred to foreign markets like watches, calculators or cameras (Bartlett/Ghoshal 1990) because they are independent of the cultural background of the consumers and their preferences. Afterwards, the trend spread to products in which the consumer preferences did not converge that easily. Direct investment in R&D facilities abroad and change of corporate behaviour and organisation was the consequence of these tendencies. Facilitated and accompanied by a rapid development in the necessary information technologies and services, multi-national companies (Buckley/Casson 1991, Casson/Singh 1993) developed global strategies for their operations. This "global sourcing" (Soete 1993) for the whole range of economic activities of a company concerns marketing and production as well as the R&D departments. Global sourcing also means recruiting personnel internationally and taking advantage of access to natural resources, product components, capital, skills, technology, and know-how on a global basis. At present, however, in most areas, there is still a relatively strong "national" dimension of R&D activities.

In his survey of the internationalisation of the German economy and especially of German multinational firms Wortmann (1991) shows motives and strategies behind the performance of R&D abroad. He distinguishes between R&D-related motives, if the introduction or expansion of R&D is done at the location which is most efficient within the framework of the corporate R&D system and motives unrelated to R&D:

1. R&D-related motives:
   - to support local production, especially for the adaption of technologies to local market and production requirements,
   - to generate new technologies, especially where certain foreign regions have a particular innovative potential,
   - to complement own R&D,
   - to have "listening posts" for the monitoring of technological development,
   - to give a subsidiary the full responsibility for all entrepreneurial functions in a specific product area ("product mandate").

2. R&D-unrelated motives:
   - to react flexibly to the policies of national government, like the procurement of companies performing R&D in the country (e.g. in the field of telecommunications),
   - to fulfill the requirements of national governments in special fields, for instance when local R&D (clinical testing in pharmaceuticals) is a precondition for approval to enter the market.

Reinforced by the shortening of product cycles, international networking as a mix of cooperation and competition were seen as a solution and strengthened the global linkages. This tendency is marked by a trend to strategic alliances and a growth in numbers of joint ventures with R&D activities (Soete 1993, 178). These kinds of cooperation are mostly between companies of the highly industrialized economies of the world. Again, advantages for the companies are seen in shorter distances to resources, markets, higher education institutes and R&D institutes, the knowledge about markets and consumers' needs or behaviour, but also in being able to identify and use cultural differences.

Another fact is the increase of mergers and large-scale acquisitions across national boundaries during the last years (Hagedoorn/Shakenraad 1991a, 5) which force companies to decentralize R&D or to find other ways to adapt to the new situation and to be politically more independent. But it depends very much on the region and its infrastructure where the decentralisation of laboratories takes place. This "techno-globalism" (Soete 1993) evoked concern about the guaranteed access to certain product components, e.g. VLSI. Because of the high costs for development, the entry costs for new competitors are too high, so that in some cases monopolistic situations might occur (OECD 1991). Mutual dependencies have increased in general.

Free access to scientific institutions and knowledge was mentioned as a major reason to internationalize R&D, but the governmental cooperation in areas of publicly financed research is barely reflected. Nevertheless, tensions about a limited and discriminatory access to publicly financed RTD programmes occurred. Programmes like the European EUREKA or the Japanese "Human Frontier Program" are seen as a step to lessen these tensions by providing an improved access to knowledge on an international level.

2.4   Human resources

One of the critical factors in creating and diffusing technology is an adequate supply of appropriately educated and trained human resources (OECD 1991, 27). Human capital and competence cannot be bought like materials or investment goods. Technological advantage depends on the people who create the technology and is a result of a cumulative process. But without previous knowledge, no new technology can be created. The assimilation of knowledge requires prior knowledge and only those capable of creating knowledge are capable of absorbing it. In order to create knowledge, the educational system is important as the basis, to provide this is in general the role of the government.

Innovation depends as much on the formal procedures of learning as - especially in companies - on learning by doing, by using, by selling or other interaction. The insufficient numbers of trained and educated personnel is in many firms the bottleneck for the creation and development of new technologies, and the rapid realisation of first prototypes.

Companies' practice: the importance of a skilled and knowledgeable work force in a large British enterprise

The overseas parent company decided to start production in the UK in the 1930s with milling machines, that is, machinery closely related to machining centres but with a much lower degree of complexity in the original product. Introduction of numerical control of the firm's products dates back to the late 1950s (punch card techniques) and early 1960s (electronic controls). Shift in product range towards machining centres occurred in the early 1970s. Thus the British mechanical engineering firm has a profound knowledge base in this field. Most important competitive strength of the firm (according to the view of the firm's management) is its highly skilled labour force with experience in the industry. This enables the firm to manufacture a good product at a low cost to a high specification.

Firms will seek to improve and to diversify their technology by searching only in the zones that enable them to use and build upon their existing technological base. But generic technologies require fundamental changes in societal attitudes and institutions (OECD 1991, 94). As a result, the human resources and the way they are treated have an increasing impact on firms, sectoral and national impacts, and are important for area-wide competitiveness. Therefore, a work force is necessary which helps to gain and use market information for the creation and production of new goods and services in order to keep competitive strength. Company organisation and production systems will have to change further on so that it can make use of human and other resources fully and effectively. This requires new management practices, since rapid changes in customer demand, technology and science lead to rapid changes of skills and the necessity of steady development and renewal of these skills. The OECD (1991, pp. 99) stresses three main implications:

1. A higher threshold of competence is required in general.

2. There is a shift in emphasis among categories of skills. In order to make full use for example of new information technologies the whole range of activities inside the firm (from design to marketing) must be integrated and new forms of cooperation and networking are necessary; this requires new skills like the ability to communicate across business functions and technical disciplines or in problem-solving. The leveraging and development of new skills can lead to a better motivation, more initiatives and responsibility for improvements.

3. An increasing proportion of the work force needs to be re-trained more frequently than before and continuous training is necessary. The greater uncertainty of demand requires more flexibility, including the capability for continuously innovating products and services. Acquiring knowledge will be a permanent task for a labour force which has to adapt readily to new requirements and assist in the innovation process.

Personnel, especially in the R&D sector, has to be trained continuously and motivated. The change of values in many industrialized societies like the German or the Japanese (see Philipp-Franz-von-Siebold-Stiftung, Deutsches Institut für Japanstudien 1991) evokes a trend to new priorities in the life of people, e.g. more free time and leisure activities. Companies have to adapt to the situation of staff oriented more to "personal time" and "higher quality living standards" with different methods of motivation (Smekal 1993, 93) because creativeness does not automatically result from knowledge. The development of knowledge, willingness and motivation to create and design something new are as important as the existence of know-how inside the company. Bringing out corporate culture and providing a creative surrounding for R&D personnel will be one of the future tasks for an innovative enterprise.

> *Companies' practice: close relationships to universities as continuous source of know-how: new technology-based firms.*
>
> *The small (below 50 employees) R&D-intensive German firm is a supplier of tool-monitoring systems, that is, components for machine tools. The field of technology comprises mechanical engineering, software and electronics. In this niche market, there is strong competition from other German and European manufacturers, thus the firm is following a strategy of concentration on one product range, whereby it tries to extend the range of application of the product. The firm was founded in the mid 1980s. The knowledge base was founded on work of the local university laboratory. Competitive strength lies in highly specialized know-how of specific elements of product technology, which is considered to be a good base for cooperations. The product technology is very dynamic: 50 % of the products were drastically changed or introduced during 1989 to 1991.*
>
> *Ideas for product innovations come from customers, but also from inside the firm. Besides the customers, government laboratories and universities are the most important sources for external ideas and R&D inputs. Therefore, location of the firm was chosen for the proximity to higher education institutes and R&D institutes. Marked methods of sourcing technology outside the enterprise are joint R&D projects, publications and open meetings, patent disclosures, and training and hiring skilled employees.*
>
> *The firm is an interesting example of a new technology-based enterprise. The mechanical engineering sector is largely characterized by technological maturity of products. Niches for new enterprises are in technology fields that include mechanical engineering, electronics and software elements. The technology-based firm is not a producer of complete machinery, but of components of machinery, which proved to be a successful product strategy. Very high technological knowledge is required in this field, close contacts to universities and other research institutions therefore are necessary. Technology of the product must be very advanced in order to convince machine tool producers to buy instead of make.*

2.5 Environmental protection and sustainable development

The goal of environmental sustainability, and particularly the development and diffusion of innovations to help meet this goal, is primarily a public aim, which cannot be achieved without ensuring that the private sector is both viable and capable of adjusting to change. Environmentally sustainable development can be defined as a process of change in which the use of resources, the structure of investment, the orientation of technical progress and the institutional structures are made consistent with future and present needs (Brundtland-Bericht 1987).

The requirements for a shift towards environmentally sustainable development has been put forward forcefully by several studies concerned with environmental problems. Meadows et al. (1992), for example, developed a simulation model which is based on estimates of world resources, population growth, rates of technological change, and pollution sources. On the basis of this model, it is argued that a major change towards sustainable growth and technologies is necessary to avoid severe economic and social problems on a global level for both the current and future generations.

Companies' practice: merging development with environmental issues

Example: large German multi-national enterprise (transportation and traffic systems)

On the corporate level of the multi-national enterprise the topic environment was laid down in five guidelines in 1992. In essence, the group was committed to
- *the conservation of natural sources as the basis of living,*
- *the minimisation of environmental strain,*
- *providing frank, candid information,*
- *involving all employees in a continuous "environment-learning" process,*
- *the appointment of commissioners for environmental issues.*

The manager of the section "Technology" was also appointed as the group´s environmental commissioner. "Technology" is one of two areas of the corporate function of R&T (the other one is "Research"). This union of responsibilities means that social acceptance and environmental compatibility receive much greater consideration in the selection of innovative technological projects.

The interdisciplinary theme "environmental protection and sustainable development" requires environmental management which is characterized by a systemic view and by the integrative involvement of all functional areas of the enterprise. In the planning, implementation and control of all areas of firm activity, environmental management is concerned with the reduction and avoidance of environmental damages as well as the long-term assurance of entrepreneurial goals (Meffert/ Kirchgeorg 1990).

The strategic importance of an environmental orientation must not be underestimated. Environmental protection is a goal to be aimed at and is therefore an additional condition within the goal system of the company. Environmental protection and environmental policy requirements may represent either competing or complementary goals (Wicke et al. 1992, pp 23). Empirical investigations by Raffee et al. (1992) show that environmental protection is regarded by successful companies with highly professional management and modern, environmentally oriented planning and controlling instruments as being complementary to the other R&D, manufacturing, marketing, and sales goals of the enterprise.

It should be borne in mind that present developments in the environmental fields (e.g. globalization of environmental problems, increasing environmental awareness, more stringent environmental laws, etc.) are leading to reductions and shifts in the options for solving techno-scientific problems (Staudt et al. 1992, pp. 330) and presenting new challenges to R&D management in enterprises. Gerybadze (1992) points out that R&D as a business function is a critical instrument for the design of technology and therefore decisive element of a "concept of integrated environmental protection". Since R&D is an important part of the innovation process it can be regarded as the early "pointsman" for environmentally oriented products, production processes and services. The consequent consideration of environmental technologies requires the implementation of environmental items into the goals and programmes of R&D as well as the linkage with the overall R&D strategy.

However, environmental issues are only one aim among many other aims of R&D, and the significance of environmentally oriented R&D in enterprises is limited. The role of environmental protection and sustainable development seems to be underestimated by enterprises and in the long run can lead to competitive disadvantages. Deiser (1993) for example points out that a so-called "post-modern enterprise" will be able to act faster and more successfully, and will keep up a competitive advantage longer than before. Typical examples of these post-modern organisations include firms that actively generate standards that transcend the prevailing rules: instead of waiting for environmental legislation, they themselves set the pace.

2.6   Summary: main challenges for R&D management

The complexity of recent trends and their future developments makesit impossible to identify and explain the whole range of challenges R&D management has to face. Only a few tendencies which will definitely have a major impact on R&D management now and in the future were described briefly. These challenges can - pessimistically - be seen as problems which have to be solved, but also as a positive chance to find new ways and create new management tools to cope with a changing environment through research and development. To sum up, the main challenges for the management of R&D in enterprises are the following issues (see figure 2.6-1):

1. Economic challenges: global markets are dominated by demand rather than by supply. Changes in consumer demands, high quality standards and the growing competition on the international markets force companies to provide a broader range of products (diversification) or one product in a larger variety. Therefore, flexible specialisation, fast reactions to consumer demands and rapid changes in the production and assembly facilities as well as in R&D are necessary, whereas the life cycles of products and whole industries are increasingly shortening. These economic trends lead to a growing importance of time as a factor in R&D management, to higher R&D expenditure and the need for efficient and effective R&D activities.

2. Technological challenges: a growing complexity of technologies in products is the consequence of changes in consumer demands and taste. The development of technology no longer corresponds to traditional classification schemes isolating one single technology, but in the context of an early and intensive networking between different areas of science and disciplines (Grupp 1993b and 1994a). This overlapping of technologies is a challenge that has to be faced by inter- and/or multidisciplinary approaches of R&D activities combining the know-ledge of different scientific and technical disciplines. There is a shift to more science-based technologies; therefore, more research inside the companies or external knowledge from the scientific community is necessary.

Figure 2.6-1:   Main challenges to R&D management

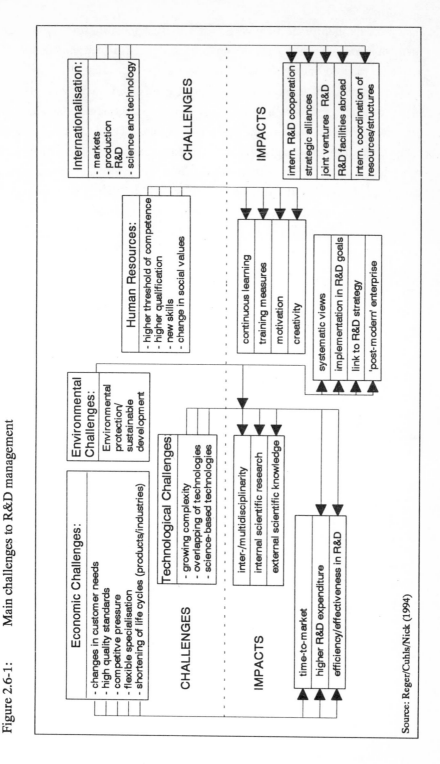

Source: Reger/Cuhls/Nick (1994)

3. Internationalisation: trade frictions are one of the limiting factors in the global trade of goods which force companies to decentralize their production and marketing and to invest abroad. Because of the increasing convergence of consumer tastes not influenced by culture, the capability to provide goods in larger varieties, and new transportation and communication possibilities, the exploration of international markets was possible. This leads to a growing competition of internationally operating companies. Global sourcing, that means combining production factors from all over the world, is a crucial driving force in the internationalisation of production as well as R&D. The internationalisation of science and technology leads to investments in decentralized R&D facilities abroad (techno-globalism) to make full use of the best available knowledge in specific technological fields, but evokes concern about free access to scientific institutions and the know-how about certain product components which are dependent on specialist knowledge.

4. Human resources: a higher threshold of competence is required in general to create new technology. Higher qualification and new skills are necessary, which are not only based on the specialized technical knowledge provided by the natural sciences, but also on social abilities, skills to communicate across functions and disciplines, problem-solving orientation and the ability to adapt to teamwork. As the amount and quality of information and knowledge increases rapidly, continuous learning and re-training of skills are necessary. As a result of a change in the social values of societies, new methods are needed to motivate personnel and improve creativity, innovation and its application in products.

5. Environmental protection and sustainable development: both goals are one of the major tasks of the future. Enterprises will have to orientate their R&D, their products and production processes towards economic as well as ecological needs. In order to fulfill these requirements R&D management needs a multidisciplinary and systemic view, has to link environmental goals with R&D aims and strategy.

3.   Basic models of R&D management

In innovation research it has often been shown (see e.g. Hauschildt 1993; Brockhoff 1992; Roussel/Saad/Erickson 1991; Rothwell 1991 and 1993; Freeman 1990), that the competitive position of single enterprises depends on a continuous, long-lasting and long-term research and development activity. However, carrying out research and development is not enough in itself to transform high innovative ability into competitive advantages. As the challenges are increasing both qualitatively and quantitatively, the firms' answer cannot consist in an increase of R&D expenditure. It is rather a question of controlling investments in R&D and the R&D process efficiently and effectively through enterprising management.

This connection between R&D activities and competitiveness is of crucial importance for government technology policy. At least in highly industrialized countries, the national competitiveness is greatly influenced by an efficient and effective utilisation of scientific and technical changes in the enterprises.

Decisions on choice, distribution of resources and the prioritisation of R&D projects are among the most complex and important issues in an innovative enterprise. The planning and controlling of the R&D processes is not only the responsibility of the R&D managers, but also of the top management, as the strategic selection of R&D projects and deployment of resources decisively influence future company successes. Management of R&D is basically different from the management of other company functions and has to deal with prejudices against it (Brockhoff 1992, pp.10):

- The research process is discontinuous, possible results are uncertain and often calculable in advance; it lies in its very nature that this process cannot guarantee a routine yield of results; routine processes, as for example in manufacturing, are more easily controlled than the uncertainty and discontinuity of R&D activities.

- R&D management often has to hear that planning is unnecessary, that it prevents creativity and is not possible in principle; these arguments however reflect the status of planning research and the attitude of the personnel in the individual enterprise and so generally cannot be justified.

- R&D management is, like innovation management, a young sub-discipline in business administration and cannot look back on a long tradition like for example accountancy.

Research and development are activities which are embedded in a more comprehensive innovation process. R&D represents a very important, but still only a part of the total innovation process (Hauschildt 1993; Rothwell 1993). This cannot be equated with invention or R&D, but includes also the introduction of a new product onto the market or the construction of a new system in the manufacturing process: "The technological innovation process includes the technical, design, manufacturing, management and commercial activities involved in the marketing of a new (or improved) product or the first commercial use of new (or improved) manufacturing processor equipment" (see Freeman 1974 cit. in Rothwell 1993). On the one hand this means that innovations must not necessarily be based on research, but that innovative ideas can come from other sources, such as customers or suppliers. Secondly, for successful commercialisation technical innovations must be accompanied by management and marketing measures. Thirdly, the success of R&D activities is a necessary, but by no means adequate condition for the commercial success of innovations.

In this chapter, the concepts of research and development, science and technology are defined and the aims and tasks of the management of R&D described. Thereafter, the question of "best management practices in R&D" will be dealt with and three different models for a modern and future R&D management will be discussed. Anticipating the results, core thesis is that there is no "best practice" that all enterprises have to or are able to follow: since the complexity of products, the manufacturing process, the technological change, customer demand, and the intensity of competition differ between and in sectors, a variety of enterprises with different competences is able to survive. However, the challenges, tasks, and approaches to R&D management are significantly changing and lead to various paradigms or generations of R&D management.

3.1 Defining research and development, science and technology

Before a discussion of R&D management issues, a definition of critical terms is necessary, since literature as well as respondents in industry use different concepts and categories. Concerning research and development (R&D), this study is based on the categories of the Frascati Manual of 1992. These definitions are used here because they are applied internationally and are a valuable pragmatic basis describing the critical elements of R&D in an appropriate way. The Frascati Manual distinguishes between basic research, applied research and experimental development (OECD 1992, pp. 69):

- Basic research is defined as "... experimental or theoretical work undertaken primarily with the aim of acquiring new knowledge of the underlying foundations of phenomena and observable facts, without any particular application or use in view." In order to identify "strategic" or "long-term application-oriented" elements of basic research (e.g. in enterprises), it is sub-divided into pure and oriented basic research:
  - Pure basic research is carried out for the advancement of knowledge without working for long-term economic or social benefits and attempting to apply results to practical problems.
  - Oriented basic research is conducted with the expectation of producing a broad base of knowledge likely to form the background for recognized, expected or future solutions.
- Applied research is "... also original investigation undertaken to acquire new knowledge. It is, however, directed primarily towards a specific practical aim or objective" (e.g. producing new or substantially improved products or processes).
- Experimental development is characterized as "... systematic work, drawing on existing knowledge gained from research and practical experience, that is directed to producing new materials, products and devices, to installing new processes, systems and services, and to improving substantially those already produced or installed".

The use of the term "science" in literature is more confusing. Schmoch et al. (part I) pointed out that in general two different approaches for defining science exist: the institutional approach differentiates between scientific institutions (e.g. like higher education institutes, R&D institutes) and industry, whereas science clearly is represented by the public and academic research sector. The cognitive approach defines science without a specific linkage to institutions. In this concept, science is closely related to systematic observation in order to discover facts and to formulate laws, to generate an organized body of (verifiable) knowledge that is derived from such observations, and to specific branches of this general knowledge such as biology, physics, etc.

If we take science "... to be the creation, discovery, verification, collation, reorganisation, and dissemination of knowledge about physical, biological, and social nature ..." (Kline/Rosenberg 1986, 287) and compare this definition with the definition of R&D according to Frascati 1992, the close relationship of basic and applied research to science is obvious. The categorisation of experimental development is more difficult and not evident, because parts of the development activities like construction of prototypes or testing equipment cannot be considered scientific. However, a certain part of experimental development overlaps with the definition of science applied here.

According to Morris (1992, 2176) the definition of "technology" includes both technical incorporation and the related processes as well as the purposeful application of scientific knowledge. Technology is a system of application-oriented means-to-an-end relationships which can be generalized; the application of such a technology is called technique (Brockhoff 1992, 22). In this sense, technology may also be defined as a bundle of certain techniques. Although technology and science are broadly overlapping, both concepts should not be confused because technology is the application of scientific and engineering knowledge to achieve a practical result like a new product or process (Roussel/Saad/Erickson 1991, pp.13).

To sum up, and as a major conclusion of the cognitive approach, R&D and science are not equivalents. However, oriented basic research, applied research and certain parts of experimental development overlap to a large extent with scientific activities. This means that a large part of scientific activities are carried out in industry. Following this approach and keeping in mind the disciplinary differentiation of science, the R&D process in enterprises regarded as a process of systematic generation of knowledge mainly has to deal with:

- the internal generation of knowledge within the firm,
- the acquisition of external knowledge which is developed by public and academic research institutes as well as by other enterprises,
- the integration of different scientific or technical disciplines to develop new or improved products or processes.

3.2   Tasks of R&D management and strategic purpose of R&D

Research and development in enterprises represent a combination of production factors which should enable the storage of previous knowledge and the generation of new technological knowledge (Brockhoff 1992, 35). The R&D activities of an enterprise aimed at increasing the knowledge base can, but need not, be carried out internally within the company. As there are contractual/formal and non-contractual/ informal methods of broadening the technological knowledge base externally, reasons of economy and limited capacity can be cogent reasons in favour of acquiring knowledge from external sources.

According to Brockhoff (1992, pp. 45) and Schneider/Zieringer (1991, pp. 25), new knowledge can be acquired on the basis of own, internal R&D or through foreign, external R&D. External R&D can be carried out as contract research and under licence or cooperatively with partners. Figure 3.2-1 gives a schematic overview. The integration of various scientific and technical disciplines as a third, technological dimension should be added to these two institutional elements, as new knowledge can be created through this union. This unification can be established either only internally or externally in cooperative form.

According to the results in chapter 2.2 it can be determined that the significance of knowledge generation through the integration of various disciplines is increasing. This development represents a new, important challenge for R&D management which is being met by enterprises at the present only inadequately (cf. chapter 4.6).

Figure 3.2-1:   Acquisition of knowledge through research and development

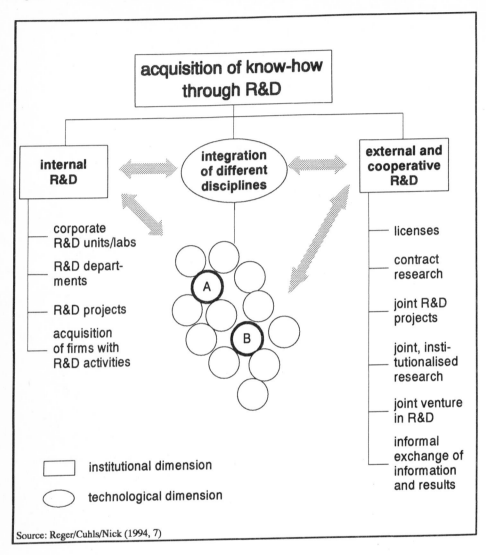

R&D management is part of the general management of the enterprise and has in principle the following five main tasks to fulfill:[1]

---

[1]   This concept of tasks of R&D management is based on Möhrle (1991, pp. 56) who distinguishes six main tasks; however, it is useful to unite the leadership and promotion of R&D employees as one task.

- A corporate R&D philosophy deals with the role of R&D in the context of the enterprise as a whole.
- The R&D policy should make fundamental decisions, develop strategies and determine goals; this applies basically to the acquisition, protection and exploitation of knowledge.
- In the planning and control of R&D, the resources for the realisation of R&D goals are determined and their results controlled; the specific characteristic of R&D planning lies in the great uncertainty about results and their possible application as well as in the expenditure of time and money involved.
- The R&D organisation includes the determination and modification of the R&D structure and its integration into the company's organisation.
- As the R&D activities are above all based on the generation and exploitation of knowledge, the leadership and promotion of R&D employees plays a special role.

In a strategic context, research and development are the basis and the operative design of the corporate technology strategy. Managing R&D strategically stands for especially integrating R&D into technology and business strategy and managing the R&D process, including its linkages throughout the corporation. The success of the R&D strategy very much depends on how far it is integrated in the overall business strategy (Kodama 1992; Roussel/Saad/Erickson 1991). Top management plays a crucial role for the integration of R&D in business strategy because it has the power of decision.

In this respect, industrial R&D has the following three main strategic purposes (Roussel/Saad/Erickson 1991, pp. 17):

1) Defence, support and expansion of existing business: existing products are modified and improved according to customer demand and adapted to different market standards or regulations; products are developed within the existing business structure.

2) Creating new business: R&D activities aim at providing opportunities for new businesses with the use of existing or new technologies.

3) Broadening and deepening technological capabilities: This concerns existing or new businesses and aims at strengthening the innovativeness and competitive position of the enterprise from a long-term view.

The strategic purpose of R&D and the R&D strategy of a company are changing according to the life cycle of industry in which the enterprise is operating. At the "embryonic stage", R&D plays a decisive role in launching new products and business and in establishing a new competitive position (see figure 3.2-2). During the "growth stage", the strategic purpose of R&D is to expand the business and to improve or sustain this competitive position. This may be carried out by extending the range of products and applications or by enlarging the application potential. In the "stage of maturity" the mission of R&D shifts to defending the competitive position by cost reduction or by extending the differentiation potential of existing products. Management may also consider deciding on a rejuvenation of business. R&D clearly and exclusively aims at cost reduction to safeguard profitability in an "aging stage". From a strategic point of view, management has to decide whether to renew the products or the manufacturing process or to abandon the products.

Summing it up, the strategic purpose and the tasks of R&D of a company are changing according to the stage of the industrial life cycle. In an early stage, R&D activities are dominated by research and are focused on product innovation, whereas in a later phase the significance of process innovation and cost reduction in R&D activities is much higher.[2]

---

[2]   See also Utterback/Abernathy (1975) and their dynamic model of process and product innovation.

Figure 3.2-2:   The mission of R&D and the life cycle of industry

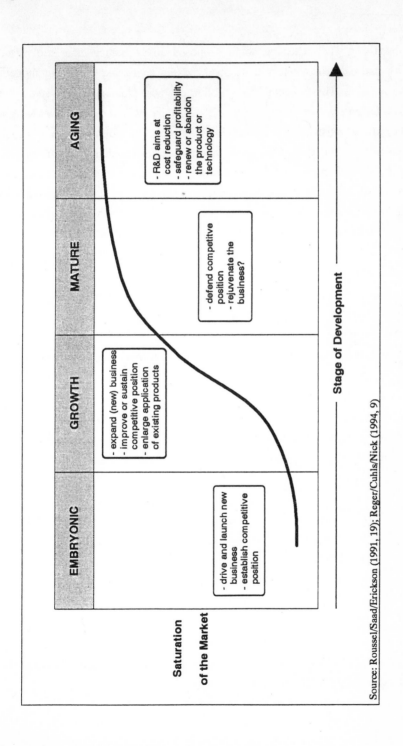

Source: Roussel/Saad/Erickson (1991, 19); Reger/Cuhls/Nick (1994, 9)

3.3   Some generalized models of R&D management

Before discussing and analysing some proposed R&D management tools (see chapter 4), one can ask whether there are generally applicable models of modern R&D management. The frequently used notion of "best practice" suggests that an ideal model for enterprises to manage their R&D activities in the one and only ideal way successfully exists. This assumption can only be followed with strong restrictions because enterprises are acting in different environments (sector, market, competition, technology) and have to face different challenges. Finding solutions and the approach to solving problems, aims and strategy of European enterprises also differ substantially: in a study about the research and technology management of more than 200 European enterprises (CEC 1994) it has been found that even firms operating in the same sector may face very different problems of technology management and often come up with different solutions. For instance, a small mechanical engineering firm with low R&D intensity rarely cooperates with universities, whereas a small mechanical engineering firm with high R&D expenditure explicitly includes cooperation with universities in its R&D strategy (Reger/Kungl 1994). Obviously, both problems and management of research and technology differ greatly according to size, market position, complexity of products and technology, customer demand, technology and R&D strategy and the available technological, entrepreneurial and organisational competences. As a conclusion, this means that a model of best management practices for R&D is an ideal image which may not be reached in practice and can only be relevant for a selected number of firms.

Rothwell (1993, 31) points out that successful innovation and R&D is "people centred": "Formal management techniques can enhance the performance of competent managers, but they are no substitute for management of high quality and ability, i.e. innovation is essentially a "people process" and simply attempting to substitute formal management techniques for managerial talent and entrepreneurial flair is not a viable option." Beneath that, innovative success is "multi-factored", there are no single factor explanations (Rothwell 1993, 28): The competence of balancing and coordinating all functions, and not doing one or two things brilliantly well, will support a successful innovation process.

Keeping these restrictions in mind three different "models" or "generations" of R&D management are presented in this chapter:

1) The model of the "Fifth Generation Innovation Process" describes different stages of the innovation process and derives from that aims and tasks for the management of innovation and R&D.

2) The model of the "Third Generation R&D" is based on experience as a consultant and describes changes in the organisation and resource allocation of R&D; this is paraphrased by a stage model which distinguishes between three different generations of R&D management.

3) The "Three Paradigms Scenario" is concerned with changes in the organisation of R&D in multi-divisional companies and institutional arrangements to balance the responsibility for R&D between the corporate and the business unit level.

These models are to serve as guidelines and stimulus for a future R&D management in European enterprises. They show not only different conceptions of R&D management but also common trends and problems in the management of R&D and their changes over the past three decades.

3.3.1   The fifth generation innovation process

Rothwell (1991, 1993) presents five generations of perceptions of the innovation process which are based on the evaluation of empirical studies and theoretical literature. Each model more or less represents the "dominantly perceived model" of innovation during several periods from the end of the 1950s to today. This model of the innovation process was selected here because it explicitly deals with R&D and the changing role of R&D in the industrial innovation process.

Rothwell's model shows an evolution from the simple linear sequential technology-push ("first generation") and need-pull imaginations ("second generation") to the more interactive coupling one which dominated up to the mid 1980s (see figure 3.3-

1). In the "coupling model", the emphasis of management lay on the integration across the R&D/marketing interface.

As fourth generation, the "integrated model" was developed from the mid 1980s onwards and marked a shift from considering innovation as a sequential process towards thinking of innovation as a parallel process (see figure 3.3-1). Emphasis of R&D management was placed on working simultaneously across business functions and on integrating the R&D/manufacturing interface technologically by CAD/CAM and organisationally by integrated development teams (so-called "rugby teams"). The "integrated model" cannot only be characterized by interfunction integration within the enterprise, but also growing integration with other companies. This includes cooperation with suppliers and customers, the creation of strategic alliances with competitors and the building up of pre-competitive research consortia partly with support from the EU and national ministries.

The "systems integration and networking model" ("fifth generation") is regarded by Rothwell as a somewhat idealized development from the fourth generation model. In this model, innovation is seen as a multi-institutional networking process (see figure 3.3-1): this encompasses strong linkages with leading edge customers, strategic integration of primary suppliers (e.g. co-development, linked CAD), and strong horizontal linkages (e.g. joint ventures, strategic alliances). The most significant feature of this model is the electronification of innovation. For the management of R&D, this means the use of interfunctional linked CAD/CAM systems and integrated supplier/assembler CAD systems, the application of simulation modelling replacing physical prototyping and expert systems as design aid. R&D management will mainly aim at higher flexibility, increasing development speed, and quality. Besides that, there are further challenges for R&D management: since the complexity of the innovation process and the number of actors are increasing, the ability to cooperate and utilize networking is of growing significance for managing R&D. This also includes "... the requirement for innovation/technology strategy to be at the leading edge of corporate strategy is greater than ever before " (cf. Rothwell 1991, 22). However, according to Rothwell this model is for most companies still in its evolutionary phase and describes the (near) future of the management of innovation and R&D.

Figure 3.3-1:   The fifth generation innovation process

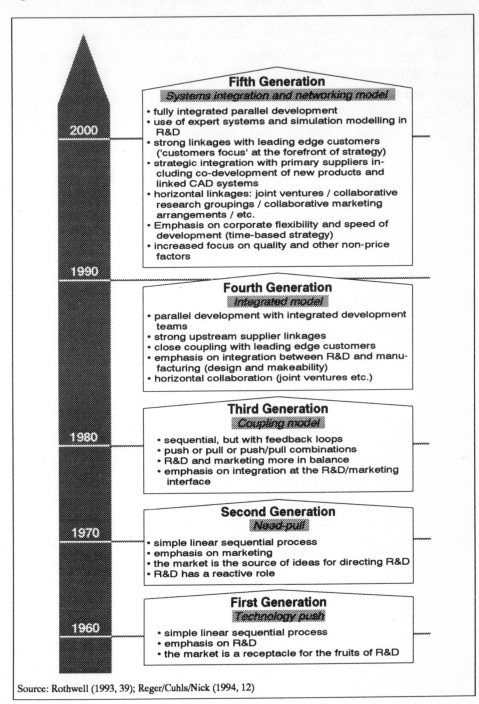

Source: Rothwell (1993, 39); Reger/Cuhls/Nick (1994, 12)

3.3.2   The third generation R&D

The model of the "Third Generation R&D" is created on the observation of the management of R&D in enterprises and the experience of a consultant by Roussel/Saad/Erickson (1991): three different generations of R&D management have appeared since the 1950s; each of them describes the management and strategic context in place, the operating principles in use, and the differences in management practices used with the different types of R&D.

The "first generation R&D management" occurs up to the mid 1960s and can be characterized by a lack of a long-term strategic framework for the management of R&D (see figure 3.3-2). There is no explicit link between business and technology/R&D strategy. R&D is treated as an overhead cost and a line item in the general manager's budget. Corporate management participates little in defining R&D programmes or projects, the results of R&D are rarely evaluated. Typically for this generation, R&D is organized into cost centres and according to scientific and engineering disciplines. R&D activities are centralized and concentrated at the corporate level, whereas incremental R&D is conducted by the business units. The main characteristics of this first R&D management generation is the lack of linkage between R&D and the corporation as well as the centralized R&D activities on corporate level.

The "second generation of R&D management" is a transition stage towards the third generation. The most distinctive difference from the first generation is the beginning of a strategic framework for R&D and the stronger linkage between business and R&D management (see figure 3.3-2). A supplier/customer relationship is established between R&D (as supplier) and the various businesses (as customers). Fundamental R&D is centralized on corporate level and incremental R&D is distributed to the business units. Nevertheless, matrix and project management are actively used. Project managers are responsible for project planning, mobilizing resources, and meeting project objectives, deadlines and budget. However, since plans for R&D are formulated on a project-by-project basis, separately and independently for each business unit and the corporation, there is a lack of integration between R&D and business strategy.

Figure 3.3-2:   Third generation R&D

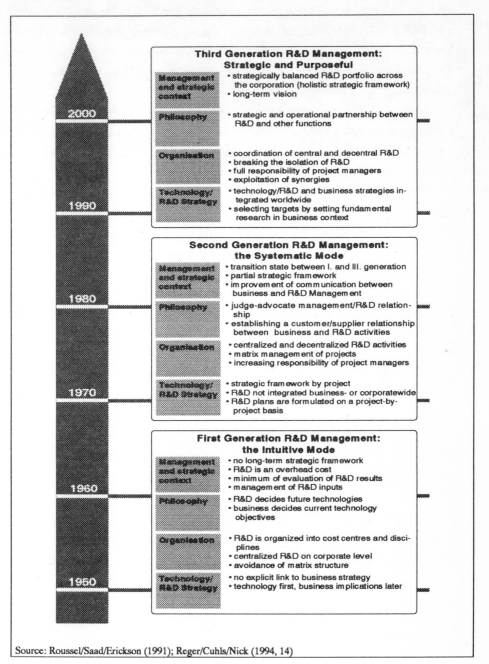

"Third generation R&D management" seeks to balance the R&D portfolio strategically across the whole corporation. General and R&D managers jointly assess and decide upon the aims, the strategy, the content and the budget of R&D. Technology/R&D strategies are integrated into the business strategies worldwide. Targets of R&D are selected by setting fundamental research in a business context and funds are allocated according to short-, medium-, and long-term needs of the business units and the corporation. Centralized and decentralized R&D are coordinated by matrix organisation, the intensive use of project management and making the project manager fully responsible for the R&D project. There is a resource-allocation principle for a strategic balancing between radical and incremental R&D activities.

This model for future R&D management clearly aims at large and multi-national enterprises and can hardly be applied to small and medium-sized enterprises (SMEs) entirely. In contrast to the model of the Fifth Generation Innovation Process, the Third Generation R&D model takes a closer look at the inside of the company and the internal factors for successful R&D management.

3.3.3   Three paradigms scenario for the organisation of R&D

The model of "Three Paradigms Scenario for the Organisation of R&D" was developed by Coombs/Richards (1993) following the model of Rothwell (chapter 3.3.1) and Roussel/Saad/Erickson (chapter 3.3.2). The third future paradigm is based additionally on an empirical study of 24 multi-divisional British enterprises. This model is focused on the organisation of strategic technology and R&D management. In particular, it deals with the balance of responsibility between the corporate and the business unit level concerning the accumulation of technological assets.

Coombs/Richards (1993) identified two traditional paradigms of R&D organisation (see figure 3.3-3). The characteristics of paradigm 1 (1950-70) are the centralisation and corporate dominance in the funding, ownership, and control of R&D. Management thinking was dominated by a technology-push focus and R&D spending grew. Paradigm 2 (from 1970 till the late 1980s) can be characterized by decentralisation and business unit dominance in the aspects of R&D mentioned. Management philosophy and practice moved towards market focus and "market-driven R&D" emerged.

However, and this is the main thesis of Coombs/Richards (1993, 387), the shift from the centralisation of R&D towards the decentralisation of R&D has a number of negative consequences. Firstly, business unit ownership of R&D is very effective at consolidating strength within an existing technological regime, but turns into a severe disadvantage if this technological regime loses competitiveness. Secondly, if new technologies emerge and destroy existing competences of the business unit, decentralized R&D may not be able to cope with this change. While decentralized, market-driven R&D activities confirm existing patterns, they ignore the need for research which is long-term oriented and beyond existing core competences of the corporation.

The negative development of paradigm 2, the increasing scale and the global character of many R&D actors, and the completion of the institutional learning process of companies are seen as decisive challenges for today's R&D management. As an answer to this, a new pattern of research and technology management is identified and visible so far only in some firms (Coombs/Richards 1993, 391). Paradigm 3 tries to combine market-driven benefits from decentralized, business-funded R&D, with technology-push benefits from a long-term oriented, centralized R&D on corporate level (see figure 3.3-3). Companies with this future R&D organisation have a mixed corporate and business unit funding for R&D with attention to subtle balance of incentives. The funding of technology is conceptually separated from the funding of products. Corporate and business unit share the ownership of R&D portfolio and resources.

The three paradigms scenario describes the decisive changes in the organisation of R&D in multi-divisional British companies. It looks at the inside of large enterprises and can hardly be applied to SMEs. The authors do not claim for paradigm 3 the possibility of application to all enterprises because the organisational arrangements differ from firm to firm, from industry to industry, and from country to country. "However, while it can be pursued to some extent in all industrial contexts, it is more appropriate and easier to apply in some contexts, and less so in others" (cf. Coombs/Richards 1993, 391).

Figure 3.3-3:   Three paradigms scenario for the organisation of R&D

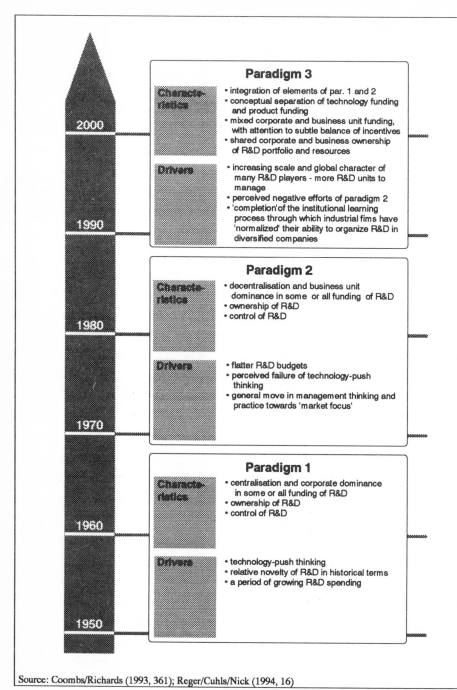

3.3.4 Conclusions

The three models presented here have common and different aims and elements. Beginning with the main differences, the model of the "Fifth Generation Innovation Process" looks at the innovation process as a whole and encompasses both internal and external factors for a successful innovative activity of companies. In contrast to the other two models, there is on the one hand a strong emphasis on cooperation activities with other firms and the use of a broad variety of instruments and forms of collaboration. On the other hand, a technological dimension is introduced in the model of the "Fifth Generation" ("systems integration and networking model") by regarding the electronification of the innovation process as a very significant feature. Besides that, this model as a whole may serve as a guide for a future management of R&D and innovation, not only for large companies but also for small and medium-sized enterprises. The other two models ("Third Generation R&D" and "Three Paradigms Scenario") take a closer look at R&D management itself and the institutional arrangements inside the company. Their model for future R&D management is clearly focused on large, multi-divisional enterprises and is not appropriate for SMEs.

All three models for a future R&D management have in common, on the one side, the concept of integrating R&D and businesses. This concerns strategic and organisational features as well as funding and resource allocation. On the other side, the relationship between long-term, centralized R&D versus short-term, decentralized R&D has to be re-defined. Taking both aspects into account, the significance of coordination and networking inside the corporation for the management of R&D is increasing. R&D management in multi-divisional enterprises has to deal mainly with the coordination of centralized and decentralized R&D, an appropriate mix of corporate and business unit funding, the integration of R&D in corporate and business strategy, the development of long-term visions and the coordination of R&D portfolio and resources between corporate and business level.

In anticipation of the results of chapter 2, a crucial challenge for the management of R&D and an adequate response is missing in the models presented. The growing complexity and the overlapping of technologies and scientific disciplines is a challenge that has to be faced by inter- or transdisciplinary approaches of R&D

activities. Knowledge of different scientific and technical disciplines has to be combined by short-term as well as institutional arrangements within the company. In this respect, networking with other enterprises, higher education institutes and non-university R&D institutes is also of growing importance.

Again, it should be emphasized, that any model for a future R&D management represents generalized images about reality and cannot be applied to all enterprises to the same extent. A model is appropriate in one context and less in another and should provide guidelines for responses to today's and future challenges to the management of R&D.

4.   Tools for R&D activities

While the issues mentioned in chapter 2 are the challenges to today's R&D management, tools for R&D activities describe how firms can respond to them. The description and discussion of these tools is analytically separated into three interfaces which are crucial to the generation of knowledge and the success of technological development. From the large number of R&D management tools mentioned in the literature, we have concentrated on the following and assigned them to the three interfaces:

-     Interface I - internal R&D activities:
      -     corporate culture and significance for R&D (chapter 4.1),
      -     organisation of R&D (chapter 4.2),
      -     development, leveraging, renewal of core competences and the role of R&D (chapter 4.3),
      -     instruments for technological forecasting (chapter 4.4);

-     Interface II - acquisition of external scientific and technical know-how:
      -     cooperation: co-development, strategic alliances, networking (chapter 4.5);

-     Interface III - scientific, technical, and functional boundaries:
      -     management of scientific, technical and functional interfaces (chapter 4.6).

Interface I, "internal R&D activities", is the integration of different modes of technology development within a corporation. For instance, this means reducing the negative effects in terms of quality, time, and cost effectiveness of departmental boundaries in enterprises. There are great differences in this respect mentioned in literature between on the one hand European and US enterprises and on the other hand Japanese firms. The latter seem to work across departmental boundaries and to exploit their core competences better than their Western competitors (see e.g. Prahalad/Hamel 1990).

The second interface, "the acquisition of external scientific and technical know-how", is the linking of technological development within the firm to the knowledge developed in the external scientific and industrial networks. Firms are using different tools like forming strategic alliances, joint ventures, contracting out research to universities, participating in pre-competitive research consortia like EUREKA, ESPRIT, RACE, BRITE/EURAM for gaining access to external know-how. Again, Japanese firms are seen as particularly efficient in using these tools (see e.g. Ohmae 1989; Prahalad/Hamel 1990).

The third interface to be discussed concerns "scientific, technical, and functional boundaries" within the firm. Barriers to successful R&D management can be the reduction of flow of information between business functions (e.g. between R&D and production) and the prevention of new knowledge through not integrating different scientific or technical disciplines. Especially the growing complexity and overlapping of technologies is developing as a more and more critical challenge to the innovativeness of European enterprises.

4.1 Corporate culture and significance for R&D (Interface I)

4.1.1 Definition: culture as system of symbols

In the literature on corporate culture, there are as many definitions as publications available. Authors from the disciplines sociology, cultural anthropology, psychology and management theory do not only use different vocabulary but also stress completely different elements and combine them to a certain definition of a "corporate culture". For an overview of different definitions see Greipel 1987, Heinen et al. 1987 or Dierkes et al. 1993.

In some cases, we have the differentiation of "corporate culture" and "organisational culture" which in general mean the same and are used in the same context. In detail, organisational culture stresses more the organisation as the most influential factor (for a discussion see Dierkes et al. 1993).

Corporate culture is defined in a simple way as "the way we do things around here" or "what keeps the herd moving roughly west" (Deal 1984, pp. 29). An often cited definition which takes into account the still unclear relation of structural and cultural aspects of organisation is the one of Allaire and Firsirotu who define "...organisational culture as a particularistic system of symbols shaped by ambient society and the organisation's history, leadership and contingencies, differentially shared, used and modified by actors in the course of acting and making sense out of organisational events. Organisational culture, thus conceived, is a powerful tool for interpreting organisational life and behaviour and for understanding the process of decay, adaptation and radical change in organisations." (cf. Allaire/Firsirotu 1984, 216; also Helmers 1993, 162).

A very popular concept using corporate culture is the creation of a "corporate identity" as the result of a target-oriented culture. Corporate identity uses some cultural elements within a company in order to have a presentation of the whole enterprise externally and to develop a "group consciousness" internally (Kobi/Wüthrich 1986, 35). Thus, to create a corporate identity is one of the aims of a target-oriented corporate culture.

In this chapter, the organisational aspect of corporate culture will not be overemphasized. Instead, corporate culture is understood as the totality of shared norms, social values and ways of thinking which all have an impact on the behaviour of personnel at every step of the hierarchy and every function of the whole enterprise (close to Kobi/Wüthrich 1986, 34).

4.1.2   Corporate culture: core of the enterprise and R&D

Corporate culture was one of the concepts en vogue during the 1980s but the concept itself and some of its aspects are not new. There is no technique or instrument to apply corporate culture as a whole concept within a company but two directions of its "use":

- The first is the understanding of the existing corporate culture in an enterprise; this knowledge may be used to define a strategy based on the existing fundament.

- The second aspect is the strategic development of a corporate culture which means stressing, improving and applying some cultural elements to make direct use of them in a strategy. This possibility will be discussed here.

Pümpin (1984) identifies direct (structural) and indirect (cultural) means to achieve strategic goals. Project plans, action plans, budgets and their allocations, the setting of personal goals, efficiency evaluation, ideal versus real comparisons can be regarded as direct and formalized instruments. They directly influence the target, whereas indirect means like symbolic actions, information, ceremonies, stories, informal contacts, promotion of identification, education or the promotion of enthusiasm at first influence corporate culture and in a second step the strategic goals (see figure 4.1-1).

Figure 4.1-1:   The use of direct and indirect methods for strategy attainment

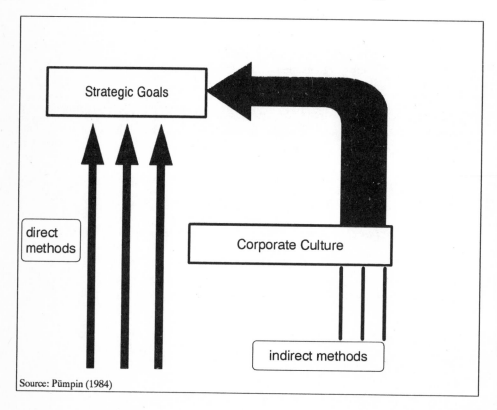

Source: Pümpin (1984)

In order to get a more pragmatic overview, some aspects of corporate culture according to Kaschube (1993, pp. 97) are mentioned. Social values and norms are in the centre of most corporate culture concepts. Social values are more abstract, stable and have a less compelling character than norms. Added to them are orientations of the cognitive base like "ways of thinking" (Krulis-Randa 1990, 6), "convictions" (Neuberger/Kompa 1986, 63) or "basic assumptions" (Schein 1985, 9). These evaluative and cognitive elements are not noticed or questioned anymore, but unconsciously influence the attitudes of all members of an organisation. They appear in symbolic forms, which can be divided into "media of symbolic exchange" (Neuberger 1985, 31, cf. in: Kaschube 1993, 98), cognitive-linguistic forms like "myths" or "legends" (Westerland/Sjöstrand 1981), interactive symbols as rites or ceremonies (Trice/Beyer 1984, Katovich 1985) or products and artefacts, e.g. subdividing available office/factory space or technologies (Pfeffer 1981).

Companies' practice: culture forming guidelines

Corporate guidelines are a means of influencing the identity and self-understanding of an enterprise. The following statement is taken from the corporate guidelines of a large German multi-national enterprise (electronics) and reveals the attitude the company has towards its employees: "Our employees are informed thoroughly. They act in a competent, entrepreneurial and responsible manner. Every employee knows how his work is supporting the business of his department or the whole corporation."

Leonard-Barton (1992) shows in her empirical study that values, norms and attitudes assigned to knowledge creation and content affect R&D activities and especially R&D projects. Therefore strategic management and the management of R&D have to take this critical role of these elements of corporate culture into consideration. R&D activities are enhanced by values and norms. The empowerment of researchers and the status of the various technical or scientific disciplines are especially critical sub-elements of values. Empowered engineers for example will create multiple future potentials for the corporation through their R&D activity. The "cultural bias" towards the historical, technical base of the corporation attracts top researchers and engineers in this core area. On the other hand, the same values, norms and attitudes can also hamper innovation (Leonard-Barton 1992, 119; see also chapter 4.3.4). If empowerment comes into conflict with the greater corporate goals, or if researchers and engineers of non-dominant disciplines are less well respected in the company, creativity can be destroyed and talented people may leave the firm.

4.1.3   Motivation of researchers as main challenge

In contrast to structural and formal aspects of an organisation which can be managed by direct instruments or techniques, corporate culture including social values and norms influences every part of an enterprise unwillingly, but cannot be steered or used as easily as a technique or an applied method (Perich 1993). Nevertheless, a well-functioning corporate culture can influence the whole company and facilitate the integration of research and development into the corporation to face the challenges of the future.

Companies' practice: corporate culture in a french multi-national enterprise

The French multi-national enterprise is one of the world's most important suppliers of telecommunication systems and services. The corporation is subdivided into divisions which are distributed over many locations throughout Europe. There are five locations with R&D activities in France, Germany, Netherlands, Spain, and Italy.

In this enterprise corporate culture is seen as one of the factors that decide about success or failure of projects. To support a common culture, every second year a meeting of the whole management is held in Paris. With this meeting corporate identity is promoted. In addition to this biennial meeting "open days" are held for all managers (approximately 2,000). For this occasion stands are set up, where the company members are able to inform themselves about the activities within the corporation. Another "open day" was held for all researchers at the facility in Stuttgart. Here open discussions were possible which revealed a number of sore points in the research process. Internationalism is an important part of the culture: English is the business language and the balances are valued in ECUs.

A strong corporate culture is supposed to have an impact on human resources and their motivation. Motivation, especially in R&D, is necessary to make people learn, to be creative or to be able to work in a team. A value-oriented management which can be the result of a strong cultural influence may give scientists and engineers the background for their work. Although general social values are changing, the individual person knows what he/she is working for. In this context, conformity in R&D has to be avoided: rotation in the job, continuous training and the employment of new personnel can be a solution to maintain a culture open to new ideas. On the other hand, if a culture is developed too strongly e.g. in a R&D department, this can lead to stereotypes, standardized work, non-creativity, resistance to any change, and problems in cooperating with other departments or groups. In such an atmosphere, creative ideas and the development of new technologies can be hampered.

In order to employ new skilled staff, the external image of a visible "good culture" is also supposed to be helpful (Dill/Hügler 1987, 197). Necessary personnel can be attracted to the company more easily if the working environment and climate in the company seems to be good. A conscious use of corporate culture later on helps to integrate new personnel, e.g. by "coaching", shaping their values, teaching the company's special language and behaviour, by ceremonies, telling stories of success, symbols or other formalized actions. For the future education and training of human resources, a strong existing culture might be quite supportive. For longer term purposes, one has to take into account which means of personnel planning and development could improve a corporate culture that fits strategic purposes. Participative management and adapted shaping of incentives (financial as well as immaterial) can strengthen a culture which underlines teamwork, decentralized organisation of R&D departments, communication between the departments, organisational learning and individual training of needed skills.

Companies'practice: personnel policy as a tool to influence culture

Example: German multi-national enterprise (automobiles)
In this enterprise R&D is divided into several research centres according to the different brands. In addition to these centres a central research facility exists. New research personnel is chosen in assessment centres. Employment starts with a rotation programme that covers a variety of different functions and departments. The idea of this programme is to provide the new employee with an understanding of the different subcultures which later enables him to deal with interface problems.

Interdisciplinary approaches to develop new technologies can be better supported if values like flexibility, openness (e.g. to other disciplines), and communication are stressed. Hence, the complexity of technology can be faced by approaches from more than one angle. In general, efficiency and effectivity can be improved if a corporate culture has the potential of coordination, integration and motivation. According to Albert/Silvermann (cf. 1984, 13) results can be:

(1) "... greater commitment to the organisation's objectives (notably quality, good consumer service, high productivity, among others);

(2) increased employee effort, pride and loyalty;

(3) lower (personal) turnover;

(4) faster implementation of plans, projects and programs;

(5) more effective problem-solving at all organisational levels;

(6) the ability to grow rapidly through directing more effort toward implementing plans, programs, and objectives and less effort toward fighting fires, plugging holes, constantly resolving conflicts ...".

Loyalty and identity with the company are the results of a strong corporate culture which is a basis for motivation for the personnel. It sets ideals and goals (e.g. by symbols, decoration, praise, parties, written down goals) to achieve which make visible the sense of the individual's own actions and work. People who have a model, who know why and what they are working for are motivated much more than others. This motivation and fruitful creativity are necessary in research and development, especially in order to transfer the developed products and knowledge to other functions and further on to market.

4.1.4   Corporate culture is no instrument

Although there is an increasing number of publications on corporate culture (Heinen et al. 1987, Greipel 1987, Dierkes et al. 1993), from their point of view, it seems to be naïve to expect general rules or recipes from science (von Rosenstiel 1993, 20).

Until now, there is no general methodology available and the two directions of describing and influencing corporate culture give no answer how to "make a culture". Pümpin/Kobi/Wüthrich (1985, pp. 9) try to apply a certain methodology on symptoms: certain elements, which are components of the general culture, can be identified, evaluated and formed. This is not a technique applied to corporate culture as a whole, but concerns some selected informative elements which Pümpin/Kobi/ Wüthrich (1985, 12) divide into

- core factors like profile of the managers (curriculum vitae, social values and mentality), rituals and symbols (ritual behaviour of management and staff, rooms and images, institutionalized rituals and conventions) or communication (style, external and internal communication);
- management factors like strategies (strategic documents, ideas), structures and processes (organisation documents philosophy, informal structures and processes) or management systems (systems, redundancy) and
- environmental factors which are marked by the economical, technological and ecological framework as well as the socio-cultural framework.

Every company needs its individual starting point and concept to develop strategies and models. To "apply a corporate culture" is not possible because of its complexity. Only individual measures are applicable. Until now, one has to identify those measures by trial and error; the successful applications can just as well be right by chance (Dierkes et al. 1993). From the ethnological (or culture anthropology) side also no result is available because data are not sufficient and no individual person but a whole corporation is looked at (Helmers 1993, 166). Maybe in the future it will be possible to use some of the methods of research in the field, especially processes of acculturation or those of Lévi-Strauss. There are still many problems left for the management of enterprises concerning corporate culture (Steger 1993, pp. 197):

- A description of a corporate culture is only possible in certain specific situations, because enterprises as "open systems" are in constant change and interaction with their environment.
- There is no culture theory available, yet; the economic disciplines tended more to influence technocratic top management advice.
- It is quite impossible to operationalize central terms.
- Large-scale expert surveys did not lead to better results than observation of "skillful persons" who intuitively combine cultural diagnosis with strategic advice.
- The danger exists that despite large expenditures only trivial results are obtained.

- It makes only sense to describe corporate culture in a context, e.g. in relation to market or competition, to compare the present state with the past or make international comparisons; this makes general statements very difficult.
- The quantification of a corporate culture's strength is impossible, no differentiation (strong versus weak) or value indicators are available.
- From a mixture of "natives and naïves", a relatively objective description may be possible if the group is able to communicate on the matter.

Figure 4.1-2:   Correspondences to be established between corporate culture, strategy, systems and environment

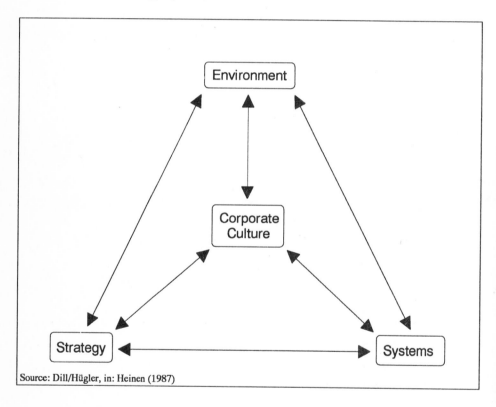

Source: Dill/Hügler, in: Heinen (1987)

As mentioned above, although the development of corporate culture as a strategic management task is nothing new (Kobi/Wüthrich 1986, 13), it is still difficult to measure. Trying to describe a corporate culture already changes it and most of the US American organisational-psychological concepts are very confusing (Kaschube 1993, pp. 133). Corporate strategy is already shaped by its culture (Heinen 1987,

44) but vice versa, new strategies do not necessarily shape the culture which is constantly changing.

A misfit analysis like that of Ansoff (Dill/Hügler 1987, 175) can also identify qualitative factors which influence the corporate culture (see figure 4.1-2). Many consultants use a set of methods by diagnosing misfits and curing some of the symptoms. But at the present stage, no one can say if they are really successful at all. The fact is that a strong "fitting" culture is one of the most important factors to face the challenges of the future. As many studies on Japanese management like Pascale/Athos (1981) prove, stressing the "soft factors" of the enterprises was a key element for the Japanese success. It made them learn, improving their knowledge steadily in different ways and supported their willingness to learn. Learning in their cultural understanding is a never-ending process and motivative factor which is a good basis for incremental and creative R&D activities.

4.2 Organisation of R&D and global R&D integration (Interface I)

4.2.1 Organisational forms of R&D

Organisational structures in companies can have a wide variety of forms: formal and informal elements which are modified and adapted to people, conditions of the environment and general requirements. Concerning research and development it is important to consider whether the organisational integration of R&D is better centralized, decentralized or a combination of both.

A more traditional possibility of organising research and development activities in an enterprise is by using linear (one-dimensional) or multi-dimensional forms. One dimensional or linear forms can be phase-oriented specialisations which divide R&D in primary functions like basic research, applied research, development of technology

198

Figure 4.2-1:   Organisational specialisation of R&D

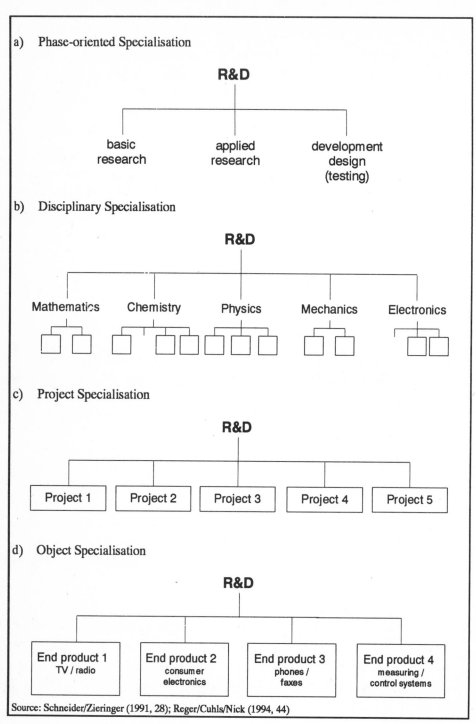

a) Phase-oriented Specialisation

R&D

basic research — applied research — development design (testing)

b) Disciplinary Specialisation

R&D

Mathematics — Chemistry — Physics — Mechanics — Electronics

c) Project Specialisation

R&D

Project 1 — Project 2 — Project 3 — Project 4 — Project 5

d) Object Specialisation

R&D

End product 1 TV / radio — End product 2 consumer electronics — End product 3 phones / faxes — End product 4 measuring / control systems

Source: Schneider/Zieringer (1991, 28); Reger/Cuhls/Nick (1994, 44)

and design, experimentation and secondary functions like patenting, documentation or literature analysis (Bleicher 1991, 160; Schneider/Zieringer 1991, 28). R&D can also be organized by scientific disciplines or by objects, like e.g. materials, components or end products (see figure 4.2-1) A fourth form can be a specialisation according to projects, e.g. the application of a certain technology, the development of a new product or its elements.

Certainly, mixed forms are also found; these are needed if formally external companies are concerned which cooperate or develop jointly or when there are financial dependencies. If the regional differentiation of a company's activities has grown to a certain extent, these criteria can also be applied (Bleicher 1991, pp. 192). Typical multi-dimensional structures are those of a matrix matching central functions and objects (or regions). The combinations can be execution-object-matrix, execution-regional-matrix or object-regional-matrix (Bleicher 1991, 165).

Figure 4.2-2:   Various dimensions of the organisational structure

I.   DIRECTION OF ELEMENTS AND RELATIONS
   1.   Object-oriented versus personnel-oriented structure
   2.   Formalized versus symbol orientation
II. CHARACTER OF REGULATION
   3.   Programmable, individual regulations versus task-oriented framework regulation
   4.   Long-term organisation versus time-limit organisation
III. CONFIGURATION
   5.   Monolithic versus polycentric configuration
   6.   Sharply ascending versus flat configuration
IV. DIRECTION OF THE STRUCTURING
   7.   Endogenous versus extraneous orientation
   8.   External shaping in the process association versus self-shaping with part autonomy

Source: Bleicher (1992, 238); Reger/Cuhls/Nick (1994, 45)

In the management concept of the University of St. Gallen, the various dimensions of an organisation are named and shall describe the extremes of organisational orientation, its character, configuration and the direction of structuring. In this model, the wide variety of organisational structures of a company are shown (see figure 4.2-2.).

The combination of internal and external organisational structures is reflected in the contrast of centralized and decentralized forms. In purely centralized companies all work on new or improved products is done in one or more central R&D facilities. No R&D activity is conducted within the divisions except for perhaps an occasional major redesign job (see figure 4.2-3). This laboratory or coordinating R&D unit is generally located at the headquarters of the company.

The other extreme is the purely decentralized company which has its research and development activities spread at different locations. In this case, the headquarters have a coordinating function but do not decide on details in R&D. More or less, general directions for product development are given by headquarters. Purely decentralized means that all work on new or improved products and processes is done within the operating divisions. In many large companies, a division may have several labs concerned with different levels of R&D (see Rubenstein 1989, 38; figure 4.2-3).

In most of the innovative, multidivisionale enterprises, there are combinations of both forms, in which there might be control competences in one laboratory and hierarchical structures in an R&D department of the company as well as decentralized or even anarchical structures in other divisions. Depending on sector, project and hierarchical structure inside the company, decisions on product development are made at the headquarters. But there is also room for own decisions and ideas in the decentralized R&D departments. In a "pure combined" company the more general, long-range, basic or exploratory work is carried out in a corporate R&D lab and the more specific, short-term applied work is conducted within the divisions (see figure 4.2-3). The degree of centralisation/decentralisation depends on several factors, in most cases a historical development, and tries to reflect the specific requirements of the company.

Figure 4.2-3:   Patterns of development of R&D in firms

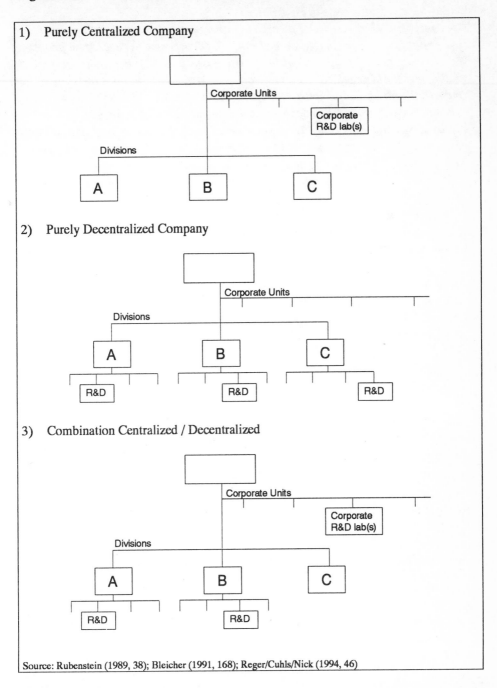

Source: Rubenstein (1989, 38); Bleicher (1991, 168); Reger/Cuhls/Nick (1994, 46)

Companies' practice: combined centralized/ decentralized R&D organisation

Multi-national enterprise in electronics

Decentralisation of research has become a major trend in the past five years. An increasing share of the budget of the central R&D department depends on financing by divisions rather than headquarters. At the central R&D laboratory of a multi-national enterprise (MNE) in electronics - somewhat of an exception in an industrial setting in the past, as basic research along the lines of academic institutes was the model - this division-dependent part of the budget was set at 70 % in 1988 and the result has been a better coordination of activities with the divisions. One recent element of this system is that the divisions or product groups are required to spend half of their research budget on stable programmes for signal processing, data compression and other core technologies that are needed for all the company's product lines.

Central facility for manufacturing technology

At the central facility for manufacturing technology (400 employees) of a large firm 80% of the work is directly funded by divisions on a project basis. 20 % is performed on the basis of annual programming that is negotiated with the division. Each group of about ten engineers is entitled to $ 25.000 of spending per year at its own discretion. Finally, each individual has 280 out of 1,600 working hours per year free for individual research.

Large Italian mechanical engineering firm

The funding of corporate R&D of an Italian mechanical engineering firm with more than 2,000 employees is divided among three sources: while 10% of funding sources are corporate, 70% of funds are contributed by business units on project basis and 20% stem from external sources; public funds play an important role hereby.

Chemical firm

A MNE in the chemical industry has a method of programming its central laboratory research that similarly gives a large say to the user divisions, yet preserves the long-term horizon of at least some substantial part of the activities. This is achieved by bi-annual programming conferences at which research managers negotiate with divisional managers.

For the global integration of R&D, decentralisation is essential and two alternative models are suggested (Booz-Allen & Hamilton 1991, pp. 68):

- The first one is the "star model" in which the R&D units outside the home country are still dependent on decisions in headquarters. This model is - on the international level - analogous to the purely centralized model on the national level. In this kind of R&D organisation, there are hardly any contacts between the R&D units abroad.

- The second model is the "network model" in which R&D units are founded without regarding national borders. Each centre concentrates on a small number of specific technological fields and is the leader for the whole therein. Contacts and decisions are more or less independent of the headquarters. Every R&D unit acts as a "centre of excellence" with equal rights. This more global view of R&D requires the integration of researchers and engineers and an appropriate human resources management.

4.2.2   Factors influencing professionalisation of R&D

The organisational structure of a company has to reflect and cope with the challenges of the future as mentioned in chapter 2, especially, (1) the increasing scale, scope and specialisation of research activities, (2) the internationalisation of R&D, (3) the increase of inter-organisational linkages in research and development associated with the growth of computer-communication networks, (4) and on-line information systems in R&D. In order to understand this development, one has to consider the organisational evolution of R&D which started with single inventors and since the beginning of this century shifted to being carried out by groups centred within the firms. Research and development became an institutionalized and integrated part of corporate activity. Three factors influenced its "professionalisation" (Howells 1990, 134): (1) the increasing scientific character of technology, (2) the growing complexity of technology, (3) and the trend towards the division of labour with the establishment of highly trained manpower and specialized research laboratories.

The object specialisation gives a clear structure setting limits: the remaining hierarchy inside and strict regulation of formal actions and competences provides - especially in large firms - an overview of the whole range of activities. For the company, it is easier to control research and development with a strict share of work. But as enterprises are growing in scale, and have to adapt to new situations in a changing world immediately and face strong competition in international markets, it is not clear if a company with this distinction of competences is capable of being innovative in future. Especially, the specialisation into the different disciplines has to be regarded with scepticism because the necessary combination of knowledge from different disciplines in order to cope with the overlap of technologies and interdisciplinarity in research is difficult to provide.

Two-dimensional (matrix) structures have an advantage in combining the knowledge of different objects (e.g. technical disciplines, end products) inside the company with different phases of R&D. The internal matrix structure of R&D can combine e.g. R&D phases with objects, objects with regions and regions with the R&D phases. A structure combining objects and R&D phases may be very helpful to cope with the growing interdisciplinarity and complexity of technology in product development, because people from different scientific disciplines can work closely together. The main task for R&D management is the coordination and matching of researchers from different disciplines and scientists with engineers and marketing people.

To sum up, the varied organisation of R&D in a company are different, often historically based responses to different internal developments as well as external challenges like internationalisation, complexity and overlapping of technology, higher competition on global and national markets, problems of human resources or the shortening of product life cycles.

4.2.3   Implications for R&D management

The effectiveness of a certain organisational form depends on the size and history of the firm, the branch, the tasks, the global aims, strategies, management, and the employees. Many details have to be taken into account and there is no "best management" practice which can be transferred from one firm to another. Mintzberg (1991, 58) points out that the organisation may be well advised to wear a "fitting form", at least for a time. With configuration, an organisation achieves a sense of order, of integration. In his point of view, the system of forces in organisations has to fit to a certain extent, but no configuration is perfect. Linear structures can still be an appropriate organisational form in small and medium-sized companies. But if a company is growing, the historically based organisation does not fit any more. For instance, the flexibility to develop rapidly and obtain economic advantages is not given and teams can hardly be integrated. Problems with communication and competences, longer distances, lack of motivation might occur. Organisational evolution will be the only answer to internal and external changes.

In multi-dimensional structures, running a project cannot be controlled as easily as in the one-dimensional structure, but combines more knowledge in the research and development process. Recently, in some sectors global internal R&D networks are occurring and within that framework, inter-organisational research and technical linkages within and between the sectors has grown. A worldwide network of R&D centres is usually the result of a long-term organisational evolutionary process (Gerpott 1990, 228). There are no (comparable) data available on the extent of globalisation in R&D except some case studies, especially in the automobile (Womack/Jones/Roos 1990) or the pharmaceutical sector (Howells 1990). The pharmaceutical company Glaxo had in 1968 two UK-based and one R&D centre abroad. This number increased until 1988 to three UK-based and six centres abroad (Howells 1990, 141). However, internationalisation of R&D strongly differs from sector to sector: according to a study on research and technology management in the mechanical engineering sector of the EU (Reger/Kungl 1994), only very few large companies are carrying out R&D activities in their units abroad.

In answer to the question which R&D phase a company should centralize or decentralize, much depends on the task and modes of R&D which has to be considered (Howells 1990, pp. 135):

1. Basic research: good information and "coupling" links with, and therefore proximity to, the head office of the company may be an advantage where the organisation sees R&D as a vital long-term strategic function.
2. Applied research: the location of R&D laboratories in a multi-divisional organisation is more likely to be associated with the individual product division where product technology is sufficiently different between each division to warrant specialized research and where good communication/contact with the divisional headquarters is seen as strategically important.
3. Development: most of these activities are oriented towards plant-level activity in terms of pilot plant, testing and prototype work.

> **Companies' practice: technology and application orientation in in the organisation**
>
> *Very often, large multi-national corporations organize their research and development according to the distinction between technology-oriented central research and application-oriented, decentral development. The following example shows a different way of organising research activities.*
>
> **Example: German multi-national enterprise (transport and traffic systems)**
> *This corporation consists of four large and independent divisions; the controlling holding company functions as the parent company of these units. While product and process development is performed within the four divisions, research activities were set up in a coherent unit on corporate level: the corporate function of Research and Technology. This holding department undertakes medium- and long-term research activities for the corporate units. As structural elements, research institutes and joint research fields have been established and are interconnected in matrix form. The research institutes operate specifically in areas relevant to the individual corporate units and their business activities. In contrast, the joint research fields deal with intra-group topics like "Transport Technology", "Materials", "Microelectronics and Microsystems", "Information Technology", "Production Research and Environment" and "Research Technology and Society". The internal knowledge transfer is especially performed by exchanging researchers and engineers between the holding's Research and Technology department and the development department of a corporate unit. Another concept is the "move-house" of a whole team with its research topics from the corporate level to the development department of a corporate unit when the results of their research reach application stage.*

According to Howells the main advantages of concentration of R&D lie in benefits of scale economies and improved research efficiency. Against this, decentralized R&D activities have the advantage of a better information flow with other business functions and a more market-oriented view. Kupsch et al. (1991) suggest the differentiation between R&D that is more concentrated on the exploration of new technologies and R&D that concentrates on issues of application. These two criteria can be developed into a matrix (see figure 4.2-4) that shows the organisational form that seems to be most appropriate to the specific combination of orientations towards either the technology or the applications.

Figure 4.2-4:   Orientation towards technology or application: organisational
                   suggestions

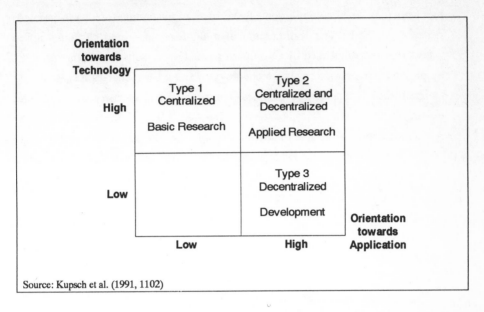

Source: Kupsch et al. (1991, 1102)

As stated above, there is rarely a "best management practice" to structure R&D activities. The organisation of R&D has to balance conflicting interests and objectives, maximize responsiveness, provide a critical mass of human and capital resources, maintain flexibility, and support ongoing and new businesses. Nevertheless, elements of a "modern" R&D organisation are provided in the literature to keep a company innovative for the future. Roussel/Saad/Erickson (1991, pp. 126) propose the following five dimensions which are to be considered to approach the optimum structure of R&D:

1. The use of internal versus external R&D resources through buying base technologies and cooperating with universities, R&D institutes, and enterprises.
2. Centralized versus decentralized control and funding of R&D have to be considered, applied, and treated separately according to the objectives of R&D, and the strengths and weaknesses of both approaches.
3. Locally concentrated versus distributed R&D resources vary according to certain situations: On the one hand, a concentrated structure of R&D is required if internal efficiency is the primary aim of R&D activities; on the other hand, a locally distributed form is needed for market proximity or response to external

constraints. In complex situations, a combination of both approaches based on the phase of R&D is needed.

4. Input-oriented (technology-oriented) versus output-oriented (market-oriented) structure of R&D: The coordination of multi-disciplinary and customer-closed tasks is best accomplished by an output-oriented organisation which is organized by products or customers. The technology-oriented form enables researchers to maintain their scientific and technical competence and to carry out long-term research.

5. A balance between the line or matrix structure for the day-to-day management and the management of R&D projects has to be found. R&D projects are a crucial organisational form for the R&D activities, therefore, project managers need full competence about the project resources.

For a successful R&D project management there are seven key practices required (Roussel/Saad/Erickson 1991, pp. 151):

- a common vocabulary for describing and characterizing R&D projects and their aims,
- clear process for jointly developed targets and results,
- process for setting priorities and allocating resources,
- backlog of ideas,
- aggressive approach to project design and setting of "milestones",
- realistic and individual project planning and information,
- appropriate project-team structure, composition, and authority.

These dimensions of an optimized R&D organisation and key factors for a successful R&D project management may serve companies as a guideline for organizing their R&D activities.

4.3   R&D management and the concept of core competence (Interface I)

In the 1980s, literature on business strategies was very much concerned with the business world and the influence of external factors on the success of enterprises. The studies by Porter on the competitive strategies of enterprises are an example of this. In recent years, however, many scientific studies have been concerned with the internal resources and competences of firms, as well as the influence of these factors on competitiveness and the development of strategies (cf. for instance Grant 1988; Rumelt 1984; Teece/Pisano/Shuen 1990).

Companies' practice: core technologies

Neither in our interviews nor in the existing literature can examples be found where the concept of core competences in the broad understanding was implemented on company level. Another approach can be seen in the core technologies which were implemented in a German multi-national enterprise (electronics) in corporate R&D. In this case the concept of core technologies was developed in order to provide a common focus for all research and development activities. Parallel to the theoretical discussion in this chapter this practical approach in corporate R&D will be introduced.

This increased concentration on firms' internal resources, "core competences" and "core capabilities" is certainly due in part to the successes of Japanese firms in the sectors of mechanical engineering, the electrotechnical industry and vehicle construction. Japanese enterprises are thought to be more capable than American or European ones of responding to changes in the market and in demand, of making more effective use of firm-specific resources, and of forming organisations that possess the ability to learn (Prahalad/Hamel 1990). On the other hand, the quest for concentration on core competences by firms can be traced back to the growth of large companies and to massive diversification efforts. Takeovers and diversification into new fields have often led to uncontrolled growth in company size and to high failure rates, so that the firms that have been bought up have had to be discarded again (Porter 1987). Concentration on core competences or core capabilities can thus be regarded as an attempt to cope with unsuccessful diversification and excessive growth (Perich 1993, pp. 48).

4.3.1   Definitions and dimensions of core competence

Understanding of the concept of core competences or core capabilities diverges; this applies equally to the question of what competences are defined as "core" competences, and to the question of differing dimensions covered by the concept. Terms used range from "distinctive competences" (Hitt/Ireland 1985), "firm-specific competence" (Pavitt 1991), "core competence" (Prahalad/Hamel 1990) to "core capabilities" (Leonard-Barton 1992), "central, strategic capabilities" (Grant 1991), "strategic competences" (Deiser 1993), "resource deployment" (Hofer/Schendel 1978) and "invisible assets" (Itami 1987).

Prahalad/Hamel (1990, 81) understand core competences as collective learning within an organisation, expressing itself particularly in the integration of numerous technology lines and the coordination of various production skills and/or experiences. The true sources of competitive advantage are seen in the management's ability to form "core competences" that enable business units to adapt to a rapidly changing environment. Possessing core competence means the ability to communicate and cooperate beyond organisational and hierarchical boundaries. A strategy of core competences considers the enterprise as a whole, rather than in terms of its various business areas.

Prahalad/Hamel compare an enterprise with a tree, growing from its roots (the "core competences") and nourishing the trunk ("core products") and smaller branches (business units); the fruits represent the end products of the business units (cf. figure 4.3-1). The core products are the physical manifestation of the core competences. The strength of the tree ("corporation") does not consist - to sustain the simile - in the leaves ("end products") but in the roots ("core competences").

Prahalad and Hamel characterize the core competences of a firm by the following three points:
- firstly, core competence gives the enterprise access potentials to numerous markets;
- secondly, core competence should contribute substantially to the usefulness of end products to customers;
- thirdly, core competence should be difficult for competitors to imitate.

Figure 4.3-1:   Competencies: the roots of competitiveness

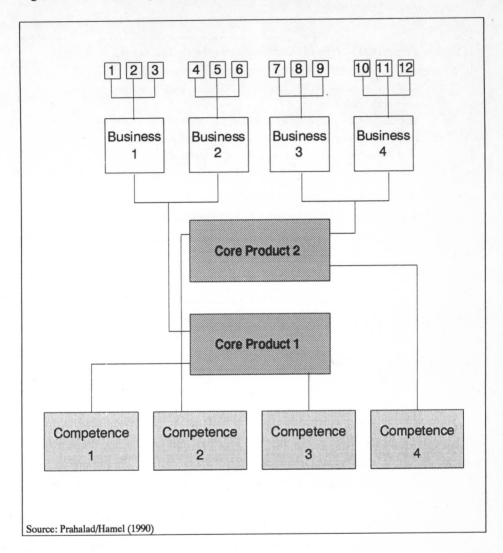

Source: Prahalad/Hamel (1990)

If there is a dominant orientation towards the markets of end products, management gets caught up in a rigid, business-unit-dominated thought pattern ("strategic business-unit mind set") and neglects to build up core competences. Thus Prahalad and Hamel put forward a concept that contrasts fundamentally with the concept of strategic business units, and draw attention both to the danger of short-term thinking and to the necessity for - and consequences of - an alternative view. "A shift in commitment will inevitably influence patterns of diversification, skill deployment,

resource allocation priorities, and approaches to alliances and outsourcing."
(Prahalad/Hamel 1990, 86).

Companies' practice: definition of core technologies in a German enterprise

Core technologies are defined in the German MNE as technologies
   -   *with an important contribution to the value added and the economic outcome,*
   -   *that are important to several departments or divisions,*
   -   *that ensure long-term innovation and growth potential,*
   -   *that are of strategic relevance for the enterprise.*

Doz/Chakravarthy (1993) follow Prahalad/Hamel's definition to a large extent, but add a dynamic perspective. Since firm-specific characteristics and capabilities may be imitated or substituted by competitors in the course of time, present competences must be developed further and new ones generated. "Core competency can be viewed then as that firm-specific attribute, which is in part the firm's resources and their embeddedness and in part the organisational context which defines how these resources are leveraged and developed" (Doz/Chakravarthy 1993, 5).

The source of core competence, according to Doz/Chakravarthy, springs from three levels of an organisation:

1) The individual level: core competence is built on the special capabilities of the employees of an organisation; the organisational embedding of these individual capabilities necessitates continuous assessment of the firm's organisation regarding the fostering of capabilities and the orientation of strategy towards "cutting edge problems".
2) The group level: another important source is to be found in groups that possess specialized knowledge and certain norms and values. This "team know-how" is often intangible, and consists in the group's ability to cooperate interdisciplinarily and tackle tasks together. Embedding this into the organisational context implies recognition and fostering of complementary skills and suitable group structures.
3) The firm as a whole (the single organisation): core competence is derived from firm-specific "tangible and intangible assets". The more systematically these "assets" are arranged, the more difficult it is for competitors to imitate them. "Assets" should be understood here in a broad sense: the technological

competence of a firm, for instance, includes technological equipment, laboratory apparatus and patents, but also the special skills of technicians and scientists.

4.3.2   Leveraging, development and renewal of competence

Core competences are established by a process of continuous improvement, and take ten years or more to build up; thus a firm which has not invested in establishing core competences will only be able to enter new markets with difficulty. Moreover, it is only possible at present to make a rudimentary estimate of the costs caused by a loss of core competence. Without a clear vision of core competences and the strategic architecture of the enterprise, it is not possible to engage meaningfully in cooperations. From a positive viewpoint, Prahalad/Hamel (1990, 87) recommend the following starting points for the formation of an innovative firm capable of learning:

- Invest in the development of core competences and core products to secure long-term international competitiveness.
- "Free" the firm's own resources: this applies not only to the distribution of capital, but even more to the distribution mechanism for highly skilled and qualified personnel. Employees who possess decisive core competences must be identified irrespective of organisational barriers, and allowed "trans-border" freedom of movement outside the individual business units.
- Extend innovation potentials: if core competences are not identified, a business unit will only pursue innovation potentials within its own business area; "interdisciplinary" innovation potentials cannot be developed in this way.

In order to maintain a competitive advantage through core competences in the long term, these must be fostered by a process of formation, development and renewal. This process has to deal with various problems. The major difficulties of the process of "leveraging" lie in identifying potentials, mobilizing the necessary resources and evaluating the relationship between potential and resources. Doz/Chakravarthy (1993, 6) mention the following ways of solving these problems:

- Identifying potentials: this process can be fostered e.g. by the spreading and distribution of resources between business units, by focusing on customer needs rather than on the product or the market, and by direct contact between developers and users.
- Mobilizing resources: the aims should be a mix of resources from different parts of the enterprise, and a new combination of existing elements. Mobilisation often runs contrary to the business unit or department's "own" policy. Possible solutions are to be found, for instance, in meetings between the board member responsible for technology and the heads of technology development and/or marketing in the business units; in addition, "urgent projects" can be defined by the Chief Executive Officer, or the best engineers can rotate between the different R&D laboratories.
- Coordination of resources and potentials: it is difficult not to limit competences too narrowly right from the start, or to place too much trust in them. As a possible solution to these difficulties, the authors suggest the initiation of "large scale projects" aiming not at a product, but at the testing and exploitation of a cross-cutting technology line which can be used in several different business areas.

Companies' practice: the process of developing core technologies

The concept of core competences or core technologies is rather new and not yet implemented by many companies. Therefore it is important not only to discuss the outcome but also the process of determining the core technologies.

In order to determine the core technologies the first question in the company discussed here concerned the technologies needed for the 300 business areas of the company. This question was to be answered by the divisions and around 400 suggestions resulted. After filtering and further processing 30 core technologies in six core technology areas were generated. To have a common understanding, terms for the core technologies were agreed on: Materials and Recycling, Processes and Energy, Components and Modules, Microelectronics, Software and Engineering, Systems and Networks. As these names already reveal, some of the categorized core technologies are closely related with each other, which supports interdisciplinary approaches. If new technologies emerge, an adaptation to the existing core technologies is tried. If this is not successful, a committee for research and development and its work groups can decide about the introduction of a new core technology. By this procedure the system of core technologies is open to changes in the technological environment.

The continuous development of competence may conflict with the process of formation. The "cultivation" or intensification of knowledge and abilities usually leads to increasing specialisation of employees and teams, which in turn complicates communication and the distribution of resources. No management instruments are suggested for the solution of these problems; Doz/Chakravarthy (1993, 10) see this aspect as a tricky tightrope walk, and give the general suggestion of leaving employees enough freedom of action to learn, while also laying down basic rules which are binding. Another aspect of the development of competence is the "aggregation" of competence into more general "metacompetences" which can be used for the renewal of the enterprise or its competences.

On the one hand, competences must be intensified and cultivated. This is intrinsically a conservative process, since the intensification is based mainly on continuity, repetition and routine, and learning and thought patterns - if they have proved successful - are continually repeated. On the other hand, however, this process also carries an implicit risk for the firm - the risk of inertia and diminishing competitive and innovative capability. In this way the firm enters the paradoxical situation of a "competence trap", as no new competences were built up (Doz/Chakravarthy 1993, 12). The challenge to management thus lies in finding a balance between the further development of competence and the inherent paradox of inertia on the one hand, and the fundamental renewal of competence on the other. Aims approached without prejudice, the simultaneous consideration of short-term and long-term developments, as well as knowledge and possibly control of the tensions created by these paradoxical processes, can be helpful in renewing competences (Hogarth/Michaud/ Doz/Van der Heyden 1991). It is also important to recognize that the learning process for the development of competence differs fundamentally from the process of renewal: the key to the management of renewal of competence lies in the speed with which an organisation can "unlearn" existing patterns (Chakravarthy/ Kwun 1990).

4.3.3   Implications for R&D management

Leonard-Barton (1992) follows the concept of core competence advanced in Prahalad/Hamel (1990), but extends this to include certain other elements and describes it as "core capabilities"; she also examines the interaction between core capabilities and R&D projects. The empirical base for her study is provided by twenty case studies of projects in five American firms (Ford, Chaparral Steel, Hewlett-Packard, a chemical firm and an electronics firm).[3]

The starting point for investigations is the paradox implicit in core competence. Whereas on the one hand the formation and development of unique capabilities represent the basis of the firm's competitiveness, the necessary institutionalisation may give rise to incumbent inertia which may lead, if the firm's environment changes, to diminished competitiveness and innovative strength (Liebermann/Montgomery 1988). The development of core capabilities both improves and impedes innovative capability at the same time:[4] "The key characteristic in paradox is the simultaneous presence of contradictory, even mutually exclusive elements" (cf. Quinn/Cameron 1988, 2). For Leonard-Barton, this paradox between the need for innovation, as well as conservation and routine, emerges clearly in R&D projects. Whereas many studies on industrial innovation concentrate on the project as an entity, Leonard-Barton examines the interface between the R&D project and the organisation, as well as the relationship between an R&D project (as an element of technology strategy) and core capabilities (1992, 112): "Observing core capabilities through the lens of the project places under a magnifying glass one aspect of the "part-whole" problem of innovation management, ...".

Leonard-Barton assumes a knowledge-based view by the firm, and gives the following definition (1992, 113): "a core capability (is) ... the knowledge set that

---

[3]   Leonard-Barton does not explicitly refer to the projects as R&D projects, but calls them "... new product and process development projects ..." (1992, 111). However, the twenty project case studies include both research and also development projects concerned with new products and new manufacturing technologies for use within the firm.

[4]   On this, compare Doz/Chakravarthy (1993), who describe this paradox as a "competence trap".

distinguishes and provides a competitive advantage." Four dimensions of knowledge are distinguished:

1) Knowledge and skills of employees: this dimension includes both firm-specific techniques and scientific understanding; the knowledge and skills of employees are decisive for the development of new products.
2) Technical systems: the knowledge embedded in "technical systems" consists in information (e.g. test series for a product extending over years) and procedures (e.g. work flows) and is the tangible result of years of accumulation, coding and structuring of the intangible "tacit knowledge" of employees.
3) Management systems: this includes formal and informal ways of knowledge acquisition (e.g. training, in-service training, cooperations) and knowledge control (e.g. report systems, incentive systems).
4) Values and norms: these are linked within the enterprise with the content and structure of knowledge, the ways and means of knowledge acquisition and the control of knowledge.

A core capability is understood by Leonard-Barton (1992, 114) as a knowledge system composed of these four dimensions, between which many interactions arise. The extent to which each of the four elements are present in a core capability may vary greatly.

The interaction between core capabilities and the R&D projects of an enterprise may continue for a few months or may go on for years, and differs in the extent to which the existing core capability at that time is oriented towards the R&D project. In her 20 case studies, Leonard-Barton shows that the extent to which project and core capability coincide ranges from very high to virtually nil, and that core capabilities may either enhance or totally impede the R&D activity. By linking the concept of core capabilities with firm-internal R&D projects, this strategic management approach acquires significance also for the management of R&D.

The more correspondence there is between the R&D project and the knowledge system, the more positive the enhancing influence of the existing core capability on the project. From Leonard-Barton's case studies it emerges clearly that R&D projects receive decisive support if they are within the area of core competence of an enterprise. Since creativity and resources are focused, and knowledge continuously accumulated in this core area, the development of new products and processes is possible here.

On the other hand, core capabilities may hamper the innovation process and cause inflexibility; these "core rigidities" represent unused knowledge systems which, because of the focusing on core capabilities, cannot be acquired. Core rigidities occur particularly in R&D projects intended to open up new areas, disciplines and capabilities for the firm. When changes occur in the firm's environment (e.g. changes in the market, in demand or in the legal framework), the inability to discard previous core capabilities can become a threat to innovativeness and competitiveness, and to the enterprise as a whole.

If core capability is separated into the four dimensions of skills/knowledge, management systems, technical systems, and values and norms, the following interactions between core capabilities (and the enhancement of R&D projects) and core rigidities (and the inability to acquire new fields) emerge (figure 4.3-2):

1) Skills and knowledge of employees:

Core capabilities: the most important element for positive support of R&D projects is excellent technical and expert skills/knowledge in the main product areas. The leaders of these R&D projects either have or need the best staff resources. Important aspects are internal tests of new products and feedback to engineers and scientists.

Core rigidities: limited resources and concentration on certain specific areas hamper the formation of interdisciplinary knowledge and capabilities. A firm with the core discipline of "mechanical engineering" will place more importance on research in this area, and will either neglect or ignore other disciplines (e.g. chemistry: new materials).

2) Technical systems:

Core capabilities: "technical systems" is understood to mean the processes, workflows and instruments ("artefacts") developed by talented researchers and used internally in the firm. This concrete knowledge of workflows can secure competitive advantages (e.g. by time-saving, high quality)

Core rigidities: if the knowledge embedded in the technical systems is outdated, the enterprises and the R&D will become inflexible. This can happen e.g. with self-developed software that is no longer compatible with other, newer products.

Figure 4.3-2:   Core capabilities and core rigidities

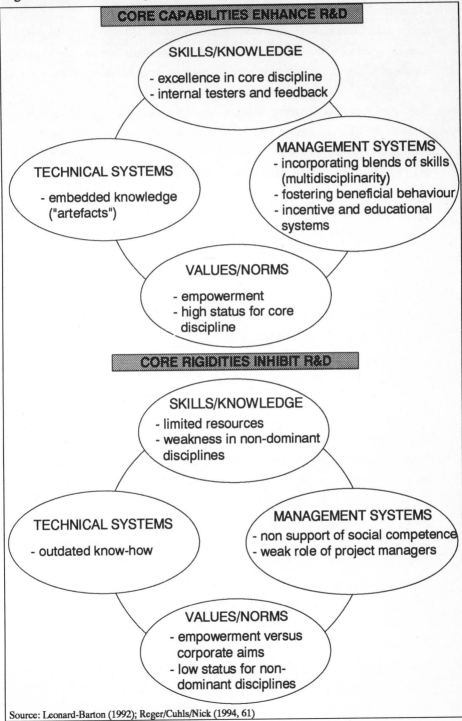

3) Management systems:

Core capabilities: management systems enhance part of the core competence if various types of skills/knowledge and personal qualities are brought together. This aspect includes incentive schemes as well as comprehensive further training systems.

Core rigidities: these occur if only specialist competence and not social competence - for instance in project leaders - is supported by incentive schemes and further training. If project leaders in R&D do not receive responsibility and acknowledgement, project management cannot become established.

4) Values and norms:

Core capabilities: the basic values and norms of an enterprise influence all R&D projects equally and have to be practically expressed in the management systems. One especially important aspect is the encouraging of a high degree of responsibility ("empowerment") of each employee working on a project. Another, equally decisive factor is the status accorded to the various disciplines of the project team: an R&D project that is considered to be particularly important and lies within the core discipline of the enterprise will motivate and attract talented researchers much more strongly than a project that lies outside the core discipline. Researchers in the core discipline may have very good career chances within the firm.

Core rigidities: these may occur both in empowerment and in the core discipline. Empowerment is a decisive factor in the success of project work, but may also come into conflict with the interests of the enterprise as a whole, and may lead to inner resignation among employees. Since R&D activities require a great deal of initiative and creativity, the central challenge for management is to combine the goals of the enterprise with the capabilities of the employees without destroying creativity and independence. Regarding the core discipline of a firm, this may lead to rigidity if product innovations require new or different technical skills and knowledge. In a self-reinforcing "vicious circle" of norms, notions and behaviour, non-dominant disciplines are "kept down" and neglected: for instance, in a firm dominated by mechanical engineers, marketing personnel and electrical engineers have a relatively low status. This lack of recognition means that interdisciplinary cooperation is hardly attempted at all. This in turn means that a common language is not developped, and internal cooperation is thus assessed as poor.[5] The low status means that researchers from "foreign" disciplines are not attracted to the firm.

The less correspondence there is between the core capability and the R&D project, the harder it becomes for project leaders to satisfy the dual aspect of core capability and still lead the R&D project. In the course of time, some core capabilities will in fact change if they impede too many projects. However, this will not happen during the course of one project, so project leaders cannot afford to just wait for "better days" to come along. In the case studies investigated, project leaders reacted in one of four different ways:

- they gave up the project ("abandonment");
- they returned to core capabilities ("recidivism");
- they reoriented and shifted the project into another area ("reorientation");
- they sealed off the project e.g. by founding a new enterprise ("isolation").

Although "core capabilities" cannot be decisively altered by a single R&D project, projects do pave the way for organisational changes by revealing "core rigidities" and by introducing new capabilities. R&D projects can be useful for the accumulation of experiences beyond conventional knowledge, which prepare the way for bigger changes. The four dimensions of the knowledge system are not equally affected by change: from technical systems to management systems, to skills/knowledge and values/norms, the dimensions become less easily influenced, less tangible and less easy to operationalize. Values and norms are closely linked with culture, and culture is hardly influenced - or influenced not at all - by management (cf. Perich 1993, 151; Barney 1986).

In order to build up a new capability into a core capability, all four dimensions of the knowledge system have to be addressed. New technical systems cannot be

---

[5]   A survey of 23 mechanical engineering firms (Kalkowski/Manske 1993) confirms these immense interface problems: between the engineers engaged in mechanical development and electrical development, considerable communication problems arose due to their different "languages" and competences. In many mechanical engineering enterprises there were in fact teams made up of personnel from development, manufacturing, assembly and sales, but the electrical design engineers were not represented in these teams.

introduced without changes in the knowledge and skills of employees, and appropriate in-service training measures have to be provided for this. Values will not change unless the desired behaviour changes are acknowledged and rewarded. "Therefore, when the development process encounters rigidities, projects can be managed consciously as the "generative" actions characteristic of learning organisations only if the multidimensional nature of core capabilities is fully appreciated" (cf. Leonard-Barton 1992, 123).

4.3.4 Conclusions: R&D projects beyond existing core areas

To some extent, the various concepts of core competence are built on one another and are complementary. On the other hand, they vary in their emphasis, their dimensions, the implications for management and the concept implementors addressed, and they have different weak and strong points.

Prahalad/Hamel's concept of core competences can be regarded as an instrument of strategic management, used to concentrate the strategies of highly diversified firms on future potentials and to focus resources. The addressees and implementors of the concept of core competences are top management. Their concept stimulates consideration of the particular capabilities of an organisation, its strengths and weaknesses. Compared to a view of a firm from the standpoint of its end products or core business areas, this concept has the advantage that it not only identifies capabilities and potentials, but makes them the basis for the assessment. However, the concept is very static and descriptive; it does not deal with the need for continuous development and renewal of core competence, nor with the elements of firm-specific capabilities or their identification. Thus, this concept cannot (yet) be operationalized for strategic management. One weak point of the concept is that the aquisition of core competence - despite a high degree of uncertainty regarding future business success - has to be prefinanced in the long term.

Companies' practice: organisational integration of core technologies

Once the core technologies are chosen it is necessary to create an organisation around them in order to support the approach. In the company considered in this chapter R&D is divided into decentralized development within the different divisions which deal with the creation and enhancement of products and processes, and centralized research dealing with the exploration of technologies. According to the idea of core technologies corporate research (ca. 1,400 employees) was transformed into a matrix structure, one dimension being the core technologies and the core technology areas while the other dimension is formed by the divisions.

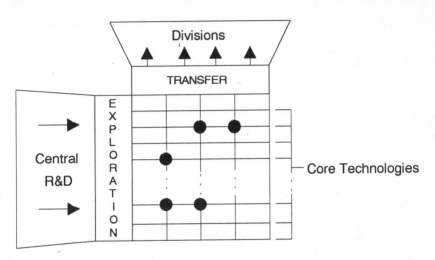

The R&D departments, each with approx. 200 researchers, are structured around the six core technology areas. Each department head is also commissioner for certain divisions, thus permitting, in cooperation with the corresponding division head, an optimal technology transfer. The departments are further subdivided into sections following the core technologies. While the department heads are responsible for the effectiveness of research in their departments, the heads of the sections have to ensure the quality and high standing of the research work as well as to optimize the distribution of resources within the core technology. A further division consists of work groups which are formed to work on important issues of the respective core technologies. The group leaders bear responsibility for the technical and scientific quality of the results and the motivation of their group members (ca. 10 scientists).

In addition to this matrix structure the committee for R&D was created that coordinates the distribution of resources between the different areas, coordinates the projects on corporate level and decides about changes within the core technologies. This committee consists of department heads as well as research commissioners of the divisions. Several work groups provide the committee with further information and are a platform for in-depth discussions of problems.

The concept of core competence gains relevance through the departure from static description and the transition to a dynamic view put forward by Doz/Chakravarthy. In order to make use of core competences as a competitive advantage in the longer term, they must be supported by a process of formation, development and renewal. In their view of this process, Doz/Chakravarthy draw attention to the risks and paradoxes which management has to be aware of if it is to meet the challenge implicit in the concept. However, the action guidelines for management contained in this concept remain relatively superficial, so that here, as with the concept of Prahalad/Hamel, the question of operationalisation is posed. Moreover, the idea of deliberately fostering the embedding of core competences into the organisational context of the enterprise remains unclear.

In her approach, Leonard-Barton attempts to link the development of core capabilities with the management of R&D projects, and is thus the only author to build a bridge explicitly towards R&D management, which is a central element of innovative capability. Core capabilities represent an accumulation of various dimensions of knowledge, and contain a paradox: on the one hand, it is core capabilities that enable innovations to take place at all; on the other hand, they hinder the exploration of new paths.

In a rapidly changing entrepreneurial environment, technology-based firms continually have to meet new challenges and re-think their previous paradigms. R&D management thus has the task of committing itself beyond existing core areas. "The time to search out and develop a new core resource is when the current core is working well" (cf. Itami 1987, 42). Here, R&D projects offer the possibility of developing the variety necessary for future innovations, and also the chance to overcome "core rigidities", and as such should be used by top management as a strategic instrument.

4.4 Technological forecasting in enterprises (Interface I)

4.4.1 Task of enhancing the information base

The techniques of technology forecasting are focused on the task of improving the company's information base. They encompass exploration and prognosis methods that can be used in the analyses of parameters affecting the development of specific technologies. These parameters can be derived out of technical, economic, and social contexts (Gerybadze 1990, 72).

For companies especially the evaluation of alternative technologies is in the centre of interest. Typical questions that are to be answered by the outcome of forecasts are the following:

- Which are the chances of specified technologies?
- Which risks evolve due to the substitution of technologies?
- How can a technology be evaluated regarding the economic needs of the enterprise?

By answering these questions forecasting prepares the ground for decisions concerning the selection of new technologies, the need for new or more diverse competences and possible sources of know-how, and thereby is the first step in a technology planning procedure (Servatius/Peiffer 1992, 73).

Companies' practice: planning process at German multi-national enterprise (automobiles)
In this enterprise general plans cover a period of five years. Additionally, a "Group Management Conference" exists, that develops strategical long-range tendencies as well as guidelines. For detailed planning a variety of tools is used, from portfolio techniques to value-analysis. However, scenarios are rarely used.

4.4.2   Techniques used in business forecasting

After several decades of intensive research in the domain of business forecasting a huge variety of techniques exists. In categorizing them we follow the structure of Porter et al. (1991). They suggest five groups of methods: monitoring, expert opinion, trend extrapolation, modelling and scenarios. A short description is given in figure 4.4-1, together with the underlying assumptions, strengths and weaknesses, and uses of the method (Porter et al. 1991, pp. 93). Additionally, a selection of specific techniques is mentioned (Porter et al. 1991; Murdick/Georgoff 1993). For Europe there are no studies concerning the degree to which the different techniques are applied (Grupp 1994a, 16). The only results are from Japan, where a study about the effectiveness and application of forecasting techniques was performed in 1990, based on a questionnaire answered by 208 research facilities. For both indicators, effectiveness as well as the degree of application, patent analysis, which can be used in forecasts covering up to five years, was considered the leading technique.

Also highly efficient are scenarios, relevance tree method, simulation and Delphi method, but as they are rather expensive and time-consuming little use is made of them. Less reliable, but inexpensive, and therefore used the most are techniques like technology portfolios and trend extrapolation. Concerning the different levels of effectiveness, as well as budget restrictions, enterprises will have to choose a method mix rather then a specific technique in order to balance the strengths and weaknesses of various forecasting methods.

Figure 4.4-1:   Forecasting methods and their characteristics

---

Monitoring:
- Description: by scanning the environment monitoring delivers information about the subject of a forecast. Therefore it is rather a method of selecting and gathering data, as well as organizing information than a specific forecasting technique. The sources of information are identified and then information is gathered, filtered, and structured for use in forecasting.
- Assumptions: information useful for a forecast is provided by the environment and can somehow be obtained.
- Strengths: useful information from a wide variety of sources is provided by monitoring.
- Weaknesses: without further selection, structure or filtering information overload may result.
- Uses: to maintain current awareness of an area and the information with which to forecast as needed. To provide information useful for structuring a forecast and for the forecast itself.
- Selected Techniques: creativity techniques (metaphors/analogies, morphological analysis, brainstorming,) technological monitoring, contextual monitoring, micro/macro monitoring, content analysis of news, patents, or scientific publications.

Expert opinion
- Description: the opinions of experts in a specific area are acquired and analysed.
- Assumptions: some individuals know significantly more about certain subjects than others. Therefore it is assumed that their forecasts are a great deal better. Group processes can be used to get a further specification of the hypothesis.
- Strengths: expert forecasts can tap high quality models internalized by experts who cannot or will not make them explicit.
- Weaknesses: first of all it is difficult to identify experts and even if they are identified their forecasts are often wrong. Questions posed to them are often ambiguous or unclear, and design of the process often is weak. Interaction among experts can be related with unforeseen social or psychological factors that affect the forecast.
- Uses: to forecast in a situation where the subject or situation to be forecasted cannot be modelled and sufficient data is missing. Experts must be identifiable.
- Selected Techniques: Delphi method, nominal group process, surveys, committees, brainstorming, EFTE (Estimate-Feedback-Talk-Estimate).

Trend analysis
- Description: mathematical and statistical techniques are used to extend time series into the future. Techniques for trend analysis vary in exactness and complication from simple curve-fitting to Box-Jenkins techniques.
- Assumptions: Past conditions and trends will continue in the future more or less unchanged.
- Strengths: substantial data-based forecasts of quantifiable parameters are offered which are especially accurate over short time frames.
- Weaknesses: It often requires a significant amount of good data to be effective, works only for quantifiable parameters, and is vulnerable to discontinuities and changing paradigms. Forecasts can be very misleading for long time frames. Trend analysis techniques do not explicitly address causal mechanisms.
- Uses: To project quantifiable parameters and to analyse adoption and substitution of technologies.
- Selected Techniques: Regression analysis, adaptive filtering, exponential smoothing, moving averages, linear regression, trend extrapolation (S-shaped growth curves, learning curve, exponential growth, linear growth), diffusion methods, lead-lag indicators.

Figure 4.4-1:   Forecasting methods and their characteristics (conclusion)

Modelling

- Description: models represent the dynamics and structure of a selected "part" of the real world. The dynamics of a model can be used to forecast the behaviour of the system being modelled. Models reach from flow diagrams, simple equations, and scale models to sophisticated computer simulations.
- Assumptions: simplified representations are able to reflect the basic structure and processes to be forecasted.
- Strengths: by isolating important system aspects from inessential details models can exhibit future behaviour of complex systems. Going through the process of modelling a better insight into complex system behaviour is provided.
- Weaknesses: faulty assumptions can be obscured by detailed models which provide a deceitful credibility for poor forecasts. Potentially important factors are neglected by the models' bias towards quantifiable over non-quantifiable factors. A missing or poor data base cannot be neutralized by a good model.
- Uses: to reduce complex systems to manageable representations.
- Selected Techniques: econometric models, historical analogy, simulation (e.g., cross-impact analysis, KSIM (Kane's Simulation) modelling, system dynamics, gaming).

Scenarios

- Description: scenarios are sets of snapshots of some aspect of the future and/or future histories leading the present to the future. The scenario set encompasses the plausible range of possibilities for some aspect of the future.
- Assumptions: the full richness of future possibilities can be represented incorporated in a set of imaginative descriptions. Usable forecasts can be constructed from a very narrow data base.
- Strengths: they can present rich, complex portraits of the possible futures and incorporate a wide range of quantitative and qualitative information produced by other forecasting techniques. They are an effective way of communicating forecasts to a wide variety of users.
- Weaknesses: They may be more imagination than forecast, unless a firm basis in reality is maintained by the forecaster.
- Uses: to integrate quantitative and qualitative information, to integrate forecasts from various sources and techniques into a consistent picture, and to provide a forecast when data are too weak to use other techniques. They are most useful in forecasting and in communicating complex, highly uncertain situations to non-technical audiences.
- Selected Techniques: specific techniques do not exist.

4.4.3 Main challenge: accelerated environmental dynamics

In the past years the interest in forecasting techniques has steadily been rising. Murdick and Georgoff (1993, pp. 2) name four possible reasons for this tendency:

- new conceptual advances in areas such as economics, theoretical and applied statistics;
- new capabilities in data accumulation, access, and processing;
- the attempt to get a better understanding of the underlying structures of events or states;
- emerging problems such as accelerated environmental dynamics and the growing importance of extended planning horizons.

As all of these points are important to the development of new and enhanced forecasting systems, the most important challenges arise from the last point. Accelerated environmental dynamics as well as the importance of extended planning horizons can be met by forecasting techniques in a variety of aspects.

As technology strategies gain in importance for the companies' well-being, economic and technical issues get more intertwined. A company using adequate forecasting techniques is able to discover new technology at an early stage of the life cycle and by adjusting to the development obtain a better market position. Information on upcoming technologies enables the company both to gain time for the development of new strategies as well as provide a timely start into the development of this technology.

Monitoring allows systematic scanning of the environment in respect to new technologies and upcoming consumer demands. Information about new technologies is derived by analysing discontinuities in development and weak signs. Another important use of forecasting is the determination of risks and chances the company will face in quickly changing markets. Forecasts can be used to investigate the relative importance of specific technologies and select the ones to pursue. With respect to the risk of substitution, the company's own can be compared with new technologies (Zahn/Braun 1992, 5). Changing consumer demands can result in the need for new technologies (market pull - technology push), therefore the understanding of technology forecasting has to be expanded by techniques of market forecasting (Benkenstein 1987, 138; Servatius 1992, 23).

As the borderlines between different technologies are becoming less clear-cut, the interdisciplinary dialogue grows in importance. Some of the forecasting techniques, e.g. the relevance tree method, can be used to visualize the interrelations of specific techniques or technologies and thereby stress the value of integrated approaches (Cuhls et al. 1993, pp. 6). Methods such as scenarios or simulations are able to reduce the complexity inherent in the loss of clear boundaries.

The rise of new technological trends and/or the decision to specialize in certain technological areas results not only in the need for changed strategies but also has an impact on the structure of the human capital needed. Forecasting enables the company to adapt personnel needs early and thereby be prepared for the shifts in technology. Adjustments are necessary when the technologies used in production are changing as well as when new technologies are implemented within the company. For R&D the right mixture of knowledge has to be gathered. An active policy concerning university contacts and internal training of researchers can be planned, based on forecasts. Also, potential users of new technologies such as computer systems have to be re-educated. A timely training might reduce the fear resulting from irregularities and changing environments. Finally, the results of forecasts are able to indicate the need for organisational adjustments (Porter et al. 1991, 308).

4.4.4   Technology assessment: problems and the use of forecasting methods

An important use of forecasting methods is technology assessment (TA). As the influence of technology on our lives and environment is rising steadily and as already discussed technology turns out to be the dominant strategic factor for both enterprises and governments, a growing need for a broad assessment of consequences and potentials of technologies can be conceived (Smits 1990, 2). Technology assessment is defined as a systematical, organized approach for analysing the technological status quo and possible lines of development. In this process direct as well as indirect technical, economic, health, ecological, human, social or other impacts of the application of a certain technology and possible alternatives are studied. The evaluation of impacts is based upon defined goals and values and may result in a desired path of further progress and guidelines for actions to be taken (Grupp 1994a). In the ideal case, TA encompasses all areas of society and environment, and the exclusion of an area should be done after thoughtful justification (Jochem 1988, 36). Also TA should start with the first identification of a new technology (prospective analysis, see Grupp 1994a), because at this stage the whole variety of alternatives is still open for discussion. In reality this rather complex ideal will hardly be reached. The first reason seems trivial, as in most cases personnel and funding are missing. Another problem is the necessity of an interdisciplinary approach; to create an comprehensive overview social as well as technical specialists have to work hand in hand. In reality often either one group or the other dominates the assessment and thereby influences the outcome. Concerning the timeliness of TA a tendency towards the performance of reactive studies has to be stated. Instead of accompanying a technology from its very beginnings especially TA in enterprises (often also called product assessment) does not start before the product is ready to be introduced into the market. By this time the variety of alternatives has dwindled to only a few.

In response to the growing importance of technology assessment, in 1991 the German Engineering Association (VDI - Verein Deutscher Ingenieure) developed a set of guidelines (VDI Richtlinie 3780, see VDI 1991) dealing with the realisation of TA in enterprises. Following these guidelines a typical TA process is structured in four steps. First, the problem to be analysed has to be defined and structured. A variety of different aspects has to be considered: the task or problem itself, the frame and background, variables to be analysed, information or data to be selected, the political, economic and ecological context, the time frame, and the analysis criteria. The second step deals with the forecast of impacts. Here the whole variety of forecasting techniques can be put into use, such as trend extrapolation, scenarios, historical analogies, simulation and so on. Besides the pure development of the technology, interactions with other technological, social, or political developments have also to be considered. The description created by the forecast is followed by the third step, an evaluation. The evaluation has to consider the technology's impacts as well as certain "values", e.g. functionality, efficiency, social welfare, security, health, natural environment and other societal and personal values. After the technology's impacts and its alternatives have been evaluated, as the last step a decision has to be made about the further path of actions which is to be realized. In the ideal case this process has to be performed every time the technology and its setting change.

Even though the prospects of an intensive use of forecasting techniques in enterprises are far-reaching, a lot of difficulties are involved with them, which will be discussed in the following section.

4.4.5 Various problems in application

In the current situation a wide variety of forecasting techniques exists which seem to be suitable for nearly every situation. Unfortunately, the use of these technologies often seems easier than it really is. Difficulties are involved with the techniques themselves, the data base available as well as with the integration with other techniques, the integration of market and technology forecasting, the integration within the organisation of the enterprise, and finally the integration of impact assessment and pure forecasts as already mentioned.

When choosing a forecasting technique it has to be first considered that not every situation is open to forecasting. Gerybadze (1990, pp. 79) makes a distinction between three cases. In the first case the event or situation that is to be evaluated is singular and/or new and everybody has the same, small amount of knowledge about it, forecasting will not result in a better base of information. In the second case, the situation still is rather new but some people know considerably more about the subject than the rest. In this case forecasting methods like Delphi or nominal group may be able to uncover additional knowledge available to these experts. An example is the Delphi Inquiry pursued recently by the Fraunhofer Institute for Systems and Innovation Research (ISI) on behalf of the German Federal Ministry for Research and Technology in 1993 (BMFT 1993). In the third case, the situation is known to a certain degree and general trends are discernible; in this case forecasting may result in a reduction of risks and thereby bring considerable advantages to the user.

The next problem that arises with the use of forecasting is the choice of a suitable technique. Murdick and Georgoff (1993, 3) summarize the problems as following:

1. The basic problem to be analysed in the forecast is not always identified.

2. The application or purpose are often unclear.

3. The list of forecasting techniques are ambiguous because they often do not:

    - specify underlying assumptions,

    - specify options for different types of input data,

    - fully identify the forecasting processes,

    - specify options for different types of forecasting outputs.

4. Resource commitments, constraints, and available data are not definitely expressed.

5. Trade-offs necessary to obtain a high benefit/cost ratio are seldom considered.

Another typical problem in choosing the right technique is the mismatch of existing data, the situation, techniques accessible and the output desired. The usual but nonetheless wrong approach starts with the problem and then selects a technique to apply. Although data is acquired by this procedure it is not guaranteed that it matches the output needed (Murdick/Georgoff 1993, 3; Porter et al. 1991, 72). A new approach first defines both the problem and the result needed before selecting and applying a certain technique.

Once the data is obtained it has to be interpreted. Often forecasters forget that forecasting techniques only provide raw material and omit to analyse the outcomes at all. Another problem is the right interpretation of the forecasting output. Typical errors are cited by Porter et al. (1991, 385):

1. Fascination with the exotic: technology forecasts often exhibit a bias towards the optimistic and neglect the realities of the market. This tendency can be easily seen in the Delphi Inquiry (BMFT 1993), where interviewees with a high level of expertise usually gave more optimistic estimations for the time of realisation of specific techniques and technologies than the ones with a middle or lower level of expertise.

2. Enmeshed with the "Zeitgeist": attention to technologies follows fashions (devaluing expert consensus), and everyone emphasizes the same pressing social and environmental needs; current example: microsystems technology.

3. Price-performance failures: the benefit/cost ratio of new technologies does not always turns out as anticipated.

4. Shifting social needs: changing demographic trends and social values are not well considered; these change user desires and market opportunities. Often forecasts are done under the ceteris paribus perspective, however, it is impossible to take grave changes into consideration.

5. Ultimate uses unforeseen: rarely do forecasters anticipate applications fully.

A lot of difficulties in forecasting also arise from environmental conditions. Parallel to the interrelation of technologies the difficulties of forecasting will increase (Servatius/Peiffer 1992, p. 76). Some of the more effective forecasting techniques, like model simulations or cross-impact methods are rather time- and capital-consuming which results in fewer applications. Finally, data acquisition still misses the easiness and flexibility needed for effective forecasting. Information is distributed over a wide range of networks and the formats are seldom compatible. Furthermore, a wide variety of sources has to be assessed to get the right data and collecting data takes a lot of time. As a result, especially SMEs do not consider using forecasts in-depth.

Companies' practice: monitoring and trend assessment at a multi-national enterprise (transportation and traffic systems)
For this enterprise monitoring technological development is the first step in discovering and assessing new and global trends. Consequently, the company has set up branch offices e.g. in Japan, USA and Russia, as well as a network of international contacts in universities and other R&D institutions. Information and data collected is discussed, filtered and evaluated by the researchers concerning the status quo of the corporation, deficits and call for action. This process results in the setting of goals for technology strategies which further on lead to concrete innovation projects. These projects, which are coordinated via the corporation's strategic plans, should foster the exploration of innovative technologies with regard to opening up existing and new business areas. Furthermore, research seminars and symposia support the exchange of empirical knowledge. Besides this, external technology trend studies e.g. like the Delphi inquiry are systematically screened and evaluated.

A great challenge to forecasting systems arises from the trend of internationalisation. In order to obtain global information the companies will be forced to create international forecasting networks. Servatius (1992, 26) mentions the characteristics of a forecasting network: R&D centres in the most important regions of the world, close contact to key customers, personal contacts to international technology experts and opinion leaders, decentralized centres of competence and international exchange of information, new communication systems (e.g. video meetings), and finally the integration of technologies into systems, as already mentioned.

The adequate analysis of a specific technology's development cannot be done with one forecasting technique (Murdick/Georgoff 1993, 2). Different time frames and stages in the technology development have to be respected as well as consumer demands. Servatius/Peiffer (1992, pp. 74) suggest four areas that can be examined by forecasts: The mere development of technology, "component" technologies (e.g. microelectronics, advanced materials, optoelectronics), technical systems in which one or more component technologies are integrated (e.g. medical technology, energy and environment technology) and finally the area of market need. Benkenstein (1987, pp. 146) suggests a concept in which several forecasting techniques are combined in order to get an integrated market and technology prognosis:

1. Problem analysis: Delphi method.
2. Analysis of environment: Delphi method, for both market and technology.
3. Trend projection: trend extrapolation, indicator systems, other qualitative forecasting techniques.
4. Scenario of the environment: Delphi method, cross-impact method, computer simulation.
5. Scenario of a specific field of interest: Delphi method, cross-impact method.

4.4.6   Implications for R&D management

As already mentioned, the pure application of forecasting techniques delivers raw material only. The forecast will have an impact if it is embedded in analysis, interpretation, communication and resulting actions (see figure 4.4-2). However, although the first two points are usually achieved rather effortlessly, communication of the results is a sore point in many companies (Gerybadze 1991, pp. 90). Organisational integration of forecasting in the R&D activities of the enterprise starts with the right monitoring system. Every member within a company should monitor his environment in respect to discontinuities or changing trends. Quality circles and service members can be "tools" in the collection of data. Using survey or Delphi methods the special knowledge existing in the company can be gathered and

Figure 4.4-2:   Process of forecasting in the enterprise

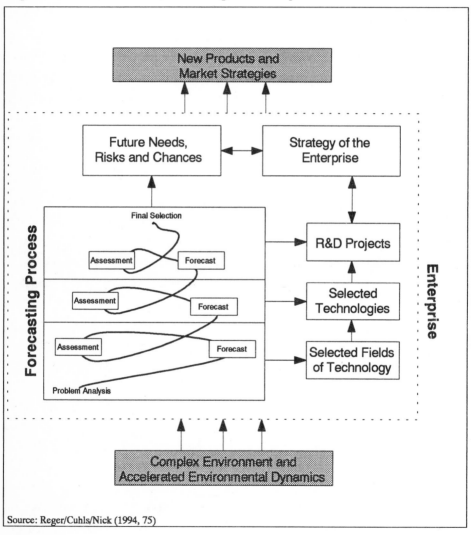

Source: Reger/Cuhls/Nick (1994, 75)

processed in a collective learning process. Interpretation of forecasts should be done by those levels of the company that need the results most, otherwise the results often will not reach their user. A bottom-up process could be initiated that integrates the forecasts from all different levels of the company. Furthermore it has to be ensured that outcomes result in action as indicated by the forecast.

Finally, the integration of technology forecasting and technology assessment has to be achieved by the R&D management. Over the last decades society's sensitivity concerning the impact of technology has increased greatly. Technology can have an impact on a broad variety of areas: social life, the emergence of new values, health, political or legal impacts such as new regulations and finally, but most important, ecological and environmental impacts (Porter et al. 1991, pp. 303). For a long time the ecological impacts of technology were externalized, the companies were not forced to take responsibility for the damage their products caused in the environment. Today only a few approaches towards a changed awareness can be noted but a sharp turn about in the situation is to be expected in the near future. Already companies in the USA are now having to pay huge amounts for the damage they caused due to more rigorous regulations within product liability. In order to take responsibility for the impact of new technologies in an early stage of their development as well as following upcoming regulations, new models of forecasting cycles have to be developed which iterate both forecasting and technology assessment. A possible approach could be the following (see also figure 4.4-2):

1. Cycle:
    a) Technology forecasting reveals new fields of technology.
    b) A technology assessment helps to select the best socio-ecological fields.
2. Cycle:
    a) Further in-depth forecasting of specific technologies selected in phase 1b.
    b) Analogous impact assessment to choose the field to pursue.
3. Cycle:
    a) Forecasting in order to select specific uses... and so on.

As the discussion in this section disclosed, technology forecasting and its application in R&D management still presents a lot of problems. While a variety of techniques have been developed that cover nearly every situation in which forecasts may be needed, the integration of these techniques nevertheless has to undergo further developments. Problems that evolve from the techniques themselves are mostly problems of the right awareness in which the technique is used.

4.5 Cooperation and networking (Interface II)

4.5.1 Different forms of collaboration

A variety of definitions for collaboration starting from "networking" to "alliances" or "cooperative agreements" exists. There are also different forms of the various collaboration activities. Regarding research and development, a more restricted definition is necessary that concentrates on collaboration as a means for R&D purposes (Herden 1992, pp. 19). In this respect, one of the most fitting definitions is the one of Dodgson (1993, 13) who regards as collaboration "...any activity where two or more partners contribute differential resources and know-how to agreed complementary aims." This includes collaborative research programmes or consortia, joint ventures, strategic alliances, shared R&D or production contracts and other forms which will be described in the following chapter. We apply this definition and concentrate on the measures and tools to gain knowledge through the means of collaboration with one or more partners.

One point of difference between all the partnering activities can be seen between vertical and horizontal collaboration. Vertical cooperations occur in the chain of production where the know-how for particular products is gained from the supply of raw material through manufacturing and assembly to marketing. Horizontal cooperation takes place between partners at the same level in the production process.

There are different approaches to classifying collaboration. For example, Dodgson (1993, 12) differentiates three forms of collaboration:

1. Infrastructural forms which are embedded in national technology and innovation systems and are created to support that system. These concern universities, governmental labs, collaborative research programmes or consortia.

2. Contractual forms which may include joint ventures or strategic alliances as well as production contracts.

3. Informal forms occur between the "invisible college" of peers; it involves informal know-how trading between scientists or engineers of different organisations.

Figure 4.5-1:   Different forms of cooperation

Form	formal/ contrac- tual	informal/ non-con- tractual	short- term	mid-term	long-term
1. Joint ventures and research corporations	X			X	X
2. Joint R&D agreements	X	X	X	(X)	
3. Technology exchange agreements	X	X	X	(X)	
4. Direct investment (minority holdings) motivated by technology factors	X			X	X
5. Licensing and second-sourcing agreements	X			X	(X)
6. Sub-contracting, production sharing and supplier networks	X		X	X	(X)
7. Research associations	X			X	X
8. Government- sponsored joint research programmes	X		X	(X)	
9. Computerized data banks and value-added networks for technical and scientific interchange		X	X	X	
10. Other networks, including informal networks		X	X	(X)	
Source: Freeman (1991); Reger/Cuhls/Nick (1994, 77)					

Freeman classifies ten forms of collaboration (Freeman 1991, 502); figure 4.5-1 illustrates which form can in the different cases be formal/contractual, informal/non-contractual and long-, mid- or short-term oriented.

In this report, we will concentrate less on explicit forms than on more general applicable tools of collaboration for companies, individuals in the companies, a group of persons, a division or a group of companies constituting a coalition (Hakansson 1987, 14) to broaden their knowledge and face the challenges of the future. This broad range of extra-corporate collaboration comprises (unlike e.g. Rotering 1990, pp. 38) contractual research by third parties (companies, public or industrial research facilities, universities, technical colleges, engineering firms) and joint R&D with or without a contractual basis and excludes the acquisition of companies, trading in licences, or the purchase of equity shares. Other activities like loose contacts to exchange information, joint technical or economic studies, jointly using measurement and test facilities, the preparation of graduation or PhD thesis, or the employment of university students as trainees or assistants, can also improve the external knowledge but are not direct collaboration (Kuhlmann/Kuntze 1991, 709; Wolff et al. 1994). Tools to gain access to external, scientific knowledge are well described in part I of this book. Generally speaking, the different forms of cooperation can be divided into:

1. Co-development as collaboration of any form to develop a new technology or product. It can take place in the form of a joint venture, research consortia, exchange agreements with other companies, cooperation inside the company, or with customers and suppliers. Co-development can be conducted on a contractual or a non-contractual basis. It is in most cases formal, although the knowledge of customers and suppliers can be informal as well.

2. Networking: Network organisations are linkages of selected partners or loosely organized systems (Mueller 1986). These connections can be formal as well as informal. There can be strong and weak ties inside the same network and one actor can belong to more than one network. Cooperative relationships and dependencies between the actors are a main factor of network stabilisation. These linkages can also be close in one respect, more distant in others. The actors of a network may consist of suppliers of equipment, components, materials, customers, customers' customers, research institutes, departments of universities, consultants or producers of complementary products and competitors (Hakansson

241

1987, 15). Many forms, including joint ventures, licensing arrangements, direct R&D collaboration on products, product sharing or sub-contracting are possible. Especially, informal networks are extremely important, because in spite of the difficulties of classifying them, they have a role analogous to "tacit knowledge" within firms (Freeman 1991, 502) and might be a major advantage for international competitiveness.

3. Strategic Alliances: These are coalitions of two or more independent companies which pursue the aim of bringing together the individual strengths in certain strategic business fields (Backhaus/Piltz 1990, 2). A principle difference to acquisitions is the independence of the partners which is maintained during the existence of the alliance. In order to suit the strategic business areas to that of the strategic partner, autonomy is partially given up; however, each company is able to pursue its own corporate policy and strategy. A strategic alliance is related exclusively to common strategic business fields and therefore differs from other forms of collaboration. In this sense, the cooperation between supplier and customer cannot be defined as a strategic alliance because it aims at different businesses. Strategic alliances are exclusively cooperations between actual or potential competitors (horizontal cooperation) and aim at realizing a relevant competitive advantage in a certain market; they may be founded on formal or non-formal contracts and have a lot to do with "trust" (Ohmae 1989, 151).

Companies' practice: strategic alliances

Large Italian firm (machine tools)
Activities of this R&D-intensive Italian firm are in the machine tool sector. Markets for standalone machinery in that sector have changed considerably conditions. While formerly split into many niche markets, under the influence of microelectronics technologies many of them have changed into volume markets. The firm, a producer of standalone machinery in former times, realized the difficulties for European producers to compete in volume markets. Product range was changed from single machines to flexible manufacturing systems. Implications for technology management resulting from that decision are an extension of the variety of technologies applied and increasing complexity in order to link the various machines to systems. Markets for these systems are small, competitors mainly European. Therefore, expansion to international markets is a very important element of the business strategy. In order to get access to the South American market, a joint venture with independent R&D was initiated there.

4.5.2   Reasons for and purposes of cooperation

Industrial research and development is regarded as a crucial source of technological innovation, thus imparting competitiveness to companies and national economies, which also holds true for small and medium-sized enterprises. The importance of cooperation in R&D between enterprises or between companies and public research institutions is steadily growing (Kuhlmann/Kuntze 1991, 709).[6]

The major reasons for collaboration are of technological or economic nature (Dodgson 1992b, 231). Kuhlmann/Kuntze (1991, 709) and Wolff et al. (1994, 43) stress the shortening of product life cycles and the increasing "technological content" of production among other things as the main issues to be answered by cooperation. Additionally, it is argued that collaboration shares the costs (DeBresson/Amesse 1991, 368; Hakansson 1987, 11) and risks involved in the technological development (Dodgson 1992a, 84) in order to respond to uncertainties (DeBresson/Amesse 1991, 368; Dickson/Lawton-Smith/Smith 1991, 147) and to be able to exploit new technology which is too cost-intensive for a single firm. The growing expenditure for R&D within the firm resulting from the growing complexity and overlapping of technologies requires different and new skills as well as inter- or multidisciplinary approaches.

There is a variety of reasons for enterprises to cooperate (EIRMA 1989 14; De Woort 1990, pp. 145; Rotering 1990; Hagedoorn/Shakenraad 1990, pp. 3 or Link/Rees 1990, 28) and there is no contradiction in the strategy of using internal and external R&D capacities (Mowery 1983). The main purposes of collaboration are not to build up high internal R&D capacities, to share the risks (especially if the risks, chances or future significance for the single company cannot be estimated), to avoid double expenditure, to use the advantages of specialisation (increasing efficiency), to use facilities and equipment of the partner, to accelerate the

---

6   Reasons for this have been discussed and analysed in a number of studies, e.g. OECD 1984; Friar/Horvitch 1985; Stankiewicz 1986; Haklisch et al. 1986; Bleicher 1989; Wigand/Frankwick 1989; Link 1989; Link/Tassey 1989; Onida/Malerba 1989; OECD 1990; Berman 1990; Rath 1990 or Rotering 1990; Mansfield 1991; for industrial networks see Lundvall 1990, and Powell 1990.

development, to combine the market position of one partner with those of the other, to enter new technology fields, to employ scientific or technical personnel and to facilitate standardisation (Wolff et al. 1994, 48).

Companies' practice: co-development as a means to share R&D-costs - German MNE and US computer company

The German company has agreed upon a cooperation with the American one in order to develop the 64 Mbit DRAM. Starting with the first concept this project will go through all stages up to the development of a prototype that is ready for production. This cooperation has become necessary as cost and time of development have steadily risen from one chip generation to the next. In this case, the development costs are estimated at about $600,000-$800,000 million per cooperation partner.

Cooperation of any kind can have a wide variety of purposes. In general, they have to solve problems one of the partners is not able to solve alone. In the case of strategic alliances the main purpose is to gain a strategic competitive advantage in certain markets. The aim of the collaboration depends very much on the sector and the size of the company (Dickson/Lawton-Smith/Smith 1991, 462).

A single enterprise is usually not equally strong in all areas of technology, therefore the in-house knowledge may be insufficient to meet all requirements. Very often, personnel with a special kind of interdisciplinary education is not available, a problem which has to be solved by combining the knowledge of different people, companies, R&D institutes or higher education institutes. In many cases, the access to special information or know-how is the motive for cooperation (Hakansson 1987, 11). Thus, new products can be developed faster, which is a competitive advantage when the life cycles of products and whole industries are shortening; the whole R&D process can be accelerated by collaboration in networks or co-development.

As competition on local as well as on global markets is increasing, a major reason to cooperate is the knowledge about and access to markets. Changes in consumer demands can be noted earlier and as more information about the market is available, faster reactions in the development, production and marketing of products are possible.

Administrative problems often furnish another argument for co-development, e.g. the question of "local content": in order not to be regarded as "imported", products are sometimes produced in a certain country using local raw materials, semi-finished goods or components to a certain extent. The trade frictions occurring in the EU on the "local content" of Japanese automobiles, for example, made Japanese manufacturers produce locally. As a consequence, the suppliers also have to produce and develop locally, which leads per force to joint production and in a second stage to joint R&D of producers and suppliers. The same is often the case in getting access to distribution channels, especially in Japan. A network can provide the necessary connections in this case and strategic alliances give more power to cope with this kind of problems.

Companies' practice: collaboration with the customers

Especially small and medium-sized enterprises (SME) of highly specialized and customized products develop their products in close cooperation with their customers. Often the customer is the one who delivers new ideas. These ideas are realized by the producer who might standardize the new product in order to complete his product line.

Example: German SME (Tool Monitoring Systems)
In this technology-oriented SME, R&D resources are organized around projects. Product development is performed in teams with responsibility resting with the project leader. The head of development coordinates the different projects. Procedures to ensure adequate linkages between R&D and other functions are very similar in cases of internal and external ideas. In the case of external ideas, after discussions with the customer, a draft design is elaborated by a team made up of members of the board, the development department and the marketing department. After formulating performance specifications a prototype is developed. The product is tested in the customers' manufacturing process. In the case of internal product ideas customers are involved in the same way in this procedure. Discussions of the new idea at the beginning of the project are due to the initiative of the firm.

Collaboration is often described as a mix of competition and sharing of knowledge (OECD 1991). It provides better possibilities to increase the standard of environmental protection, not only because of knowledge in new methods of producing "bio-products" or "cleaner" production processes which can be shared, but also because of the ecological factor as a competitive advantage. During the last years, a growing consciousness of ecological problems resulting from products and processes can be noted and products with the attribute "environment friendly" may be traded better than others.

Personnel relationships are the most important factors to make a collaboration successful. This is especially important if a product is developed jointly. In formal collaboration, it can be a helpful experience and training to work together with external partners in order to motivate the staff and make the work force learn. This training in special skills as well as in communicative and social competence can be helpful to learn for in-house teamwork. For informal collaboration and networking the personal linkages are the most important factor to keep the relationships stable and allow communication and the flow of information.

Companies' practice: joint R&D projects

Medium-sized French enterprise
External sources for innovative ideas for a manufacturer of machinery/equipment for the chemical industry are customers, competitors and CENG (Centre d'Etudes Nucléaires de Grenoble). CENG is a government laboratory whose activities lie in the field of applied research. One person divides his working hours between CENG and the enterprise, working in joint projects.

Regarding networks, Mueller (1986, 10) worked out the following main purposes:

- Networkers can accumulate influence or power by gathering and controlling information unavailable to them in hierarchical situations.
- Common interests, ideology, or social position can build a power base.
- Personal chemistry, friendship, and peer relationships are powerful forces in human situations.
- Adequate communication between people is the result of the connecting power of networks.
- Networks can be viewed as promoters of culture; norms, values, beliefs, and codes are transmitted by networks.
- Networking can be considered a necessary prelude to the establishment of an organisation; once a formal structure is created, the network disappears unless the leaders make special arrangements to preserve the subtle connections.

4.5.3   Problems of collaboration

Networks are nothing new (Freeman 1991, 499) but networks are more and more becoming part of the strategic management of R&D. Hagedoorn/Schakenraad (1992) show an increasing number of strategic technology alliances since the 1980s, especially in information technologies. Although external inputs into companies were always necessary, the cost dimension in research and development forces companies to find new forms of collaboration on a sector basis. This concerns co-development of technical products as well as every kind of networking. In networks, there seems to be the need for more interaction between industry with its more applied research and university laboratories or non-university R&D institutes with their knowledge in basic research.

Concerning strategic alliances, there is a tendency to develop global strategies and collaborate internationally, too. In the past, different experiences of companies cooperating on a long-term basis were made. Both partners have to gain advantages from strategic alliances. Expectations, especially in collaborations between Japanese and Western companies, are often very different on both sides. Western companies wanted to gain access to markets and to sell their products, whereas the Japanese partners stressed the long-term perspective of learning (Prahalad/Hamel 1990). This lead to many frictions and misunderstandings in- and outside the company, e.g. claims that the Japanese are stealing know-how, although gaining knowledge was their declared purpose for collaborating.

In spite of some empirical studies on collaboration in general (Dickson/Lawton-Smith/Smith 1991; Lawton-Smith/Dickson/Smith 1991; Hagedoorn/Schakenraad 1991; Dodgson 1993; Hagedoorn 1993; Wolff et al. 1994), very little is known about scale and scope of collaborations and evidence available is often contradictory (Dodgson 1992a, 83). Even the outcomes of collaboration are unclear. Also, little is known about the importance of technological issues for collaboration; one exception, but with a small sample, is Herden (1992).

> **Companies' practice: the combination of various cooperation forms**
>
> *Big enterprises especially are linked to a variety of different partners for cooperations. Two examples are described in the following.*
>
> **Large German enterprise (mechanical engineering)**
> *This enterprise produces machines for working with sheet metal. The biggest market is for standard machines, a branch with tough price competition. Based upon the standard machines customized versions can be developed. Niche markets are usually avoided. Besides bilateral contacts with other companies the enterprise uses a broad variety of cooperational forms: direct R&D contracts, transfer of personnel especially between the company and universities or other research institutes, and cooperations for single projects. In the interviewee's opinion German enterprises are open to cooperations but very cautious not to lose know-how. For strategic alliances, the danger of a one-sided dependence exists.*
>
> **French multi-national enterprise (telecommunication systems and services)**
> *The German research facility of this company also maintains a variety of cooperations. There are strong links to universities, e.g. in Stuttgart, Darmstadt, Aachen and Karlsruhe. Their main purpose is the exchange of know-how. Co-development takes place in a pre-competitive setting. Here, especially the participation in EU projects was mentioned. The cooperation with (direct) competitors is usually limited to pre-competitive phases. Besides the danger of losing knowledge, strict anti-trust regulations were mentioned as a reason not to cooperate too much during competition phases.*

An exception are collaborations and networks between industry and the scientific community which are publicly supported. For example, a programme of the German Federal Ministry of Research and Technology (BMFT) to support "Research Cooperations between Industry and Science" showed positive results. Between 30 and 40 percent of the enterprises taking part in that programme mentioned as "very important" an improvement in their know-how, a broadened view of problems and faster innovations in the area of cooperation (Wolff et al. 1994, 31). Another study which was conducted under the auspices of the MONITOR/SPEAR programme of the Commission of the EU examined the "value added" from gaining knowledge through multinational university-industry partnerships (De Freitas et al. 1992). In this survey, it was found that the perception of the value added resulting from research projects is different among researchers, industrialists and policy-makers, and the conditions were identified under which this value added is higher.

According to a study on the impact of "European Technology Policy in Germany" (Reger/Kuhlmann 1995), the "Second Framework Programme of the Community in the Field of Research and Technological Development" definitely increases the willingness of German enterprises to cooperate across borders. Participation of firms in EU supported consortia stabilizes and reinforces cooperation at a European level; this applies particularly to cooperation between European enterprises. Especially innovative SMEs are offered an opportunity to expand their European business relationships to include cooperation in the area of R&D.

Management of and communication between the collaborating partners seem to be the most difficult features (Gemünden/Hillebrands/Schaettgen, 19). In some cases, collaboration can lead to anti-competitive and inflexible, innovation-reducing situations (Dodgson 1992a, 84) or resistance because of the "not-invented-here-syndrome" (Dickson/Lawton-Smith/Smith 1991, 151).

Collaboration in all its forms can help to face the challenges of the future, if the right partner is chosen, the aims and time frames of both partners are stated clearly, the intellectual property rights are clarified, management problems are solved and an innovative and open management has a positive attitude towards collaboration (Wolff et al. 1994, 51; Dodgson 1992 a, 85; Stankiewicz 1986, 50). Other preconditions are that communication and interface coordination are working, common attitudes and perceptions are achieved, personnel involved is really willing to cooperate and is trained to work together in teams, that there is the necessity to share costs, risks, know-how about technologies, temporarily extended capacities or the need for interdisciplinary knowledge (Kuhlmann/Kuntze 1991, 710; Wolff et al. 1994, 51; Jain/Triandis 1990, pp. 135; Cuhls 1993), and that both partners gain from working together.

It depends very much on the purpose of the collaboration, the actors or the sector which form of collaboration should be chosen. General advice cannot be given. Especially for co-development and strategic alliances, it is necessary to define the goals and details of the collaboration in advance, and to evaluate, supervise and control them during the projects. Formal, contractual forms of co-development have their limits of application and effectiveness. Problems, especially in the case of SMEs, can be the risk of losing competitive advantage or corporate independence, the risk of prematurely introducing jointly developed products to the market and too high expenditure to be spent by the SME for conducting external R&D (Kuhlmann/Kuntze 1991; 711, Wolff et al. 1994, 52).

In informal networks, there are no obvious obligations to continue, but linkages are stabilized by mutual duties. In general, every company is related to a certain network (DeBresson/Amesse 1991, 369), but their success for knowledge creation depends on the strength of the ties between the partners and how they are used.

Companies' practice: networking and cooperation with universities

Respondents tend to use contracts with a university department for particular research projects, not primarily as a means to acquire important knowledge for specific business reasons, but as a way to establish their presence in important networks. Indirectly this leads to improvements in the firm's intelligence and scanning function. But respondents stress the importance of close contacts with bright new talent as being the most important reason for maintaining their positions in "scientific" networks. Participation by the larger corporations in European and national RTD programmes is similarly aimed at strengthening the position in networks more than at direct innovation or business benefits.

Examples:

Small Portuguese start-up (industrial automation)
The firm has a close relationship and a number of joint projects (namely in EU programmes) with the local university (Aveiro University) and also occasional cooperation with other universities and research centres. This relationship is used both as a source of information about recent evolution in its areas of activity and as a support to some development activities, namely standing in for the absence of more research-oriented internal activities.

German multi-national enterprise (electronics)
The enterprise maintains close connections to universities in order to monitor emerging technologies closely. Within the company, there are around 200 professors who also teach at universities, not only in Germany but throughout the world. Hundreds of contracts allow post-graduate researchers and students to do their research on the companies' account, both in the company and at their home universities. Close cooperations exist with the universities at the enterprises' main locations. There are further associations with important American universities such as MIT, Carnegie Mellon University and University of California, Berkeley.

Synergetic creation of knowledge through interaction, dynamic technological accumulation and social learning are all central aspects of networks of innovators (DeBresson/Amesse 1991, 366), but collaboration is not an easy task. Goals, advantages and in- and output for both sides have to be reflected in advance and later on permanently. In order to remain competitive, and to gain competitive advantages, companies have to identify, integrate and benefit from external knowledge and collaborations of any form.

4.6   Management of scientific, technical and functional interfaces (Interface III)

4.6.1   Defining the management of interfaces

The management of interfaces is often understood as the integration of the different activities of business functions in enterprises (Brockhoff 1989, 1). Since the creation of business functions necessarily leads to interfaces, the task of management is to overcome the division of objectives, strategies, and actions as well as to coordinate these items. Concerning R&D, the question of interface management in enterprises is focused on coordination problems between R&D and marketing. These disturbances can eat up the advantages of specialisation or ignore customer requirements. Reasons for these interface problems between market and R&D mainly are a lack of internal communication, cultural differences between the business functions, different perceptions of changes in the enterprises' environment, and an unsystematical benchmarking of competitors (Brockhoff 1989).

However, with respect to the crucial role of science and technology for R&D activities, the management of interfaces here encompasses functional interfaces as well as interfaces between scientific and technical disciplines. Since the technology of the coming decades will be characterized by an increasing role of science-intensive and interdisciplinary areas, an important task of R&D management will be generating knowledge by uniting different technical and scientific disciplines.

Companies' practice: the importance of interdisciplinary approaches

The following quote of the head of R&D of a German multi-national enterprise supports the importance interdisciplinarity has for the success of innovations:

"The success of an innovation is determined firstly by the degree to which the new product meets the customers' wishes, secondly, if the product is brought to market fast enough and in third place - and this is of special importance today - if one is able to work together interdisciplinarily, meaning the collection of different disciplines in a single team. New technologies and markets seldom rise from the middle of established markets or disciplines, but from the borderlines of different markets or technologies. Here the strength of a centralized research and development department can be seen: it provides all disciplines under a common roof, meanwhile the divisions have to be more specialized."

4.6.2   Challenges from the growing overlapping of technologies

Under the heading of "interdisciplinarity" all cooperative activities beyond the borders of two different disciplines are summarized (part III). From the point of view of an individual discipline-bound scientist who struggles with a specific problem in his field of research, help from and cooperation with scientists from other disciplines, who are dealing with related problems, are a form of interdisciplinary work and the process of knowledge production in his own discipline is improved. The cooperation between different disciplines emerges from the role of technology in modern societies. As technologies are to a large extent the application of results from scientific research, new technologies can be generated by the cooperation of different disciplines. In this manner, applicable new technologies can be created. These cross-point technologies are emerging technologies which do not fit into the traditional classification of natural sciences any more (Grupp 1993a, 1993c) but are overlapping to a certain extent as described in chapter 2 (see figure 2.2-1). The progress in the development of such technologies is thus dependent on the cooperation of scientists from different scientific disciplines.

Several types of interdisciplinarity can be identified (see for a detailed discussion part III). Multidisciplinarity, according to Jantsch (1970), is the weakest form of cooperation within research projects and has to be excluded from the types of interdisciplinary research, as there is no real exchange of theories and methods, but only a gathering of results emanating from the work in single disciplines. If a cooperation takes place without coordination of different disciplines in one project, it can be called pluridisciplinarity and if the methods of one dominating discipline are adopted by others, this might be called crossdisciplinarity. The expression transdisciplinarity is used in cases when disciplines are melted to study the same problem. What all forms of interdisciplinarity have in common is that there has to be a certain intellectual exchange between the participating disciplines which is applied methodically or to a specific subject.

Three different challenges for managing interdisciplinarity as a subject of growing importance for R&D management could be identified. Increasing efficiency is the first challenge: in this case, there is one scientist who from the perspective of his discipline is struggling with a specific problem in his field of research. He is dependent on help from other disciplines dealing with related problems. Therefore, the process of knowledge production in this particular discipline is improved by the cooperation. Authors like Jantsch (1970) and Lenk (1978, 1980) point to the fact that the improvement of efficiency in solving problems within one single discipline remains crucial.

With the development of modern industrialized societies, there is a second group of problems like environmental pollution and unforeseen impacts of the application of new technologies, which are in part a logical and dismal consequence of the success of scientific discovery. These and other global challenges already mentioned in chapter 2 reach far beyond the borders of single scientific disciplines and are also of growing importance for enterprises. As a consequence, scientists from various disciplines in industry and at universities have to work together in order to find solutions for the currently urgent problems (Weizsäcker 1978; Ditfurth 1984; Kocka 1987; Maier-Leibnitz 1992; Robson 1993).

The third area of cooperation between different disciplines emerges from the role of technology in modern societies and enterprises. Technology is to a large extent the application of results from scientific research as comprehensive studies by Spiegel-Rösing/de Solla Price (1977) and Grupp/Schmoch (1992c) show. As scientific research offered more basic results than application techniques, it is often difficult to match these outcomes to technical problems and apply them in products. Consequently, as the traditional concepts of technologies and disciplines are no longer applicable to emerging technologies (Grupp 1993b, see also chapter 2), there is the need for scientists and engineers from various disciplines to cooperate in order to develop new technology.

4.6.3   Managing interdisciplinarity

Many forms of interdisciplinary work are possible within a company and in cooperation with external sources. These forms exist in large company-specific varieties. One possibility to face the challenges of overlapping technologies mentioned in literature is the employment of the "right" personnel. In industry, this seems to be successful to a certain extent, if people fitting the requirements can be found at all. In some areas, there is still some resistance against employing interdisciplinarily educated staff as it is assumed that they are "generalists". As described above, interdisciplinarity does not mean knowledge of everything, but detailed specialisation in one or more fields and maybe added information from other scientific disciplines. Therefore, they often face difficulties in acceptance and end up in lower positions than others (see Kilburn 1990, and part III for a detailed discussion).

Interdisciplinarity in research and development depends mainly on the personnel involved in R&D projects. Therefore, most of the techniques are concerned with the management of human resources, which means employing people with a broader education, re-training staff in new scientific and technical areas, attracting researchers from other disciplines than the company's core ones, and creating incentive systems to stimulate overlapping cooperations. Special instruments concerning aspects of human resources are the following:

1. First, the employment of people with an interdisciplinary education brings the knowledge of already combined scientific fields into the company. Researchers who have a very detailed know-how from one or more scientific areas are already trained to combine different methods, ways of approaching problems, different

scientific languages and thoughts. Cooperation with other researchers inside the company is facilitated and the development of rather new products or processes has a broader basis.

2. Secondly, internal and external training provides personnel in special areas with different know-how. Seminars, courses, participation in conferences or providing time for reading can be some of the means to keep and increase the level of in-house knowledge while working together cooperatively. In this case, the interdisciplinarity is found within one single person who is expert in one technological field and gains knowledge in a different one in order to combine them and bring out new methods, techniques or ideas which may lead to the development of new technologies or products.

3. The third category of measures concerns the ability of technology fusion and of teamwork. Social competences, teamwork, and creativity methods can be trained as well as specialists' knowledge. One form of gathering know-how in order to develop or improve a technology or product are quality circles (which do not only improve quality, anymore) as well as other forms of teamwork bringing together the knowledge of different hierarchies and - if possible - different departments and sectors of an enterprise (Cuhls 1993). Given the freedom to decide on and improve products and processes, the workforce will be better motivated to find new solutions. Teamwork uses synergies and mobilizes the in-house competence and knowledge of a firm. It should not only be applied to the R&D department, but can also consider recommendations coming from production and marketing.

4.6.4   Simultaneous engineering

Another concept which seems to be used in Japan very often and is gaining more and more attention in Western enterprises is called "simultaneous engineering". Other names for the same concept are "concurrent engineering", "simultaneous development", "overlapping engineering" and "concurrent design" (Gerpott 1990b).

Simultaneous engineering can be defined as the development of products and production techniques not sequentially, but simultaneously, by in-house project teams as well as by integrating suppliers and customers (Eversheim 1989, pp.5). It is an organisational strategy which requires internal cooperation and coordination across business functions (see figure 4.6-1). Externally, there is a need for a trusting cooperation with the supplier's and customer's areas of development and production. Through parallel planning of the new product and the production process at the same time, a very early determination of the main production components is possible. The aim of simultaneous engineering is to increase the quality of products and production facilities and to reduce the concept-to-launch period and costs of the innovation process.

Simultaneous engineering is a tool which tries to combine the knowledge across functional and disciplinary borders in order to plan and develop a new product and bring it to market. Concerning external cooperations, it tries to integrate know-how from different sectors. In this management concept, one development project is divided into work packages, structured and coordinated so that these packages can be developed parallel at the same time in different business functions (or sectors) by coordinating overlapping areas (Bullinger et al. 1989; Pantele/Lacey 1989; Gerpott 1990b), using new information technology and other means of communication. Interdisciplinary teams not limited to one business function have to be created in order to get the optimal combination of all value chain phases (Töpfer/Mehdorn 1993, pp. 80; see figure 4.6-1). In sequentially organised projects, only step-by-step development from one department to the next was applied and as one scientist had to wait for the preceding step it could take a long time until a product was launched onto the market. Simultaneous engineering also needs teamwork competences of the personnel involved and, if possible, interdisciplinarily educated persons who understand a common terminology.

256

Figure 4.6-1:   Simultaneous engineering

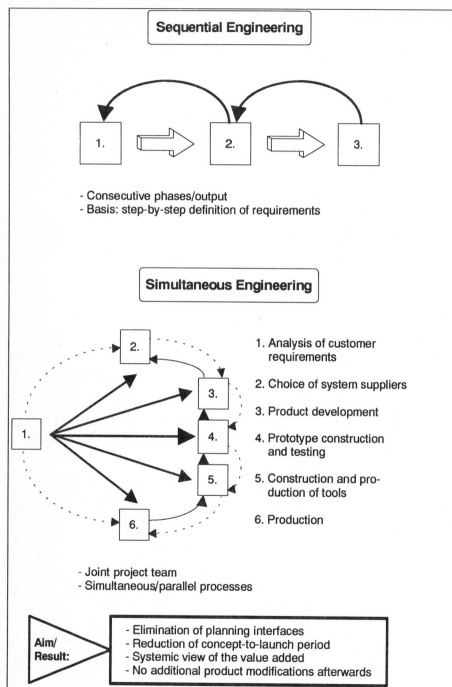

Source: Töpfer/Mehdorn (1993, 82); Reger/Cuhls/Nick (1994, 91)

The following elements are crucial for the concept of simultaneous engineering (Gerpott 1990b):

- overlapping in time/parallel development of products and production factors;
- early comprehensive coordinated and market-oriented planning of critical quality peculiarities of a new product (quality function deployment);
- the development resources for producers of the means of production and suppliers of components have to be included;
- project-oriented, function-integrating cooperative development organisation.

Many Western companies still rely more on breakthrough approaches than on fusion of existing technologies (Kodama 1992). However, in a world where the maxim "one technology one industry" is no longer applicable, a singular breakthrough strategy is inadequate; companies need to include both the breakthrough and fusion approaches in their technology strategies. Therefore, learning not only of technological specialities but also of social techniques, creativity methods and other integrative means to facilitate teamwork will be unavoidable in the future.

In the domain of interdisciplinary oriented research and development in companies, the concept of simultaneous (or concurrent) engineering is very helpful recently. In principle, the planning, creation, development and design of products is conducted simultaneously (from the time perspective) with a strong flow of information from one scientist, engineer, manager or project group to another involved in that specific project. As the product cycles are shortening rapidly, the use of simultaneous engineering for reduced development times, mobilizing all kinds of in-house know-how, might be one of the main future competitive advantages.

Teamwork in general is a well appreciated approach to bring together the in-house know-how of different disciplines or to collaborate with external persons in order to integrate their knowledge. Working in a team has advantages as well as disadvantages: the success of groups depends very much on the circumstances of their introduction, the team members, their competence and willingness to cooperate, and the management incentive system. The often mentioned synergies of teamwork are often not reached, especially if the participants of a team are not able to adapt to other's opinions or the situation of being responsible for decision-making. If teamwork is not promoted or rewarded by incentive systems it will not be successful. Nevertheless, making use of creativity techniques and being open to inter-social and technical learning helps to integrate team members and to become an innovative and learning organisation (e.g. Womack/Jones/Roos 1990; Imai 1991; Warnecke 1992; Töpfer/Mehdorn 1993; gfmt 1993). The philosophy of the Total Quality Management concept is based on this way of thinking.

Companies' practice: simultaneous engineering in a British mechanical engineering firm

In a large British mechanical engineering firm, adequate linkage between R&D and other functions is ensured by simultaneous engineering; this method proved very successful in reducing the concept-to-launch period to only twelve months in the development of the latest type of series. From the experience of that development, success can be attributed to
- *correct market intelligence,*
- *possible cost parameters known in advance,*
- *design controlled by cost and market needs,*
- *design project undertaken by project team,*
- *suppliers and customers involved throughout the project.*

The special kind of teamwork used in simultaneous engineering is necessary for that specific approach. For Europe, there are at present no data available on how successful the whole concept might be in terms of parallel combining the in-house knowledge and information flow. However, there are already positive results available concerning the shortening of time for the development of products (Hoeschen 1989; Pantele/Lacey 1989). Thus, the concept of simultaneous engineering is an instrument to face the challenge of shortening product cycles (Gerpott/Wittkemper 1991, 121) and to accelerate the concept-to-launch period within firms. However, simultaneous engineering with its different parallel working groups needs a lot of coordination which must not be underestimated because there are no organisational buffers.

4.6.5 Implications for R&D management

Regarding the increasing role of science-intensive areas and the overlapping of technologies, the management of interfaces should encompass scientific, technical, and functional aspects. A new approach combining all these aspects is the concept of simultaneous engineering. This concept is an organisational strategy which does not necessarily require the usage of extensive computer systems (Eversheim 1989, 24). Moreover, the set up of an interdisciplinary project team plays a decisive role which contains, so far needed, personnel from various technical disciplines and/or business functions, from suppliers or customers.

Managing interdisciplinarity in R&D has a lot to do with a proper management of human resources. This means employing people with a broader education, re-training staff in new scientific and technical areas, attracting researchers from other disciplines than the company's core ones and creating incentive systems to stimulate overlapping cooperations.

5.   General conclusions and recommendations

As the review of the literature in this study shows, a broad variety of publications exists on challenges for enterprises and the management of R&D in general as well as on single tools for R&D activities. Since publications often deal with either economic, scientific and/or technological challenges or R&D management and tools, this study tried to unite the different approaches. It describes how companies use different tools as a response for different challenges. In most cases, one tool is used for a variety of challenges and one challenge requires the usage of several tools. Additionally, three models for the management of R&D are presented which characterize the changes in industrial R&D management and its challenges in the time span since the late 1950s and point out comprehensive dimensions for a modern R&D management in enterprises.

Nevertheless, some important open research questions appeared from the literature review, which will be shortly described before presenting some implications for the research and technological development (RTD) policy of the European Union (EU).

5.1   Open research questions

A crucial challenge for the management of R&D and an adequate response is missing in the three generalized models of R&D management presented: the growing complexity and the overlapping of technologies ("technology fusion"). Knowledge of different scientific and technical disciplines has to be combined by short-term as well as institutional arrangements within the company and a model for R&D management should include this dimension. Moreover, most models for R&D management are based upon observations in large international and multi-divisional enterprises. Although there are many studies which investigate the special innovative behaviour and the role of small and medium-sized enterprises (SMEs) for a national system of innovation, a model regarding changes over time and explicitly created for the management of innovation and R&D in SMEs was not found.

Literature about managing interfaces in companies is mainly concerned with functional barriers and less with disciplinary ones. Studies on interdisciplinary research activities in industry show different results: whereas some studies show that industrial R&D laboratories are more accustomed to interdisciplinary research activities than e.g. universities, investigations on mechanical engineering firms (Kalkowski/Manske 1993) show problems especially in the cooperation between mechanical and electronic engineers in technology development. The management of disciplinary interfaces concerning mainly questions of culture, organisational structures and human resources may be an important area for further research.

Concerning organisational aspects of multi-national enterprises (MNEs), the relationship between centralized and decentralized R&D, long-term application oriented research and short-term development, corporate and business sponsored R&D is re-defined. Whereas this re-definition and the underlying challenges seem to be identified, further research may be required for the creation of modern instruments for their coordination and the institutional implementation. SMEs, which do not often conduct their technology development in separate development departments, and especially new technology-based firms managing organisational change as well as maintaining and getting an "innovative, learning organisation" is an important subject of further research. SMEs are increasingly overtaxed by recognizing technological trends and by uniting the management of innovation with organisation.

The concept of core competences is often named in literature as an interesting approach to re-thinking corporations due to present and future challenges. This concept tries to concentrate the corporate strategies on visions and future market potentials by regarding the company from its core competences and not from its business units. However, the elements of core competences are not sufficiently operationalized, the process of identification within the company as well as the allocation of resources is unclear. Further research may be necessary to bring this interesting concept to an operational level and to evaluate the impacts on resource allocation and organisation in the company.

The discussion in chapter 4.4 disclosed that technology forecasting and its application in R&D management still presents a lot of problems. While a variety of techniques have been developed that cover nearly every situation in which forecasts may be needed, planning techniques are often overemphasised and too lavish for use in companies. An interesting, new research question is the institutionalisation of technological forecasting as a process of organisational learning as well as the coordination of technical and market trends. Additionally, the integration of technology forecasting and technology assessment has to be fostered. This can be done by further research dealing with the development of integrated forecasting and assessment systems for use in enterprises.

5.2 Issues for technology policy of the European Union

The challenges to the enterprises characterized in chapter 2 of this report also present new challenges to the research and technological development policy of the European Union (EU). New issues derive from the fusing of technology, increasing globalisation and ecological problems.

Since various fields of technology are progressively fusing and overlapping, technology as the basis for industrial innovation and competitiveness at the beginning of the 21st century cannot be understood or dealt with from a conventional point of view. For instance, in order for "nanotechnology" to function as a fruitful base technology for future innovation processes and new generations of technology, transdisciplinary interactions are necessary with electronics, information technology, materials science, optics, biochemistry, biotechnology, medicine and micro-mechanics. The science-intensive and overlapping technology of tomorrow requires the sustained support of appropriate fundamental research. This does not only increase the importance of the classic transfer from basic research to industrial research; the feedback transfer from industrial problems into basic research also acquires new significance. Whereas the dissemination of results from basic research is a well-known task for policy activities of the European Commission, the transfer from industrial requirements into the scientific community can become a new task.

The globalisation of markets, production, reseach, and technology will limit the possibilities of regional and national technology policy, whereas RTD policy on the level of the European Union will be of growing significance. This will lead to a stronger need for coordination between the member states and the institutions of the EU. Additionally, European RTD policy in future will have to promote not only R&D cooperation within Europe, as it has done until now, but will have to envisage specifically the support of cooperation with partners in the "triad" (USA, Japan) and with developing countries. This may also include the dissemination of publicly available scientific results from countries outside the EU concerning technological and managerial issues.

The path of development followed by the developed industrialized nations until now cannot be continued in the long term, due to the consumption of resources and the damage to the climate. Public technology policy will have the important task of preparing the "turning of the ways" onto acceptable paths. This implies the necessity to link visionary applications of new technologies with new research tasks, without eroding the present responsibilities of the actors. Public RTD policy can make an important contribution by an intelligent combination of classic research promotion, stimulation of demand, the establishing of appropriate frame conditions and stable, long-term signals to science and industry. The global nature of challenges will mean that the Commission of the EU, as a transnational authority, will be pressed by a growing number of urgent problems that can no longer be dealt with at the level of single countries. The transnational share in the shaping and planning of research and technology will continue to grow. The sooner the European Union, in cooperation with the member states, recognize and acknowledge the ecological challenges, the sooner they can be met, thus making a contribution towards strengthening the competitive situation of Europe on the world markets.

The incorporation of these aspects in new R&D management practices on the firm level is a major challenge to RTD policy. As a consequence, the RTD policy of the EU should not only support the technological competence, but also the entrepreneurial competence and the learning ability of European firms. A future R&D policy should encompass not only the solutions of technical problems but at the same time the companies' management of R&D and innovation. Therefore, the European RTD promotion should boost the entrepreneurial competence and the learning ability of the enterprises with appropriate instruments. There are many such starting points:

1) Cooperation: the instrument of promoting cross-border cooperation has proved a success in the EC Framework Programmes. However, more attention should be paid to the composition of the research consortia. Cooperation in two directions of the value added chain is required: on the one hand, the cooperation between suppliers and users, and on the other hand between manufacturers and customers. A promotion of cooperation between direct competitors will not be advisable on the whole, as the danger of loss of know-how predominates at least with the enterprises specialized in niche markets like e.g. machine tools manufacturers. The promotion of cross-border cooperation should contain instruments to manage cooperations (above all SMEs), which support a participation in programmes of the EU and can lead to an increased knowledge for inexperienced enterprises.

2) Linking technology with strategic planning: the use of new technology can be linked with strategic planning and promoted by public technology policy. Such an approach was used e.g. in the Norwegian BUNT programme (Business Development Using New Technology) which was funded by the Royal Norwegian Council for Scientific and Industrial Research (NTNF). The participating companies were supported in developing strategic analyses by specially trained consultants before new technology was implemented within the firms.

3) Project planning: R&D projects and the application of new technologies require good planning, which should also be a part of the promotional concept: costs for a systematic company planning, for the setting-up of inter-departmental or interdisciplinary project teams and for the utilization of complex planning instruments should be financially supported. The projects supported by the EU could be divided e.g. into two phases (planning and development phase) and financed separately: in a "planning phase" before the start of research or development work the task in hand will be determined through preparatory market studies and the selection of suitable technologies and organisation structures. In the "development phase" the direct R&D activity is the focal point.

4) Technology forecasting: some of the more effective forecasting techniques are too resource-intensive for a single, especially small, company. Similar to the "Delphi inquiry" pursued recently in Germany (following a Japanese model), technology-oriented forecasts could be initiated by the EU in order to get a

macro-picture of technological development in Europe. An interactive process of forecasting not only has to be implemented at company level but on a national or European scale, too. As an example for the successful management of a national process of forecasting the Japanese MITI and its "Think Tanks" might suffice. These expert groups figure out the general trends in technology and provide companies with tentative visions of the future while the companies select the specific technology fields they are going to work on. A collective learning process further is launched by cooperative research projects of several companies. Both the selection of partners and the overall coordination of these projects is performed through MITI.

5) Managing interfaces: Kodama (1992, 72) works out that the most important factor for a fusion strategy is how well senior management incorporates three fusion principles: demand articulation, intelligence gathering and collaborative R&D. MITI's industrial policy which promotes technology fusion very actively through legislation and government-funded research projects also helps to stimulate interdisciplinary approaches: over 75 research associations have been formed to encourage diffusion of technologies and the creation of intercompany engineering infrastructure through tax incentives and direct sponsorship. Furthermore, the application of concepts like e.g. simultaneous engineering, which reduces the concept-to-launch period and supports functional and interdisciplinary cooperation, may be supported by the Commission.

To sum up, the success of increasing innovativeness of enterprises does not depend only on technical solutions but also on the management of R&D and innovation of the individual enterprise. A modern European RTD policy should therefore encompass not only the technological areas (what or which technology should be promoted?) but also companies' management of R&D and innovation (how or which instruments, methods or approach should be promoted?).

PART III

U. Schmoch, S. Breiner, K. Cuhls, S. Hinze, G. Münt

The Organisation of Interdisciplinarity -
Research Structures in the Areas of Medical Lasers and
Neural Networks

Executive summary of part III

The technology of the coming decades will be characterised by an increasing role of science-intensive and interdisciplinary areas. Against this background, the present study aims at the exploration of typical structures of interdisciplinary areas, especially for determining problems of communication and organisation as well as approaches for their solution.

According to an evaluation of the respective literature, main causes for interdisciplinarity are
- first, improvement of efficiency,
- second, the solution of urgent problems of mankind,
- third, the introduction of results from scientific research in technological applications,
- fourth, small interdisciplinarity, i. e. the re-integration of specialised branches within a discipline, and
- fifth, search for new paradigms in the final phase of an old scientific paradigm.

Interdisciplinarity can be divided into different types such as multidisciplinarity, pluridisciplinarity or crossdisciplinarity according to the organisation and intensity of the interdisciplinary co-operation. Many authors see a growing importance of transdisciplinarity which denotes the merger of two disciplines into a new discipline and thus the most intensive form of interdisciplinarity.

The literature on interdisciplinarity is chiefly written from the perspective of academic institutions and, first of all, deals with problems of reputation and the high risk of failure of interdisciplinary projects. According to these sources, the problem of interdisciplinary communication seems to be the main barrier between academic institutions and industry, and obviously a gap in culture between the scientific community and industry in this regard exists. As a major shortcoming of the existing literature, there is almost no theoretic work that deals with the organisation of interdisciplinary co-operation either in science or in industry.

Former theories are based on the assumption of a quite strict division between the scientific community and industry. Recent studies introduce as a new element the emergence of techno-scientific communities in science-intensive areas which comprise academic as well as industrial researches. This approach seems to be an appropriate analytical tool for the analysis of interdisciplinary co-operation in science-intensive areas of research.

The problem of interdisciplinary co-operation is analysed in further detail on the basis of two case studies for the areas of medical lasers and neural networks. Each study starts with a bibliometric analysis on the basis of patents and scientific publications which proves to be helpful for the assessment of the scientific and technological performance and for the identification of major actors in the field and thus the description of characteristic institutional structures. In the second part of the case studies interviews with typical actors are carried out which include industrial enterprises, academic institutions, and other public research centres which are located in large and small countries of the EU.

The field of medical lasers is characterised by a dynamic, even euphoric development during the eighties and a stagnation, but also consolidation in recent years. The stagnation is primarily due to the fact that the market for medical lasers is not as broad as originally forecast and that the impact of laser beams in many areas of applications is not yet sufficiently explored. Against this background, future research activities will be focused first, on the identification and exploration of new application areas and, second, a deeper examination of the interaction mechanisms between laser beams and biological tissue.

The field of neural networks originated in the forties; a real breakthrough was observed only in the second half of the eighties. Therefore, the research activities on the academic and industrial side still increase. In some years, a certain stagnation comparable to the area of medical lasers can be forecast; the recession, however, will be less distinct because of the generally broader market potential. Future areas of research concern, first, the identification of marketable applications and their introduction into practice; second, the further theoretical development of artificial networks, third, the development of neuro-computers, thus very large networks; and fourth, the deeper exploration of the structures and mechanisms of biological networks and the transfer of the respective results on artificial networks. Only the latter area is characterised by a real "big" interdisciplinarity. The continuation of the biology-oriented research will, in the long run, be important for the further progress of the field.

The following conclusions and recommendations are based on common findings for the specific areas of medical lasers and neural networks. Both areas are characterised by the emergence of a techno-scientific community which establishes an interdisciplinary network of industrial and academic actors. Within these networks, the members do not work on the same problems, but a quite clear division of labour can be observed, concerning a different orientation on the involved disciplines, but also the dimension of an applied versus a basic orientation. In periods of economic recession, the function of universities in basic research gets even more important, because many industrial enterprises reduce their respective activities and favour an orientation towards application.

As to the disciplinary orientation, a strong tendency towards a division of research according to traditional disciplines even in interdisciplinary areas can be observed. In the case of medical lasers there still exists a quite strict division into, on the one hand, technical, system-oriented research and, on the other hand, biomedical research. In neural networks, the activities are generally divided into computer science and neuro-biology. Structures of "small" interdisciplinarity within natural sciences or within life sciences predominate with, e.g., teams of physicists and electrical engineers or biologists and physicians. Only few institutions aim at the real integration of distinctly different disciplines. These institutions, however, generally prove to have a decisive function for the progress of the area. Against this background, the promotion of interdisciplinarity should aim at the organisation of an efficient dialogue between institutions of different disciplines and especially support those institutions which bear the risks of a real interdisciplinary approach.

The results of the project confirm the outcome of the literature analysis that industrial companies have less problems to organise interdisciplinarity. This is true at least for the two cases which are analysed in this study. Possibly, neither of these two fields need "big" interdisciplinarity in an industrial research environment and the results would have been different for other research areas. Companies, however, work in the applied part of interdisciplinary fields, where the disciplinary differences generally are not as big. For example, the manufacturers of medical lasers have to integrate physicists, engineers in electronics and technicians in precision mechanics, but no physicians. Industrial research teams in neural networks generally consist of physicists, electrical engineers and computer specialists, but seldom biologists. The big interdisciplinary gaps between, e. g., physics and medicine or computer science and biology appear in the early stages of a new techno-scientific field and thus primarily on the level of basic research. In consequence, first of all academic institutions - thus the target group of Interface II - is confronted with problems of "big" interdisciplinarity. The disciplinary structures in universities, however, are much more rigid than in industrial enterprises, and the set-up of interdisciplinarity institutes is generally quite problematic. In consequence, the active promotion of interdisciplinary approaches in academic institutions by external bodies is crucial for the development of advanced techno-scientific areas.

The above considerations have decisive consequences for the planning of new RTD programmes. According to these results, it is not only important to verify the assumptions concerning the European technical and scientific performance in an ex-ante evaluation. In addition, it is necessary to explore the existing structures of involved actors and their respective function within a techno-scientific community. On this basis, it is possible to decide deliberately which types of institutions should be combined - or not combined - in common projects.

In both case studies, institutional approaches seem to be quite a promising instrument of promotion. In contrast to RTD projects where small groups of different institutions are combined for a quite short period on a project basis, the institutional approach aims at linking medium-sized institutional groups with a limited, but long-term perspective and more flexible targets. In these long-terms arrangements it is important that the original aims of research can be modified according to intermediate results. The reorientation should be discussed within the institutional group in workshop-like meetings and with the participation of experts from the side of the Commission.

In dynamic research areas with a large number of research actors, it is important to achieve a sufficient co-ordination. For that purpose, the establishment of networks and the set-up of databases are appropriate tools which are already successfully used in EC programmes such as MHR4 or ESPRIT. A further instrument - also already promoted by the Commission - is the exchange of personnel.

Conferences and publications are effective tools for the dissemination of existing RTD results. Most interview partners, however, emphasise the problem of quality. In the case of conferences, this orientation can lead to a reduction of frequency and higher investments in the preparation of the remaining conferences. In addition, small workshops on topical problems can be helpful. In the case of publications, their financing within the projects has to be considered, because the preparation of articles of high quality and with an orientation to special target groups is time-consuming.

In both case studies, the problem of bureaucratic structures in the application procedures for RTD programmes and the delays of respective decisions are mentioned by the interview partners. In face of the very large number of tenders and the complexity of the structure of actors of different national origins, one has to think in more detail about whether it is possible to achieve a more effective application procedure. A major aim of these considerations should be approaches to reach those institutions which have a high scientific performance but little experience in European application procedures.

An interesting common outcome of both case studies is the high scientific performance of institutions from small and less-favoured countries, whereas the technical performance of these countries is low. These results can be interpreted as a lack of coupling between the academic and industrial sector, especially in less-favoured countries. For an improvement of this situation, public promotion can aim at a better knowledge transfer from the public research sector to existing industrial enterprises. A further promising approach is the promotion of young technology-oriented enterprises as spin-offs of universities. In any case, the support of less-favoured regions should include leading-edge, science-intensive technologies on the basis of existing research activities in the public sector.

All in all, the study confirms the increasing importance of interdisciplinarity and emphasises its key function for advanced areas of technology. Especially in academic institutions, however, distinct barriers to interdisciplinarity often exist, so that promotion by external organisations is a decisive element of a successful set-up of interdisciplinary research.

1.   Introduction to part III

The present study was performed within the framework of the programme VALUE II of the European Union. VALUE II aims to promote the dissemination and exploitation of results of research and technical development (RTD) achieved in activities of the EU. The measures of VALUE II are grouped within 3 areas:

- research/industry interface (Interface I)
- research/scientific community interface (Interface II)
- research/society interface (Interface III).

The present study was carried out in the second group, the research/scientific community interface: thus the general focus of the activities within this area is the dissemination of knowledge, achieved in EU research programmes, to the European scientific community.

The analysis has to be seen against the background of a general literature review on constraints and opportunities for the dissemination and exploitation of R&D activities documented in part I. According to these findings, the next years will be characterised by the emergence of interdisciplinary technologies especially in science-intensive areas. Actual innovation systems, however, are still largely discipline-bound, a statement which applies first of all to the academic sector, thus, the target group of Interface II. Therefore, the existing innovation systems have to change towards interdisciplinary structures in order to meet the requirements of the future.

This study starts with a review of the literature on the problem of interdisciplinarity. Definitions and different types of interdisciplinarity are introduced and typical structures of interdisciplinary research described. The review, however, reveals that most respective publications remain on quite a general level, and there is an obvious lack of information on detailed institutional and organisational structures of interdisciplinarity.

Against this background, two case studies are carried out in the areas of medical lasers and neural networks in order to achieve more practice-oriented knowledge on the organisation of interdisciplinarity. Each case study comprises an explanation of the causes of selection, a technical description, a bibliometric analysis and - as the most important element - a field study on the basis of interviews. The necessary methodological explanations are discussed by the example of the first case study, the medical lasers. The reader interested in methodology should therefore refer to that chapter.

In a final chapter, common results of both case studies are discussed. A special focus is on conclusions which are interesting for activities of the Commission.

2. Interdisciplinarity: a literature review

Today's organisation of scientific research in universities is dominated by the division of labour into scientific disciplines. Scientific research, teaching and training are generally focused on specific subjects the discipline mainly deals with; students and future researchers are trained to look at problems from a special limited perspective, to apply common theoretical and empirical methods to matters which are closely related to the discipline's traditional field of research. Consequently, each generation of discipline-bound scientists is educated to enlarge the inherited body of knowledge and to improve the research methods of their single discipline, just as their teachers did. Thus, scientific progress is put forward in the narrow channel of established theory and empirical testing which is commonly regarded as "state of the art" in each discipline. "Progress", in this perspective, means a gradual change and modification of the ruling theories and methods. Above all, it is a further diversification and specialisation of research focus and interest (Hübenthal 1989; Kocka 1987).

There are, however, strong efforts which are aiming towards an integration of research activities across the borders of different disciplines. "Interdisciplinarity" has become a keyword for the meanwhile wide-spread conviction that, although the division of labour in scientific research has proved so successful in history, in sharing knowledge, theoretical frameworks and methods with other fields of research single disciplines would not only benefit from co-operation for their own discipline-bound interests, but also contribute to the solution of urgent problems of society. Literature on this subject is vast and cannot be completely reviewed. We are concentrating here on the questions emanating from interdisciplinarity as far as science-based technological innovations are concerned (for an almost complete bibliography and an excellent introduction into the subject see Klein 1990)[1].

---

[1] In this context, it is interesting to take a closer look at the scientific (predominantly philosophical) work done by East European researchers who are discussing the problems of the discipline-bound development of science on the background of Hegel's dialectic method, thus, contrasting the processes of disintegration and integration of scientific work and knowledge. Most surprisingly they arrive at almost the same conclusions as West European philosophy and practice (Gott et al. 1984; Kröber 1983; Schulze 1981; Wessel 1983).

2.1 Emergence of disciplines in science and need for (re)integration

Since the emergence of science as an application of methods for thinking and problem solution, the organisation of scientific work headed towards a separation into single disciplines (Hübenthal 1989). In their time philosophers such as Aristotele, Francis Bacon, d'Alambert, Leibniz and Kant struggled to restore the lost unity of science by contemplating on ways to find a common basis for all kinds of scientific thinking. Their theories, nowadays summarised under the heading of epistemology, recurred to the formal descriptions of logic and mathematics but never managed to cope with the spread of scientific activities into various isolated fields. The rise of ideas of enlightenment led to an explosive increase in the development of theory and the body of knowledge. Especially the knowledge about nature grew at an increasing pace thanks to the revolution in the natural sciences stirred by the discovery of "laws of nature" by Newton and others. Soon, it was recognised that the division of labour in science could not be stopped. Specialisation turned out to be the most efficient way to deal systematically with the explosive increase in the amount of knowledge. Different research areas emerged. Each of them focused on a specific part of knowledge; each of them developed own theoretical frameworks and methods that fitted well in their specific perspectives and subjects (Vosskamp 1984). Division of labour and diversification became common features of scientific development and brought about the evolution of the specialised scientist. Up to now this development has not come to an end, which is probably due to the outstanding success of this method to stimulate and control the creation of new knowledge that is applicable to the solution of problems and thereby increases wealth and prosperity[2].

The emergence of disciplines, however, did not come along as an isolated process which deeply changed the nature of scientific discovery, but was accompanied by the

---

[2] It is important to note that apart from the more structural and institutional point of view there emerged a functional differentiation within each discipline that has led to the well-known distinction between "basic" or "pure" and "applied" science (Mulkay 1977). This aspect will be further dealt with below.

development of a scientific culture that was closely connected with single disciplines. Far beyond distinctive theories and methods, each discipline cultivated a unique social behaviour makig it discernible from others. The organisation of lectures, the foundation of institutions for research, the emergence of a faculty spirit that decides on the admission of new faculty methods and, thus, on the career of young scientists and even the formation of ideas have been decisively influenced by this culture (Huber 1991). Kuhn (1972) called these specific paths in the creation of knowledge and the evolution of science paradigms, i.e. trajectories of only gradual change in the inherited traditions of single disciplines. Meanwhile this gradual evolutionary process has led to the emergence of nearly 4,000 different subjects in scientific work in almost 30 disciplines (Kaufmann 1987; Kocka 1987). Another aspect which results from the process of scientific specialisation is broadly discussed by Snow (1967) who in his book "The Two Cultures" complains about the negative and disruptive separation of the natural sciences and humanities. Since then both fields of research have developed specific theoretical and empirical methods which can hardly be reconciled. However, each time in history when the development of scientific research hits at insurmountable barriers, each time individual thinkers revolutionised thinking within and beyond the borders of disciplines, and each time when new areas were successfully explored, the traditional structures of disciplines tried to adapt to the new ideas or to integrate them.[3]

Although it was never achieved to restore the former unity of sciences, the ideal philosophers had striven for, there is a lot of insight and motivation to co-operate beyond the borders of scientific disciplines to share views and findings with colleagues from other areas of scientific research. It is quite obvious that the need for co-operation is expressed by scientists representing almost all branches of scientific activity. People like Heisenberg (1984) or Weizsäcker (1978), philosophers, biologists, and sociologists from different countries commonly propose a joint effort of all disciplines to overcome the isolated development of knowledge production in favour of a broader based strategy to tackle problems.[4]

---

[3] E.G. Hübenthal (1989) points out how Einstein's thinking revolutionised the natural sciences, thus altering perspectives simultaneously in physics, chemistry, and biology.

[4] For a review of statements and opinions see Hübenthal (1989); Kocka (1987);and Mittelstraß (1994).

All co-operative activities beyond the borders of different disciplines are generally summarised under the heading of "interdisciplinarity". Before we further investigate the various forms, structures and institutional arrangements of interdisciplinarity research a short look at the common purpose of this form of co-operative scientific activity should disclose similarities and differences in motivation. Main causes for interdisciplinarity are:

First, interdisciplinary research can be looked upon from the perspective of a discipline-bound scientist who struggles with a specific problem in his field of research. He is searching for some kind of help from other disciplines which are dealing with related problems. Co-operation in this case aims at improving the process of knowledge production in his own discipline; it is efficiency-increasing. Authors like Jantsch (1970) and Lenk (1978, 1980) point to the fact that the **improvement of efficiency** to solve problems within single disciplines remains crucial.

Second, there is a group of problems which have come along with the development of modern industrialised societies. Environmental pollution, the problems that arise from nuclear fusion or the avoidance of war are in part a logical and dismal consequence of the success of scientific discovery. As science has adopted the role of a general problem-solver during the last century, it is expected that scientists will deliver **solutions to** these **urgent problems of mankind.** The range of these global problems, however, reaches far beyond the borders of single scientific disciplines. Consequently, scientists from various disciplines are forced to work and to bring out solutions together[5]. Probably because of the widespread public acknowledgement of these problems, national governments have started initiatives for problem-bound interdisciplinary research on specific subjects. The book of van den Daele et al. (1979) deals with the influence of government on national research agendas especially in the area of interdisciplinary projects.

A **third** area of co-operation between different disciplines emerges from the role of technology in modern societies. Technology is commonly regarded as a general

---

[5] See e.g. Weizsäcker (1978); Ditfurth (1984); Kocka (1987); Maier-Leibnitz (1992); Robson (1993).

instrument of problem solution. The influence of technology in daily life is pervasive, there is almost no sphere which does not rely on technical products. As findings in the field of innovation research have shown[6], technology is to a large extent the **application of results from scientific research**. However, new scientific solutions were often steered by problems in the application of new technology, but practical problems generally do not fit in traditional disciplinary categories. More than once, scientific research offered only basic results which could not be matched to technical problems immediately. According to a study sponsored by the U.S. National Science Foundation in the sixties, called TRACES, which looked at the dependence of innovation in industry on basic science, the transfer of results from science to industry often takes as many as 30 years and relies on the close interaction of scientists from different disciplines[7]. Two typical situations have to be mentioned: a new product or process is generated by an integration of findings of different disciplines, or a basic technical solution largely based on one discipline - often called basic function - is applied in areas of other, external disciplines.

As the description of part I of the theoretical and institutional background of the science/technology interface has shown, knowledge transfer between science and industry takes various paths and urges co-operation from different disciplines and institutions. In this context, Grupp (1993b) investigated the development and structure of technology at the threshold of the 21st century. What he found out sharply contrasts with traditional concepts of technology. The emerging technologies will no longer fit common classification schemes because single technological developments will not evolve in isolation but rely on an early and intensive networking between different areas of science, and, thus, different disciplines. Consequently, new technological developments will not be put on track unless scientists and engineers from all disciplines work together.

Technology, as well as its scientific foundations, does not only have to cope with technical problems. Technological development is embedded in a broad socio-economical and political system that judges technological progress according to

---

[6] See e.g. the comprehensive study edited by Spiegel-Rösing/de Solla Price (1977); Grupp/ Schmoch (1992); or Spinner (1994).

[7] For a detailed account of the TRACES study cf. Stankiewicz (1987) and part I, chapter 4.1.

criteria which differ significantly from that of pure technical feasibility. Thus, science-based technology cannot ignore the complexity of problems which exist in daily life. As mentioned above, these problems generally do not fit the discipline-bound organisation of science. The progress in the development of technology is, therefore, crucially dependent on and tied to the co-operation of scientists from different disciplines. This third aspect will be at the centre of the discussion below.

A **fourth** aspect of interdisciplinary work deals with co-operation within single disciplines and might be called **"small interdisciplinarity"** (Hübenthal 1989, 20). This kind of co-operation has come up because of an excessive division of labour even within disciplines. Scientists have to work on interdisciplinary fields within their own discipline because otherwise their specialisation does not allow them to stay in touch with related areas of research. However, this study applies a broader meaning of the term small interdisciplinarity. Co-operation between disciplines which have a relatively high affinity, such as physics and electronics, are considered as small interdisciplinarity. Co-operation between disciplines which are distinctly different, such as physics and medicine, or computer science and biology, is called "big" interdisciplinary research.

A **fifth** cause of interdisciplinarity is linked to typical structures of scientific development. As discussed above, disciplines are based on commonly accepted paradigms and the respective production of knowledge follows quite clear trajectories. In the final phase of a scientific paradigm, the members of the respective scientific community try to leave the field and **search for new paradigms**. These scientific revolutions can generally only be achieved by falling back on findings and methods of other disciplines (cf. Kuhn 1972). Of course, this simplified model of strict paradigms which can only be overcome by scientific revolutions does not describe the scientific knowledge production in a realistic way, because branchings of disciplines and "micro-radical" shifts within a discipline can be observed as well (cf. Mulkay 1977). Nevertheless, interdisciplinarity has a key function for achieving decisive new steps of scientific knowledge.

2.2   Definition of different types of interdisciplinary research

Interdisciplinarity is a concept which has evolved up to the present discussion from its earliest beginnings in the era of Kant when the problem of scientific specialisation emerged. Since then, it underwent several changes in definition and still today there is still no exact definition of what interdisciplinarity means (Hübenthal 1989; Klein 1990). Furthermore, other closely related concepts are often used, which mostly prove to be sub-categories of interdisciplinarity.

According to Jantsch (1970) **multidisciplinarity** represents the weakest form of a co-operation of different disciplines in research projects. In general, multidisciplinarity does not belong to the types of interdisciplinary co-operation because there is no real exchange of theories and methods, but **only a gathering of results** emanating from the work in single disciplines.

Pluridisciplinarity means **co-operation without co-ordination** of different disciplines in one project. **Crossdisciplinarity** describes the integration of two or more disciplines wherein one discipline dominates, and therefore the other disciplines adopt the related methods. An example is the dominance of information science with regard to biology in neural networks (cf. chapter 4.4.3).

Transdisciplinary presupposes (on the basis of applied theories and methods) the **melting of disciplines** which are studying the same problems (cf. Jantsch 1970; Gibbons 1993; Mittelstraß 1994). From an institutional perspective, Lenk (1980) defines the type of closest interdisciplinary work when a new discipline is born out of the "marriage" of single disciplines as the result of a complete fusion of common theories and methods.[8]

Whatever type of definition one is inclined to favour, what all definitions of interdisciplinarity have in common is that there must be some kind of intellectual exchange between the participating disciplines, either with regard to a specific

---

[8] It is worth noting that scientists from Eastern Europe use definitions which only differ slightly from those mentioned above (see e.g. Gott et al. 1984; Kröber 1983).

subject or methodically (Vosskamp 1984); thus multidisciplinarity is excluded. As a common understanding for the term **interdisciplinarity** is necessary this study proposes a pragmatic definition. A co-operation of different disciplines for a common research task is called interdisciplinary research. This definition does not specify the concrete way the co-operation is organised. In the following this broad definition is applied for interdisciplinary research.

Most interestingly during the last decades, a number of interdisciplinary theories have emerged that focus directly on the application of different disciplinary perspectives to wide-ranging problems such as cybernetics or systems theory (Hübenthal 1989).

Beyond the philosophical discussion about what interdisciplinarity really is a number of interdisciplinary research centres have been established - in most cases in proximity to universities. The "Centre for Advanced Studies" at Princeton University or the "Centre for Interdisciplinary Research" ("Zentrum für interdisziplinäre Forschung") at the University of Bielefeld (Germany) might serve as examples for this kind of institutionalised interdisciplinarity which might even start with the scientific training of students (Kocka 1987).

2.3 Interdisciplinary research for technological development

So far the discussion of interdisciplinary research has mainly focused on the sphere of scientific research at universities. Following a broader concept of science (see e.g. part I, chapter 2) industry and independent research laboratories are engaged in scientific research, too. Thus, science is no longer confined to the realms of honourable scholars contemplating in their ivory towers but has become a decisive input into modern technology. Although there is some technological development in university laboratories (think, for example, of the engineering faculties at universities), technology is generally created and applied to products in industrial laboratories. These industrial R&D laboratories have developed as part of the modern industrial process of production and are first and foremost concentrating on the solution of practical problems with the help of scientific knowledge and methods (see, e.g., Freeman 1982). Quite different from university as far as organisation and motivation are concerned, industrial R&D laboratories do not only develop technology but engage in applied or even basic research and thus create new knowledge in the natural sciences (see, e.g., Grupp/Schmoch 1992b).

There is the common notion that university-bound science and technology belong to different cultures of thought and practice. The expression "science community" serves as a synonym for the professional and social distinction of the group of scientists who work on their respective fields of research which are organised in disciplines and faculties and generally characterised by a certain inertia (Layton 1977; Stankiewicz 1986). Dasgupta/David (1992) emphasise the cognitive and methodological difference between scientists working in industry or at universities. They believe some characteristic features to be a constitutive element of the emergence of distinctive research cultures in industry and at university. As crucial factors they regard the socio-economic arrangements that determine the disclosure of knowledge and the reward systems.

Work in R&D laboratories which form the institutional equivalent to faculties and departments in universities is, to a larger extent, determined by the dynamics of practical technical problems which normally do not reflect the structure of the division of science in disciplines. In general, technical problems do not exactly fit the classification scheme of disciplines, thus belonging to several disciplines at the same time. In this context, Mittelstraß (1994, 313) introduces the notion of an asymetry of problem and discipline development. Consequently, **industrial R&D laboratories** must be much more **accustomed to multi- or interdisciplinary research activities** (Layton 1977). This same aspect is also highlighted by Majer (1978) who surveyed the composition of research teams in R&D laboratories in industry. He found out that, in general, they consist of scientists and engineers from different disciplines.

The following pages will deal with a number of questions which focus on the multidimensional relationship between industry and the science community in the field of technology:

One aspect will be, whether appropriate forms or concepts of interdisciplinary research organisation exist in industrial R&D laboratories which are different from those in universities. Another question asks whether there are barriers and difficulties in technological research projects which have their origins in the division of science into faculties and last but not least which kind of co-operation university and industry are engaged in to overcome the differences between the two spheres of science and technology. Special attention is, of course, paid to interdisciplinary approaches.

2.4 Interdisciplinarity in science and technology

Nowadays, the term "technology" describes much more than the narrow conception of an adaptation of technical equipment to practical problems. Technology has reached the significance and function of a social subsystem which is tightly intertwined with all sorts of social relationships, thus, with politics and the economy (Layton 1977; Freeman 1982). Progress in technology relies on the consideration of a broad range of problems in related spheres. Ropohl (1976, 1978) therefore expresses the need for a more holistic, socio-economic view for planning and developing future technology.

Tijssen (1992) concludes from his study of interdisciplinary structures in science and technology that modern technological developments are heavily dependent on a clear-cut definition of practical problems which have to be solved by an intensive interdisciplinary collaboration. Tijssen studies the **emergence of interdisciplinary research fields** with the help of a combination of a bibliometric co-classification analysis and interviews with experts. He found out that the definition of a field of new problems has led to the evolution of a vast network of intellectual relations between single disciplines which have never co-operated before. However, as Tijssen himself admits, his quantitative results may be in some cases misleading, because the exact intellectual contribution of single disciplines to the development of new unique interdisciplinary fields of research can hardly be isolated; consequently a distinction between multidisciplinarity and interdisciplinarity is nearly impossible.

The problem of an exact separation of interdisciplinarity from multidisciplinary co-operation in technology was also part of a study published by Dror (1993) that deals with multitechnology innovations as the driving force for technology evolution and growth. Dror traced back the US patent applications between 1975 and 1984 and singled out those which have been classified as belonging to two different areas of technology. Although it is difficult to decide whether patent applications reflect a multi- or interdisciplinary research co-operation, the results overwhelmingly prove the close relationship between economic growth in single technologies and their emergence as the research outcome of a melting of formerly unrelated technologies. The application of patent analysis to the socio-economic background of technology does not only point to the importance of multi- or interdisciplinary technological research for the solution of economically relevant problems, but focuses also on the emergence and evolution of new technological fields out of formerly single disciplines, i.e. the evolution of transdisciplinary fields. As the results of the aforementioned study of Grupp et al. (1993b) on the development of technology at the threshold of the 21st century imply, future technology cannot be classified according to traditional fields of research and cleary seperated disciplines.

What both studies of Tijssen and Dror however lack, due to the limitations of the methods used, is an assessment of how the bringing together of different technologies is institutionally organised. There is no hint whether the emergence of new technological fields starts within the scientific community or within single disciplines or whether the idea is grasped at in industrial R&D laboratories which are closer to the market.

In the context of the **institutional organisation of interdisciplinary research** we turn to the second field of questions which deal with the barriers that hamper an effective interdisciplinary research co-operation due to the organisation of science in disciplines.

A review of the literature reveals that the there is **almost no theoretical work that deals with the organisation of interdisciplinary co-operation** - either in science or industry. We agree with the verdict of German sociologist Renate Mayntz (1985, 18) who concludes that literature on R&D management is vast, but does not reflect at all the necessary theoretical quality which is crucial for the discussion.

For example, Hanson's (1979) report on the interdisciplinary research efforts to develop and manufacture the first instant photographic film and the special camera at Eastman Kodak mainly focuses on the organisational problems that arise from the notorious shortage of time. His report is a description of different management methods to solve various technical problems, but evades the questions what kind of intellectual contribution each discipline lent to the final solution and how the differences in knowledge and method were melted to form a new true really interdisciplinary team.

Similarly, articles by Hoch (1990) and Kilburn (1990), which describe the functions and problems of Interdisciplinary Research Centres (ICRs) in Great Britain, are predominantly concerned with the questions of strategy and management. Although both authors acknowledge the necessity "to develop from various angles, the scientific 'knowledge base' underlying a potentially key generic technology" (Hoch 1990, 115), they fail to give a detailed account of how the potential for new generic technologies is conceived and later exploited in interdisciplinary co-operation. Both articles, however, - in accordance with Hanson (1979) - point to the various social and organisational difficulties which emerge from the need to break through the barriers of established customs and hierarchy within companies. Kilburn (1990), as an expert consultant in the field of **interdisciplinary research,** points to the fact that the **risk of failure** for this kind of research is fairly **high**. Consequently, interdisciplinary work should be organised in small and highly flexible teams of specialists, who have experience not only in the discipline they usually belong to, but also in some kind of team work. In the case of failure, interdisciplinary scientists often end up with **diminished career opportunities**. Therefore motivation and incentive should be above-average to overcome the **low reputation** that is normally attached to this kind of work.

Interestingly, these problems seem to reflect a basic problem that will emerge if new organisational structures of interdisciplinary research have to overcome the barriers and resistance of traditional structures. As Stankiewicz (1986, 29) describes, similar **problems and resistance** are also common **within the scientific community,** because of a lack of reputation for interdisciplinary research among colleagues and of gloomy career opportunities.

Interdisciplinary research in industry, however, is closely related to the emergence of the industrial R&D laboratory which, for the first time, integrated the spheres of disciplinary science and the needs of daily life via engineering and the development of technology, as is shown in the seminal work of Freeman (1982). Thus,

interdisciplinary research (even if it does not fulfil the exact definition stated above) is much **more common in industry,** because firms have employed a number of scientists and academics who got their scientific training from different disciplines and faculties. In order to get better insights into the process of the co-ordination of these scientists in the industrial innovation process, Majer (1978, 83) asked German firms from different industries in a survey from which disciplines the scientists involved got their training. The results show, firstly, that the dependence on science varies from industry to industry. Secondly, nearly all of the surveyed industries do not only rely on one single scientific discipline. In general, there is a predominance of engineers, but scientists from the natural sciences and humanities also belong to the teams of researchers who are responsible for industrial innovations.

Consequently, as technical problems determine the research agenda, interdisciplinary research is naturally practised in industrial R&D laboratories and scientists are constantly forced to look beyond their own disciplines. Thus, the emergence of a sclerotic structure of single disciplines is avoided in industry. However, recent strategic innovation concepts which stress the need to increase the concentration on the internal resources of companies, the so called "core competencies" (Prahalad/Hamel 1990), point out that their application may lead to obstacles to interdisciplinary research as a negative effect (Leonard-Barton 1992). So the need to assure a continuous improvement of interdisciplinary research has to be taken into account even more for future concepts (see part II, chapter 4.3).

This means, however, that teaching and research at universities does not match to these prevailing interdisciplinary structures in industry, as long as teaching and training of young scientists concentrate on single disciplines; then traditional borders between universities and industry will survive. Thus **the problem of interdisciplinarity seems to be a major barrier of university-industry co-operation.**

The obvious **gap in culture between the scientific community and industry** is further stressed by Stankiewicz (1986, 29), who in his book about university-industry relations, points to the barriers in thinking and communication which are largely due to the discipline-bound organisation of science at university. Industrial researchers often think that this fragmentation of science was established by historical accident, prevents science from coping with urgent problems and is therefore artificial and outdated.

Stankiewicz, however, fiercely defends the discipline-bound organisation of science at universities. Although he agrees upon the fact that an efficient bi-directional transfer of knowledge between university and industry is decisive, he prefers to stick to disciplinary of organisation. Disciplines efficiently perform their function as an academic structure which directs and monitors the progress in science within the frame of a social structure. In his view, problems arising from interdisciplinary research between universities and industries are not necessarily due to the discipline-bound organisation, and thus cannot be remedied by abandoning this structure.

Böhme et al. (1983) analysed the conditions under which scientific specialities could be managed for socially useful purposes without damage to their discipline-bound development. Their study focuses on the appropriate degree of **coexistence between discipline-bound and interdisciplinary research**. They come to the conclusion that there are multiple needs for multi- or interdisciplinary research on each stage in the evolution of a single discipline. Although these needs should never be neglected, specialisation within each discipline is nevertheless necessary. Böhme et al. (1983) therefore propose that in the early stages of a new development within a discipline specialisation must be further pursued until its own scientific paradigms have emerged and the new branch has matured. Consequently, basic research should be confined to university, while applied research and development might benefit from a multi- or interdisciplinary approach which includes industry. This view of the innovation process, however, deeply ignores its complex structure. Universities, industries and a whole network of research institutions work together on all stages of the development from basic research, applied research and development (see, e.g., Grupp 1992b; Grupp/Schmoch 1992a).

At last, we turn to our third question which asks whether there are, apart from all the difficulties presented above, any known forms of co-operation between university and industry. Therefore we refer to a study published by Rappa/Debackere (1992). They analysed the flow of information and the diffusion of knowledge within so-called "technological communities". These technological communities are contrasted with the "scientific communities". They are "defined as the group of scientists and engineers, who are working on an interrelated set of technological problems and who may be organisationally and geographically dispersed but who nevertheless communicate with each other" (Rappa/Debackere 1992, 21; see also Debackere/Rappa 1993 and 1994, and Häusler et al. 1994). The authors depart from a question raised by Nelson (1992) about the motivation of scientists working with competing companies to share and exchange knowledge on newly emerging technologies with competitors and academics from universities. Rappa and Debackere come to the conclusion that there is a significant and fruitful information exchange beyond the borders of discipline-bound research at universities and industrial intramural R&D activities which is often multi- or interdisciplinary in character. In their study they chose as a basis the newly emerging interdisciplinary field of neural networks.

Their analytical strategy is twofold: on the one hand they focus on the type of information and the types of scientists who publish this information. Their results show that the members of this "technological community" hold, on average, doctorates or other comparable degrees in science, which proves that neural networks are strongly "science-based". Although the field of neural networks is dominated by electrical engineers, there are also large groups of physicists, biologists and mathematicians, thus underlining the interdisciplinarity of this field. The community communicates through published papers, conferences, patents and personal contacts. Academics from universities are slightly older and publish more papers, whereas scientists from industry hold more patents, but all in all, the structures are quite similar.

On the other hand, Rappa and Debackere looked at the dynamic structure of this information network and found out that academic scholars usually engage earlier in a new emerging field of technology. Industry, however, largely dominates the later stages, a finding that is in accordance with results for other non-interdisciplinary technologies (Grupp/Schmoch 1992c).

As a consequence, the study of Rappa and Debackere shows that interdisciplinary co-operation between university and industry takes place via the network of "technological communities" but changes and evolves over time, thus reflecting the underlying different structures between the scientific community and industry. The binding element of a technological community is the common interest in a complex technological problem which is attractive for academic scientists as well. In part I, therefore, we suggested to call them techno-scientific communities. The strong common interest obviously stimulates the members of the community to overcome the above discussed hampering factors of interdisciplinary co-operation.

3.   Medical lasers

3.1   Reasons of choice

Within the limited scope of the present study, only two case studies could be carried out, so that an appropriate choice of topics was crucial. For the choice, different criteria were taken into account:

First, the selected area should have a distinct interdisciplinary character where disciplines with normally low proximity have to be integrated.

Second, interdisciplinarity should be linked to technological applications and the above discussed typical situations (cf. section 2.1).

Third, the area should have a clear science-intensive character, so that a potential for the emergence of techno-scientific communities exists.

Fourth, the chosen area should not be purely historic, but still up-to-date.

Fifth, in order to minimise the risk of a bad selection, precursor studies justifying the expectation of relevant results should exist.

Sixth, the area should have a proximity to already existing RTD activities of the Commission.

In the area of medical lasers, two quite different disciplines, physics and medicine, have to be integrated. The interdisciplinary approach is necessary, because a basic functional technology of one discipline is applied in the area of a different discipline, one of the above discussed "standard" situations. Laser technology itself as well as modern medicine are science-intensive, so that there is a high probability of the emergence of a techno-scientific community. The area is still up-to-date; intensive actual research can be observed. Several recent studies on the knowledge transfer from science to technology based on the example of medical lasers, clearly indicate that also an analysis of the aspect of interdisciplinarity will lead to interesting results

(Grupp/Schmoch 1992a; Vianen/van Raan 1992; Noyons et al. 1994). Finally, the introduction of new medical techniques is a major field of activity of the European Commission, especially in the programmes MHR4 and BIOMED1.

3.2   Technological description[9]

3.2.1   History and principles

The term "LASER" is an acronym for 'Light Amplification by Stimulated Emission of Radiation' that means a source of high-energy light which is initiated by the bundling of a certain kind of radiation.

The first successful construction and implementation of a laser apparatus took place in 1960, when T.M. Maiman tested a ruby laser in the Hughes Laboratories in California. This first implementation of laser technology marked a starting point for the application, development and diffusion of a thoroughly new technique to a variety of technical areas. These potential fields of application are the cutting, boring and welding of materials, the improvement of measurement techniques for instruments, information technology and medicine. Since its beginning in the 1960s, progress in laser technology expanded at an ever increasing pace. Especially the exploding development and improvement of new types of lasers - that is, the use of quite different laser materials (see below) - offered possibilities for new and different areas of application.

Looked upon from the perspective of application, laser technology is a young area of research. Its theoretical foundation, however, goes back to the first two decades of this century. In his seminal work on the quantum theory of radiation, Einstein revised

---

[9]   The authors of this study would like to thank Dr. F. Frank for his helpful and illuminating comments on this subject.

Max Planck's theory of the quantum effect and thereby predicted - as a side-effect - the possibility of stimulated emission of radiation. Following the assumptions of Bohr's theoretical atomic model, Einstein concluded that conventional sources of light (such as light bulbs) are emitting a spontaneous photon radiation. In Bohr's model single electrons revolve around the atomic nucleus (which consists of protons and - in general - neutrons) on different levels (orbits). Each of these levels represents a specific energy. Thus, once these electrons absorb any kind of energy (in light bulbs this "energy" comes with the heating of the coil), they change from lower to higher levels ("orbits"). As this "jump" of orbital electrons results in energetic instability, the atoms tend to reduce the energy of their electrons by forcing them back to lower orbits. The change from higher to lower levels of energy is accompanied by the emission of a photon - the energetic equivalent of light in quantum theory (see figure 3.2-1 for the explanation of absorption and the two different types of emission).

Figure 3.2-1:   Absorption, spontaneous and stimulated emission of photons

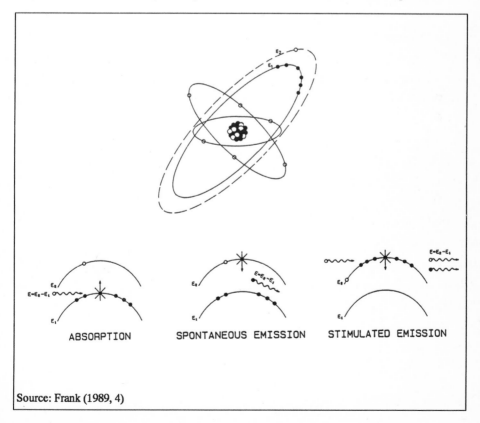

Source: Frank (1989, 4)

The difference between a 'spontaneous' and a 'stimulated' emission of a photon refers to the probability with which the electrons may stay in higher orbits. Normally electrons stay longer than necessary on the higher energetic levels and thus, in a 'spontaneous' emission, they return to lower levels at a lower speed. In contrast, the 'stimulated' emission uses this inertia of high energetic electrons to return to lower energy levels. Using free-wheeling photons of a specific wavelength which hit atoms with electrons on higher energy levels, these electrons instantly return to the more

Figure 3.2-2:   Model of a laser resonator with the excitation and amplification principle

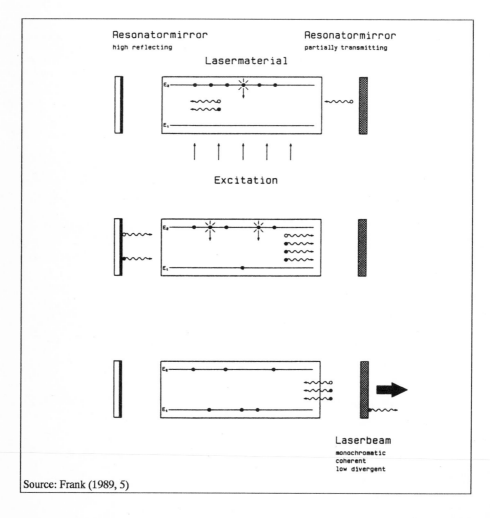

Source: Frank (1989, 5)

stable lower levels. In this process they are emitting a photon of the same wavelength and phase like the free-wheeling photon that caused the emission. In comparison to the 'spontaneous' emission the 'stimulated' emission generates a photon second to the initiating one and at a far higher speed.

For the practical realisation of this accelerated 'stimulated' emission, researchers constructed an apparatus that consists - in its core parts - of a laser-active medium enclosed between two mirrors - the resonator. The laser-active medium - in the first laser, this was a ruby rod - must be a substance with a large potential of electrons that can be excited by the absorption of energy and which can instantly release this energy by the 'stimulated' emission of photons. The mirrors at both ends of the medium serve as reflectors of the photon radiation, thus amplifying the photon emission within the medium. One of the mirrors, however, is semi-permeable, so that a part of the photon radiation leaves the laser as a focused beam of high energy light (see figure 3.2-2 for the model of a resonator).

3.2.2 Properties of laser light and different types of lasers

Regardless of the type of laser medium used, there are certain characteristics of laser light that make it quite different from conventional light sources (such as light bulbs).

First, laser light is monochromatic; that means that all emitted photons are of the same wavelength. Second, the laser beam is temporally coherent, so that all photons are in phase. Third, all photons move in parallel and in the same direction; this results in a highly collimated beam of low divergence. In total, these three characteristics of laser light are responsible for the high energy densities which allow for a broad variety of potential applications.

Different lasers can be characterised by the type of laser medium they use. Since the first use of solid-state laser materials such as ruby, a broad range of different materials has been discovered and tested which are appropriate for application to laser resonators. In addition to ruby, neodym-yttrium-aluminium-granate (Nd:YAG) and Er:YAG (Er: Erbium) proved to be efficient laser materials in the group of solid-state lasers.

In the group of gas lasers the carbon dioxide (CO_2)-laser is dominant for welding, boring and cutting of materials in industrial production, because of its high energy beams. Besides this type of laser there is a variety of gas lasers which use inert gas as laser medium such as argon, helium and other noble gases. During the last years a new type of gas laser has been developed: The Excimer-laser uses a laser medium that consists of two gases such as argon, xenon, chlorine or fluorine which form one molecule if excited and then decay to elements while emitting photons. The Excimer-laser is especially used in medical applications such as ophthalmology.

Figure 3.2-3: The spectral wavelengths of different types of lasers

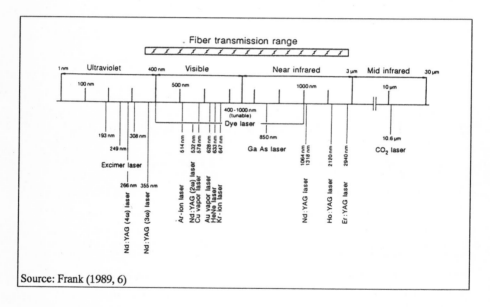

Source: Frank (1989, 6)

Third, there is a group of semiconductor lasers which use a special property of semiconductors that makes stimulated emission possible. This effect, forecast by the mathematician and physicist John von Neumann in 1953 (Sietmann 1993, 85), is used to build small-scale lasers which fit into CD-players and other information technology equipment. Fourth, there are dye lasers which use special dyes as laser medium for special applications where specific wavelengths are required which cannot be produced by the above described materials.

Each laser medium emits photon radiation at a specific wavelength. Figure 3.2-3 shows the spectrum of laser radiation which covers the range from ultraviolet via visible light to infrared radiation. While Excimer-lasers emit photons in the short-wave ultraviolet range at about 200-300 nm, CO_2-lasers produce a radiation of about 10.600 nm. The commercially most important solid-state lasers emit photons at about 1000-3000 nm.

Besides the wavelength, the power density of beams is of special importance for the practical use of lasers. Strictly speaking, the average power of lasers depends on two factors (regardless of the wavelengths): the energy of laser beam pulses and the pulse frequency so that the average power (P_{av}) equals the product of pulse energy (E) and pulse frequency (f)

$$P_{av} = E \times f$$

Average power in laser beams varies between some milliwatt (mW) for gas and semiconductor lasers and some kilowatt (kW) for CO_2-lasers. These numbers refer to continuous wave (cw) lasers; that means they are steadily emitting photons at a constant rate. There are, however, a lot of pulsed laser modes where the average power remains the same, peak power, however, can reach up to 1 terawatt (TW) in CO_2-lasers.

A medium in the resonator is normally excited to higher energy levels by the help of arc lamps or other lasers. As these so-called 'pump-sources' do not instantly excite the laser medium to its highest energy potential, the storage of excitation energy and its sudden release in very short (e.g. some nanoseconds) but highly energetic laser pulses is possible. These so-called 'q-switch' or 'mode locking' lasers allow cutting, boring and welding of any kind of material.

Unfortunately, only a small range of wave lengths of this radiation can be guided through fibers by using the effect of successive total internal reflection (see fig. 3.2-3 for the fiber transmission range). In all other cases, laser beams have to be guided by reflection on mirrors which lead to power losses and handling problems if applied to hidden surfaces.

3.2.3   Lasers in medical applications

As can be seen from the above statements, the application in medicine is just one of several different potential application areas. Medical applications thereby make broad use of lasers as a source of heat or other forms of highly concentrated energy. Already in 1963, thus three years after the first laser source built by Maiman, Goldman used the new source of light for medical purposes (Berlien et al. 1989). Since that time, the interest in this special area of application has steadily grown.

A survey of the broad range of special applications in medicine should be based on an understanding of the basic underlying principles of interaction between laser light beams and biological tissue.

Figure 3.2-4:   Causes and effects of laser-tissue interaction

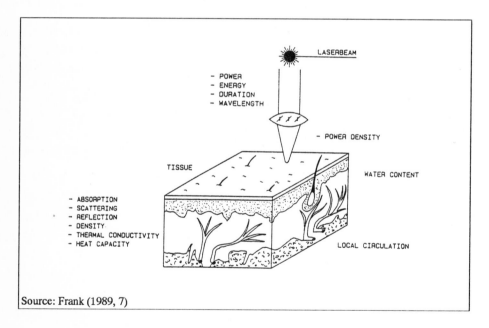

Source: Frank (1989, 7)

The **effect of laser radiation on biological tissue** depends on a variety of biological and physical parameters. As figure 3.2-4 shows, the impact of laser light on tissue is influenced by power (energy and duration) and wavelength as physical parameters.

On the other hand, the water content of the tissue, its structure and the blood circulation affect the results of the laser-tissue interaction.

Depending on the interaction time (IT) of laser radiation and on the power density (PD), three types of interaction can be distinguished (Frank 1989, 7):
- Photochemical effects (IT: 10 s to 1.000s, PD: 10^{-3} to 1 W/cm^2)
- Photothermal effects (IT: 1 ms to 100s, PD: 1 to 10^6 W/cm^2)
- Photoionizing effects (IT: 10 ps to 100ns, PD: 10^8 to 10^{12} W/cm^2)

An extremely long interaction time and low power densities lead to photochemical transformations of the tissue. The photosensitised oxidation uses the absorption of light and the effects of an injected photosensitiser for intramolecular chemical reactions that help to eradicate tumours selectively. At present, research is concentrated on finding and testing of different types of photosensitisers that enable the laser-initiated photochemical reactions. Unsöld/Jocham (1988) have shown that the use of the photosensitiser HpD (haematophyrine derivative) does not only stimulate photochemical reactions in the field of photodynamic therapy, but also allows for a detection of malignant tumour cells in tissue with the help of fluorescence (see also Unsöld et al. 1990). Another example for photochemical effects is the localisation and stimulation of nerves. This is called 'biostimulation'.

Figure 3.2-5:   Thermal tissue alterations following laser irradiation

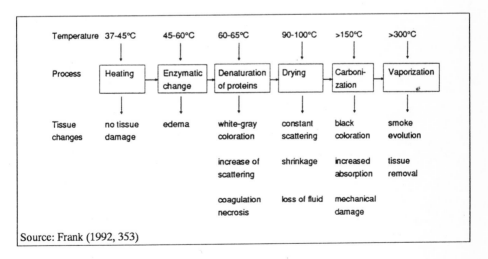

Source: Frank (1992, 353)

When the interaction time decreases and power density increases, photochemical effects are more and more substituted by photothermal effects. Photo thermal effects result from the massive conversion of laser light into heat and are used in surgery for tissue removal and tissue coagulation.[10] Figure 3.2-5 shows the effects of different heating stages on biological tissue.

Figure 3.2-6: Absorption coefficient of tissue and threshold energy density for non-thermal photo ablation depending on wavelength
— Absorption coefficient of H_2O
--- threshold energy density for tissue ablation (mJ/mm^2)

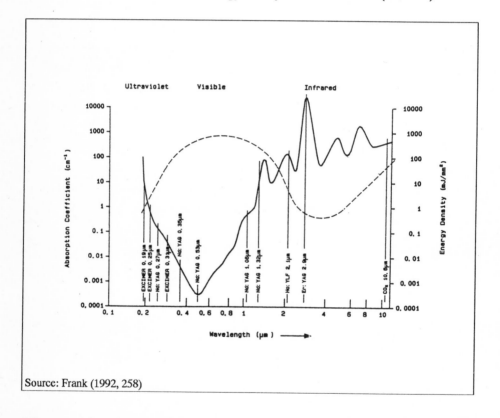

Source: Frank (1992, 258)

The conversion of laser light into heat largely relies on the absorption of radiation in biological molecules. Biological tissue consists - to a large extent - of water.

---

[10] It is quite clear that photochemical reactions are based on the conversion of radiation into heat, too. The difference, however, lies in the dominant form of reaction. In photochemical reactions chemical effects other than tissue burning are predominant.

Consequently, the absorption coefficient of H_2O, depending on the respective wavelength of radiation, roughly represents the heating capacity of biological tissue. Figure 3.2-6 shows the absorption coefficients of H_2O and the threshold energy density for tissue ablation for several types of lasers. As can be seen from the diagram, the ultraviolet radiation emitted by the group of Excimer-lasers and the Ho-laser (Ho: holmium) and Er-laser- (Er: erbium) radiation is largely absorbed in biological tissue. Both parts of the wavelength spectrum are therefore suitable not only for photothermal, but also for photoionising effects - the latter is generated by power densities exceeding the threshold of 10^7 W/cm^2. In this case, non-linear effects lead to the dissolution and ionisation of material. The dissolution of tissue is called 'photo ablation', a process that breaks the intramolecular bonds in tissue. Photo ablation is used for precise non-necrotic cuts in surgery. The ionisation of tissue leads to a strong expansion of the free electrons and the ionised tissue (plasma), which suddenly bursts. This process is called 'photo disruption'. Photo disruption is largely used for the smashing of gallstones, kidney and ureter stones.

Table 3.2-1:   Types of lasers and their potential applications

TYPES OF LASERS AND THEIR POTENTIAL APPLICATIONS

	ANGIOPLASTICITY	LITHOTRIPSY	OPHTHALMOLOGY	SURGERY	ENDOSCOPIC IMAGING	BIO-STIMULATION
EXCIMER (193nm-400nm)	+		++			
ARGON (488nm-514nm)	+		+	+		
He-Ne (632nm)	+/-					+
Ga-ARSENID (910nm)						+
Nd:YAG (1064nm)	+	+	+	++	+	
CO2 (10600nm)				+		
DYE LASERS	+	+		+		

Source: Frank (1992, 353)

Whereas the above description was confined to general biophysical principles, this part should provide a general **survey of the types of lasers used in medicine**.

According to the above distinction between photochemical, -thermal and -ionising effects of laser radiation, we will describe below which kind of effect is mainly used in the fields of angioplasty, lithotripsy, ophthalmology, surgery (in general) and biostimulation. Furthermore, we will relate the fields of application with the corresponding types of lasers (see table 3.2-1 for a matrix of best fit between types of lasers and fields of application). Endoscopic imaging does not fit the selected distinctive criteria mentioned above. Endoscopic imaging with laser serves as a supportive function for other medical applications. Often endoscopic imaging does not rely on laser light sources, but on conventional light. The remaining five fields of application can be roughly divided into biostimulation, which relies on photochemical reactions, surgery and angioplasty, which take advantage of the photothermal effects, and lithotripsy and ophthalmology, which use the photo disruptive and -ionising effects of laser radiation.

In angioplasty laser light is guided through fibers to arteries in order to dissolve blockages in blood circulation which would otherwise lead to heart failure. The most commonly used type of laser for this application is the Nd:YAG laser which allows the photo thermal as well as the photo ablative destruction of the blockages. Sometimes other solid-state lasers such as the Ho-laser are used. The radiation emitted by these lasers is even more absorbed in tissue cells.

The application of lasers in general surgery has started early with the development of the high energetic solid-state and CO_2-lasers. The cutting and removal of large volumes of resistant tissue needs high energy beams which are strong enough to heat the tissue cells beyond their respective temperatures of dissolution. One of the most recent applications is the thermal coagulation of prostate hyperplasy (Muschter et al. 1993) with a Nd:YAG laser in the special field of urology.

Lithotripsy comprises the destruction or fragmentation of gallstones, kidney and ureter stones. This process depends on the almost entire absorption of laser energy which leads to the disruption and fragmentation of material. As the laser light for lithotripsy has to be guided via fibres to hidden spaces, the solid state lasers with radiation within the fibre transmission range (see figure 3.2-3) are preferred.

In ophthalmology, the recently developed Excimer-laser and the Er- and Nd- solid state lasers prevail. The surgical application to eyes relies even more than in lithotripsy on the almost total absorption of radiation in very small volumes of tissue. The conversion of radiation into heat must be confined to small, precisely defined areas - otherwise the surrounding tissue of the eyes will be severely damaged. The use of lasers in ophthalmology is therefore confined to applications such as the so-called 'cornea-shaping' and the cutting of the cornea to reduce eye pressure - so the risk of conventional surgery can be reduced. In ophtalmology, lasers are also used for diagnostic purposes. For example the curvature of the cornea or the structure of the retina can be analysed by laser instruments.

The above-mentioned list of potential fields of application for laser technology falls short of being comprehensive. Laser technology has revolutionised a lot of traditional fields of medicine and has improved many conventional techniques, thus providing a source of progress in medicine. Besides the mentioned applications, there are other fields such as gynaecology or children surgery where laser technology plays an important role in medicine, but where lasers are economically of minor importance (Willital 1989) or where the respective techniques belong to the field of general surgery (such as in gynaecology).

All in all, a broad variety of applications of lasers in medicine is available.

3.3   Bibliometric analysis

In the present study, the analysis of interdisciplinarity is chiefly based on interviews with experts. Due to cost limitations, the number of interviews is relatively small, all in all eight per field. In consequence, the choice of relevant interview partners is crucial for the validity of the outcome. The standard procedure for getting interview partners in new, relatively unknown areas is to read some articles and thereby to identify some relevant experts. During interviews with these experts, recommendations concerning further interview partners are collected. This approach is quite time-consuming and often leads to the choice of less relevant partners, so that quite a high number of interviews is necessary.

Against this background, the basic institutional structures of both fields were examined by means of bibliometric analyses based on patents and on scientific publications. This approach has proved to be very effective for the identification of relevant institutions and experts. In the context of the present study, this approach was helpful, because the interview partners should not only represent major institutions in the area from a technical and scientific perspective, but also include institutions of different European countries. Without the tool of bibliometrics, the aspect of international structures is quite difficult to explore. As a side-effect, the bibliometric analysis does not only highlight institutional structures, but an assessment of country performances and major trends is possible as well.

In part I, chapter 5.4, we have shown that patents and scientific publications are produced during the whole technology life cycle, i.e. in the first innovation stages and also after the introduction into the market place. Patents reflect primarily applied R&D activities; scientific publication basic and applied research and less experimental development.

The patent analysis was carried out on the basis of patent applications at the European Patent Office, because European patents represent a selection of inventions of relatively high technical and economic quality. Furthermore, the situation at the European Patent Office (EPO) is quite balanced, so that it is appropriate for country comparisons. Nevertheless, a certain regional advantage of European countries compared to the United States and Japan has to be taken into account. (For further methodological details cf. Schmoch et al. 1988; Grupp/Soete 1993, 13-21; OECD 1994).

The search strategy in the patent database World Patent Index Latest (WPIL) was performed by a combination of the keyword "laser" and the classification code A61 (medical science) of the International Patent Classification (IPC). Thus, all potential applications in the medical area were included.

As already mentioned above, the first medical application of lasers in dermatology took place in 1963 already. Nevertheless, a broader use in this area could not be observed before the middle of the seventies. Since about 1976, a moderate number of patent applications on medical lasers were registered, and since about 1981, the figures distinctly increased (Schmoch/Schwitalla 1989; Noyons et al. 1994). The

European Patent Office was opened in 1978 so that - due to phase-in processes - valid statistics can be carried out since the beginning of the eighties. The respective statistics show a quite steady increase of the EPO applications for the countries of the European Union up to 1990 and a clear decrease for the last observation year 1991 (figure 3.3-1). Due to a delay of the publication of patent applications of 18 months after the first registration (priority application), more recent data were not yet available. A similar structure with an increase until the end of the eighties and a decrease at the beginning of the nineties can be observed for the United States and Japan as well. For the other countries, the decrease already starts in the middle of the eighties.

Figure 3.3-1:   Patent applications at the EPO of major countries in the area of medical lasers (Database: EPAT, * projection)

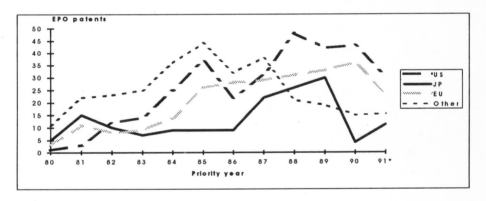

Thus, the patent analysis indicates that the application-oriented innovation activities in medical lasers have passed a - first (?) - maximum at the end of the eighties and, at present, the R&D activities obviously decrease. As to the interpretation of this outcome, it has to be taken into account that patents in the area of medical lasers reflect first of all innovations of technical equipment, whereas "methods for treatment of the human or animal body by surgery or therapy and diagnostic methods practised on the human or animal body" are explicitly excluded from patentability (Art. 52, par. 4 of the European Patent Convention).

Among the countries of the European Union, the patent activities are distinctly concentrated on Germany; France and Great Britain are - on a much lower level - at second position (figure 3.3-2). The patent numbers of the other nine countries of the European Union are nearly negligible. Also on the level of single European countries, the decrease of the innovation activities since about 1988 or 1989 is clearly visible.

Figure 3.3-2:   Patent applications at the EPO of EU countries in the area of medical lasers (Database: EPAT, * projection)

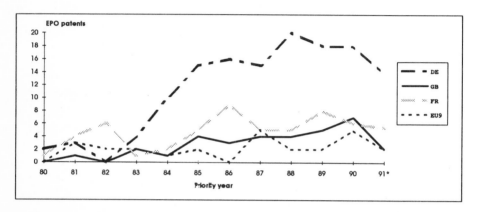

The patent applicants located in the European Union are documented in table A1-1 of the appendix for the most recent period from 1990 to 1991. According to this list, the German dominance in the patent activities is based on a variety of different companies such as Aesculap, Siemens, Messerschmidt-Bölkow-Blohm (MBB) or Schott. In the case of France, the participation of the public or semi-public institutions Centre National de la Recherche Scientifique (CNRS), Commissariat à l'Energie Atomique (CEA) and Institut National de la Santé et de la Recherche Médicale (INSERM) is remarkable. Some French companies, however, such as Cheval Frères or Euroceltique appear in the list as well. In the case of the United Kingdom, isolated patents come from several companies such as Diomed or Elopak. In the European sample, only two patents are taken out by universities.

As the European patent applications already decreased at the beginning of the nineties, a second list for 1988 and 1989 was drawn, as well, in order to see whether the most recent list is sufficiently representative (table A1-2). The comparison of both lists shows, once again, a broad diversity of institutions with quite a low concentration at the top of the list. Only some companies such as MBB, Aesculap,

Alcon, or Zeiss can be found in both lists; but in general, the fluctuation of companies with only one patent is very high. In the upper ranks, the prominent position of Rodenstock at the end of the eighties has to be mentioned.

In table A1-3 the structure of applicants from countries outside the European Union is documented as well. Once again, the concentration at the top end is relatively low and a large variety of companies with only one or two patents can be found. Compared to the situation in the EU, there are relatively more hospitals and universities with own patent activities.

The quite similar structures in all lists with a low concentration on the top positions can be taken as an indication that most companies concentrate on small sub-fields. In the present situation, medical lasers do not seem to be sufficiently interesting for high R&D investments. It has to be noted that the degree of concentration even diminished since the middle of the eighties (cf. Schmoch/Schwitalla 1989, 25).

Table 3.3-1:   Search strategy for medical lasers in the database PASCAL carried out in English abstracts and titles (* right hand truncation)

| Intersection of LASER* with |
| MEDIC*, SURGERY, SURGICAL, THERAPY, PHOTOTHERAPY, TUMOR, GLAUCOMA, CARDIOVASCULAR, RETINA, MACULA, ARTER*, ENDOSCOP*, CATARACT*, or OPHTHALMOLOG* |

In contrast to patent databases, publication databases generally do not cover all areas of science and technology, but only selected parts. Therefore, it is necessary to check to what extent a certain topic is reflected in different databases. The present investigations could build on a publication of Vianen/Raan (1992) who already carried out a bibliometric analysis for medical lasers. They compared the databases PASCAL, INSPEC, BIOSIS and SCI. They got quite good experiences for the PASCAL database and used a pure keyword strategy, which was taken over for the present study. It is based on a combination of the keyword LASER with typical areas of medical applications (table 3.3-1).

Figure 3.3-3:   Publications in the database PASCAL in the area of medical lasers for major countries

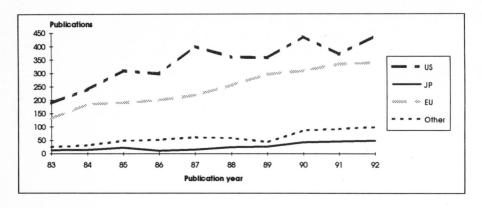

Figure 3.3-4:   Publications in the database PASCAL in the area of medical lasers for EU countries

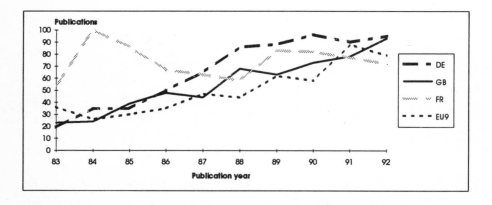

The main advantage of the database PASCAL is the relatively broad coverage of different scientific areas. As for the representation of medical lasers, it is important that publications in biology, medicine, physics, and applied sciences and technology are included. A major disadvantage of PASCAL is the unbalanced coverage of journals as to their national origin, leading to a bias towards French publications. In consequence, the relative position of France in country comparisons is too strong. The results of the analysis in PASCAL is documented in figures 3.3-3 and 3.3-4.

As already mentioned, Vianen/Raan (1992) performed a similar keyword search in the Science Citation Index (SCI). They achieved relatively poor results compared to

PASCAL, because until recently only the titles, not the abstracts, of the publications were available for text searches. Against the background of these experiences, the searches in SCI were redone with a different strategy. Therein, the potential medical applications were not described by keywords, but the search with the term LASER was carried out in a sub-database of the SCI concerning clinical sciences. This strategy led to relevant results and was much more successful than the exclusively keyword-based approach. The respective results of a country comparison in the eighties are documented in figures 3.3-5 and 3.3-6.

Figure 3.3-5:   Publications in the database SCI in the area of medical lasers for major countries

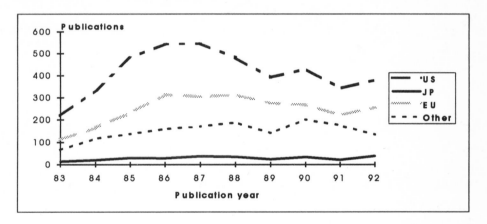

As to the global trends for the United States, Japan, the European Union and other countries, the results in PASCAL and SCI are only partly comparable. First, the ranking of these four groups of countries is the same, but the absolute position is quite different. In SCI, the other countries have a much stronger position then in PASCAL, and also the publication numbers of the United States are relatively higher. Nevertheless, both data bases show quite a low position for Japan, whereas in the patent analysis the Japanese figures sometimes nearly reach the level of the EU. These contradictory results indicate that the Japanese activities in the area of medical lasers have a strong focus on technical equipment, whereas the respective scientific research is relatively weak.

A second difference between the results of PASCAL and SCI is the general increase of the PASCAL graphs, whereas the statistics in SCI show a stagnation or decrease since about 1987, especially for the United States. This latter outcome supports the similar findings of the patent analysis, where the stagnation begins a little bit later in about 1989. The most probable explanation for the trend differences of PASCAL and SCI is the relatively pure journal coverage of PASCAL at the beginning of the eighties, especially of English language journals which were continuously completed during the eighties.

Figure 3.3-6:   Publications in the database SCI in the area of medical lasers for EU countries

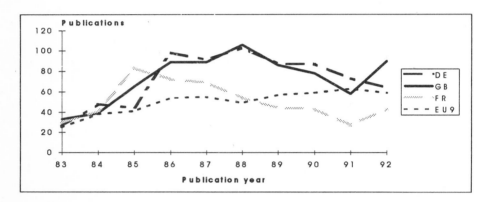

As to the EU countries, the results of both databases are quite comparable, with the major exception of the strong position of France in PASCAL. All in all, the statistics of SCI seem to be more realistic. In comparison to the patent analysis, Germany is not dominating in the scientific area and has a level equal to Great Britain. Furthermore, the scientific activities of the other nine EU countries are much stronger than the technological performance reflected in patents. To sum up, a major result of the bibliometric analyses is the relatively balanced distribution of scientific activities in the EU, whereas the technological realisation is obviously concentrated in Germany.

Similar to patent databases, it is possible to draw up institutional lists in publication databases as well. The preparation, however, is much more complex, first, because the number of publications is distinctly higher than that of patents and, second, the names of the different institutions are less uniform than in the legally oriented patent databases. In consequence, a lot of work has to be invested in database cleaning.

A major advantage of the SCI database is the recording of the institutions of all co-authors of an article so that co-operations become visible. In most other publication databases, only the first institution is mentioned leading to a decisive reduction of institutional information. In the case of the SCI, the co-operations of different institutions are not visible in ranking lists and can only be seen by looking at single records. A detailed analysis of the co-operation structures in form of matrices or by means of multidimensional scaling is extremely time-consuming and could not be realised within the limited scope of the present project. Therefore, the co-operation structures were analysed in a qualitative way by scanning the records of recent publications.

The co-publications of institutions reveal multiple international co-operations, but the dominance of local networks is striking, a result which is confirmed for the area of neural networks, too. For that reason, the institutional list in table A 1-4 is not arranged according to institutions, but according to the cities with the most frequent publications. The list shows furthermore not only the main institutions, but additionally in many cases the respective departments. As to the institutional structures, publication databases are more complex than patent databases, but give much more detailed information.

The institutional ranking list according to patents or publications have to be interpreted with caution, because different propensities to patent and to publish exist. Furthermore, the limitation of the lists to the most recent years can lead to a certain distortion, as the comparison of tables A1-1 and A1-2 already illustrates. Nevertheless, these institutional lists highlight the most important institutions in technology and in science. For the selection of interesting interview partners, different criteria were taken into account:

First, major institutions in the area of technology as well as science should be selected. Second, different types of institutions should be represented in the sample, especially industrial enterprises, universities and other public or semi-public research institutions. Third, the institutions should not be exclusively located in the three largest countries of the EU, but should reflect the activities in other countries as well, where the scientific activities are not at all negligible, according to the publication statistics.

Table 3.3-2:   Institutions selected for interviews in the area of medical lasers

- Dornier-Medizintechnik GmbH, Germering, Germany (Dr. Frank)
- G. Rodenstock Instrumente GmbH, Ottobrunn, Germany (Dr. Dolabdjian)
- University Hospital Leuven, Belgium (Prof. Dr. Rutgeerts)
- Hospital San Raffaele, Laser Medicine Research Group (LMR), Milan, Italy (Dr. Gobbi)
- University of Aalborg, Department of Medical Informatics and Image Analyses, Laboratory for Experimental Pain Research, Denmark (Prof. Dr. Arendt-Nielsen)
- National Medical Laser Centre, University College London, Medical School, United Kingdom (Prof. Dr. Bown)
- Gesellschaft für Strahlen- und Umweltforschung (GSF), Zentrales Laserlabor (ZLL), Neuherberg, Germany (Dr. Dr. Unsöld)
- Centre du Laser et de l'Optronique en Médicine (CLOM, INSERM), Lille, France (Prof. Dr. Brunetaud)

These criteria, of course, cannot lead to an unambiguous choice, but a variety of potential institutional sets is left open. Finally, the eight institutions documented in table 3.3-2 were picked out. As the technology side in the EU is concentrated in Germany, the two German companies Dornier and Rodenstock were selected, the first representing surgical lasers, the second ophthalmologic applications. Both companies are located near Munich and thus belong to the respective local network. The scientific side is represented by four universities or hospitals and two public research centres, so that all types of institutions are reflected in the sample. As to the national distribution, the activities outside Germany, the United Kingdom and France are represented by institutions in Italy, Belgium and Denmark. All in all, the quite small sample of interviews includes a variety of different aspects which are important for the understanding of interdisciplinary structures in the European Union.

3.4   Interview results

3.4.1   Main activities of interview partners

The **Dornier-Medizintechnik** passed through different changes of ownership. Originally, it belonged to Messerschmitt-Bölkow-Blohm (MBB) which was, first of all, engaged in military aircraft and space technology. At that time, the MBB-Medizintechnik was nearly exclusively concerned with medical lasers chiefly in the area of surgery. In the middle of the eighties, MBB was taken over by the Daimler concern, a change with no major impact on the activities of the medical department. At the beginning of the nineties, Daimler acquired the company Dornier, a further aircraft manufacturer with its own medical department. The activities of Dornier in medical technology were chiefly concentrated on kidney lithotripters and ultrasound technology. MBB and Dornier became part of the Deutsche Aerospace (DASA), wherein both medical departments were merged with the name Dornier-Medizintechnik. Within this new department, the medical lasers represent only a minor activity. At the end of 1993, the Dornier-Medizintechnik was sold to the German company group Jenoptik. The interview within this project was still carried out in the era of Dornier-Medizintechnik.

The activities of MBB in the field of medical lasers started at the beginning of the seventies; the first apparatus was commercialised only in 1978. The activities of MBB and later of Dornier concentrate on surgical applications in different non-ophthalmologic areas. The company mainly sells Nd:YAG lasers. Until the middle of the eighties, MBB was a leading company in the sector on a European and a world-wide scale; but in recent years, especially American companies have become important competitors. The business in surgical lasers is not as profitable as forecasted in the eighties due to several reasons: apart from the already mentioned rivalry of other companies, the experiences in the eighties have shown that surgical lasers are in competition with other methods, for example the traditional scalpels or electrical surgery. Therefore, it is important to identify applications which cannot be realised by other methods. A further problem from the perspective of manufacturers is the relatively low price per apparatus leading to a low absolute turnover and profit compared to more expensive equipment like lithotripters or magnetic resonance scanners. In addition, medical lasers have a high durability so that they are only replaced after many years. The latter aspects are, of course, advantages for users of surgical lasers.

The company **Rodenstock Instrumente** works in the area of optics for ophthalmological purposes. It produces glasses, spectacle-frames or equipment for eye specialists, for example slit lamps. Against this background, the laser activities of Rodenstock are concentrated on application for ophthalmological purposes. For therapeutical applications, the company produces different types of gas lasers, for example argon lasers, and Nd:YAG lasers. For diagnosis, laser diodes and helium, neon or argon lasers are used. A leading product in this area is the so-called scanning laser ophthalmoscope (SLO) for the scanning of the eye ground. All in all, the laser market for ophthalmological purposes seems to be more prosperous than the surgical area, because more exclusive fields of applications exist which cannot be replaced by other methods. Nevertheless, the profits are limited due to strong competition from different manufacturers, especially the German companies Zeiss and Aesculap and the American company Coherent.

At the **University Hospital of Leuven,** all types of medical lasers are used. The interview was conducted with Professor Dr. Rutgeerts who is responsible for the department of endoscopy, and therefore the research is concentrated on endoscopic lasers. In Leuven, the first clinical tests with lasers were already performed at the end of the seventies. The topical activities of the department are focused on endoscopes with several laser fibres with enhanced characteristics for the removal of diseased tissue.

The laser medicine research group at the **Hospital San Raffaele in Milano** was established at the end of 1992, so it has been in existence only a short time. The activities chiefly concern the conception and realisation of new medical lasers, first of all in the area of ophthalmology. The group is relatively small and comprises four persons. At present, the group works on different topics: the development of a photo coagulator for ophthalmology, but eventually also for surgery, is nearly finished. A further aim is the development of a Nd:YAG laser with diode stimulation which can replace argon-krypton lasers in ophthalmology and dermatology.

The laboratory for experimental pain research of the **University of Aalborg** belongs to the Department of Medical Informatics and Image Analysis. The work of the group is located in the project area of electro-physiology and biomechanics and is focused on basic research. In the special field of experimental pain research, lasers are used for the stimulation of pain sensitive receptors, e.g., on the skin surface. Thus, the lasers are first of all used in dermatology. The main advantage of lasers is the generation of well-defined signals, so that the level of pain perception can be exactly determined. Although this method is actually first of all applied for experimental purposes, it may be used for pain diagnosis, later on.

The **National Medical Laser Centre** belongs to the Department of Surgery of the **University College London**, Medical School. It was founded in 1984. The research under the direction of Professor Bown aims first of all at the exploration of new medical application areas of lasers by laboratory experiments as well as clinical tests. The group does not develop own technical equipment. At present, the major work concerns a variety of laser applications in cancer therapy, e.g. the interstitial laser photo-coagulation or the photo-dynamic therapy. Furthermore applications in dermatology and in the therapy of artery restrictions are explored.

The **"Zentrales Laserlaboratorium (ZLL)" in Neuherberg near Munich** was founded in 1973 and became part of the then "Research Centre for Environment and Health" (*GSF - Gesellschaft für Strahlen- und Umweltforschung*; today: *GSF - Forschungszentrum für Umwelt und Gesundheit*). The ZLL was one of the first institutions to explore medical applications of lasers. The centre carries out own scientific activities as contract research on behalf of clinics, universities or industrial enterprises. The work comprises the development of new technical equipment as well as laboratory experiments and clinical tests. At present, the main activities concern the areas of photo-therapy and photo-diagnosis, endoscopic laser surgery and different types of analysis. Especially the area of photo therapy is relatively new and the respective research has a quite basic character. For example, the so-called photo-dynamic therapy uses lasers for the stimulation of photochemical reactions in tissues. For that purpose, it is necessary to introduce photosensitive substances into the circulation. The research concentrates first of all on the detection of appropriate photosensitive substances and their interaction with different types of lasers.

The **Medical Laser Institute in Lille** was founded in 1978 and originally belonged exclusively to the public research organisation *Institut National de la Santé et de la Recherche Médicale* (INSERM). It is located in the building of a large hospital centre and near the medical faculty of the University of Lille. In order to co-ordinate their activities and to get a common institutional and legal framework, the clinic, the medical faculty and INSERM have founded the *Centre du Laser et de l'Optronique en Médecine* (CLOM). In consequence, the laser institute has three different financial sources, INSERM chiefly for research projects and the faculty for the personnel; the hospital pays for medical services and buys laser equipment. The institute has the departments of dermatology and of gastroenterology; but the research comprises all application areas of medical lasers with the major exception of ophthalmology. At present, the activities chiefly concentrate on dermatology, endoscopy and gynaecology. The work comprises experimental laboratory research, e.g. animal experiments, and clinical tests in hospital as well as the development of own technical equipment. For example, the institute developed its own laser apparatus for the treatment of skin inflammations or improved a CO_2 laser.

All in all, the selected interview partners represent a broad variety of activities in all areas of medical lasers concerning the development of new technical equipment as well as experimental research and clinical tests.

3.4.2   Future research trends

All interview partners confirm the result of the bibliometric analysis, which shows an enormous increase of the R&D activities in the eighties and a decrease in recent years. The increasing R&D activities correspond to a dynamic - even euphoric - stage, whereas the current situation is characterised by a certain disillusionment, but also a consolidation and higher realism. As a consequence, several institutions involved, especially manufacturers, have left the field. As an example, the Medical Laser Centre in Berlin described the applications in the area of stone destruction still in 1989 in a quite optimistic way (LMZ 1989) and forecasted a broad market potential, but most of these applications have proved to be not competitive with traditional techniques.

Against this background, the future activities in the area of medical lasers will be characterised by two main trends. First, it will be necessary to look for new application areas and to check the existing application ideas in a detailed way. From the perspective of the manufacturers, it will be very important to identify those applications which are linked to broader market potentials in order to stabilise the economic situation. The role of the non-industrial institutions will be to analyse further applications with a medium- and long-term perspective. In any way, a variety of new applications in ophthalmology, dentistry, dermatology or minimal invasive surgery seems to be realistic. Additionally, quite new applications such as the photo dynamic therapy or the use of lasers in biochemical diagnosis seem to be promising, too.

The second main trend will be a more generally oriented research on the interaction between laser beams and tissue. Chiefly, medical specialists see a need for a better understanding of the detailed mechanisms and long-term impacts. According to their opinion, many applications failed because of a precipitate introduction into the market without a sufficient knowledge of the underlying mechanisms. This more basic understanding will be important for the development of new applications and the comparison of laser-based techniques with conventional methods. In the early euphoric phase of medical lasers, this important second branch was not sufficiently developed.

3.4.3   Structures of interdisciplinary research

The organisation of interdisciplinary research is partly based on internal structures, partly on external contacts and co-operations. The specific situation of the examined institutions is quite different according to the specific institutional conditions and the main areas of activity. Therefore, each institution will be discussed separately, and at the end of this section, a common picture of interdisciplinary research in the area of medical lasers will be elaborated.

The medical lasers section within **Dornier-Medizintechnik** consists of about 30 persons including all areas of activities such as development, production, marketing and administration. The research is carried out exclusively by physicists. A first area of activity is the development of new technical equipment wherein the laser source itself is generally bought from specialised manufacturers. The main problem of medical lasers are not the beam source, but the control systems and the conception of a compact, mobile apparatus. Furthermore, the development of appropriate peripheral equipment is crucial, such as transmission fibres, couplings or handles. The second area of research is the identification of new application areas. Against the background of the above described commercial problems, the importance of this second area is growing. For both areas, a close co-operation with medical specialists is indispensable. At the very beginning of Dornier in medical lasers, at that time headed by MBB, first prototypes were put at the disposal of clinics and sometimes self-employed physicians, and the MBB researchers assisted and observed the work for long periods of several months. Thus, the MBB physicists acquired a certain level of medical knowledge from the physicians in the hospitals, and the physicians for their part learned from the physicists. In consequence, both partners could profit from their relation. The attempt of MBB to employ a physician proved to be not helpful, because the "industrial doctor" was not acknowledged as a valuable expert by the physicians in the hospitals.

From the perspective of Dornier, the hospitals (or university hospitals) are the most important external partners. At present, the presence of Dornier staff in hospitals is not as extensive as in the early periods, but still necessary. The medical specialists are especially important for the identification of new areas of application. Whereas in the early periods most of the external partners of Dornier, respectively MBB, were located in the Munich area, the network was enlarged and other specialists in Lübeck or Berlin were included. Apart from universities, there exist or existed co-operations with medical laser centres such as the *Zentrales Laserlaboratorium* in Neuherberg (ZLL), the Medical Laser Centre in Lübeck (MLL) or the Medical Laser Centre in Berlin (LMZ Berlin). Dornier was one of the founding members of the LMZ Berlin; other founding members are the companies Zeiss, Aesculap and Braun as well as the state of Berlin. The advantage of such research centres is the common sharing of research expenditures which is chiefly advantageous in the area of basic research. In the area of applied research, however, there is always the danger that the know-how of one partner is taken over by another partner. All in all, the concentration of activities in research centres seems to be useful for avoiding a duplication of research activities.

To sum up, interdisciplinarity is a crucial element of the research activities of Dornier. It is chiefly organised by a co-operation with external partners whereby the relations to clinics are the most important ones. Furthermore, the company collaborates with specialised research centres in the area of medical lasers. Most of the co-operations are carried out within Germany, whereas the contacts to foreign partners are less extensive. Of course an exchange of ideas with foreign partners takes place, but formal co-operations in terms of laboratory experiments or clinical tests are seldom. There is no real co-operation with manufacturers of laser sources, because the necessary know-how is brought in by the Dornier specialists themselves who are generally physicists with experiences in the area of laser systems. The laser source manufacturers only act as suppliers, and they influence the work of the producers of medical laser systems by the introduction of new sources, for example diode lasers or dye lasers. The outcomes of the application research for medical lasers generally do not have any feedback to the research in the area of laser sources. The example of Dornier is discussed in a quite extensive way, because it seems to be quite characteristic for the structures of different actors in the field of medical lasers.

The company **Rodenstock Instrumente** has about 30 employees in the development department which cover all types of activities, not only medical lasers. The staff belongs to the areas of electronics, optics, informatics or precision engineering, but not to physics. Hence the structure of the staff is different to that of Dornier with a focus on physicists. In consequence, a certain internal communication between the different disciplines is necessary. The differences, however, are not really fundamental, so that there are no critical communication problems. As to the collaboration with medical specialists, external co-operations with clinics and physicians are necessary, similar to the situation of Dornier. In ophthalmology self-employed physicians play a more important role than in the area of surgery. As a typical pattern of co-operation, a physician gets a laser apparatus for three months free of cost and prepares a report on his experiences in return. For Rodenstock, the penetration of the market was easier than for Dornier, because it was already active in the production of other ophthalmological equipment and the respective distribution channels already existed. For more basic research projects, the company has intensive co-operations with clinics and universities in the southern area of Germany, especially with the Institute for Medical Lasers (ILM) in Ulm. Furthermore, common research projects with the GSF - "Forschungszentrum für Umwelt und Gesundheit", Department of Applied Optics in Germering are undertaken, for example concerning the development of a system for monitoring of ophthalmological surgery on screen. The co-operation with producers of laser sources seems to be more intensive than in the case of Dornier - perhaps because the staff of Rodenstock does not include physicists. But the co-operation with manufacturers of laser sources are clearly less important than that with clinics, universities or research centres. The co-operation with institutions of foreign countries concern - similar to Dornier - first of all an exchange of information and less joint research projects.

In the **University Hospital Leuven,** 15 persons work in the area of endoscopy, thereof 6 scientists, all of them physicians. Within the department, no physicists, engineers or technicians are employed. In consequence, the research in the area of endoscopy is focused on laboratory experiments, for example animal experiments, and chiefly clinical work. The aspect of interdisciplinarity with non-medical disciplines only comes in by way of a co-operation with external partners, first of all producers of medical laser systems. The Leuven hospital collaborated first of all with the above presented German manufacturer MBB/Dornier and some French companies such as Satelec. In this regard, Leuven represents the other side of a collaboration between manufacturers and clinics. For non-ophthalmologic lasers, it is not customary that the manufacturers give any financial advantages to clinics. The clinics even have to buy the equipment for their research. Hence the co-operation with manufacturers is less attractive. For that reason, the endoscopic research group, in recent years, has a growing co-operation with the faculty of physics of the University of Leuven with the major advantage of short distances in the case of technical problems. For the future, the establishment of a central laser laboratory for the clinic with the integration of technical specialists is projected, in order to achieve a higher independence.

The **Laser Medicine Research Group (LMR)** at the hospital San Raffaele in **Milan** consists of 4 members, three electrical engineers and one engineer with mechano-optic orientation. Thus, there is no physician in the research group itself. In consequence, the activities concentrate on the development of new medical laser systems. The group, however, belongs to the hospital and has a close relation to the clinical work, especially to the Department of Ophthalmology (Prof. Brancato). Therefore, interdisciplinary research can be internally realised within the clinic without the necessity of including external partners. Nevertheless, co-operations with Italian universities, especially Milan, Pavia and Florence, exist. Co-operations with manufacturers of medical laser systems do not concern research activities, but chiefly the production and marketing of the equipment developed by LMR.

By comparison to the above described institutions, the situation at the **Laboratory for Experimental Pain Research in Aalborg** is completely different, because the research does not aim at the development of new laser systems or applications. The research has a very basic character and the laser is mainly used for measuring purposes. Nevertheless, the structures in Aalborg are very interesting for this study, i.e., in which way interdisciplinary research should be organised. The research activities take place within the Department of Medical Informatics and thus belong to the area of biomedical engineering. In most countries, universities offer supplementary training courses of biomedical engineering after basic studies in mechanics or electrical engineering.

In Aalborg, the students start from the very beginning with an interdisciplinary education in engineering as well as biomedicine. Thus, the basic education comprises disciplines such as economics, mathematics, biology and physics, and the later phases concentrate on biomedicine. A major aim of the studies is the communication between different disciplines. All in all, in Aalborg real transdisciplinary research is realised, because interdisciplinarity is not performed by a collaboration of specialists from different disciplines, but by researchers with an integrated education in different disciplines. This new quality of transdisciplinary research would be very fruitful for the development of new medical laser systems as well.

The **National Medical Laser Centre** at the **University College London** comprises about 15 persons, most of them with a medical education, but researchers with purely scientific backgrounds such as biochemistry are also represented. The necessary technical knowledge is acquired by the practical work in the Centre. In addition, a close co-operation exists with two specialists of the Department of Medical Physics, who exclusively work in the laser area. In this situation, external co-operations with manufacturers are slowly beginning to exist. The work of the centre is about evenly divided between experimental laboratory work on understanding the effects of laser light on living tissue and the clinical work. This integration of laboratory and clinical work can be regarded as the greatest strength of the centre. Clinicians and scientists are working together and taking the results of the laboratory experiments straight into the clinic.

In contrast to the situation in London, the **Central Laser Laboratory (ZLL)** of the GSF in **Neuherberg** is explicitly oriented on interdisciplinarity, on the one hand physics and similar areas and on the other hand medicine. The head of the laboratory, Dr. Dr. Unsöld, is a physicist and assistant professor in medicine. The laboratory has broad technical equipment at ist disposal, including different types of lasers, complete laboratory and surgery equipment and the own breeding of experimental animals. The other employees of the laboratory, at present about 15 persons, are mainly physicians, but also physicists, biologists, chemists and engineers in precision mechanics. The work within the ZLL is focused on the development of new or improved laser systems and laboratory experiments. Clinical research is realised in co-operation with several hospitals especially in the Munich area. Thus, the laboratory is largely independent and only needs external co-operations for clinical studies. Furthermore, nearly all German manufacturers of medical lasers have used the laboratory because of its good technical equipment. Joint research projects chiefly concerned the development of new complex systems, such as Rodenstock's scanning laser ophthalmoscope.

The **Medical Laser Institute in Lille** has an independent structure similar to that of the ZLL. In the institutes, 11 scientists and about the same number of technicians and other personnel is employed. The scientists comprise 3 physicians, 2 engineers and 6 PhD students in the areas of biomedicine and biomedical engineering. Thus, the research team reflects the interdisciplinary orientation of the work, which includes laboratory experiments and clinical studies as well as own developments of laser systems. In recent years, however, the research on technical equipment aims at the improvement of existing apparatus, not at the generation of completely new systems. The Centre has bought different laser systems from several manufacturers, first of all French manufacturers like Satelec. At present, there is no French producer anymore. The Centre was not engaged in close research co-operations with manufacturers, but gave licences of its own developments to French manufacturers. Contacts to external institutions, for example the Medical Laser Centre in Berlin, concern first of all the exchange of information. Furthermore, the head of the Centre, Professor Brunetaud is member of the Société Française des Lasers Médicaux which aims at the systematic promotion of research and the training of physicians in order to achieve a broader diffusion of medical lasers.

The interviews have revealed the existence of a variety of institutions which are active in the field of medical lasers and which organise the "big" interdisciplinarity between physics and medicine in quite different ways. It is, however, possible to elaborate some main structures. As a first major outcome of the analysis, there is no intensive communication between, on the one hand, actors in the area of medical lasers and, on the other hand, actors in the area of laser beam sources. The main linkage between these two groups is the transfer of new types of laser sources to potential applicants whereof the usefulness is checked for medical applications. This situation is depicted in figure 3.4-1.

The major actors in the field of medical lasers are manufacturers, hospitals or university hospitals, universities - in general with close linkages to hospitals - self-employed physicians and public or semi-public research centres. These different actors constitute an innovation-oriented network, respectively a techno-scientific community. The interactions between these institutions include an exchange of information as well as direct research co-operations. It is interesting to note that Meyer (1992) found quite similar actor structures for the research networks built in the framework of the MHR4 programme.

A first type of a typical research co-operation is the application-oriented research and development concerning laser systems of the manufacturers and the respective laboratory tests and clinical studies of universities, hospitals and self-employed physicians. Thus, the linkage of different disciplines is realised by the collaboration of different institutions.

In addition to these direct co-operations, many universities and hospitals perform own research activities independently of manufacturers. This latter activity has a more basic character; but in terms of the Frascati definitions the term "basic research" would not be appropriate, because "basic research is ... undertaken primarily to acquire new knowledge ... without any particular application or use in view" (OECD 1993). In the area of medical lasers every research is oriented to applications - perhaps with the exception of the above described experiments in Aalborg. In consequence, the independent research at universities and hospitals should be called "generally directed applied research" in contrast to "specific applied research", a distinction which was suggested for the new version of the Frascati Manual, but which was not included, because the experts involved could not agree on a common definition. In the case of independent research of universities or hospitals, the respective institutions try to organise interdisciplinarity by mixed research teams or by the co-operation of different groups within one institution. Some universities and hospitals perform purely medical research, wherein the involved researchers try to achieve a certain basic knowledge of laser physics by practical experience and reading. The outcome of the interviews, however, clearly shows that this approach can only be a temporary solution and that in the long run the establishment of substantial supplementary activities in laser physics is necessary.

Figure 3.4-1:   Actor structures in research for medical lasers

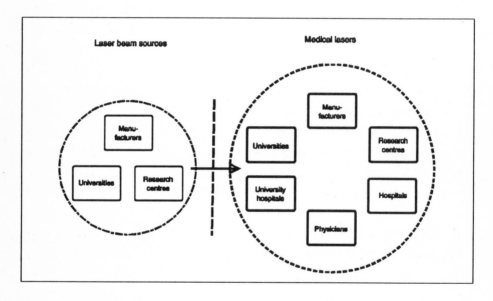

Some universities and hospitals, especially the laser research centres, undertake own developments of medical laser systems. In contrast to manufacturers, they have closer direct linkages to medical specialists and their research is more generally directed. In some cases, like the ZLL in Neuherberg, there exist joint research projects of industrial and non-industrial institutions for system developments. In most countries, however, several non-industrial institutions develop their own technical equipment without any linkage to national manufacturers.

One has to be aware that in the application-oriented area of medical lasers, many research activities have a strong dissemination aspect. The co-operations between manufacturers and hospitals do not only aim at clinical studies, but are also important marketing instruments. Many hospitals and research centres offer training courses for interested physicians in order to achieve a broader spread of the technology. The aspect of dissemination is very important for the future prospects of medical lasers and should not be neglected.

3.4.4   Problems of interdisciplinarity

At first sight, the organisation of interdisciplinarity in the area of medical lasers seems not to be very problematic. Indeed, the interviews show that the interdisciplinary co-operation within the area of technical equipment, comprising physicists and engineers in electronics, precision mechanics or optics, works quite well. However, clear barriers between technical and biomedical disciplines exist, which are reflected in a quite strict separation of the organisational structures. There are, for example, the technical specialists on the side of the manufacturers and the medical specialists on the side of the hospitals. Within the hospitals, a clear distinction of the medical and technical departments can be observed. Among the interview partners, only some institutions have really interdisciplinary teams within one organisational unit, the ZLL in Neuherberg and the CLOM in Lille. Many interview partners see very different scientific and organisational cultures of the technical and medical areas leading to communication problems.

The quite strict and closed structures in the medical area seem to be a decisive problem, so that the introduction of new ideas from external disciplines largely depends on the initiative of single, open-minded persons. This general statement does not apply to all countries in the same way; for example, the structures in Germany and France seem to be more rigid than in Denmark.

Only in Denmark, a clear transdisciplinary approach already in the stage of university education is visible, whereas in other countries biomedical engineers have chiefly a technical education and got only a limited supplementary knowledge in biomedicine.

From the perspective of the technical specialists, the physicians have an insufficient knowledge of technical problems which sometimes is expressed in quite naive expectations of the performance of technical systems, or in a very slow adaptation to new systems. From the perspective of the physicians, the technicians do not sufficiently see biomedical problems, for example, they underestimate the problems of long-term effects on tissue. Interestingly, the least problems of communications between technical and medical experts seem to exist in ophthalmology, obviously because the respective medical specialists need a broad understanding of optics.

In any case, there seems to be a need for a better mutual understanding and a more intensive dialogue. The existing structures of single manufacturers and a variety of highly engaged physicians have proved to produce a variety of important results so that these structures should not be called into question. Nevertheless, really interdisciplinary research centres like the CLOM in Lille or the ZLL in Neuherberg have a key function for achieving major shifts in the two main lines of future research, the identification of new applications and the basic understanding of the interaction of laser beam and tissue.

3.4.5   Areas of public promotion

The situation of public support for medical lasers on the national level is not comparable in different member countries of the European Union. The German Ministry for Research and Technology (BMFT, since 1994 BMBF) recently launched a specific programme for medical lasers, and in France medical laser research is financed in the framework of the National Research Association INSERM. In addition, the research activities are supported by specific sources, for example through the general research budget of a hospital. In most other countries, no specific promotion from the side of the government exists, so that the main part of the budget comes from the already mentioned specific sources. Only since recently the basic research at the University of Aalborg has been getting major funds from the government, which, however, is not a usual situation. The Danish government generally prefers the promotion of applied research. In view of this **generally uncertain budgetary situation in most EU countries**, every support is helpful for many institutions so that a promotion from European Commission would play a decisive role.

Nevertheless, the different interview partners have different, sometimes contradictory demands on the orientation of public promotion, especially from the side of the European Commission. Nearly all institutions underline a positive role in supporting co-operative research projects, especially for bringing together research teams of different disciplines and of more basic and more applied orientation. The above discussion on future trends of medical laser shows that this orientation will be decisive for the further development of the area. Many institutions see the necessity for co-operation also against the background of a limited market. Co-operations can help to achieve a sufficient economy of resources and a "critical mass" of the research teams.

The manufacturers suggest that a support programme for medical lasers should be, already from the beginning, accompanied by an advisory board wherein experts of the industry are represented in a sufficient way. This instrument has been actually established for the German research programme on medical lasers in order to guarantee an orientation on research topics which have a sufficient proximity to industrial applications. The manufacturers additionally mention the not yet unified admission procedures of medical apparatus as a major barrier for a co-operation with other European partners.

Nearly all interviewed institutions want to have a less rigid definition of the aims of research projects. Due to the long delays from a first proposal to the actual realisation of the project, the priorities of manufacturers can change, and a strict binding to former targets would lead to more or less irrelevant results. From the perspective of more basic research institutions, it is not possible to define all outcomes of a research project in advance so that the necessity of a clear definition of research targets in the proposal is an enormous limitation. In any case, it would be very helpful during the execution of a research project, if the targets can be modified, for example in consultation with an expert group of the Commission.

Many - not all - interview partners complain about the application procedures for public research programmes especially for the European programmes. Major points of criticism are the complex and very bureaucratic requirements of the application, so that a participation in a call for tender is very time-consuming. As a further problem, insufficient expertise of the decision-making committee is mentioned. In this context the admission procedures of the German Research Association (DFG) are pointed out as a positive example where competent experts decide on the bids. The sometimes long delays between the application and the grant of research projects are criticised as well. Some institutions have gained the impression that lobbyism is a decisive element for getting research contracts from the Commission. These arguments, of course, are largely influenced by subjective experiences. Nevertheless, they show that the Commission should think in more detail about possibilities to reach also those institutions which have a high quality of research, but which are less experienced in application procedures of European programmes.

Because of the variety of research activities in Europe, the **organisation of workshops and conferences** is a further decisive instrument of promotion. In that context, the respective disciplinary forums in the MHR4 programme (cf. Vinck/Laredo 1992, 108) are positively appreciated. As major purposes of conferences, the information on activities of other groups, the presentation of own results and the establishment of personal contacts and of networks are mentioned. The major focus of the respective activities should not be a multiplication of conferences and meetings, but the achievement of a higher quality. Some interview partners see, in the present situation, a higher quality of conferences in the United States and a lower level of those in Europe.

Some institutions favour a promotion of the exchange of specialists, for example of PhD students and chiefly postdoc scientists. Thus, the respective orientation of existing EC programmes is confirmed.

Problems concerning the establishment of networks are sometimes not due to insufficient European activities, but to insufficient national support. For example, the National Medical Laser Centre in London aimed at a participation in a European network which was supported by an EUREKA project and invested a lot of time in the preparation. The centre had to stop this project because the British government withdrew its support.

As to the **dissemination of already existing RTD results** of EC programmes, the support of publications and conferences are appropriate media. All interviewed institutions do actively publish - a main criteria for their selection - or participate in conferences. But, as already mentioned, the quality of conferences has to be sufficiently high to attract the interest of the scientists. The results of the interviews clearly show that in the area of medical lasers, a network of specialists of academic and industrial institutions exists who communicate through publications, conferences or direct personal contacts; hence a techno-scientific community according to the definition of Rappa/Debackere (1992) has been established.

The bibliometric analysis has revealed that a broad variety of institutions perform active research in the area of medical lasers. Against the background of the above discussed scientific and economic problems, a co-ordination of these activities is crucial in order to achieve a higher efficiency. The suggested instruments of co-operative research projects and conferences are - without any doubt - important means. The analysis of the area, however, has shown that decisive problems, such as the interaction of laser beam and tissue in different applications, cannot be solved within short-term projects. Therefore, the establishment of long-term, but temporary networks of different research institutions seems to be an appropriate tool. This type of **institutional approach** beyond the scope of specific RTD programmes has already been discussed in part I of this book. The area of medical lasers is an appropriate example for this instrument of promotion. One could imagine the establishment of several networks of about 10 manufacturers, research centres and hospitals with an international and interdisciplinary structure wherein, because of the long-term character, only a general orientation is given at the beginning and the precise intermediate steps are agreed on the course of the common work by a discussion of the participating institutions and experts from the side of the Commission. This long-term orientation would reduce the bureaucratic load and improve the mutual understanding of the partners, and in consequence, improve the efficiency of research.

A further instrument for the co-ordination of research activities can be the establishment of a **register of European research groups** in the area of medical lasers and a documentation of their major projects. This approach has to be seen as a supplement to conference activities, because not all projects can be presented in the limited framework of conferences. On the basis of such a register it would, for example, be possible that a research group with the main focus on applications in dermatology can compare its orientation and results with those of other groups in the same area. The authors of this report, at any rate, got the impression that a broad duplication of research activities exists.

All in all, the results of the bibliometric analysis and of the interviews underline the necessity of a promotion especially of interdisciplinary aspects. On the basis of related research activities, a solution of the present problems can be forecast. It should be called to mind that the present economic problems are largely due to positive characteristics of medical lasers, i.e. the low price and the high durability, so that medical lasers are, in any case, an important step forward for medical diagnosis and therapy.

4.   Neural networks

4.1   Reasons of choice

The choice of neural networks as second area of analysis was based on the criteria already described in section 3.1, i.e. distinct interdisciplinarity, context with technological applications, clear science intensity, topicality, existence of precursor studies and proximity to EC programmes.

In detail, the area of neural networks has a highly interdisciplinary character, comprising different disciplines such as physics, informatics, mathematics and electrical engineering. These areas, however, have still a certain proximity, so that in some respect the above mentioned concept of "small interdisciplinarity" seems to be an appropriate description. Against this background, the main reason for the choice of neural networks was the relevance of respective activities in biology and psychology, both disciplines being clearly distinct from disciplines oriented towards mathematics and physics. At the beginning, it was not clear whether findings of biologists were only relevant in early stages or whether they still have a decisive impact on the development of this area. The positive decision was mainly influenced by a publication of Rappa/Debackere (1992) on communication structures in the area of neural networks. In this article, they published a table of the disciplinary affiliation of the involved scientists which is reproduced in table 4.1-1. According to this list, about 16 per cent of the academic researchers and hardly 4 per cent of the industrial researchers belong to the disciplines of biology or psychology, so that at least on the academic side, a distinct participation of these areas in recent years is documented. The study of Rappa/Debackere is focused on North America, and it is not clear if biology has a similar position in Europe. Therefore, one important aspect of the present study is the examination of the impact of biology on the area of neural networks in Europe.

Neural networks are a typical example of the situation in which a new technology is generated by the integration of different disciplines. Thus, neural networks are linked to technological applications, but the structures are different to medical lasers, where interdisciplinarity is the result of the application of a basic technology in a different discipline.

Neural networks are clearly a science-based area, and the already mentioned article of Rappa/Debackere (1992) documents the emergence of a respective techno-scientific community.

Table 4.1-1:   Major field of highest academic degree for academic and industrial respondents in a survey of Rappa/Debackere (1992) in the field of neural networks

Major field of highest academic degree	Respondents with an academic affiliation (N = 283)		Respondents with an industrial affiliation (N = 112)	
	N	% of total	N	% of total
Electrical engineering	99	35.0	57	50.9
Physical sciences	51	18.0	30	26.8
Computer science	44	15.5	10	8.9
Biological science and engineering	31	11.0	1	0.9
Mathematics	18	6.4	8	7.1
Psychology and cognitive science	15	5.3	3	2.7
Neural networks	12	4.2	1	0.9
Other	13	4.6	2	1.8

Neural networks are a quite young and dynamic area of a high topicality. There are, however, sufficiently long time series for analytical purposes. A former analysis of Schmoch/Koschatzky (1991) has shown that R&D activities on the technical side enormously increased since the middle of the eighties (cf. also Raan/Tijssen 1993). The considerations in the next section on technical aspects will show that neural networks open up completely new perspectives for information technology and perhaps will even establish a new paradigm.

As to the last criterion of choice, the proximity of neural networks to European RTD activities is high; they are already promoted within ESPRIT.

To conclude, neural networks are a very interesting topic for the analysis of interdisciplinarity.

4.2   Technological description

4.2.1   History and principles

An increase in efficiency and capability of conventional data processing techniques was often realised by miniaturisation, and thus, a higher integration of the devices. This approach leads to reduced propagation times or an increase of density. But the existing technology increasingly approaches physical limits. Due to different barriers set by thermodynamics, quantum mechanics and electromagnetic theory, further miniaturisation is restricted. Furthermore, material limits, especially of the primarily used material silicon, have to be considered.

But several computational tasks are still going beyond the capability of existing technology. Therefore, researchers are looking for new solutions. Different ways are being pursued. One of them, which is becoming increasingly popular at present, is the concept of neural networks. Neural network research is based on the idea of simulating the functions of the human brain which may be considered as a highly developed information processing system, much more complicated and efficient than any computer (Nicolini 1991).

The architecture, and thus the functioning of conventional information processing machines and the human brain are totally different. Whereas computers are built according to the von Neumann architecture, the brain uses principles of parallel processing. Both systems have their special strengths and weaknesses. Up to now, conventional computers demonstrate their superiority to the human brain primarily in the area of problem solution by using clearly defined algorithms. But they fail in the area of fuzzy problems, that means problems with limited chaotic influence as for instance, pattern recognition (Kinnebrock 1992, 8-10), which cannot be solved by means of classical logic.

Neural networks are information processing devices - sharing their structure and nomenclature with the biological original. They consist of a large number of highly connected elements. These elements - the neurons - are simple non-linear processing modules, whereas the connecting elements have information storage and programming functions. But these structures represent only a very coarse and simplified idealisation of reality (Abu-Mostafa/Psaltis 1987; Hinton 1992; Collins 1993).

The idea of simulating information processing principles as realised by the human brain was born already in the 1940s by McCulloch/Pitts. In 1943, they opened the discussion on "neuro-logical networks" (McCulloch/Pitts 1943). They developed a model of neural activity according to which the neuron is adding exciting and inhibiting impulses being received by the neighbouring cells. An action potential will be set off only if the sum of the electrical impulses reaches a specific threshold.

A lot of research activities took place in the 1960s. This period was followed by a phase of disillusionment because of exaggerated expectations of the capabilities of neural networks. Due to the discontent with other methods of artificial intelligence we can observe, since about the beginning of the eighties, an increasing interest in the development of neural networks (Hart 1992).

Figure 4.2-1:   Model of a biological neuron

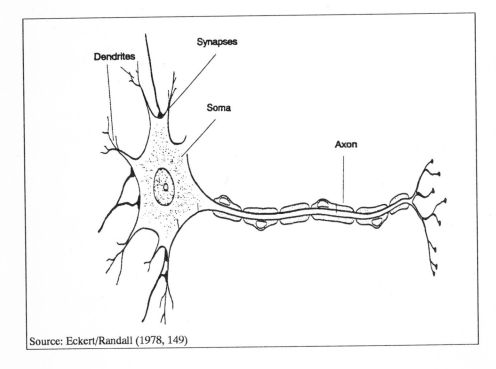

Source: Eckert/Randall (1978, 149)

For the understanding of the concept of neural networks, it is helpful to describe some basic assumptions adopted from the biological knowledge about the functions of the human brain. The human brain comprises about 10^{10} neurons. Each neuron is connected with approximately 10^3 other cells. All neurons and their inter-connections form a neural network. A single neuron consists of the cell body (*soma*) - responsible for realising the essential functions of metabolism, and two types of branches - a considerable number of *dendrites,* serving as information receiver and one *axon,* transmitting information to other neurons (figure 4.2-1). The point where two neurons become inter-connected and the information passes on to the next neuron is called the *synapse.* The synapse is separated from the following cell by the synaptic gap.

Transfer of information is realised by electrochemical impulses, moving through dendrites towards the cell body and away through the axon. When these impulses reach the synapses, "certain chemicals are released. These are called neurotransmitters and are related to hormones. The neurotransmitters diffuse across the synaptic gap and affect the cell membrane on the other side. The effect can be either to enhance or inhibit the receptor cell's own tendency to emit impulses" (Brunak/Lautrup 1990, 38). If the resulting impulse exceeds a certain threshold, an action potential is sent off and the impulse continues. These impulses can move in one direction only. The direction is determined by the synapse, which always acts as "one-way valve".

"Not all synapses are equally effective in transmitting neuronal signals: some are strong, others are weak. The effectiveness of a synapse can be altered by the signals passing through it so that synapses can more or less permanently learn from the activities in which they participate" (Brunak/Lautrup, op.cit.).

Artificial neural networks have to be seen as a very coarse model of their natural equivalents only. They consist of a large number of simple processors - the "neurons" or "nodes"- which are interconnected in a complex network consisting of several layers, thus separating the input and output function (Figure 4.2-2).

Figure 4.2-2: Typical configuration of an artificial neural network

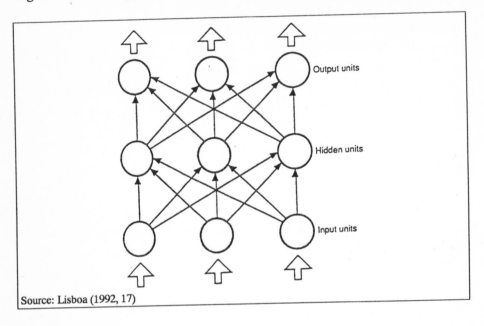

Source: Lisboa (1992, 17)

The function of the system is simulated by mathematical models. Input signals x_n reach the "synapses", in artificial neurons their exhibitory and inhibitory effects are simulated by positive or negative weights. That means, the exhibitory effects are simulated by multiplying the input values by positive values and the inhibitory effects are realised by multiplying the input values by negative values. All weighted input data are added, and if the sum of all input data exceeds a certain threshold, an activity potential is set off through the axon (Figure 4.2-3). The output of this neuron then becomes one of the input signals for a different neuron, whereas the output and input signals occur in two states (0, 1) only. "0" means that no activity potential is set off and "1" that an activity potential is set off (Kinnebrock 1992, 14-17; Brause 1991, 36- 39; Hinton 1992, 134-135).

The most important advantage of neural networks is their capability to learn by training. At the beginning of the training, the network is fed with information on a set of target data, e.g. in a case of pattern recognition with clearly written numbers; then, the network is confronted with fuzzy information, e.g. badly readable numbers. During the training output failures are recognised and reported back to the input layer. To improve the result the weights are changed, connections delivering the right information are strengthened and those sending false information become weakened. This procedure is repeated until an optimal concurrence between target and output data is realised. When the net is well trained it is able to react correctly to unknown patterns as well (Dechau 1989, 55; Müller 1993, 103). But changing tasks require a new training. At present different training algorithms are known, e. g., the back propagation algorithm or the Boltzman learning algorithm.

Figure 4.2-3:   Representation of a formal neuron

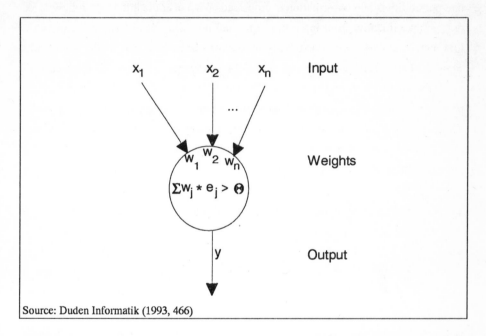

Source: Duden Informatik (1993, 466)

The effective simulation of natural neural networks through artificial neural networks requires software as well as hardware developments. In principle, it is possible to simulate neural networks with conventional computer architecture, but this is very time-consuming.

4.2.2   Principal models

The information-processing properties of neural networks depend mainly on two factors: the network topology defined as the scheme used to connect elements or nodes together, and the algorithm (the rules) employed to specify the values of the weights connecting the nodes. When looking for criteria to classify neural networks, one possibility is how information is processed. Whenever the information flow is led only in one direction from input to output and no recurrence of signals is possible, the neural networks are called *feed-forward networks*. The first model which was capable of classifying known patterns was the *perceptron*, which still is the archetype of this category of neural networks (Brause 1991, 81). The first and most simple perceptrons have only synaptic junctions between the input and output layer. Therefore, they are only successful for those pattern-recognition problems that can be solved by means of a single-layer structure. One possible way of overcoming this restriction was to include so-called *hidden layers* between the input and the output layer. The number of hidden layers that is needed depends on the complexity of each specific problem. The hidden neurons in multilayer perceptrons can be arranged in innumerable ways to suit the nature of the problem. Currently, there is no standardised mode by which the optimal perceptron can be tailored to a given problem. A large part of contemporary research is directed towards finding rules of thumb for network architecture as well as a proper theory (Brunak/Lautrup 1990, 124). In order to adapt synaptic strengths and thresholds to a given problem, the *back-propagation algorithm* is one possible method to train the multilayer perceptron. This algorithm is used "to adjust the network's many parameters in light of the mistakes made in the training examples. If the network gives the wrong answers, one, so to speak, sends the mistake back through the network. This *back-propagation* adjusts the values of all the strengths and thresholds in a way that next time the network is shown the same example it will be closer to producing the right answer than before" (ibid, 128). After training, the network is able to classify new data by generalising from the examples given during the training phase. Mathematically, the perceptron interpolates between the examples it has seen (ibid 133; Lisboa 1992, 17). The more examples it has seen the better the generalisation is. Deciding on the architecture best suited for the problem and training a network are very slow and difficult processes, but a trained perceptron is quick.

A typical algorithm for so-called recursive networks is the Hopfield network. All nodes of a Hopfield network are connected to one another by weights. The "activity of any one neuron is determined by the overall signal received from all of the other neurons in the network according to whether or not this signal exceeds a given threshold" (Lisboa 1992, 11). The nodes have an all-or-nothing function, meaning that a node is always fully 'on' or 'off'. The state of the network is always represented by patterns of activity of the nodes. The links between the nodes determine the network activity. The networks' intention is to minimise the so-called energy function following the "principle of least action, which drives physical systems in equilibrium with their environment to states of least energy" (ibid, 12). The Hopfield network is a powerful algorithm for optimisation problems.

4.2.3   Application of neural networks

Neural networks have a broad range of possible application fields in industry, production and services. Whenever fuzzy information processing for a non-linear representation is required, neural networks are a possible solution. As non-linear representations exist in many fields in science and economy, any list of applications can only give a brief overview of the potential use. Some successful applications of adaptive systems belong, according to Kinnebrock (1992, pp. 103), to

- automatic control
- robotics
- health care
- chemistry
- economy and financial services
- meteorology
- computer science
- communication science.

Major tasks of neural networks are signal processing, especially pattern recognition, image interpretation as well as voice generation and recognition. Because of their robustness and adaptability, neural networks are useful for identifying letters and numbers with low quality writing and hand writing, fields in which conventional optical character recognition software is not applicable. Regarding image interpretation, neural networks are widely applied for military applications, such as location and classification for example of airplanes, submarines and helicopters. First civil applications are "robotic eyes" and signal classification (Kratzer 1990, 172).

Because of their learning ability and fault tolerance, neural networks represent one possibility of realising voice generation and recognition in combination with a voice recognition chip. The first network for voice generation was developed in 1986 by Sejnowski/Rosenberg at the John Hopkins University and is well known as *NETtalk*. NETtalk consists of three layers and uses back propagation for learning to pronounce the words (Kinnebrock 1992, 105). Concerning voice recognition, a comparably successful application as recognition of voice is not known, because of dialects and different pronunciation, which are very difficult to identify.

Control and robotics is one of the most important fields of application for neural networks. Implemented neural applications already exist which never could have been realised using conventional control methods (ibid., 108). One well-known example for demonstrating the capability of neural networks is the broomstick balancing machine (Kratzer 1990, 173). With the help of a neural network, a control system is built that is able to balance a broomstick placed on a free movable wagon. Another application was demonstrated by Widrow/Nguyen in 1990. They used two back-propagation networks to simulate the parking of a trailer in front of a loading rack (Nguyen/Widrow/Truck, 1990).

Neural networks are also applied successfully as *diagnostic systems in quality control* as one possible way of using their signal processing capability already described above. Although only a small number of systems are used so far, they already provide a wide range of different fields of application, e.g. airplanes, gearboxes, engines, medical substances, nuclear power plants, or detection of computer virus (Schöneburg 1992, 162).

4.3   Bibliometric analysis

By analogy with medical lasers, the bibliometric analysis for neural networks is based on the one hand on patents representing technology and on the other hand on scientific publications representing science. Details of the methodology used can be found in section 3.3. The searches were carried out with the terms "neural network" and synonyms such as "neural net", "neuron network", "neural circuit", "neural computer", etc. Most hits of the determined samples, however, are due to the basic expression "neural network".

The patent searches were carried out on the basis of patent applications at the European Patent Office recorded in the database EPAT. For the interpretation of the results, it has to be taken into account that according to article 52, paragraph 2, point C, "programs for computers" are not patentable. However, new software developments closely linked to an improvement of hardware are patentable, according to the legal practice of the last years. This means in the special case of neural networks that theories and mathematical methods are generally not patentable, but most software developments have already such a close linkage to hardware that patent protection is possible. Although the roots of neural networks trace back until the beginning of the forties, visible patent activities started not earlier than in 1987 (cf. figure 4.3-1). It is, of course, possible that first developments in this area were described by different expressions, for example "artificial nerves", "biological computers" etc. In any case, a common terminology and thus the emergence of a new technological area began in 1987 and has enormously increased since that time. The highest patent activities are recorded for the United States and in second position for Japan, followed by the European Union. Within the EU, the German and French figures have almost the same level, whereas the British figures especially in the most recent years are quite low. The patent activities of the other nine countries of the EU are nearly negligible (figure 4.3-2).

On the science side, the searches were first of all performed in the database INSPEC which is specialised on electrical engineering, electronics, control technology, computers, information technology and physics. Parallel searches were made in the Science Citation Index (SCI) in order to check the journal coverage of INSPEC and the validity of the respective results. Furthermore, INSPEC records only the first institution of a publication, so that institutional co-operations remain invisible. A last argument for the additional use of the SCI is the broader coverage of biology and medicine, which might be important for the complete description of neural networks.

Figure 4.3-1:   Patent applications at the EPO of major countries in the area of neural networks (Database: EPAT)

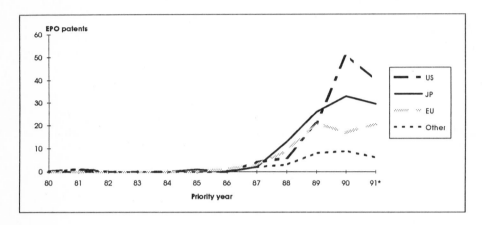

Figure 4.3-2:   Patent applications at the EPO of EU countries in the area of neural networks (Database: EPAT)

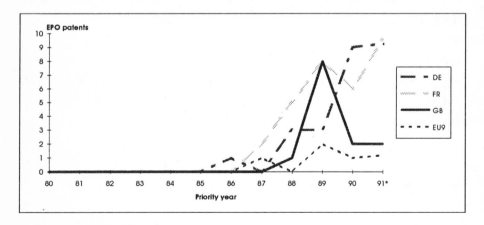

The searches in INSPEC and SCI lead to very similar results as to the main trends and the relative country positions (cf. figures 4.3-3 to 4.3-6). The absolute figures in SCI, however, are much lower than in INSPEC, because, first, only titles and no abstracts or index terms are available for searches and, second, the coverage of the areas of electronics and information technology is insufficient (for further details see Schmoch et al. 1993a). All in all, the publication activities start nearly parallel to the patent activities. The publications begin one or two years earlier, when a delay of about one year between the reception of an article at the journal and its publication is taken into account. The publication statistics confirm the leading position of the United States. Like in medical lasers, the relative position of Japan is much lower in science than in technology, whereas the relative position of the European Union and of the other countries is getting stronger. Within Europe the result of the patent analyses concerning a comparable level of Germany and France is confirmed; but now, Great Britain has the highest publication numbers, which might partly be due to a language bias in INSPEC. Nevertheless, the scientific performance of Great Britain seems to be better than the technological performance. As a further result of the publication statistics, a quite high activity level of the other nine countries of the European Union is recorded. In this regard, the situation is once again comparable to medical lasers.

Figure 4.3-3:   Publications in the database INSPEC in the area of neural networks for major countries

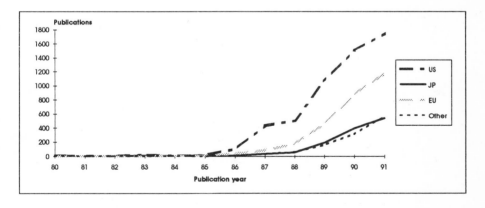

As neural networks are a new emerging area, the absolute patent numbers are still quite low leading to limited institutional lists. Within the European Union, a variety of companies with one or two patents appears, and only a few companies such as Philips, Thomson CSF or Siemens show higher patent activities (cf. table A 2-1). The applicant list for non-EU countries shows that the higher patent numbers of Japan and the United States are due to a broader basis of companies involved, and in the case of US patents also to several universities. At the top of the list, the third position of the chemical company Du Pont is remarkable.

Figure 4.3-4:   Publications in the database INSPEC in the area of neural networks for EU countries

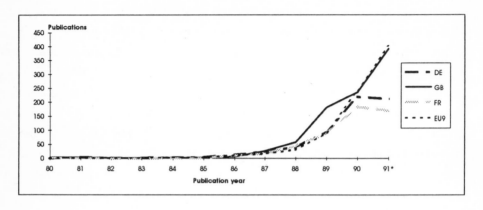

Figure 4.3-5:   Publications in the database SCI in the area of neural networks for major countries

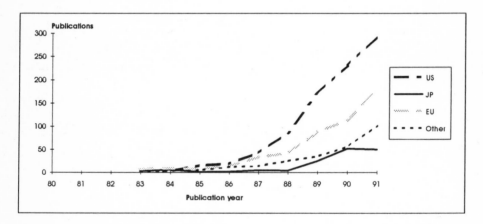

The institutional list based on INSPEC reveals a broad variety of universities being active in the area of neural networks, but also some companies such as British Telecom, GEC Marconi or Siemens are recorded (table A 2-3). Once again, a representation according to major cities - and only in addition major institutions - was chosen in order to show that in many cases departments in electronics, mathematics, computer science, psychology or neuro-biology work in a close local proximity. In contrast to the situation of medical lasers, very few publication activities of public research institutes apart from universities are documented. A major exception is the German Research Centre GMD. Therefore, this type of institution was not included in the interviews.

Figure 4.3-6:   Publications in the database SCI in the area of neural networks for EU countries

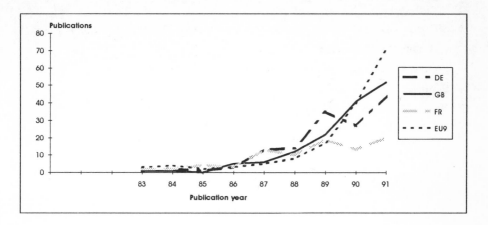

The institutional list generated on the basis of SCI publications leads to a similar picture as INSPEC. Only in some cases additional clinical or biological departments are identified. Although the number of publications recorded in INSPEC is higher than in SCI, the number of institutions in table A2-4 is a little bit higher than in table A2-3. First, the INSPEC list was generated only for 1992, the SCI list for 1991 to 1992, and, second, in SCI multiple institutions per publication are often recorded.

Like for medical lasers, the co-operation structures were roughly analysed by a scan of SCI records. According to this, there is again a focus on local partners; but the co-operations with external partners, especially international partners, seem to be more frequent than in the area of medical lasers. Finally, the institutions documented in table 4.3-1 were selected for the interviews. All in all, eight interviews were conducted, three of them with the enterprises British Telecom, Siemens and Philips. The other interviews were made with 5 universities in 5 different countries, so that the international structures of this area are well reflected in the selection of interview partners.

To sum up, the bibliometric approach was helpful to identify major actors in the field. In the case of neural networks it would have been even more interesting than in the field of medical lasers to draw a map of national and international networks, but due to time restrictions this approach could not be realised.

Table 4.3-1   Institutions selected for interviews in the area of neural networks (interview partner in brackets)

- Siemens AG, Central Research and Development Department (ZFE), Munich, Germany (Dr. Ramacher)
- Philips, Laboratoire d'Electronique Philips (LEP), Limeil Brévannes, France (Mr. Pergrale)
- British Telecom (BT), Systems Research Division, Ipswich, United Kingdom (Prof. Gell)
- University of Bochum, Institut für Neuroinformatik, Germany (Prof. von der Malsburg)
- University of Genoa, Department for Biophysics and Electronic Engineering, Italy (Prof. Caviglia)
- University of Nijmegen, Department of Medical Physics and Biophysics, the Netherlands (Prof. Gielen, Dr. Kappen)
- Centre for Neural Networks, King's College London, United Kingdom (Prof. Taylor)
- Interdisciplinary Centre for Neural Networks (ICNN), University of Leuven, Belgium (Prof. Orban, Dr. van Hulle, Prof. Bollé et al.)

4.4 Interview results

4.4.1 Main activities of interview partners

The following description of the main activities of interview partners follows the order of table 4.3-1 and in consequence, starts with three manufacturers followed by the description of the universities.

The activities of **Siemens** in the area of neural networks started in 1987 with a strategic study on the use of neural networks for the targets of the company. As an outcome of this study, two research groups were established with a focus on

- application and optimisation of neural networks for industrial processes (Prof. Schürrman, 4 collaborators) and
- development of neural computers (Dr. Ramacher, 2 collaborators).

At present, three major research groups exist, two, concerning industrial applications, one in Munich (18 collaborators), the other in Princeton (USA, 24 collaborators), and a third group on neural computers (8 collaborators). Furthermore, a variety of very small research groups exist in different departments aiming at special applications, e.g. in the areas of central production and logistics, automation, medical technology or power plant control. All in all, the different researchers in neural networks represent one of the largest industrial research groups of the world in this area. Because of the special interview partner, Dr. Ramacher, the discussion was focused on neural computers which represent one of the most advanced activities in the field of neural networks. The computer called "Synapse" consists of 8 processors, each simulating 16 parallel working nodes. On this hardware basis, it is possible to simulate very large neural networks with up to 8,000 nodes. By such large networks, a high processing speed can be achieved, e.g., pattern recognition in real time can be realised. Up to now, only a small U.S. American company has realised a similar neural computer, but with a lower performance than the version of Siemens. The conception of the hardware aims at sufficient flexibility in order to support any type of neural networks and training algorithms. This flexibility is important, because for different applications different types of networks are optimally suitable. The new hardware of the neural computer, of course, implies the development of new software solutions as well. Further details of the new computer are described in Müller (1993) and Meyer (1993).

It is interesting to look at the timing of the development of this advanced neural computer in more detail. The conception of the system was elaborated in the period of 1988 to 1990; as a next step, a prototype was developed which was realised in 1993. Each of the three above mentioned research groups will get one prototype for testing. The next step was the production of a small series of about 20 computers. These apparatus were given to interested departments within Siemens and to some external partners, mostly universities. At the beginning of 1994 it was decided to start commercial production at Siemens Nixdorf in Dresden. The price for the commercial product will be around 350.000 DM for the basic version. The price for the small series was less than that in order to give research units the opportunity to test the innovation.

The **Laboratoire d'Electronique Philips (LEP)** is one of five large research laboratories of Philips and is located near Paris. The research activities of LEP are focused on 5 areas:
- architecture of microsystems,
- detection and photonics,
- video communication,
- digital systems processing,
- professional imaging systems.

The activities concerning neural networks are associated to "architecture of microsystems" and comprise about 10 researchers. But also in the other areas, research on neural networks is carried out, e.g., in professional imaging systems. Further related work is performed in the laboratories of Aachen and Eindhoven. The activities of LEP in neural networks started in about 1986. These early activities chiefly concerned theoretical work in order to achieve a sufficient level of knowledge. Meanwhile, the research has reached an application-oriented stage. The orientation on application in recent years is not only linked to a sequential research cycle from basic to applied research, but to a change of the policy of Philips in the context of general economic problems. In consequence, those activities are promoted where a quick introduction into the market can be expected. Major areas of activity are:

- recognition of handwriting, e.g. the recognition of signatures on medical prescriptions,
- distinction and recognition of sound sources, e.g. for the automatic volume control of car radios depending on the noise of the engine,
- control of vacuum cleaners in dependence of the specific application conditions,
- processing of images, e.g. the evaluation of ultra-sound or X-ray images,
- image recognition for industrial applications, e.g. for fault detection in the production of integrated circuits.

These examples are enumerated in order to illustrate that already today a variety of applications with the expectations of considerable sale volumes exist. The research activities of the LEP team, first of all, concern the identification of appropriate network types for the different applications and the development of the respective hardware, especially microchips, and software. The identification of appropriate network types and their adaptation to specific applications requires an adequate theoretical knowledge as well as broad practical experiences.

British Telecom (BT) is the largest telecom network operator of the United Kingdom. In the eighties, research and development activities of BT were carried out in a common department; in 1990, they were separated into two departments whereof the research department comprises 300 persons. The research department is divided into the systems research division, the networks division and the software-application division. The activities concerning neural networks are located mainly in the systems research division (about 70 collaborators), and therein in the sub-field of self-organisation (at present 12 researchers). The activities in neural networks started in about 1986, i.e., before the reorganisation of BT, and were focused on applications in the areas of speech and vision. As BT has broadened its scope towards advanced network services and applications, the focus of the neural network research has broadened as well. At present, the BT research concerns mainly the coordination and control of telecommunication networks and information systems. The work of the research department helps to acquire knowledge and to find solutions for so-called meta-tasks, i.e. general tasks. The results are linked, according to the new organisation structure, to work in the development departments; in many cases, general solutions are adapted to specific problems. Therefore, a real "marketing" of the research results is necessary.

The **Institute for Neural Informatics** at the **University of Bochum** was set up in 1989 as an independent unit which is not associated with a special faculty. The foundation has to be seen in the context of the general boom of neural networks at the end of the eighties. The institute comprises about 15 researchers. About 80 % of the work at the institute can be characterised as applied research, about 20 % as basic research. Because of the proximity of basic and applied research in neural networks, many results of the basic research can be directly transferred into applications. The basic research is chiefly focused on the exploration of principles of vision, i.e. the neuro-biology of vision. On the side of application, the issue of pattern recognition - as an equivalent to the basic research on vision mechanisms - is analysed as well as the topics of diagnosis of sound and the optimisation of process control.

The major activities in neural networks at the **University of Genoa** are located in the **Department of Biophysical and Electronic Engineering**. It has been established in 1982, while the activities on neural networks started in 1987. The department comprises 36 professors in total (full, associate, and assistant professors). About 10 professors are engaged in neural networks. The respective work aims at five main topics:
- VLSI artificial neural networks: neural modules and learning networks
- neurocomputing
- neural algorithms for signal processing
- biologically inspired: artificial sensorial systems, machine vision (modules and systems)
- neurobiology of neural networks.

Thus, the work comprises the basic study (including biological neural networks), the modelling and the implementation of neural networks; they are especially simulated and designed, so that they are optimally adapted to different hardware conditions. More than 60 % of the research can be characterised as applied research.

The **Department of Medical Physics and Biophysics** at the **University of Nijmegen** started its research activities on neural networks in 1988. At present, the department employs 29 persons, thereof 6 permanent scientists, 12 doctorate students and 5 postdoc students. The research includes studies on artificial as well as on biological neural networks. A major topic is the exploration of processes in the co-ordination of arm and leg movements as well as eye movements. In addition, problems concerning the navigation or orientation of human beings are analysed; a further area concerns bioelectricity. As to artificial neural networks, training processes are examined. In applied research the results on biological movement control are used for robotics, and information recorded in an international cancer database is analysed in order to identify optimal therapies for individual persons. Up to now, this selection was primarily made on the basis of statistical evaluations. Finally, the analysis of the reliability of neural networks is a major research topic. The respective processing is carried out by the implementation in conventional hardware which, at least at present, makes sufficiently high processing speed possible.

The **Centre for Neural Networks at King's College London** was founded in 1990 and integrates the respective activities of the departments of mathematics, physics, electronics and computer science. The Centre aims at a co-ordination of education and research in the area of neural networks. The research activities are focused on theoretical aspects of artificial neural networks and their application for speech analysis, artificial eyes, control, medical diagnosis, and forecast, e.g. for financial issues. A further activity concerns the hardware development of specific chips. The research group is quite large and comprises all in all about 45 persons with a high share of doctorate students. This quite large group of researchers explains the broad variety of research topics.

Since 1992, the **Interdisciplinary Centre for Neural Networks** of the **University of Leuven** co-ordinates the already existing respective activities of the Institute for Theoretical Physics, the Institute for Electrical Engineering and the Laboratory for Neural and Psychophysiology of the medical faculty. In the Institute for Electrical Engineering, a research group with the head Prof. Vandewalle performs basic research on neural networks from the perspective of computer science and electrical engineering. The activities comprise the topics:
- identification and control,
- system analysis of neural networks,
- speech recognition,
- implementation.

The Institute of Theoretical Physics with the head Prof. Bollé carries out abstract model-theoretic considerations of neural networks. The main interest is a further development of the model structure of the above mentioned Hopfield networks.

The Laboratory for Neural and Psychophysiology headed by Prof. Orban consists of 3 research groups. The first group examines issues of neurology and presently aims at a mapping of ape brains. The second group examines similar topics for human beings, but because of restricted possibilities of practical experiments, the work has to be based on model development and analogies to animal experiments. The third research group, headed by Dr. van Hulle, works on artificial neural networks. The activities concern their modelling and the massive-parallel implementation for pattern recognition and motion control in analogy to the human brain. Furthermore, the group tries to describe the function of brain cells by means of back-referring networks. The Laboratory for Neural and Psychophysiology represents, with 18 scientists, the largest research group within the Interdisciplinary Centre for Neural Networks.

To sum up, the different interview partners represent a large variety of activities in of neural networks including concrete applications as well as (oriented) basic research. Especially, it was possible to include the respective activities in biology, so that the whole spectrum of interdisciplinarity is reflected in the sample.

4.4.2   Future research trends

After a stagnation period in the seventies, the research activities on neural networks started again in the middle of the eighties and, in the meantime, have reached a considerable volume. The first stimuli came from the United States; many European research institutes and manufacturers, however, started in 1987 and 1988 as well. The United States are still leading in this field, but the performance of European research is considerable. The evaluation of the literature, the bibliometric analysis and, first of all, the interviews lead to the following distinction of four main lines concerning future research activities.

First, a large part of the activities is focused on the identification of appropriate applications and the development of respective small networks. These activities concern the development of software as well as hardware, i.e. the design of microchips. This part of research is decisive for the success of neural networks, because a relatively quick introduction into the market is possible. On this basis, the research for more advanced solutions can be financed.

The second line of research concerns a further development of the theory on neural networks, e.g. for the development of new and efficient algorithms or the assessment of reliability. Furthermore, a more systematic theoretical basis is necessary for supporting the choice of appropriate network types for specific applications.

The third area of research concerns the development and analysis of very large networks, i.e. neuro-computers. In this area, a quick market success cannot be expected, but in the long run, this type of computer will have a non-negligible market share and at least partly replace the von Neumann computers. In this regard, neuro-computers may constitute a new technological paradigm of information technology.

The research in the area of neuro-biology represents the fourth line of research on neural network. This line can be again divided into basic and applied activities. The basic biological research concerns the improvement of knowledge on the structure of neurons and the human brain or, e. g., the mechanisms of vision. The more applied work aims at the transfer of knowledge from biology to informatics and a more realistic modelling of biological networks by artificial networks. Strong indications exist that these activities will lead to a new generation of neural networks with a much higher efficiency than the existing ones. According to the results of the interviews, this biology-oriented research is more developed in the United States than in Europe.

All in all, the area of neural networks is characterised by a close proximity of basic and applied research. The prospect of a quick introduction into the market will be a decisive support for the research activities in this area and a major incentive to carry out not only applied research, but strategic, long-term activities as well.

The present situation is characterised by a high dynamism which attracts a large number of research institutions. It can be forecast that in some years, many institutions will not be sufficiently competitive and leave the area. In consequence the scientific performance as measured in the number of scientific publications will stagnate, or even decrease, similar to the situation in medical lasers. This "recession", however, will be less distinct, because the potential markets of neural networks are broader than those of medical lasers.

4.4.3   Structures of interdisciplinary research

The interview at the Central Research and Development Department of **Siemens** was performed with Dr. Ramacher, the head of the research group on neuro-computers. In consequence, the following description of interdisciplinary structures at Siemens exclusively concerns the situation in this group which consists of 2 physicists and 6 electronic engineers. The communication between physicists and engineers within the group works well, and problems chiefly arise in communications with external partners, especially other departments of Siemens. These communication problems concern not so much the interdisciplinary approach of the group, but the unusual holistic approach which comprises the development of the original conception of a system up to the realisation of a final product. Normally, quite a strict differentiation exists between research, development, and production with closed communities. According to Dr. Ramacher, a clear trend towards computers for specialised applications is visible, so that the main problems of interdisciplinarity will concern the communication with external applicants. In this regard, the situation is quite similar to the structures of medical lasers, where interdisciplinarity is introduced by the application of a basic technology in a different discipline.

At present, there are no direct contacts to neuro-biologists, but only an indirect observation of this area through the universities of Bochum and Berlin. From the perspective of the industrial researchers, the basic functions of neurons are already known. As the respective progress of research is quite slow, a decisive impact on artificial networks is expected only in a long-term perspective. According to Dr. Ramacher, physicists are the most appropriate researchers at the interface between biology and informatics, because the analysis of complex systems and their modelling is a main element of their education.

Similar to the situation of Siemens, the research staff of **LEP** comprises specialists in electronics and software, but no biologists. For the application-oriented needs of Philips, there are sufficiently advanced types of networks which can be directly introduced into practice. Against this background, several linkages to external academic co-operation partners have been set up, for example the universities of Grenoble and London or the Ecole Polytechnique Paris, but exclusively in the area of electronics and informatics, not biology. The main problems of communication between different disciplines arise, similar to Siemens, when neural networks should be used for special applications, e.g. in the medical area (automatic image analysis for medical purposes). In these situations, it is important to find an open-minded partner on the application side. In France, a special association for biomedical technology was founded for promoting the communication between respective companies and interested physicians.

The systems research division of **British Telecom** comprises in total about 70 employees, chiefly electrical and mechanical engineers and physicists, but also biologists, economists, and jurists. The special research activities on neural networks are carried out by 9 permanent employees of British Telecom and further 6 so-called short-term fellows of different European universities for relatively short-term projects. These contractors guarantee a good communication to academic research groups and a sufficient flexibility as to the research tasks. Like in the cases of Siemens and LEP, the research exclusively concerns artificial networks so that communication problems with biologists do not exist. Nevertheless, a different aspect of communication problems related to interdisciplinarity have to be noted. They appear in the communication between natural scientists and engineers, on the one hand, and economists, on the other hand. Due to a strong orientation on market needs, economists are not only employed in the marketing divisions, but also in the research division. This orientation is also reflected in the above mentioned necessity of a marketing of research results within the company. The consideration of economic needs already in the stage of research is a quite interesting model for other companies as well. It implies, however, the willingness of the engineers and natural scientists for an interdisciplinary dialogue with economists, a problem which is often overlooked.

The **Institute for Neural Informatics at the University of Bochum** primarily employs physicists, but also mathematicians, computer scientists, electrical engineers and biologists. In addition, a few philosophers, linguists and physicians work in the institute. The interdisciplinary composition reflects the above discussed interdisciplinary orientation of the research within the institute on biological as well as artificial networks. In consequence, a really "big" interdisciplinarity within the institute is realised. The institute undertakes a lot of information exchange or direct research co-operations with a variety of research institutes of national and international origin. Examples are the Max Planck Institute for Brain Research in Frankfurt and the universities in Ilmenau, Hamburg, Bonn, Bielefeld, but also Paris, Sterling or Madrid. Outside Europe, co-operations with the University of Southern California, the University of Jerusalem or the University of Washington are important. This long list demonstrates that the communication with external partners - once again of different disciplinary orientation - is an important element in the area of neural networks.

In addition to contacts to academic institutions, the institute has intensive co-operations with different industrial partners such as Siemens, Daimler-Benz, Volkswagen, Opel, Ford, Hoesch, Mannesmann or Henkel concerning different application areas such as navigation, sound analysis or process control. In this regard, the institute in Bochum represents - as already mentioned in the context of Siemens - a bridging institution for industrial enterprises to neuro-biological aspects.

The research at the **Department for Biophysics and Electronic Engineering** at the **University of Genoa** mostly concerns artificial neural networks, but the neuro-biological topics are also addressed. As the activities are largely oriented on application, the research group chiefly consists of electronic engineers and only a few bio-engineers. The necessity of a co-operation between neuro-biology and computer science is acknowledged, and the necessity of a detailed study of biological problems is seen as crucial for the future development. Most of the external contacts concern other universities in Italy such as Milan, Bologna, Pavia or Rome and increasingly in other European countries, such as Darmstadt, Bonn, Bochum,Twente, or Paris, with an orientation on microelectronics, computer science, and biology. Furthermore, the institute has a close relationship to industrial companies such as ST Microelectronics, ELSAG Bailey, Automa, ILVA (a big Italian steel company), or the French SEMA group.

The activities at the **Department of Medical Physics and Biophysics at the University of Nijmegen** concern on the one hand projects on artificial networks and on the other hand biological networks. This double orientation, de facto, leads to the division into two research groups, wherein the projects on artificial networks are primarily conducted by physicists and engineers and those on biological networks by biologists, physicians and physicists. Thus, physicists seem to have a certain bridging function between biological and artificial networks. Altogether, the structures of interdisciplinary research are comparable to those at the University of Bochum, where both branches of research are carried out in parallel. The main external contacts concern other Dutch universities, first of all Utrecht and Amsterdam, but also external institutions such as the universities in Madrid, Bochum, Genoa, Leuven, Zurich, Paris or Milan. Furthermore, co-operations with Japanese and American partners exist. It is interesting to note that the activities within the Netherlands are co-ordinated by the Foundation for Neural Networks, so that an unnecessary duplication of research activities is avoided. In addition to the academic co-operations, different projects are carried out for industrial partners such as Shell or Fokker. Some industrial projects are executed in form of co-operative projects with several industrial partners and sometimes participation of the public sector.

The internal research of the **Centre for Neural Networks at the King's College London** chiefly aims at artificial neural networks, which is reflected in the composition of the research team consisting of mathematicians, physicists, computer scientists, and electrical engineers. Thus the internal disciplinary structures are comparable to those of the University of Genoa, but the relative weight of engineers compared to more theoretically oriented scientists is lower. Furthermore, the Centre actively tries to carry out projects with a biological orientation by external co-operations with the universities of Cambridge, Amsterdam, or London. Hence, the "big" interdisciplinarity is realised by common projects with external partners. In addition, the centre is very active in the area of collaborative research projects and informal contacts with external partners in the United Kingdom, Europe and also the United States. These co-operations do not only concern academic institutions, but also a variety of companies.

The **Laboratory for Neuro and Psychophysiology at the University of Leuven** within the Interdisciplinary Centre for Neural Network (ICNN) represents, among the interviewed institutions, the most intensive approach to interdisciplinarity between computer science and neuro-biology. The 18 scientists at the laboratory come from the disciplines of biomedicine, biology, mathematics and informatics. In the laboratory, the three main lines of research on neuro-biology on the basis of animal experiments, the neuro-biology of human beings and of the modelling and implementation of artificial neural networks exist in parallel. The work is carried out in different projects, but a major aim of the head of the institute, Prof. Orban, is the organisation of a systematic communication between these three research groups where the results of the experimental and theoretical work are regularly discussed. This systematic exchange of ideas leads to a mutual learning and a mutual control of the research orientation. In addition to this intensive internal communication, the laboratory co-operates with the two other members of the Centre who come from the Faculty of Electrical Engineering and of Theoretical Physics (cf. the more detailed description of these activities in section 4.4.1). The two other institutes within the Centre predominantly represent the side of artificial networks. Because of the generally basic orientation of the Laboratory for Neuro- and Psychophysiology, only little contract research for companies is carried out, especially Philips and the Belgium telecommunication company Belgacom. Therefore, most external co-operations and contacts concern academic institutions, especially leading institutes such as the King's College in London or the Institute for Neural Informatics in Bochum (cf. the respective descriptions above). Each of the three sections of the ICNN knows those institutes which work in the same areas of specialisation quite well.

To sum up, the area of neural networks is characterised by a clear division of labour between a variety of actors. The division of labour does not only concern the different disciplines *computer science* and *biology,* but also the dimension of *applied* versus *basic research.*

The most application-oriented group, of course, are the manufacturers, who focus their activities on a quick introduction of existing networks into marketable applications. For most of them, the more theoretical stage of knowledge appropriation at the end of the eighties is finished, and the present activities aim at concrete technical developments. The necessary theoretical side in this science-intensive area is chiefly introduced by external academic partners. Thus, the co-operation of manufacturers and universities largely reflects the dimension of applied versus basic research. Nevertheless, the manufacturers carry out basic research activities concerning small neural networks and first of all, as the example of Siemens illustrates, large neural networks for the development of neuro-computers. At present, the latter activities are chiefly undertaken by manufacturers, but universities will be involved in the stage of a test of prototypes. In this special case, Siemens took the risk of a long-term engagement, because neuro-computers seem to have an enormous market potential and will induce a decisive advance of the whole area of information technology.

The second group of actors are university institutes and laboratories which are mainly engaged in artificial networks, thus in computer science and has only limited activities in biological networks. The University of Genoa and King's College London stand for this group. It is, however, under-represented in the sample of interview partners, because the selection was chiefly made for studying the interdisciplinary co-operation between computer science and biology. In reality, most academic institutions belong to this group as the results of the bibliometric analysis clearly illustrate (cf. tables A2-3 and A2-4). Within the network of actors, the function of this group is the bridging between basic and applied aspects of artificial neural networks and in this regard, they are interesting co-operation partners for manufacturers.

The third group are institutes with a pure biological - sometimes even psychological - orientation which work on biological neural networks and introduce interdisciplinarity by external relations to institutes in computer science. According to the bibliometric analysis, this third group is the smallest one in the techno-scientific community of neural networks. It has to be noted that there are many more institutes carrying out research in neuro-biology; they aim at medical purposes or perform pure basic research without any explicit orientation. As the biological institutes in neural networks also belong to the scientific community of neuro-biology, the results of the "external" neuro-biological institutes can be indirectly introduced into the stock of knowledge for neural networks.

The fourth group of actors is located at the interface of artificial and biological neural networks. Among the interview partners, this group is represented by the institutes in Bochum, Nijmegen and Leuven. It has the decisive strategic function to prevent a dissociation of the research on artificial networks from its biological basis. In consequence, these institutes have a difficult, but crucial mediating role. As described above in section 4.4.2, there are strong indications that progress in the exploration of biological networks will lead to substantial progress of artificial networks within the next years.

The techno-scientific community of neural networks with the four strategic groups of actors is depicted in a schematic way in figure 4.4-1. Each of the four groups has a specific function, and it is not possible to assign different ranks of quality. It is noteworthy that in the present economic recession, the role of universities for the maintenance of an adequate level of basic research is increasing. This applies to the basic research of institutes oriented on computer science, e.g. concerning the development of improved algorithms, as well as on biological institutes which explore the mechanisms of biological networks.

Figure 4.4-1:   Actor structures in research for neural networks

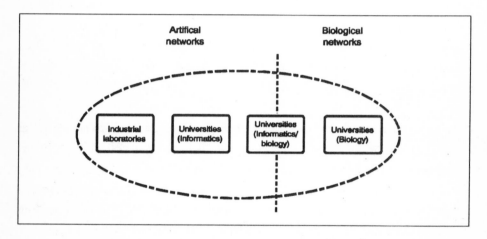

Already at the present stage of development, artificial neural networks generate interesting results and are, in problems of fuzzy logic, an interesting alternative to conventional von Neumann computers. A further improvement of the underlying algorithms will lead to an enhanced performance of the existing types. Against this background, there is the danger of under-estimating the impact of biological research on the advance of the field, because the results are not directly visible and introduced in marketable products, but only through multiple intermediate steps. From this angle, the explicit promotion of interdisciplinarity is an important element for the research in neural networks.

4.4.4 Problems of interdisciplinarity

In the area of neural networks, the main problems of interdisciplinary co-operation emerge in the relation of computer specialists and biologists. Biologists consider themselves first of all as pure natural scientists who aim at a systematic collection of observable facts. In the case of neural networks, this research leads to a very complex picture of the mechanisms of biological networks. In contrast, specialists in artificial networks, especially physicists, try to achieve adequate models which are necessarily linked to simplifications in order to reduce the complexity. The problems do not only concern a different orientation of research and different "languages" leading to communication problems, but also the mutual respect. The situation is rendered more difficult by the fact that there are only a few projects which can be carried out jointly. In general, a clear separation of projects on artificial and on biological networks emerges.

Against this background, enormous explicit efforts are necessary to guarantee a fruitful mutual knowledge transfer. As to the institutional arrangement of such a knowledge transfer, only universities seem to be able to achieve a successful realisation. This phenomenon can be explained by the generally basic orientation of the biological research, which cannot be sufficiently appreciated by application-oriented partners, especially researchers of industrial laboratories. Academic institutions, however, often have conflicts with their environment organised on strictly disciplinary lines. A good example is the Institute for Neural Informatics in Bochum, which was set up not on the initiative of the university, but of the Federal State of Nordrhein-Westfalen. In the following years, the affiliation of the two heads of the institutes to other faculties, the so-called co-optation, proved to be quite difficult. In the case of Nijmegen, the students of the Department of Medical Physics and Biophysics partly belong to the Faculty of Medicine, partly to the Faculty of Natural Sciences. The students have to meet chiefly the requirements of examination of their specific faculty, and in times of financial constraints the faculties primarily try to protect their core activities and less "peripheral" interdisciplinary areas. This latter type of problems concerns, first of all, the real interdisciplinary institutes integrating biology and computer science.

The establishment of institutes with a strong orientation on artificial networks is less difficult, because artificial networks are generally accepted as a sub-area of informatics. But even there, the establishment of specialised institutes needs a specific effort and often requires complex forms of organisation, e.g., the Centre for Neural Networks at King's College London has to link the interests of the four different departments of mathematics, physics, electronics, and computer science. In view of the increasing necessity of combining these disciplines in information technology, their still traditional structure is hardly understandable.

Besides the barriers between biologists and computer specialists, certain communication problems exist between physicists and engineers because of their orientation on basic respectively applied research. It is undisputed that physicists have a prominent role in the modelling of artificial networks and the transfer between biological and artificial networks. There exists, however, the danger of an arrogance towards "simplistic" engineers, and it is important for interdisciplinary co-operation that the different functions within a team are mutually respected. In any case, the experiences of engineers concerning the concrete implementation of artificial nets are indispensable as well.

Further problems of interdisciplinary co-operation which are not specific for the case of neural networks could be observed in the context of implementations of neural networks in practice, as already discussed by the examples of Siemens and LEP. This type of problems mainly concerns manufacturers; the situation is comparable to that of medical lasers.

The positive example of British Telecom reveals as a further problem of interdisciplinarity the dialogue between natural scientists and engineers on the one hand and economists on the other hand. These problems and the resulting insufficient communication between research and marketing seems to be typical for European companies, whereas in Japan these departments are co-ordinated in a more efficient way (see e.g. Cuhls 1993).

All in all, the organisation of the "big" interdisciplinarity between biology and computer sciences involves the greatest problems in the research on neural networks and can only be realised by a deliberate effort. At present, this effort is made by some highly committed individuals who can only continue their work with sufficient external promotion.

4.4.5 Areas of public promotion

The public promotion of neural network research on the national level is distinctly better than in the area of medical lasers. For example, the Italian government established an 8-year programme on technologies for bioelectronics with a sub-area for neural and sub-micron electronics, and a small special programme for neural networks is projected. Also in Germany, the United Kingdom and the Netherlands the support from the national public sector is generally sufficient. In addition, most of the academic institutes get supplementary funds through contract research for industrial partners. Only in the case of the Laboratory for Neuro- and Psychophysiology in Leuven may financial problems arise in the near future. At present, the basic infrastructure and the personnel costs are financed by the university, and the projects by the Belgium Science Foundation. Due to the bad fiscal situation of the Belgium state, several projects will probably be cut back. These financial problems have to be seen against the background of the clear orientation on basic research at the interface of biology and computer science, so that additional funds cannot be acquired through contract research.

All interview partners have already participated in EU programmes, especially ESPRIT. Most institutions generally appreciate the support by the EU, but in detail many interview partners expressed critical points similar to those already mentioned in the area of medical lasers. As a major topic, the enormous bureaucracy linked to project applications, but also during the execution of a project is mentioned. In this context, the focus on formal requirements and the negligence of scientific quality is complained about. A further point of criticism is the demand for clearly defined research targets at the beginning of the project, which hampers really advanced research with a largely experimental character and the risk of failure. Many interview partners, also of industrial origin, see a shift of focus within ESPRIT from basic to applied research, whereas in the still quite early stage of neural networks a substantial support of basic research is still necessary. Another problem are the quite long delays of decision on applications by the EU managers. In this context, the research promotion of the NATO is mentioned as a positive example, because of low decision times and a clear orientation on the scientific quality of the applications. Many interview partners, however, see the extremely high number of applications and the problem of an appropriate administration. Some of the interview partners even worked for the Commission as experts for the evaluation of project applications and understand the more complex situation of an international body compared to a national government. Nevertheless, it seems to be necessary to thoroughly think about how the application procedures can be simplified and accelerated, and how the programme structures can become more flexible.

The situation in the area of neural networks is characterised by a multiplicity of activities in all European countries which is even stronger than in the area of medical lasers. Therefore, it is necessary to achieve a sufficient co-ordination of the research activities, and all interview partners welcome international co-operations. So this explicit orientation of European RTD programmes is generally welcomed. Nevertheless, the criteria for the set-up of international consortia are criticised which often seem to be determined by guidelines such as a balanced national distribution, inclusion of sufficient industrial participants etc. This can lead to the establishment of artificial consortia wherein the special faculties of the partners are not appropriate for the project contents. In this context, the interview partners see risks in the establishment of interdisciplinary consortia, even if the project has no interdisciplinary character.

Within the framework of ESPRIT, there are already intensive activities for the establishment of networks and an exchange of information in order to avoid a duplication of research. At present, an international network called NEURONET is co-ordinated by Prof. Taylor of King's College London. Starting at the beginning of 1994, a further project will support the set-up of a database, the publication of newsletters and the organisation of workshops. These co-ordination activities are highly appreciated by all interview partners. In addition, special associations for neural networks were established in most European countries, so that additional measures seem not to be necessary.

As to the dissemination of existing RTD results, the above described networks are efficient instruments of promotion. Furthermore, all interview partners actively publish and attend conferences. A major problem in the area of neural networks, however, is the extremely high number of publications and the too big conferences because of the large number of active institutions. In consequence, only publications of high quality and published in well-reputed journals are noticed. This means for the dissemination of RTD results of EU programmes that respective publications have to be prepared with care and that a financing of scientific publications within the programme should be considered. As to conferences, some interview partners see a higher quality of American conferences compared to European ones, although the scientific quality of the results is comparable. Therefore, the enhancement of the quality of conferences should be a main target of the Commission. In this context, some interview partners complain that the same well-reputed experts appear in all meetings, and new ideas are not introduced ("travelling circus"). In the present situation, the experts generally prefer the organisation of small workshops, where topical problems can be discussed in an intensive way.

Especially academic institutions often use the exchange of personnel for the communication of RTD results. Therefore, the support of the respective EU programmes for human capital and mobility, e.g. ERASMUS, are considered as very positive.

To sum up, the existing instruments of EU promotion for neural networks work quite well and are largely used by the involved institutions. Major points of criticism are the complexity of the application procedure, a lack of flexibility in the execution of the projects and an obvious neglect of basic research in ESPRIT in recent years. At the same time, other activities such as the establishment of a European network are highly appreciated.

In addition to the instruments already existing, one should think in more detail about an institutional approach, similar to the suggestion for medical lasers in section 3.4.5. Such an institutional arrangement could comprise about 15 academic as well as industrial institutions which are linked together for a longer, nevertheless limited period. The members of this institutional group do not necessarily work on the same project, but follow a main orientation, e.g. the exploration of a vision, with about three or four different approaches. Similar to the example of Leuven, parallel work on the biological level, on the modelling of artificial networks and the development of new algorithms and on the practical implementation of artificial networks could be carried out. A major element of such an institutional arrangement should be regular workshop-like meetings where the intermediate results are discussed by all involved groups so that a mutual reorientation can take place. As a side effect of such an arrangement, the problem of an appropriate location of biological research for neural networks could be solved. At present, this type of research can be associated neither with ESPRIT nor with a medical or biological programme, strictly speaken. An important element of this approach is the long-term perspective and the possibility of an intermediate reorientation, so that a sufficiently stable perspective and at the same time a high flexibility can be achieved.

In this context, one interview partner mentioned the Japanese Real World Computing Programme as a positive example because of its long-term orientation. This programme is projected for a period of 10 years, with a first stage of 5 years oriented on basic research and a second phase with the implementation of these results in practice. This concept, however, is based on a sequential model of the innovation process and it seems to be more appropriate to carry out, right from the beginning, applied and basic research in parallel. Besides, the Japanese programme seems also to be quite bureaucratic.

In summary, the quality of the industrial and academic research in neural networks in Europe is high and, up to now, a clear backlog compared to the United States or Japan is not visible. In this very dynamic area, it will, however, be necessary to continue the different existing approaches of promotion and even to add new instruments such as institutional arrangements. In any case, neural networks seem to be a key area for catching up in information technology.

5.   General conclusions and recommendations

The following conclusions and recommendations are based on common findings for the specific areas of medical lasers and neural networks. Both areas are characterised by the emergence of a techno-scientific community which establishes an interdisciplinary network of industrial and academic actors. Within these networks, the members do not work on the same problems and a clear division of labour can be observed. This division concerns a different orientation on the involved disciplines, but also the dimension of an applied versus a basic orientation. In periods of economic recession, the function of universities in basic research becomes even more important, because many industrial enterprises reduce their respective activities and favour an orientation on application.

As to the latter aspect, both case studies illustrate that basic and applied research activities have specific functions within the network and have to be carried out in parallel. In this context, the information-theoretic approach of David et al. (1993) for the analysis of different types of research is helpful. According to the cited authors, the outcomes of basic research cannot be directly measured by monetary quantities, because "basic research results rarely lead directly to new processes or products without substantial modification." Basic research rather generates orientation knowledge which helps to identify promising areas for applied research and, also important, less prosperous areas. Applied research provides information on potential products or processes, and based on these results, development realises marketable products. These different functions become directly visible in the two selected case studies. Especially the orientation function of basic research in biomedicine for medical lasers and biology in neural networks is obvious. In consequence, the evaluation of basic research activities should not consider direct monetary outcomes, because this approach chiefly reveals secondary effects, the so-called spin-offs. It is, however, necessary to examine how far the information-theoretic approach is useful for areas of basic research which are not linked to a techno-scientific community.

Concerning the disciplinary orientation, a strong tendency towards a division of research according to traditional disciplines can be observed even in interdisciplinary areas. In the case of medical lasers, a quite strict division into, on the one hand, technical, system-oriented research and, on the other hand, biomedical research still exists. In neural networks, the activities are generally divided into computer science and neuro-biology. There are first of all structures of "small" interdisciplinarity within natural sciences or within life sciences with, e.g., teams of physicists and electrical engineers or biologists and physicians. Only few institutions aim at the real integration of distinctly different disciplines. These institutions, however, generally prove to have a decisive function for the progress of the area. Against this background, the promotion of interdisciplinarity should aim at the organisation of an efficient dialogue between institutions of different disciplines and especially support those institutions which bear the risks of a real interdisciplinary approach.

The results of the project confirm the outcome of the literature analysis that industrial companies have less problems to organise interdisciplinarity. This is true at least for the two cases which are analysed in this study. Possibly, neither of these two fields need "big" interdisciplinarity in an industrial research environment and the results would have been different for other research areas. Companies, however, work in the applied part of interdisciplinary fields, where the disciplinary differences generally are not as big. For example, manufacturers of medical lasers have to integrate physicists, engineers in electronics and technicians in precision mechanics, but no physicians. Industrial research teams in neural networks generally consist of physicists, electrical engineers and computer specialists, but seldom biologists. The big interdisciplinary gaps between, e. g., physics and medicine or computer science and biology appear in the early stages of a new techno-scientific field and thus primarily on the level of basic research. In consequence, first of all academic institutions - thus the target group of Interface II - are confronted with problems of "big" interdisciplinarity. The disciplinary structures in universities, however, are much more rigid than in industrial enterprises, and the set-up of interdisciplinary institutes is generally quite problematic. In consequence, the active promotion of interdisciplinary approaches in academic institutions by external bodies is crucial for the development of advanced techno-scientific areas.

In this context, the orientation of the academic education plays a major role, and the example of the University of Aalborg with an explicitly transdisciplinary approach in the area of biomedical technology can be a model where different disciplines are introduced in a balanced way and interdisciplinary communication is systematically trained.

The above considerations have decisive consequences for the planning of new RTD programmes. According to these results, it is not only important to verify the assumptions concerning the European technical and scientific performance in an ex-ante evaluation. In addition, it is necessary to explore the existing structures of involved actors and their respective function within a techno-scientific community. On this basis, it is possible to decide deliberately which types of actors should be combined - or not combined - in common projects.

On the basis of the interviews, it was not possible to determine clearly whether the participation in interdisciplinary research teams promotes or hampers the career perspectives of the researchers. The career perspectives are influenced by a large variety of factors wherein interdisciplinarity is only one element. Furthermore, the institutional arrangements of the interview partners largely differ according to the type of institution and the national framework so that, at least in this quite small sample, a clear result cannot be achieved. Therefore, this aspect is not mentioned in the case studies. Nevertheless, there are some indications that interdisciplinary research has often a negative - or at least no positive - impact on the scientific career of academic researchers.

In both case studies, institutional approaches seem to be quite a promising instrument of promotion. In contrast to RTD projects, where small groups of different institutions are combined for quite a short period on project basis, the institutional approach aims at linking medium-sized institutional groups with a limited, but long-term perspective and more flexible targets. In these long-term arrangements, it is important that the original aims of research can be modified according to intermediate results. The reorientation should be discussed within the institutional group in workshop-like meetings and with the participation of experts from the side of the Commission.

In dynamic research areas with a large number of research actors, it is important to achieve a sufficient co-ordination of the work. For that purpose, the establishment of networks and the set-up of databases are appropriate tools which are already successfully used in EC programmes such as MHR4 or ESPRIT. A further instrument - already promoted by the Commission as well - is the exchange of personnel.

Conferences and publications are effective tools for the dissemination of existing RTD results. Most interview partners, however, emphasise the problem of quality. In the case of conferences, this orientation can lead to a reduction of frequency and higher investments in the preparation of the remaining conferences. In addition, small workshops on topical problems can be helpful. In the case of publications, their financing within the projects has to be considered, because the preparation of articles with high quality and with an orientation on special target groups is time-consuming.

In both case studies, the problem of bureaucratic structures in the application procedures for RTD programmes and the delays of the respective decisions are mentioned by the interview partners. In face of the very large number of tenders and the complexity of the structure of actors of different national origin, one has to think in more detail about whether it is possible to achieve a more effective application procedure. A major aim of these considerations should be approaches to reach those institutions which have a high scientific performance but little experience in European application procedures.

An interesting common outcome of both case studies is the high scientific performance of institutions from small and less-favoured countries, whereas the technical performance of these countries is low. These results can be interpreted as a lack of coupling between the academic and industrial sector, especially in less-favoured countries. For an improvement of this situation, public promotion can aim at a better knowledge transfer from the public research sector to existing industrial enterprises. A further promising approach is the promotion of young technology-oriented enterprises as spin-offs of universities. In any case, the support of less-favoured regions should include leading-edge, science-intensive technologies on the basis of existing research activities in the public sector.

All in all, the study confirms the increasing importance of interdisciplinarity and emphasises its key function for advanced areas of technology. Especially in academic institutions, however, distinct barriers to interdisciplinarity often exist, so that support by external organisations is a decisive element for a successful set-up of interdisciplinary research.

Appendix

Part 1: Medical lasers

Table A 1-1:   Applicants at the European Patent Office (EPO) from EU countries
in the area of medical lasers for 1990 to 1991
Source: Database WPIL (Questel)

3 AESCULAP AG
3 MESSERSCHMITT-BOELKOW-BLOHM GMBH
3 SIEMENS AG
2 OMEGA UNIVERSAL HOLDINGS LTD
2 SCHOTT GLASWERKE
1 ADIR & CIE
1 ALCON PHARM LTD
1 BASF AG
1 BAUSCH & LOMB IRELAND
1 BOEHRINGER MANNHEIM GMBH
1 BUCHMANN OPTICAL EN
1 CHEVAL FRERES SA
1 CNRS CENT NAT RECH SCI
1 COMDENT GMBH
1 COMMISSARIAT ENERGIE ATOMIQUE
1 DIOMED LTD
1 DORNIER MEDIZINTECHNIK
1 ECLIPSE SURGICAL TECHNOLOGIES
1 ELOPAK LTD
1 EURO IND LTD
1 EUROCELTIQUE SA
1 FA CARL ZEISS
1 FIDIA SPA
1 FR KONSTRUKTIONSELEMENTE ZAHNPROTHETIK
1 GIP EXERCICE
1 INSERM INST NAT SANTE & RECH MED
1 JENOPTIK JENA DDR GMBH
1 KEYMED MED & IND EQ
1 LAICA LASER TECHN V
1 MEDIZINISCHES LASERZENTRUM LUEBECK
1 ROFIN SINAR LASER GMBH
1 SCI GENERICS LTD
1 SOC NAT MOTEURS AVIATON
1 TECHNOLAS LASER TECH GMBH
1 TECHNOMED INT
1 TELEMIT ELECTRONIC GMBH
1 UK ATOMIC ENERGY AUTHORITY
1 UNIV ALICANTE
1 UNIV VICTORIA MANCHESTER
1 WOLF R GMBH

12 FREE INVENTORS

Table A 1-2:   Applicants at the European Patent Office (EPO) from EU countries
in the area of medical lasers for 1988 to 1989
Source: WPIL (Questel)

5 MESSERSCHMITT-BOLKOW-BLOHM GMBH
4 RODENSTOCK G INSTRU
2 FA ZEISS CARL
1 AESCULAP AG
1 AKZO PATENTE GMBH
1 ALCON PHARM
1 AMERSHAM INT PLC
1 BIOTRONIK MESS-&
1 BRITISH TELECOM PLC
1 CENT INT RECH CANCE
1 CONSIGLIO NAZ DELLE RICERCHE
1 DENTAURUM WINKELSTR
1 DORNIE MEDDIZINTECH
1 FRAUNHOFER-GES FORD ANGE
1 GEN ELECTRIC CGR SA
1 GENERAL ELECTRIC CGR SA
1 HARTMETALLWERK MAIE
1 HERAEUS GMBH W C
1 INST OPHTHALMOS SA
1 KEYMED MED IND EQUI
1 LENTIA GMBH
1 LEUVEN RES & DEV
1 NAT RES DEV CORP
1 RAP RECH AUTO PRUFT
1 RED KITE TECHN LTD
1 SCI GENERICS LTD
1 SIEMENS AG
1 SINERGY SA
1 SOCOP NAHRUNGSMITTEL HANDELSGES
1 STORZ K & CO GMBH
1 TECHNOMED INT
1 TELEMIT ELTRN GMBH
1 THOMSON COMP MICROO
1 ULRICH DARDENNE-STI
1 UNIV COLLEGE LONDON

18 FREE INVENTORS

Table A 1-3:   Applicants at the European Patent Office (EPO) from non-EU
                countries in the area of medical lasers for 1990 to 1991
                Source: Database WPIL (Questel)

6 COHERENT INC
5 ALLERGAN INC
5 EASTMAN KODAK CO
5 GEN HOSPITAL CORP
5 LASERSCOPE
4 CANDELA LASER CORP
4 KOWA CO LTD
4 MASSACHUSETTS INST TECHNOLOGY
3 BARD INC C R
3 CIBA GEIGY AG
3 LASER ENG INC
2 ADVANCED SYSTEM INC
2 BOSTON ADVANCED TECHNOLOGIES INC
2 EYE RES INST RETINA FOUND
2 HUGHES AIRCRAFT CO
2 IBM CORP
2 L'ESPERANCE MEDICAL TECHNOLOGIES INC
2 MEDITRON DEVICES INC
2 PHOENIX LASER SYSTEMS INC
2 PREMIER LASER SYSTEMS INC
2 SCHNEIDER
2 SLT JAPAN CO LTD
2 SORENSON LAB INC
3 SUMMIT TECHNOLOGY INC
2 SURGICAL INC
1 ACCULASE INC
1 ALBERTA INC
1 ALCON SURGICAL INC
1 AMERICAN MEDICAL SYSTEMS INC
1 AMERICAN TELEPHONE & TELEGRAPH CO
1 AMOCO CORP
1 ANGELASE INC
1 ARIA CORP
1 AURORA LASER INC
1 BAXTER INT INC
1 BRIGHAM & WOMENS HOSPITAL
1 CEDARS SINAI MEDICAL CENT
1 COLORADO LASER MARKING INC
1 COMMONWEALTH SCI & IND RES ORG
1 DANFORTH BIOMEDICAL INC
1 DE BEERS IND DIAMOND
1 DYNAMET INC
1 ENDO TECHNIC CORP
1 FUJI OPTICAL SYSTEMS
1 GEBR SULZER AG
1 GENERAL ELECTRIC CO
1 GEORGIA TECH RES CORP

1 GLYCOMED INC
1 GORE & ASSOC INC W
1 GREEN CROSS CORP
1 HAMAMATSU PHOTONICS KK
1 HEALTH RES INC
1 HERAEUS LASERSONICS INC
1 INTELLIGENT SURGICA
1 INTERFACE BIOMEDICAL LAB CORP
1 IRIS MEDICAL INSTR INC
1 ISHIKAWAJIMA HARIMA JUKOGYO KK
1 JTT INT INC
1 LASAG AG
1 LASB LASER CORP
1 LASERSURGE INC
1 LENTEC CORP
1 LTV AEROSPACE & DEFENCE CO
1 MATSUTANI SEISAKUSHO KK
1 MEGADYNE MEDICAL PROD INC
1 MINNESOTA MINING & MFG CO
1 MYRIADLASE INC
1 NESTLE SA
1 NIM INC
1 PFIZER HOSPITAL PROD GROUP INC
1 PHOENIX LASER SYST
1 SHIMADZU CORP
1 SONY CORP
1 SUNRISE TECHNOLOGIE
1 TOPCON CORP
1 TOSOH CORP
1 TRIMEDYNE INC
1 UNIV COLUMBIA NEW YORK
1 UNIV CONNECTICUT
1 UNIV INDIANA FOUND
1 UNIV TEXAS SYSTEM
1 US DEPT OF ENERGY
1 US SURGICAL CORP
1 VIVASCAN CORP
1 WARNER LAMBERT CO
1 YEDA RES & DEV CO LTD

38 FREE INVENTORS

Table A 1-4:   Medical lasers, institutions located in the European Union related to publications of 1991 and 1992 in the database SCI, ranking according to major cities

Major Cities

84 London, GB	19 UNIV COLL HOSP	3 NO INFORMATION
		10 NATL MED LASER CTR
		2 DEPT RADIOTHERAPY
		1 DEPT ANAT & DEV BIOL
		1 DEPT CONSERVAT DENT
		1 DEPT GASTROENTEROL
		1 DEPT ORAL & MAXILLOFACIAL SURG
		1 INFLAMMAT GRP
	10 MOORFIELDS EYE HOSP	7 NO INFORMATION
		2 DEPT RETINAL DIAGNOST
		1 DEPT CLIN OPHTHALMOL
	9 GUYS & ST THOMAS HOSP	1 NO INFORMATION
		3 DEPT SURG
		2 DEPT CONSERVAT DENTSURG
		2 DEPT PAEDIAT CARDIOL
		1 DEPT OBSTET & GYNAECOL
	8 KINGS COLL SCH MED & DENT	1 NO INFORMATION
		2 DEPT SURG
		2 HARRIS BIRTHRIGHT RES CTR FETAL MED
		1 DEPT CARDIOL
		1 DEPT CLIN BIOCHEM
		1 DEPT OPHTHALMOL
	7 ST BARTHOLOMEWS HOSP	3 PROFESSORIAL SURG UNIT
		1 DEPT CARDIOL
		1 DEPT RADIOL
		1 DEPT RHEUMATOL,INFLAMMAT & ARTHRITIS GRP
		1 WILLIAM HARVEY RES INST

6 UNIV COLL & MIDDLESEX HOSP MED SCH

3 DEPT RADIOL

2 NATL MED LASER CTR

1 DEPT SURG

4 INST OPHTHALMOL — 4 NO INFORMATION

4 ST THOMAS HOSP — 2 NO INFORMATION

1 DEPT OPHTHALMOL

1 LAMBETH WING EYE DEPT

3 CHEST HOSP — 1 NO INFORMATION

2 DEPT THORAC MED

1 DEPT ANAESTHET

1 DEPT CARDIOTHORAC SURG;

1 DEPT OPHTHALMOL

3 HAMMERSMITH HOSP — 2 DEPT RADIOL

1 DEPT PATHOL

3 INST UROL — 3 NO INFORMATION

3 ROYAL COLL HOSP — 3 DEPT SURG

3 ROYAL POSTGRAD MED SCH — 1 DEPT HISTOCHEM

1 DEPT HISTOPATHOL

1 DEPT MED PHYS,DERMATOL UNIT

2 NATL HEART & LUNG INST — 2 DEPT CARDIAC MED

2 QUEEN CHARLOTTES & CHELSEA HOSP — 2 DEPT OBSTET & GYNECOL

2 ST MARYS HOSP — 2 DEPT SURG

2 WESTMINSTER MED SCH & HOSP — 1 NO INFORMATION

1 DEPT SURG

1 MARYS HOSP — 1 NO INFORMATION

1 QUEEN MARY & WESTFIELD COLL — 1 INTERDISCIPLINARY RES CTR BIOMEDMAT

1 ROYAL MARSDEN HOSP — 1 NO INFORMATION

1 WHIPPS CROSS HOSP & CHEST CLIN — 1 NO INFORMATION

51 Paris,FR — 21 UNIV PARIS 12, HOP HENRI MONDOR — 4 NO INFORMATION

5 SERV EXPLORAT FONCTIONNELLES

5 INSERM

			3 FRAUENKLIN
			2 DEPT CARDIOVASC SURG
			2 DEPT SURG
			1 DEPT MED
30 München, DE	7 TECH UNIV MÜNCHEN KLINIKUM RECHTS ISAR		1 NO INFORMATION
			3 DEPT INTERNAL MED 2
			1 DEPT VASC SURG
			1 INST ALLGEMEINE PATHOL & PATHOLANAT
			1 UROL KLIN
	6 UNIV MÜNCHEN, KLINIKUM GROSSHADERN		1 NO INFORMATION
			2 HALS NASEN OHRENHEILKUNDE KLIN & POLIKLIN, M
			1 ORTHOPAD KLIN
			1 FRAUENKLIN
			1 INST SURG RES
	4 UNIV MÜNCHEN, AUGENKLIN		2 NO INFORMATION
			1 DEPT OPHTHALMOL
			1 H WACKER LAB MED LASER APPLICAT
	3 KLINIKUM MUNCHEN BOGENHAUSEN		1 MED KLIN 1
			1 DIV CARDIOL
			1 INST PATHOL
	2 MBB MED TECH		2 NO INFORMATION
	2 STADT KRANKENHAUSES MÜNCHEN HARLACHING		2 GASTROENTEROL ABT
	2 UNIV MÜNCHEN,DERMATOL KLIN & POLIKLIN		2 NO INFORMATION
	1 GSF MÜNCHEN		1 CENT LASER LAB
	1 INST & POLIKLIN STRAHLEN- THERAPIE & ONKOL		1 NO INFORMATION
	1 UNIV MÜNCHEN		1 NO INFORMATION
	1 UNIV MÜNCHEN INNENSTADTKLINIKEN		1 INST NEUROPATHOL

24 Utrecht, NL	18 UNIV HOSP	9 INST HEART & LUNG,DEPT CARDIOL
		2 DEPT NEUROL,RES LAB
		1 ,INST MOLEC BIOL & GENET
		1 CTR BIOSTAT
		1 DEPT DERMATOL
		1 DEPT MED INSTRUMENTAT
		1 DEPT NEUROSURG
		1 DEPT RADIOL
		1 JANUS JONGBLOED RES CTR
	6 INTERUNIV CARDIOL	6 NO INFORMATION
22 Amsterdam, NL	17 UNIV AMSTERDAM,ACAD MED CTR	1 NO INFORMATION
		8 CTR LASER
		2 DEPT GASTROENTEROL
		2 DEPT RADIOL
		1 DEPT EXPTL SURG
		1 DEPT PLAST RECONSTRUCT & HAND SURG
		1 DEPT PATHOL
		1 DEPT EAR NOSE & THROAT
	5 FREE UNIV AMSTERDAM HOSP	1 INST EXTRAMURAL MED RES
		1 DEPT REHABIL MED
		1 DEPT PULM MED
		1 DEPT PATHOL
		1 DEPT OTORHINOLARYNGOL
19 Heidelberg, DE	18 UNIV HEIDELBERG	6 FRAUENKLIN,GYNAKOL RADIOL ABT
		4 AUGEN KLIN
		2 INST MED BIOMETRIE & INFORMAT
		1 ABT INNERE MED
		1 ABT KARDIOL
		1 CHIRURG KLIN
		1 DEPT PAEDIAT,DIV NEONATOL
		1 INST ANGEW PHYS
		1 KINDERKLIN
	1 THORAXKLIN HEIDELBERG ROHRB.	1 CHIRURG ABT

19 Lille, FR	5 CTR HOSP REG & UNIV	2 CTR LASERS & OPTRON MED
		1 SERV OTORHINOLARYNGOL
		1 ,MALAD APPAREIL DIGEST CLIN
		1 CTR TRAITEMENT LASER
		1 CTR MULTIDISCIPLINAIRE TRAITMENT LASER
	5 HOP CARDIOL LILLE	1 NO INFORMATION
		1 SERV CHIRURG CARDIOVASC B
		1 SERV CHIRURG CARDIOVASC A
		1 SERV CARDIOL B
		1 DEPT ANESTHESIE
	5 INSERM	1 NO INFORMATION
		3 UNITE 279
		1 INST PASTEUR
	2 CNRS	2 LAB SPECTROSCOPIE MOLEC LILLE
	2 LAB SPECTROSCOPIE HERTZIENNE	2 NO INFORMATION
19 Milano, IT	9 UNIV MILANO	7 CLIN OCULIST
		1 DEPT OBSTET & GYNECOL L MANGIAGALLI
		1 INST VASC SURG & ANGIOL
	3 IST NAZL STUDIO & CURA TUMORI	2 DIV ENDOSCOPY
		1 SERV FIS SANITARIA;
	3 CTR AMBROSIANO	1 NO INFORMATION
		2 MICROCHIRURG OCULARE
	1 POLITECN MILAN	1 IST FIS,CTR ELETTR QUANTIST & STRUMENTAZ ELETTR
	1 FATEBENEFRATELLI HOSP	1 DEPT UROL
	1 CLIN S AMBROGIO	1 NO INFORMATION
	1 QUANTA SYST INC	1 NO INFORMATION
		1 DEPT MED PHYS
		1 DEPT OPHTHALMOL,
		1 DEPT SURG

18 Berlin, DE	7 FREIE UNIV BERLIN, KLINIKUM STEGLITZ	2 KINDERCHIRURG ABT,
		1 INST MED TECH PHYS & LASERMED
		1 DEPT GASTROENTEROL
		1 DEPT GENET MOLEC
		1 DEPT INTERNAL MED
		1 DEPT PAEDIAT SURG
	3 FREIE UNIV BERLIN,KLINIKUM CHARLOTTENBURG	3 AUGENKLIN
	3 SCHLOSSPK KLIN	3 AUGENABT
	1 DEPT CARDIOTHORAC SURG	1 NO INFORMATION
	1 HUMBOLDT UNIV	1 FAC MED. INNERE
	1 KLINIKUM BERLIN	1 KINDERKLIN 3
	1 LASER MED CTR GMBH	1 NO INFORMATION
	1 TECH UNIV BERLIN,KLINIKUM RUDOLF VIRCHOW	1 AUGENKLIN
17 Bonn, DE	16 UNIV BONN	7 FRAUENKLINIK & HEBAMMEN-SCHULE
		3 INST PATHOL
		2 NUKL MED KLIN
		2 INST ANGEW PHYS
		1 CHIRURG KLIN
		1 UROL KLIN
	1 GASTROENTEROL PRAXIS	1 NO INFORMATION
13 Erlangen, DE	13 UNIV ERLANGEN NURNBERG	3 MED KLIN (NO INFORMATION)
		5 DEPT OPHTHALMOL
		2 HOSP EYE
		1 UROL KLIN
		1 NEUROCHIRURG KLIN
		1 INST BIOMED STAT
13 Leuven, BE	7 KATHOLIEKE UNIV, HOSP GASTHUISBERG	2 DEPT OBSTET & GYNAECO
		2 DEPT CARDIOL
		2 DEPT UROL
		1 DEPT RADIOL
	5 KATHOLIEKE UNIV, CLIN ST LUC	5 DEPT GYNECOL INFERTIL RES UNIT
	1 KATHOLIEKE UNIV	1 DEPT DIDACT PHYS

11 Lübeck, DE	9 MED UNIV	2 DERMATOL & VENEROL KLIN
		2 CHIRURG KLIN
		2 INST PATHOL
		2 INST ANAT
		1 DEPT RADIOL
	2 MED LASERZENTRUM	2 NO INFORMATION
	LUEBECK GMBH	
9 Manchester,	6 UNIV	4 DEPT PHYS
GB		2 DEPT PATHOL SCI
	3 N MANCHESTER GRP HOSP	1 DEPT RADIOL
		1 DEPT NEUROSURG
		1 DEPT NEURORADIOL
9 Ulm, DE	9 UNIV	3 FRAUENKLIN
		2 INST LASERTECHNOL MED
		2 INNERE MED KARDIOL ANGIOL
		PNEUMONOL ABT4
		2 AUGENKLIN
9 Valencia, SP	7 UNIV	1 NO INFORMATION
		2 DEPT QUIM FIS
		1 DEPT SURG
		1 DEPT QUIM INORGAN
		1 DEPT BIOL ANIM
		1 DEPT ANAT
	1 HOSP DR PESET	1 DEPT CLIN CHEM
	1 CTR INVEST BIOMED	1 NO INFORMATION
	APLICADAS	
7 Aalborg, DK	5 UNIV	5 DEPT MED INFORMAT
	2 HOSP	1 DEPT UROL
		1 DEPT MED INFORMAT

Part 2: Neural networks

Table A 2-1:   Applicants at the European Patent Office (EPO) from EU countries
in the area of neural networks for 1990 to 1991
Source: Database WPIL (Questel)

8 SIEMENS AG
7 PHILIPS
6 THOMSON CSF
3 BODENSEEWERK GERAETETECH GMBH
2 BASF AG
2 BRITISH TELECOM PLC
2 KINGS COLLEGE LONDON
1 ATP-ARBEITSGRUPPE
1 BRITISH TEXTILE TECHNOLOGY GROUP
1 COMMISSARIAT ENERGIE ATOMIQUE
1 DAIMLER-BENZ AG
1 ERNO RAUMFAHRTTECH GMBH
1 PURPLE ELEKTROCHEMISCHE IND GMBH
1 SERVICES PETROL SCHLUMBERGER
1 STANDARD ELEKTRIK LORENZ AG
1 TELMAT INFORMATIQUE EURL
1 UK SEC FOR DEFENCE

3 FREE INVENTORS

Tabel A 2-2:   Applicants at the European Patent Office (EPO) from non-EU
countries in the area of neural networks for 1990 to 1991
Source: Database WPIL (Questel)

15 IBM CORP
10 MATSUSHITA ELEC IND CO LTD
8 DU PONT DE NEMOURS & CO E I
6 CANON KK
6 EASTMAN KODAK CO
6 FUJITSU LTD
6 HITACHI ENG CO LTD
5 INTEL CORP
5 MASSACHUSETTS INST TECHNOLOGY
5 MOTOROLA INC
4 GENERAL ELECTRIC CO
4 UNIV BOSTON
4 YOZAN INC
3 SONY CORP
3 TOSHIBA KK
2 ADAPTIVE SOLUTIONS INC
2 AMERICAN TELEPHONE & TELEGRAPH CO
2 FUJI PHOTO FILM CO LTD
2 HONEYWELL INC
2 HUGHES AIRCRAFT CO
2 MITSUBISHI DENKI KK

2 NCR CORP
2 TOYOTA KOKI KK
2 UNIV IOWA STATE RES FOUND INC
1 ALLEN-BRADLEY CO
1 APPL ELTRN VISION
1 ARINC RES CORP
1 ATLANTIC RICHFIELD CO
1 AUSTRALIAN ELECTRO OPTICS PTY
1 AUTOMATION TECNHNOLOGY INC
1 CALIFORNIA INST OF TECHN
1 CORNELL RES FOUND INC
1 DAINIPPON SCREEN SEIZO
1 ENERGY CONVERSION DEVICES INC
1 FUJI PHOTO FILM KK
1 GAMMA-METRICS
1 HCS IND AUTOMATION BV
1 HNC INC
1 HONDA GIKEN KOGYO KK
1 IMPACQ TECHN INC
1 IRVINE SENSORS CORP
1 KAWASAKI STEEL CORP
1 KOMATSU SEISAKUSHO KK
1 LERNOUT & HAUSPIE SPEECHPRODUCTS
1 LUMINIS PTY LTD
1 MICROELTRN & COMP
1 MILLTECH-HOH INC
1 NAT SEMICONDUCTOR CORP
1 NEC CORP
1 NEUROMED SYST INC
1 NEUROSCIENCES RES FOUND INC
1 NIPPON TELEG & TELEPH
1 NISSAN MOTOR CO LTD
1 OREGON GRADUATE INST SCI & TECHN
1 PRAXAIR TECHNOLOGY INC
1 R & D ASSOC
1 RCA LICENSING CORP
1 ROCKWELL INT CORP
1 SCITEX CORP LTD
1 SEIKO INSTR INC
1 SHARP KK
1 STANFORD TELECOM IN
1 TELECTRONICS NV
1 TEXACO DEV CORP
1 THINKING MACH CORP
1 TOA MEDICAL ELECTRONICS CO LTD
1 UNIV FLORIDA
1 UNIV GEORGIA RES FO
1 UNIV OF TEXAS SYST
1 UNIV SYDNEY
1 UNIV UTAH
1 US DEPT ENERGY
1 WACOM KK
1 WESTERN THUNDER

7 FREE INVENTORS

Table A 2-3:   Neuronal networks, institutions located in the European Union related to publications of 1992 in the database INSPEC, ranking according to major cities and to some major institutions

Major Cities

30 London, GB	8 King's College Univ.	3 NO INFORMATION
		3 DEPT. OF ELECTRON. & ELECTR. ENGINEERING
		1 WHEATSTONE LABORATORY
		1 DEPT. OF MATHEMATICS
	7 Univ. College	4 DEPT. OF COMPUTER SCIENCE
		2 DEPT. OF ANATOMY
		1 DEPT. OF PSYCHOLOGY
	6 Imperial College	3 NO INFORMATION
		3 DEPT. OF ELECTRON. & ELECTR. ENGINEERING
	1 Queen Mary & Westfield College	1 DEPT. OF COMPUTER SCIENCE
	1 R. Holloway & Bedford College	1 DEPT. OF COMPUTER SCIENCE
	1 St. George's Hospital Med. School	1 DEPT. OF PHYSIOLOGY
	1 City Univ.	1 DEPT. OF ELECTRON. & ELECTR. ENGINEERING
	1 Polytechnic of Central	1 INDEPENDENT CONTROL CENTRE
	1 Thames Polytechnic School of England	1 NO INFORMATION
	1 MRC Cognitive Development Unit	1 NO INFORMATION
	1 School of Economy	1 NO INFORMATION
	1 Citibank Na.	1 INVESTMENT UNIT, TREASURY
26 Ipswich, GB	26 British Telecom Laboratories	23 NO INFORMATION
		1 NF. SWITCHING & PROCESS.
		1 SPEECH & LANGUAGE TECHNOL. SECT.
		1 IMAGE PROCESS. SECT.
22 Roma, IT	15 Univ.	4 NO INFORMATION
		4 DIPARTIMENTO DI FISICA
		3 DIPARTIMENTO DI MATEMATICA
		3 INFN
		1 DIPARTIMENTO DI PSICOLOGIA

	4 CNR	4 ISTITUTO DI PSICOLOGIA
	1 ENEA	1 NO INFORMATION
	1 Fondazione Ugo Bordoni	1 NO INFORMATION
	1 Pontificial Gregorian Univ.	1 NO INFORMATION
21 München, DE	9 Technische Univ.	1 NO INFORMATION
		5 INST. FOR NETWORK THEORY & CIRCUIT DESIGN
		2 DEPT. OF PHYSICS
		1 INST. FUR INFORMATIK
	2 Ludwig-Maximilians-Univ.	1 NO INFORMATION
		1 INST. OF NEUROPATHOLOGY
	9 Siemens AG	3 NO INFORMATION
		6 ZENTRALE FORSCHUNG UND ENTWICKLUNG
	1 Kratzer Automatisierung GmbH	1 NO INFORMATION
21 Oxford, GB	20 University	2 NO INFORMATION
		9 DEPT. OF THEORETIC PHYSICS
		6 DEPT. OF PHYSICS
		2 DEPT. OF ENG. SCIENCE
		1 DEPT. OF EXPERIM ENTAL PSYCHOLOGY
	1 Europe LTD.	1 NO INFORMATION
20 Genova, IT	15 Univ.	10 DEPT. OF BIOPHYS. & ELECTRON ENGINEERING
		4 DEPT. OF PHYSICS
		1 DEPT. OF COMMUN. COMPUT. & SYST. SCIENCE
	5 CNR	5 ISTITUTO PER I CIRCUITI ELETTRONICI
20 Milano, IT	9 Univ.	1 NO INFORMATION
		8 DIPARTIMENTO DI SCI. DELL'INFORMAZIONE
	8 Poltecnico	3 NO INFORMATION
		4 DIPARTIMENTO DI ELETTRONICA
		1 DEPT. OF NUCLEAR ENGINEERING
	1 Cattolica Univ.	1 NO INFORMATION
	1 Advanced Computing Systems	1 NO INFORMATION
	1 Cefriel	1 NO INFORMATION

18 Paris, FR	5 Ecole normale superieure	1 NO INFORMATION
		2 LAB. DE PHYSIQUE STAT.
		2 LAB. DE PHYS. THEORIQUE
	3 Univ. Rene Descartes	3 ECOLE DES HAUTES ETUDES EN INF.
	2 Ecole nat. superieure des Telecommun.	1 NO INFORMATION
		1 DEPT. IMAGES
	2 Ecole superieure de Phys. et de Chimi	1 NO INFORMATION
		1 LAB. D'ELECTRON.
	1 Inst. Pasteur	1 NO INFORMATION
	1 XI Univ.	1 LRI (ORSAY)
	1 Telecom	1 CNRS
	1 Univ. Pierre et Marie Curie	1 LAB. D'INF. DES SCI. DE LA TERRE
	1 Soc. anonyme des Telecommun.	1 DIV. OPTRONIQUE ET DEFENSE,
	1 Thomson	1 CSF/SDC
15 Leuven, BE	15 Katholieke Univ.	4 NO INFORMATION
		5 INST. VOOR THEOR. FYSICA
		2 DEPT. OF ELECTR. ENGINEERING
		2 DEPT. OF METALL. & MATER. ENGINEERING
		2 LAB. VOOR NEURO- EN PSYCHOFYSIOLOGIE
14 Cambridge, GB	13 Univ.	7 NO INFORMATION
		2 COMPUTER LABORATORY
		1 DEPT. OF CHEMISTRY
		1 DEPT. OF ENG.
		1 PHYSIOLOGY LABORATORY
		1 INST. OF ASTRONOMY
	1 Sci. Generics Ltd.	1 NO INFORMATION
11 Uxbridge, GB	11 Brunel Univ.	4 DEPT. OF ELECTRON. & ELECTR. ENGINEERING
		3 DEPT. OF DESIGN
		3 DEPT. HUMAN SCI.
		1 DEPT. OF MANUF. & ENG. SYST.

10 Sheffield, GB	9 Univ.	2 NO INFORMATION
		6 DEPT. OF AUTOM. CONTROL & SYST.
		1 DEPT. OF ELECTRON. & ELECTR. ENGINEERING
	1 City Polytechnic	1 SCHOOL OF ENG. INF. TECHNOL.
10 Stuttgart, DE	8 Univ.	1 NO INFORMATION
		5 INST. FUR MIKROELEKTRONIK
		1 INST. FUR HOCHFREQUENZTECHNIK
		1 INST. FUR THEOR. PHYS. UND SYNERGETIK
	1 Max-Planck-Institut	1 FESTKORPERFORSCHUNG
	1 Fraunhofer-Institut	1 MANUF. ENG. & AUTOMATION
10 Napoli, IT	4 Univ.	3 DIPARTIMENTO DI INF. E SISTEMISTICA
		1 DIPARTIMENTO DI SCI. FISICHE
	4 CNR	3 ISTITUTO PER LA RICERCA SUI SISTEMI INFORMATICI PARALLELI
		1 ISTITUTO DI CIBERNETICA
	2 INFN	1 NO INFORMATION
10 Newcastle, GB	10 Univ.	2 NO INFORMATION
		7 DEPT. OF CHEM. & PROCESS ENGINEERING
		1 DEPT. OF ENGLISH LANGUAGE
9 Nijmegen, NL	8 Univ.	3 NO INFORMATION
		4 DEPT. OF MED. PHYS. & BIOPHYS.
		1 FAC. OF MATHEMATICS & INFORMATICS
	1 Catholic Univ.	1 DEPT. OF ANALYTIC CHEMISTRY
8 Bochum, DE	8 Ruhr-Univ.	4 INST. FUR NEUROINFORMATIK
		2 INST. FUR MATHEMATIK
		1 INST. FUR PHYSIOLOGIE
		1 LEHRSTUHL FUER NACHRICHTEN-TECHNIK
8 Athen, GR	3 NRCPS 'Demokritos'	3 INST. OF INF. & TELECOMMUN.
	3 Nat. techn. Univ	3 DEPT. OF ELECTR. & COMPUT. ENGINEERING

	1 Pliroforiki Ltd.	1 NO INFORMATION
	1 Amper Sa Inf. Syst.	1 NO INFORMATION
8 Pisa, IT	4 Univ.	4 DIPARTIMENTO DI INGEGNERIA DELL'INF.
	3 CNR	2 ISTITUTO DI ELABORAZIONE DELLA INF.
		1 INST. OF CLINICAL PHYSIOLOGY
	1 INFN	1 NO INFORMATION
8 Torino, IT	3 Univ.	1 NO INFORMATION
		1 ISTITUTO DI ECONOMIA POLITICA
		1 DEPT. OF THEOR. PHYSICS
	3 Politecnico	2 NO INFORMATION
		1 DIPART. DI SIST. DI PRODUZ. ED ECON. DELL'AZIENDA
	2 CSELT	2 NO INFORMATION
8 Warwick, GB	8 Univ.	3 NO INFORMATION
		4 DEPT. OF ENGINEERING
		1 SCHOOL OF IND. & BUS. STUDIES

Other Major Institutions

6 GEC	3 NO INFORMATION
MARCONI	3 HIRST RES. CENTRE
6 GMD	6 no dept
3 ALCATEL	3 DIN, ALCATEL ALSTHOM RECHERCHE
3 PHILIPS	2 RES. LABS., EINDHOVEN
	1 RES. LAB. AACHEN
3 THOMSON	2 LAB. ELECTRON. DE RENNES
CSF	1 SDC, PARIS

Table A 2-4:   Neuronal network, institutions located in the European Union related to publications of 1991 to 1992 in the database SCI, ranking according to major cities and to some major institutions

Major Cities

52 London, GB	17 Imperial college	2 NO INFORMATION
		4 DEPT ELECT ENGN
		4 DEPT COMP SCI
		3 CANC RES FUND,BIOMOLEC MODELLING LAB
		2 DEPT CHEM
		2 DEPT PHYS
	14 Kings college	2 NO INFORMATION
		8 DEPT MATH
		2 WHEATSTONE LAB
		2 CTR NEURAL NETWORKS
	10 UNIV COLL	8 DEPT COMP SCI
		2 DEPT ANAT
	2 R.Holloway & Bedford college	2 DEPT COMP
	2 School of Economy	2 NO INFORMATION
	2 HIRST RES CTR	2 LONG RANGE RES LAB
	2 HAMMERSMITH HOSP	2 MRC,CYCLOTRON UNIT;
	1 Brunel Univ.	1 DEPT ELECT ENGN
	1 CHARING CROSS HOSP	1 DEPT CLIN NEUROSCI
	1 British Telecommun	1 NO INFORMATION
37 Paris, FR	15 Univ.	3 NO INFORMATION
		3 INST NEUROSCI,DEPT NEUROSCI VIS,
		2 NEUROPHYSIOL LAB
		2 RECH INFORMAT LAB
		1 ECOLE HAUTES ETUDES INFORMAT
		1 LPNHE;
		1 UFR MATH
		1 ACCELERATEUR LINEAIRE LAB
		1 OCEANOG DYNAM & CLIMATOL LAB
	10 CNRS	1 NO INFORMATION

		4 MATH LAB
		2 PHYS THEOR LAB
		2 NEUROSENSORY PHYSIOL LAB
		1 INST ELECTR FONDAMENTALE,CNRS
	5 Ecole super Phys & Chim ind.	2 NO INFORMATION
		3 ELECTR LAB
	2 ECOLE NORM SUPER	2 DEPT PHYS
	1 Coll.	1 PHYS CORPUSCULAIRE LAB
	1 Ecole cent	1 LAB GIC
	1 Inst Pasteur	1 NO INFORMATION
	1 CTR NATL ADM METEOROL	1 NO INFORMATION
	1 CONSERVATOIRE NATL ARTS & METIERS	1 NO INFORMATION
28 Oxford, GB	27 Univ.	2 NO INFORMATION
		8 DEPT. OF PHYSICS
		8 DEPT. OF THEORETIC PHYSICS
		3 DEPT. OF ENG. SCIENCE
		2 PHYS. CEM. LAB.
		2 DEPT EXPTL PSYCHOL
		1 PHYSIOL LAB,
		1 NUCL PHYS LAB.
	1 MRC	1 ANAT NEUROPHARMACOL UNIT
24 Leuven, BE	23 Katholieke Univ.	7 INST THEORET FYS
		6 DEPT ELEKTROTECH., ESAT
		5 NEURO & PSYCHOFYSIOL LAB,
		2 DEPT MET & MAT ENGN
		1 ESAT MICAS
		1 DEPT MATH
		1 MICROELECTR LAB
	1 Lab Control Syst	1 NO INFORMATION
22 Rom, IT	14 Univ.	5 DIPARTIMENTO FIS
		4 DIPARTIMENTO MATEMAT
		3 INFO COM DPT
		1 IST FISIOL UMANA;
		1 INST PSYCHOL
	2 CNR	2 INST PSYCHOL

	1 Catholic Univ. Sacred Heart	1 INST CARDIOL
	4 INFN	2 NO INFORMATION
		1 SEZ
		1 IST SUPER SANITA
	1 SIP	1 DG PO PDE
19 Barcelona, ES	12 UNIV AUTONOMA	5 CTR NACL MICROELECTR
		3 DEPT STRUCT & CONSTITUENTS MATTER
		1 DEPT INFORMAT
		1 DEPT FIS FONAMENTAL
		1 FIS ALTES ENERGIES LAB
		1 UNITAT ENGN QUIM
	6 UNIV POLITECN CATALUNA	3 DEPT TEORIA SENAL & COMUN
		2 DPTO ELECTR
		1 CSIC,INST CIBERNET
	1 ESCOLA TECN SUPER INGN TELECOMMUN	1 NO INFORMATION
19 München, DE	12 Techn. Univ.	2 NO INFORMATION
		5 INST NETWORK THEORY & CIRCUIT DESIGN
		4 DEPT PHYS
		1 INST ORGAN CHEM
	1 Univ München, Klinikum Großhadern	1 INST KLIN CHEM
	6 Siemens AG	2 NO INFORMATION
		4 CORP RES & DEV
16 Ipswich, GB	British Telecommun	11 NO INFORMATION
		2 INFORMAT SWITCHING & PROC,
		1 MATH CONSULTANCY GRP
		1 DNR
		1 DIV SYST RES,
	4 NRCPS 'Demokritos'	1 NO INFORMATION
		2 INST INFORMAT & TELECOMMUN
		1 INST NUCL PHYS
13 Göttingen, DE	9 Univ.	5 INST THEORET PHYS,
		2 INST PHYSIOL
		2 DRITTES PHYS INST

	2 Max - Planck - Inst.	2 INST BIOPHYS CHEM
	2 UNIV KLINIKUM	1 No dept
		1 NEUROPHYSIOL ABT
9 Bologna, IT	5 INFN	5 NO INFORMATION
	4 Univ.	3 DIPARTIMENTO FISICA
		1 DEPT BIOL,BIOPHYS LAB
8 Amsterdam, NL	5 Univ.	1 NO INFORMATION
		2 DEPT EXPTL ZOOL
		2 DEPT AQUAT ECOL;
	2 NL Inst. Brain Res.	2 NO INFORMATION
	1 Natl. Inst. Nucl. Phys. & High Energy Phys.	1 NO INFORMATION
8 Erlangen, DE	8 Univ. Erlangen-Nürnberg	1 NO INFORMATION
		3 INST ALLG. & THEORET. ELEKTROTECHNIK
		2 INST ORGAN CHEM
		1 ELECT ENGN
		1 INST PATTERN RECOGNIT
8 Glasgow, GB	5 Univ.	1 DEPT CELL BIOL
		1 DEPT CHIM GEN & INORGAN
		2 DEPT MECH ENGN
		1 DEPT MED CARDIOL
	2 UNIV STRATHCLYDE	2 DEPT ELECTR & ELECT ENGN
	1 Western Infirm & Associated Hosp.	1 TENNENT INST OPHTHALMOL
8 Newcastle, GB	8 UNIV	7 DEPT CHEM & PROC ENGN
		1 DEPT ELECT & ELECTR ENGN
8 Trieste, IT	4 Univ.	3 DIPARTIMENTO FISICA
		1 DEEI
	4 INFN	4 NO INFORMATION
8 Uxbridge, GB	8 Brunel Univ.	3 DEPT HUMAN SCI
		3 DEPT ELECT ENGN & ELECTR
		1 DEPT MFG & ENGN SYST;
		1 ASPEX MICROSYST
7 Berlin, DE	Freie Univ.	2 FACHBEREICH PHYS,AG BIOPHYS
		1 INST PHYSIOL
	Bundesanstalt Arbeitsmedizin	1 NO INFORMATION

	Rudolf Virchow Krankenhaus	1 NEUROCHIRURG KLINIK
	HUMBOLDT UNIV	1 DEPT PHYS 4
	TECH UNIV	1 INST ANGEW INFORMAT
7 Granada, ES	7 Univ	3 DEPT ELECTR & TECNOL COMPUTADORES
		1 DEPT SOCIOL & PSICOL;
		1 DEPT FIS APLICADA
		1 DEPT FIS MODERNA
		1 DPTO CIENCIAS COMPUTAC & INTELIGENCIA ARTIFICIAL
7 Manchester, GB	7 Univ	2 INST SCI & TECHNOL,DEPT COMPUTAT
		1 DEPT COMP SCI
		1 DEPT MED BIOPHYSWOLFSON IMAGE ANAL UNIT
		1 DEPT PHYSIOL SCI
		1 DEPT PSYCHOL
		1 DEPT THEORET PHYS
6 Cambridge, GB	4 Univ.	1 PHYSIOL LAB
		1 DEPT ENGN,
		1 DIV INFORMAT ENGN
		1 INST ASTRON
	1 MRC	1 MOLEC BIOL LAB
	1 Royal Greenwich Observ.	1 NO INFORMATION

Other Major Institutions

9 GEC Marconi LTD.	9 Wembley, GB	9 HIRST RES CTR
5 PHILIPS	2 Aachen, DE	2 FORSCHUNGSLAB
	2 Limeil Brevannes	2 LABS ELECTR
	1 Eindhoven	1 RES LABS
4 ALCATEL ALSTHOM RERCH	2 Marcoussis, FR	2 DIA
		2 DIN

Part 3: Interviews

Table A 3:   Guideline for interviews on interdisciplinary co-operation in research-intensive areas

General information on the institution

- size (turnover, employees)
- divisions, sectors, location of medical lasers/neural networks within the institution
- competitors

Significance of interdisciplinary co-operation and its development in time

- emergence of the research area medical lasers/neural networks (time, location, research team)
- reasons for the necessity of interdisciplinary co-operation
- involvement of traditional scientific disciplines
- focus of the interdisciplinary work (knowledge generation, technical application)
- time of entrance of the institution into the research area
- significance of present interdisciplinary co-operation in comparison to former activities
- shift in emphasis and/or enlargement of the research area into new areas (of application)
- estimation of the regional distribution of interdisciplinary activity in this area within Europe
- self-assessment compared to European and extra-European competitors.

Organisation of interdisciplinary research

- targets, form and duration of the organisation of interdisciplinary research within the institution (form of projects, line or matrix organisation)

- participation of researchers of the interdisciplinary teams in conferences, meetings and workshops; publication activities (frequency, targets)
- direct contact to and co-operations with other enterprises, institutes, research centres, clinics etc. (frequency, duration, targets)
- dependency on the co-operation with external researchers
- significance of local, regional, national and international communication networks

Personnel structure of interdisciplinary research teams

- disciplinary origin of the researchers
- average age of the researchers and position within the enterprise and the time of entrance into the interdisciplinary team
- average length of stay in the research team
- position within the institution when leaving the interdisciplinary team, career prospects
- financial incentives and other privileges
- promotion of the exchange of researchers between academic and industrial institutions

Problems

- type and frequency of problems which result from the interdisciplinary character of the research
- communication problems between different disciplines

Public promotion

- necessity and preferred type of public promotion (budgetary, project-oriented, institutional, etc.)
- assessment of existing RTD programmes of the EC (necessity of research throughout Europe, organisation, targets)
- appropriate starting-points for European activities, recommendations
- form of industrial participation in public research programmes.

References

Albert, U./Silverman, M. (1984):
Making Management Philosophy a Cultural Reality, Part 1: Get Started, Part 2: Design Human Resources Programs Accordingly. In: Personnel, Vol. 61, No. 1, pp. 12-21 and No. 2, pp. 28-35.

Allaire, Y./Firsirotu, M. E. (1984):
Theories of Organizational Culture. In: Organization Studies, Vol 5, No. 3, pp. 193-226.

Allesch, J./Preiß-Allesch/D./Sprengler, U. (1988):
Hochschule und Wirtschaft. Bestandsaufnahme und Modelle der Zusammenarbeit, Köln.

Atkinson, H./Rogers, Ph./Bond, R. (1990):
Research in the United Kingdom France and Germany, SERC, London.

Backhaus, K./Piltz, K. (1990):
Strategische Allianzen - eine neue Form kooperativen Wettbewerbs? In: Backhaus, K./ Piltz, K.: Strategische Allianzen, Düsseldorf/ Frankfurt.

Barney, J.B. (1986):
Organizational Culture: Can it be a Source of Sustained Competitive Advantage? In: Academy of Management Review 11(3), pp. 656-665.

Bartlett, Chr./Ghoshal, S. (1990):
Internationale Unternehmensführung - Innovation, globale Effizienz, differenziertes Marketing, Frankfurt/ New York.

Becher, G./Kuhlmann, S./ Kuntze, U. (1989):
Forschungs- und Technologiepolitik für kleine und mittlere Unternehmen in ausgewählten Industrieländern, Karlsruhe (FhG-ISI).

Benkenstein, M. (1987):
F & E und Marketing: Eine Untersuchung zur Leistungsfähigkeit von Koordinationskonzeptionen bei Innovationsentscheidungen, Wiesbaden.

Berman, E. M. (1990):
The Economic Impact of Industry-Funded University R&D. In: Research Policy, Vol. 19, pp. 349-355.

Bleicher, K. (1989):
Zum Management zwischenbetrieblicher Kooperation: Vom Joint Venture zur strategischen Allianz. In: Bühner, R. (ed.): Führungsorganisation und Technologiemanagement. Festschrift für Friedrich Hoffmann zum 65. Geburtstag, Berlin, pp. 77-89.

Bleicher, K. (1991):
Organisation: Strategien - Strukturen - Kulturen, Wiesbaden.

Bleicher, K. (1992):
Das Konzept integriertes Management, Frankfurt/M., New York.

Blume, S. (1992):
Insight and Industry. On the Dynamics of Technological Change in Medicine, Cambridge, MA/London.

BMFT (1988):
Bundesbericht Forschung 1988, Bonn.

BMFT (1990):
Faktenbericht 1990 zum Bundesbericht Forschung, Bonn.

BMFT (1993a):
Bundesbericht Forschung 1993, Bonn.

BMFT (ed.) (1993b):
Deutscher Delphi-Bericht zur Entwicklung von Wissenschaft und Technik, Bonn.

Böhler H. et al. (1989):
Der Technologie-Transfer in einer strukturschwachen Region. Stand und Ausbauempfehlungen, Bayreuth.

Bösenberg, D./Metzen, H. (1993):
Lean Management, Vorsprung durch schlanke Konzepte, 3. durchgesehene Auflage, Landsberg/Lech.

Bräunling, G./Allesch, J. (1982):
Technologie-Transfer in ausgewählten Industrieländern. Report to the German Federal Parliament, Karlsruhe.

Bräunling, G./Maas, M. (1988):
Nutzung der Ergebnisse aus öffentlicher Forschung und Entwicklung. Report to the CEC, Karlsruhe.

Brockhoff, K. (1989):
Schnittstellen-Management: Abstimmungsprobleme zwischen Marketing und Forschung und Entwicklung, Stuttgart.

Brockhoff, K. (1992):
Forschung und Entwicklung. Planung und Kontrolle, 3. Auflage, München.

Brundtland-Bericht (1987):
Weltkommission für Umwelt und Entwicklung. Unsere gemeinsame Zukunft. Deutsche Ausgabe edited by V. Hauff, Greven.

Brynjolfsson, E. (1992):
The Productivity of Information Technology: Review and Assessment, MIT Sloan School Working Paper # 130.

Buckley, P.J./Casson, M. (1991):
The Future of the Multinational Enterprise, London.

Bullinger, H.-J. (ed.) (1989):
Forum für Management in Forschung, Entwicklung und Technologie, Tagungsunterlagen, München.

Bullinger, H.-J. (1992):
Neue Produktionsparadigmen als betriebliche Herausforderung. In: IAO-Forum, Bullinger, H.-J. (ed.): Innovative Unternehmensstrukturen, Berlin/Heidelberg.

Bush, V. (1945):
Science, The Endless Frontier, Washington, D.C.

Cabinet Office (1991):
R&D '91, Annual Review of Government Funded, Research & Development, Cabinet Office, London.

Cabinet Office (1992)
R&D '92, Annual Review of Government Funded, Research & Development, Cabinet Office, Office of Science and Technology, London.

Casson, M./Singh, S. (1993):
Corporate Research and Development Strategies: The Influence of Firm, Industry and Country Factors on the Decentralization of R&D. In: R&D Management, Vol. 23, No. 2, pp. 91-107.

Chakravarthy, B./Kwun, S. (1990):
The Strategy-Making Process: an Organisational Learning Perspective. Working Paper, Carlson School of Management, University of Minnesota.

Cheese, J. (1991):
Attidudes to Innovation in Germany and Britain: A Comparison, Centre for Exploitation of Science and Technology (CEST), London.

Cohen, W. M./Levinthal, D. A., (1989):
Innovation and Learning: The Two Faces of R&D. In: The Economic Journal, 99, September, pp. 569-596.

Collins, P./Wyatt, S., (1987):
Citations in patents to the basic research literature. In: Research Policy, Vol. 17, pp. 65-74.

CEC (ed.) (1994):
Research and Technology Management in Enterprises: Issues for Community Policy. Report prepared for the Strategic Analysis in Science and Technology (SAST) Unit of the Directorate-General for Science, Research and Development of the CEC (includes 13 single reports). Brussels/ Luxembourg.

Coombs, R./ Richards, A. (1993):
Strategic Control of Technology in Diversified Companies with Decentralized R&D. In: Technology Analysis & Strategic Management, Vol. 5 (4).

Corsten, H. (1987):
Problems with Cooperation Between Universities and Enterprises - A Comparative Study on Size of Enterprise. In: Technovation, Vol. 6, pp. 195-301.

Cuhls, K. (1993):
Qualitätszirkel in japanischen und deutschen Unternehmen, Heidelberg.

Cuhls, K./Grupp, H./Breiner, S. (1993):
Methodology for Identifying Emerging Technologies - Recent Experiences from Germany. Paper contributed to 1993 R&D Dynamics Network Meeting, Kyôto, Japan.

Dasgupta, P.S./David, P.A. (1994):
Towards a new economics of science. In: Research Policy, Vol. 23, pp. 487-521.

David, P.A./Mowery, D./Steinmüller, W.E. (1992):
Analysing the economic payoffs from basic research. In: Economics of Innovtion and New Technology, 2 (4), pp. 73-90.

Debackere, K./Rappa, M. (1994):
Technological communities and the diffusion of knowledge: a replication and validation. In: R&D Management, 24, 4, 355-371.

De Freitas, J.E./Gonard, T./Kuhlmann, S./Morandini, C./Tsipouri, L. (1992):
Analysis of the Value Added due to Multinational University-Industry Partnerships in EC Research Projects, Athens.

De Woot, P. (1990):
High Technology Europe. Strategic Issues for Global Competitiveness, Oxford/Cambridge, Mass.

Deal, T.E. (1984):
Unternehmenskultur: Grundstein für Spitzenleistungen. In: ATAG (ed.): Die Bedeutung der Unternehmenskultur für den Erfolg ihres Unternehmens, pp. 27-42, Zürich.

Deiser, R. (1993):
Post-conventional Strategic Management: Criteria for the Postmodern Organization. Paper for the 11th International SMS Conference in Toronto, October 1991, Vienna.

Dickson, K./Lawton-Smith, H./Smith, S. L. (1991):
Bridge Over Troubled Waters? Problems and Opportunities in Interfirm Research Collaboration. In: Technology Analysis & Strategic Management, Vol. 3 (1991) No. 2, pp. 143-156.

Dierkes, M./Rosenstiel, L. von/Steger, U. (ed.) (1993):
Unternehmenskultur in Theorie und Praxis, Frankfurt/New York.

Dill, P./Hügler, G. (1987):
Unternehmenskultur und Führung betriebswirtschaftlicher Organisationen - Ansatzpunkte für ein kulturbewußtes Management. In: Heinen, E. (ed.): Unternehmenskultur, Perspektiven für die Wirtschaft und Praxis, München/Wien.

Ditfurth, H.v. (1984):
Wir sind nicht nur von dieser Welt, Munich.

Dodgson, M. (1992 a):
Technological Collaboration: Problems and Pitfalls. In: Technology Analysis & Strategic Management, Vol. 4, No. 1.

Dodgson, M. (1992 b):
The Strategic Management of R&D Collaboration. In: Technology Analysis & Strategic Management, Vol. 4, No. 3.

Dodgson, M. (1993):
Technical Collaboration in Industry, London/New York.

Döge, P. (1992):
Im Osten nichts Neues. In: Wechselwirkung, Nr. 57, pp. 29-35.

Dosi, G. (1982):
Technological Paradigms and Technological Trajectories. In: Research Policy, Vol. 11, No. 3, pp. 147-162.

Dosi, G. (1988):
Sources, Procedures, and Microeconomic Effects of Innovation. In: Journal of Economic Literature, XXVI, pp. 1120-1171.

Doz, Y./Chakravarthy, B. (1993):
The Dynamics of Core Competency. Paper presented at the International Workshop "Evolution in Technology Management", October 1993 in Warth, Fontainebleau.

Durand, T. (1992):
Dual Technological Trees: Assessing the Intensity and Strategic Significance of Technological change. In: Research Policy, Vol. 21, pp. 361-380.

Durand, Th. /Kandel, N. (1989):
Les Relations Grandes Entreprises - PME en Matière de Technologie et de R&D. In: Commission of the European Communities/T.I.I. (eds.): Partnership Between Small and Large Firms, London, pp. 342-345.

EIRMA (European Industrial Research Management Association) (1989):
Cooperative R&D in Industry, Paris (Working Group Reports No. 38).

Enos, J. (1958):
A Measure of the Rate of Technological Progress in the Petroleum Refinig Industry, In: Journal of Industrial Economics, June.

Ernste, M./Meier, V. (eds.) (1992):
Regional Development and Contemporary Industrial Response, London/New York.

eurostat (1992):
Europa in Zahlen, Amt für amtliche Veröffentlichungen der Europäischen Gemeinschaften, Brussels/Luxembourg.

Eversheim, W. (1989):
Simultaneous Engineering - eine organisatorische Chance. In: Verein Deutscher Ingenieure (VDI) (1989): Simultaneous Engineering. Neue Wege des Projektmanagements, VDI Berichte 758, Düsseldorf.

Ferrata, R./Bonisoli, A./Carlo, C. (1992):
Pre-Feasibiltity Study on the Research /Scientific Community Interface. Report to the CEC, Milano.

Fleischmann, G./Esser, J. (eds.) (1989):
Technikentwicklung als sozialer Prozeß, Frankfurt.

Freeman, C. (1974):
The Economics of Industrial Innovation, 1st edition, London.

Freeman, C. (1982):
The Economics of Industrial Innovation, 2nd edition, London.

Freman, C. (1987):
Technology Policy and Economic Performance: Lessons from Japan, London/New York.

Freeman, C. (1988):
Japan : A New National System of Innovation? In: Dosi et al. (eds.): Technical Change and Economic Theory, London/New York, pp. 330-348.

Freeman, C. (1990):
The Economics of Innovation, Aldershot.

Freeman, C. (1991):
Networks of Innovators: A Synthesis of Research Issues. In: Research Policy, Vol. 20, pp. 499-514.

Friar, J./Horvitch, M. (1985):
The Emergence of Technology Strategy. A New Dimension on Strategic Management. In: Technology in Society, Vol. 7, pp. 143-178.

Geisler, E./Rubenstein, A. H. (1989):
University-Industry Relations: A Review of Major Issues. In: Link, A. N./ Tassey, G. (eds.): Cooperative Research and Development. The Industry-University-Government Relationsship, Boston, pp. 43-62.

Gemünden, H.G./Hillebrand, G./Schaettgen, M.,
Management grenzüberschreitender Kooperationen kleiner und mittlerer Unternehmen. Non-published report of Universität Fredericiana zu Karlsruhe, Institut für Angewandte BWL und Unternehmensführung.

Gerpott, T. J. (1990a):
Globales F&E-Management. In: Die Unternehmung, Vol. 44, No. 4, pp. 226-246.

Gerpott, T. J. (1990b):
Simultaneous Engineering. In: Die Betriebswirtschaft, Vol. 50, No. 3, pp. 399-400.

Gerpott, T. J./Wittkemper, G. (1991):
Verkürzung von Produktentwicklungszeiten. In: Booz - Allen & Hamilton (ed.): Integriertes Technologie- und Innovationsmanagement, Berlin.

Gerybadze, A. (1982):
Innovation, Wettbewerb und Evolution, Tübingen.

Gerybadze, A. (1991):
Technological Forecasting. In: Technologie-Management: Ein Erfolgsfaktor von zunehmender Bedeutung, Zürich, pp. 71-100.

Gerybadze, A. (1992):
Umweltorientiertes Management von Forschung und Entwicklung: In: Steger, U. (ed.): Handbuch des Umweltmanagements, München 1992.

Gesellschaft für Management und Technologie (gfmt) (ed.) (1993):
Personal-Management, Der Mensch in der schlanken Fabrik, Tagungsbericht, München.

Gesellschaft für Wirtschaftspublizistik (GWP) (ed.) (1991):
High-Tech-Marketing, Düsseldorf.

Gibbons, M./Johnston, R. (1974):
The Role of Science in Technological Innovation. In: Research Policy, Vol. 3, pp. 220-242.

Gibbons, M. (1993):
National Innovation Systems in Transition: Some lessons for Germany. In: Bundesministerium für Forschung und Technologie (ed.), Anforderungen an das Innovationssystem der 90er Jahre in Deutschland, Bonn.

Grant, R.M. (1991):
The Resource-Based Theory of Competitive Advantage: Implications for Strategy Formulation. In: California Management Review, Spring.

Greipel, P. (1988):
Strategie und Kultur: Grundlagen und mögliche Handlungsfelder kulturbewussten strategischen Managements, Stuttgart.

Grenzmann, Ch./Marquardt, R./Wudtke, J. (1991):
Forschung u. Entwicklung in der Wirtschaft 1989, SV - Gemeinnützige Gesellschaft für Wissenschaftsstatistik mbH im Stifterverband für die Deutsche Wissenschaft, Essen.

Grupp, H. (1991a):
Dynamics of Science-Based Innovation in Northern America, Japan and Western Europe, presentation at the 3rd International Conference on Science and Technology Policy Research, NISTEP, Oiso (Japan), March.

Grupp, H. (1991b):
Innovation Dynamics in OECD Countries: Towards a Correlated Network of R&D-Intensity, Trade, Patent and Technometric Indicators. In: OECD (ed.): The Technology Economy Programme (TEP); Technology and Productivity, The Callenge for Economic Policy, Paris, pp. 275-295.

Grupp, H. (1992a):
Competitive Trade Advantage of EC Nations as a Function of their Science and
Technology Production. In: Van Raan et al. (eds.): Science and Technology in a
Policy Context, Leiden, pp. 327-355.

Grupp, H. (ed.) (1992b):
Dynamics of Science-Based Innovation, Heidelberg/New York.

Grupp, H. (1993a):
Dynamics of Science-Based Innovation in Northern America, Japan and Western
Europe. In: Okamura, S./Sakauchi, F./Nonaka, I. (eds.): Science and Technology
Policy Research: New Perspectives on Global Science and Technology Policy: The
Proceedings of NISTEP the Third International Conference on Science and
Technology Policy Research, Tôkyô, pp. 179-194.

Grupp, H. (ed.) (1993b):
Technologie am Beginn des 21. Jahrhunderts, Heidelberg.

Grupp, H. (1994a):
Kritische Technologie: Technikbeobachtung und -vorausschau als Bestandteil der
Technikfolgenabschätzung. In: Bechmann, G. and Petermann, T. (eds.):
Veröffentlichungen der Abteilung für angewandte Systemanalyse (AFAS), Vol. 2,
Frankfurt.

Grupp, H. (1994b):
The Measurement of Technical Performance of Innovations by Technometrics and
its Impact on Established Technology Indicators. In: Research Policy, Vol. 23, pp.
175-193.

Grupp, H. (1995):
Science, High Technology and Competitiveness of EC Nations. In: Cambridge
Journal of Economics, Vol. 19, pp.209-223..

Grupp, H./Albrecht, E./Koschatzky, K. (1992):
By Way of Introduction: Alliances between Science Research and Innovation
Research. In: Grupp, H. (ed.): Dynamics of Science-Based Innovation, Berlin et al.,
pp. 3-18.

Grupp, H./Schmoch, U. (1992a):
At the Crossroads in Laser Medicine and Polyimide Chemistry. Patent Assessment of
the Expansion of Knowledge. In: Grupp, H. (ed): Dynamics of Science-Based
Innovation, Berlin et al., pp. 269-301.

Grupp, H./Schmoch, U. (1992b):
Perception of Scientification of Innovation as Measured by Referencing between
Patent and Papers. Dynamics in Science-Based Fields of Technology. In: Grupp, H.
(ed.): Dynamics of Science-Based Innovation, Berlin et al., pp. 73-128.

Grupp, H./Schmoch, U. (1992c):
Wissenschaftsbindung der Technik. Panorama der internationalen Entwicklung und sektorales Tableau für Deutschland, Heidelberg.

Grupp, H./Soete, L. (1993):

Analysis of the Dynamic Relationship between Technical and Economic Performances in Information and Telecommunication Sectors, Vol. I: Synthesis Report. Report to the European Commission, Karlsruhe/Maastricht.

Hack, L. (1989):
Determinationen/Trajekte vs. Konfigurationen/Projekte. In: Fleischmann/Esser (1989), pp. 71-104.

Hagedoorn, J. (1993):
Understanding International Business: Globalization, Corporate Flexibility and Networks of Innovation. Paper of the Workshop, "European Management and Organisation in Transition", Strasbourg.

Hagedoorn, J./ Schakenraad, J. (1990):
Interfirm Partnerships and Cooperative Strategies in Core Technologies. In: Freeman, C./Soete, L. (eds.): New explorations in the Economics of Technological Change, London, pp. 3-37.

Hagedoorn, J./Schakenraad, J. (1992):
The Economic Effects of Strategic Partnerships and Technology Cooperation. In: Second Framework Programme for Research and Technological Development (1987-1991), Evaluations and Reviews, Vol. 2, Brussels.

Hakansson, H. (1987):
Industrial Technological Development - A Network Approach, London/Sydney/ Dover/ New Hampshire.

Hakansson, H. (1989):
Corporate Technological Behaviour. Co-operation and Networks, London/New York.

Haklisch, C./Fusfeld, H./Levenson, A. (1986):
Trends in Collective Industrial Research. New York University, Center of Science and Technology Policy, New York.

Hassink, R. (1992):
Regional Innovation Policy: Case-Studies from the Ruhr Area, Baden-Württemberg and the North East of England, Utrecht.

Hauschildt, J. (1993):
Innovationsmanagement, München.

Heinen, E. (ed.) (1987):
Unternehmenskultur, Perspektiven für die Wirtschaft und Praxis, München/Wien .

Helmers, S. (1993):
Beiträge der Ethnologie zur Unternehmenskultur. In: Dierkes, M./Rosenstiel, L. von/Steger, U. (eds.): Unternehmenskultur in Theorie und Praxis, Frankfurt/New York.

Henfling, M. (1981):
Theorie technischer Innovationen in der industriellen Fertigung, Gernbrunn.

Herden, R. (1990):
Die Bedeutung der zwischen- und überbetrieblichen Zusammenarbeit als Voraussetzung für das Entstehen und die Entwicklung innovativer Produkte und Prozesse. Report to the Ministry of Economy of Baden-Württemberg, Karlsruhe.

Herden, R. (1992):
Technologieorientierte Außenbeziehungen im betrieblichen Innovationsmanagement, Heidelberg.

Hitt, M./Ireland, R.D. (1985):
Corporate Distinctive Competence, Strategy, Industry and Performance. In: Strategic Management Journal, No. 6, pp. 273-293.

Hoeschen, R.-D. (1989):
Simultaneous Engineering als strategische Herausforderung. In: Bullinger, H.-J.: Forum für Management in Forschung, Entwicklung und Technologie, Tagungsunterlagen, München, pp. 97.

Hofer, C.W./Schendel, D. (1978):
Strategy Formulation: Analytical Concepts, St. Paul.

Höft, U. (1992):
Lebenszykluskonzepte. Grundlage für das strategische Marketing- und Technologiemanagement, Berlin.

Hogarth, R./Michaud, C./Doz, Y./Van der Heyden, L. (1991):
Longevity of Business Firms: a Four-stage Framework for Analysis. INSEAD Working Paper 91/55/EP/SM, Fontainebleau.

Hornbostel, S. (1991):
Drittmittel im Fach Physik - ein Indikator für Forschungsleistung? In: Phys. Bl., Vol. 47, Nr. 2, pp. 123-125.

House of Lords (1993):
Faraday Programme, Select Committee on Science and Technology. Session 1992-93, 4th Report, London: HMSO, HL Paper 50

Howells, J. (1990):
The Location and Organisation of Research and Development: New Horizons. In: Research Policy, Vol. 19, pp. 133-146.

Hübenthal, U. (1991):
Interdisziplinäres Denken, Versuch einer Bestandsaufnahme und Systematisierung, Stuttgart.

Hughes, Th.P. (1986):
The Seamless Webb: Technology, Science, etcetera, etcetera. In: Social Studies of Science, Vol. 16, pp. 281-292.

IIT Research Institute (1968):
Technology in Retrospect and Critical Events in Science, Washington, D.C.

Imai, M. (1991):
Kaizen - Der Schlüssel zum Erfolg der Japaner im Wettbewerb, München.

Irvine, J., Martin, B.R. (1984):
Foresight in Science. Picking the Winners, London/Dover.

Itami, H. (with Roehl, T.) (1987):
Mobilizing Invisible Assets, Cambridge.

Jain, R.K./Triandis, H.C. (1990):
Management of Research and Development Organizations. Managing the Unmanageable, New York.

Jantsch, E. (1970):
Inter- and Transdisciplinary University. A Systems Approach to Education and Innovation, Policy Sciences, Vol. 1, pp. 403-428.

Jochem, E. (ed.) (1988):
Technikfolgenabschätzung am Beispiel der Solarenergienutzung, Frankfurt.

Johnsten, N. (1992):
The Working Group on Innovation, Final Report, UK R&D Scoreboard, June.

Kalkowski, P./Manske, F. (1993):
Innovation im Maschinenbau. Ein Beitrag zur Technikgeneseforschung. In: SOFI-Mitteilungen January 1993, Göttingen.

411

Kamin, J.Y./Bijaoui, I./Horesh, R. (1982):
Some Determinants of Cost Distributions in the Process of Technological
Innovation. In: Research Policy 11 (2), pp. 83-94.

Kaschube, J. (1993):
Betrachtung der Unternehmens- und Organisationskulturforschung aus
(organisations-) psychologischer Sicht. In: Dierkes, M./Rosenstiel, L. von/Steger, U.
(eds.): Unternehmenskultur in Theorie und Praxis, Frankfurt/New York.

Kayser, P. (1987a):
Den Technologietransfer vertraglich absichern! In: Kayser, P. (ed.),
Technologietransfer Forschung-Industrie, Dokumentation eines Expertengespräches,
Berlin, pp. 4-67.

Kayser, P. (ed.) (1987b):
Technologietransfer Forschung-Industrie, Dokumentation eines Expertengespräches,
Berlin.

Kennedy, P. (1993):
Preparing for the Twenty-First Century, New York 1992.

Kilburn, K. D. (1990):
Creating and Maintaining an Effective Interdisciplinary Research Team. In: R&D
Management, Vol. 20, No. 2, pp. 131-138.

Kleinknecht, A. (1989):
Firm Size and Innovation, Observations in Dutch Manufacturing Industries, Small
Business Economics.

Kline, S.J. (1985):
Innovation is not a Linear Process. In: Research Management, Vol. 28, pp. 36-45.

Kline, S.J./Rosenberg, N. (1986):
An Overview of Innovation. In: Landau/Rosenberg (1986), pp. 275-306.

Kobi, J.-M./Wüthrich, H. A. (1986):
Unternehmenskultur verstehen, erfassen und gestalten, Landsberg/Lech .

Kocka, J. (ed.) (1987):
Interdisziplinarität, Praxis-Herausforderung-Ideologie, Frankfurt/Main.

Kodama, F. (1992):
Technology Fusion and the New R&D. In: Harvard Business Review, July-August,
pp. 70-78.

Kreikebaum, H. (1992):
Integrierter Umweltschutz (IUS) durch strategische Planungs- und Controlling-Instrumente. In: Steger, U. (ed.): Handbuch des Umweltmanagements, München.

Krupp, H. (1984):
Basic Research in German Research Institutions, Excluding Universities and the Max-Planck Society. In: Proceedings of the Japan-Germany Science Seminar, Japan Society for the Promotion of Science, Tokyo, pp. 73-109.

Kuhlmann, S. et al. (1991):
The University-industry and Research-industry Interfaces in Europe, edited by the CEC, Brussels/Luxembourg.

Kuhlmann, S. (1992):
Thematic Evaluation of Community Support Frameworks for Research and Technology Development in Greece, Fraunhofer Institute for Systems and Innovation Research, Karlsruhe, December.

Kuhlmann, S./Kuntze, U. (1991):
R&D Cooperation by Small and Medium-Sized Companies. In: Kacaoglu, D. F./ Niwa, K. (eds.): Technology Management. The New International Language, New York 1991.

Kulicke, M. (1988):
Technologieorientierte Unternehmensgründungen. In: Dose, N./Drexler, A. (eds.): Technologieparks, Opladen, pp. 77-88.

Kupsch, P. U./Marr, R./Picot, A. (1991):
Innovationswirtschaft. In: Heinen, E. (ed.) (1991): Industriebetriebslehre, Wiesbaden.

Laudan, R. (1984):
Cognitive Change in Technology and Science. In: Laudan, R. (ed.): The Nature of Technological Knowledge. Are Models of Scientific Change Relevant?, Dordrecht/Boston/Lancaster, pp. 83-104.

Laudan, R./Rosenberg, N. (eds.) (1986):
The Positive Sum Strategy. Harnessing Technology for Economic Growth, Washington, D.C.

Lawton-Smith, H,./Dickson, K./Smith, S. L. (1991):
"There are two sides to every story": Innovation and Collaboration within Networks of Large and Small Firms. In: Research Policy, Vol. 20, pp. 457ff.

Legler, H./Grupp, H./Gehrke, B./Schasse, U. (1992):
Innovationspotential und Hochtechnologie, Technologische Position Deutschlands im internationalen Wettbewerb, Heidelberg.

Lenk, H. (1978):
Philosophie als Fokus und Forum. In: Lübbe, H. (ed.): Wozu Philosophie?
Berlin/New York.

Lenk, H. (1980):
Interdisziplinarität und die Rolle der Philosophie. In: Zeitschrift für Didaktik der
Philosophie, Vol.1, pp. 10-19.

Leonard-Barton, D. (1992):
Core Capabilities and Core Rigidities: A Paradox in Managing New Product
Development. In: Strategic Management Journal, No. 13, pp. 111-125.

Leyden, D.P./Link, A.N. (1993):
Tax Policies Affecting R&D: an International Comparison. In: Technovation, Vol.
13, No. 1, pp. 17-25.

Liebermann, M./Montgomery, D.B. (1988):
First-mover Advantages. In: Strategic Management Journal, No. 9, pp. 41-58.

Link, A. N./Rees, J. (1990):
Firm Size, University Based Research, and the Returns to R&D. In: Small Business,
No. 2, Economics, pp. 25-31.

Link, A. N./Tassey, G. (ed.) (1989):
Cooperative Research and Development. The Industry-University-Government
Relationship, Boston et al.

Lundvall, B.-A. (1988):
Innovation as an Interactive Process: from User-Producer Interaction to the National
System of Innovation. In: Dosi, G. et al. (eds.): Technical Change and Economic
Theory, London/New York, pp. 349-369.

Lundvall, B.-A. (1990):
Explaining Inter-Firm Cooperation and Innovation: Limits of the Transaction Cost
Approach. Paper presented at the workshop "Networks. On the Socio-Economics of
Inter-Firm Cooperation", Social Science Center Berlin, 11-13 June, 1990.

Lundvall, B.-A. (1992):
National Systems of Innovation, London.

Machlup, F. (1962):
The Production and Distribution of Knowledge in the United States, Princeton, NJ.

Maier-Leibnitz, H. (1992):
Science and the Humanities, A Plea for Interdisciplinary Communication. In:
Interdisciplinary Science Reviews, Vol. 17, No. 2, pp. 171-177.

Majer, H. (1978):
Industrieforschung in der Bundesrepublik Deutschland. Eine theoretische und
empirische Analyse, Tübingen.

Mansfield, E. (1986):
Microeconomics and Technological Change. In: Landau/Rosenberg (1986), pp. 307-
326.

Mansfield, E. (1990):
Academic Research and Industrial Innovation. In: Research Policy,Vol. 20, pp. 1-12.

Martin, B. (1989):
International Comparison of Government Expenditure on Academic and Related
Research, 1975-1987, Science Policy Research Unit (SPRU), University of Sussex,
Brighton.

McKelvey, M. (1991):
How Do National Sytems of Innovation Differ? Working Paper No 79,
LIUTEMA/T/WP-91/0079.

McKelvey, M. (1992):
Technologies Embedded in Nations? Genetic Engineering and Technological Change
in National Systems of Innovation. Conference paper presented at 1992 EAEPE
Conference "Structural Change and Regulation of Economic Systems: Integration,
Disintegration and Globalization", November 4-6(th), Paris.

Meadows, D.H./Meadows, D.L./Randers, J. (1992):
Beyond the Limits to Growth, London.

Meffert, H./Kirchgeorg, M. (1990):
Marktorientierte Unternehmensführung im Europäischen Binnenmarkt. Perspektiven
aus der Sicht von Wissenschaft und Praxis, Stuttgart 1990.

Merkle, E. (1975):
Die Analyse technologischer Entwicklungen auf der Grundlage von
Patententwicklungen. In: Raffée, H. Wiedmann, K.-P. (eds.): Strategisches
Marketing, Stuttgart.

Merrifield, B. (1979):
Stimulating Technological Innovation - Nurturing the Innovator. In: Research
Management, Vol. 12, Nov., pp. 12-14.

Meyer-Krahmer, F. (1989):
Der Einfluß staatlicher Technologiepolitik auf industrielle Innovationen, Baden-
Baden.

415

Meyer-Krahmer, F. (1990):
Science and Technology in the Federal Repulic of Germany, London.

Meyer-Krahmer, F. (1993) (ed.):
Innovationsökonomie und Technologiepolitik, Forschungsansätze und politische
Konsequenzen, Heidelberg.

Meyer-Krahmer, F./Kuntze, U. (1992):
Bestandsaufnahme der Forschungs-und Technologiepolitik. In: Grimmer, K./
Häusler, J./Kuhlmann, S./Simonis G. (eds.): Politische Techniksteuerung, Opladen,
pp. 95-118.

Meyer-Krahmer, F./Walter, G. H. (1993):
Modelle des Technologie-Transfers. In: Wüst, J. (ed.): Technologietransfer am
Rande gemeinnütziger Forschungseinrichtungen, Karlruhe.

Meyers, S./Marquis, D.G. (1969):
Successful Industrial Innovation, Washington, D.C.

Mittelstraß, J. (1994):
Grundlagen und Anwendungen - Über das schwierige Verhältnis zwischen
Forschung, Entwicklung und Politik, in: Chem.-Ing.-Tech. 66, No. 3, 309-315.

Mintzberg, H. (1991):
The Effective Organization: Forces and Forms, Sloan Management Review, Winter,
pp. 54-67.

Möhrle, M.G. (1991):
Informationssysteme in der betrieblichen Forschung und Entwicklung,
Bad Homburg.

Morris, C. (ed.) (1992):
Academic Press Dictionary of Science and Technology, San Diego.

Mowery, D.C. (1983):
The Relationship Between Intrafirm and Contractual Forms of Industrial Research in
American Manufacturing, 1900-1940. In: Explorations in Economic History, Vol.
20, pp. 351-374.

Mowery, D.C. (1988):
The US National Innovation System: Origins and Prospects for Change. in: Research
Policy, Vol. 21, pp. 125-144.

Mueller, R.K. (1986):
Corporate Networking - Building Channels for Information and Influence,
New York.

Murdick, R. G./Georgoff, D. M. (1993):
Forecasting: A Systems Approach. In: Technological Forecasting and Social Change, Vol. 44, pp. 1-16.

Nature (1993):
How will Britain run its science now? In: NATURE, Vol. 361, 18 February 1993.

Nelson, R.R. (1988):
Institutions supporting technical change in the United States. In: Dosi et al. (eds.): Technical Change and Economic Theory, London/New York, pp.312-329.

Neuberger, O./Kompa, A. (1986):
Firmenkultur I. In: Psychologie Heute, Vol. 13, No. 6, pp. 60-68.

Noyons, E.C.M./Van Raan, A.F.J./Grupp, H./Schmoch, U. (1994):
Exploring the Science and Technology Interface: Inventor-Author Relations in Laser Medicine Research. In. Research Policy, Vol. 23, pp. 443-457.

OECD (1980):
Frascati Manual. Proposed Standard Practice for Surveys of Research and Experimental Development, Paris.

OECD (ed.) (1984):
Industry and University. New Forms of Cooperation and Communication, Paris.

OECD (1989):
Industrial Policy in OECD Countries, Annual Review, Paris.

OECD (1990):
Technology/Economy Programme (TEP). Draft Background Report. Chapter 4: Innovation-Related Networks and Technology Policy-Making, Paris.

OECD (ed.) (1991):
Technology in a Changing World, Paris.

OECD (1992):
Frascati Manual 1992. Proposed Standard Practice for Surveys of Research and Experimental Development. Preliminary versions of August and September 1992, Paris.

OECD (1993):
Main Science and Technology Indicators, Paris.

OECD (1994):
Frascati Manual 1993. Proposed Standard Practice for Surveys of Research and Experimental Development, Paris.

Ohmae, K. (1989):
The Global Logic of Strategic Alliances. In: Harvard Business Review, March/April, pp. 143-154.

Onida, F./Malerba, F. (1989):
R&D Cooperations between Industry, Universities and Research Organizations in Europe. In: Technovation, Vol. 9, pp. 131-193.

Pantele, E.F./Lacey, C. E. (1989):
Mit "Simultaneous Engineering" die Entwicklungszeiten kürzen. In: io Management Zeitschrift, Vol. 58, No. 11, pp. 56-58.

Pascale, R. T./Athos, A. G. (1981):
The Art of Japanese Management, Middlesex.

Pavitt, K. (1984):
Sectoral Patterns of Technical Change: Towards a Taxonomie and a Theory. In: Research Policy, Vol. 13, pp. 343-373.

Pavitt, K. (1991):
Key Characteristics of the Large Innovating Firm. In: British Journal of Management, No. 2, pp. 41-50.

Pavitt, K. (1992):
What Makes Basic Research Economically Useful? In: Research Policy, Vol. 20, pp. 109-119.

Pavitt, K. (1993):
What Do Firms Learn From Basic Research? In: Foray, D./Freeman, C. (eds.): Technology and the Wealth of Nations. The Dynamics of Constructed Advantage, London/New York.

Pavitt, K./Robson, M./Townsend, J. (1987):
The Size and Distribution of Innovating Firms in the U.K.: 1945 - 1983. In: The Journal of Industrial Economics, XXXV.

Perich, R. (1993):
Unternehmungsdynamik. Zur Entwicklungsfähigkeit von Organisationen aus zeitlich-dynamischer Sicht, 2.Auflage. Bern/Stuttgart/Wien.

Pfeiffer, W./Bischof, P. (1982):
Produktlebenszyklen - Instrument jeder strategischen Produktplanung. In: Steinmann, H. (ed.): Planung und Kontrolle, pp. 133-166.

Phillipp-Franz-von-Siebold-Stiftung, Deutsches Institut für Japanstudien (1991):
Miscellanea, Individualität und Egalität in Familie und Unternehmen, Tôkyô.

418

Phillips, A. (1971):
Technology and Market Structure, Lexington.

Porter, A. L./Roper, A.T./Mason, T. W./Rossini, F. A./Banks, J. (1991):
Forecasting and Management of Technology, New York.

Porter, M.E. (1980):
Competitive Strategy: Techniques for Analyzing Industries and Competitors.
New York.

Porter, M.E. (1987):
From Competitive Advantage to Corporate Strategy. In: Harvard Business Review,
May-June, pp. 43-59.

Porter, M.E. (1990):
The Competitive Advantage of Nations,
London/Basingstoke.

Poser, H. (1990):
Wissen und Können. Zur Geschichte und Problematik des Wissenschaftstransfers. In:
Schuster, H. J. (ed.): Handbuch des Wissenschaftstransfers, Berlin/Heidelberg/New
York.

Powell, W. W. (1990):
Neither Market nor Hierarchy: Network Forms of Organization. In: Straw,
B.N./Cummings, L.L. (eds.): Research in Organizational Behaviour, Vol. 12, pp.
295-336.

Prahalad, C.K./Hamel, G. (1990):
The Core Competence of the Corporation. In: Harvard Business Review, May-June,
pp. 79-91.

Price, W.J./Bass, L.W. (1969):
Scientific Research and the Innovative Process. In: Science, Vol. 164, No. 16, May,
pp. 802-806.

Puck, A. (1987):
Kriterien der Zusammenarbeit zwischen Wissenschaft und Industrie. In: Kayser, P.
(ed.): Technologietransfer Forschung-Industrie, Berlin.

Pümpin, C. (1984):
Unternehmenskultur, Unternehmensstrategie und Unternehmenserfolg. In: gdi impuls,
No. 2, pp. 19-30.

Pümpin, C./Kobi, J.-M./Wüthrich, H. A. (1985):
Unternehmenskultur, Basis strategischer Profilierung erfolgreicher Unternehmen. In:
Die Orientierung, No. 85, Schweizerische Volksbank, Bern.

Quinn, R./Cameron, K. (1988):
Organizational Paradox and Transformation. In: Quinn/Cameron (eds.): Paradox and Transformation, Cambridge.

Raffee, H./Förster, F./Fritz, W. (1992):
Umweltschutz im Zielsystem von Unternehmen. In: Steger, U. (ed.): Handbuch des Umweltmanagements, München.

Rammert, W. (1992):
Research on the Generation and Development of Technology: The State of the Art in Germany. In: Dierkes, M./Hoffmann, U. (eds.): New Technolgy at the Outset, Frankfurt/New York, pp. 62-89.

Rammert, W. (1993):
Technik aus soziologischer Perspektive, Opladen.

Rath, H. (1990):
Neue Formen der Unternehmenskooperation, Hamburg.

Reger, G./Cuhls, K./Nick, D. (1994):
Best Management Practices and Tools for R&D Activities, edited by the European Commission, Brussels/Luxembourg.

Reger, G./Kuhlmann, S. (1995):
European Technology Policy in Germany. The Impact of European Community Policies upon Science and Technology in Germany, Heidelberg.

Reger, G./Kungl, H. (1994):
Research and Technology Management in Enterprises: Issues for Community Policy. Case Study on the Mechanical Engineering Sector. Brussels/Luxembourg.

Richmond, Sir M. (1993):
Science and wealth creation, NATURE, Vol 362, 15 April.

Rickerby, D.S./Matthews, A. (1991):
Market Perspectives and Future Trends. In: Rickerby, D.S./Matthews, A. (eds.): Handbook of Surface Engineering, Glasgow/London, pp. 343-364.

Robson, M (1993):
Interdisciplinary Efforts are Needed as Researchers Battle Environmental Threats. In: The Scientist, p.12.

Ropohl, G. (1979):
Eine Systemtheorie der Technik, München/Wien.

Ropohl, G. (1989):
Ein Systemmodell der technischen Entwicklung. In: Fleischmann/Esser (1989), pp. 1-28.

Rosenberg, N. (1976):
Perspectives on Technology, Cambridge et al.

Rosenstiel, L. von (1993):
Unternehmenskultur - einige einführende Anmerkungen. In: Dierkes, M./Rosenstiel, L. von/Steger U. (ed.) (1993): Unternehmenskultur in Theorie und Praxis, Frankfurt/ New York.

Rotering, Ch. (1990):
Forschungs- und Entwicklungskooperationen zwischen Unternehmen. Eine empirische Analyse, Stuttgart.

Rothwell, R. (1991):
Successful Industrial Innovation: Critical Factors for the 1990s. Extended version of a paper presented to the Science Policy Research Unit's 25th Anniversary Conference, Brighton, University of Sussex, 3-4 July.

Rothwell, R. (1994):
Issues in User-Producer Relations: Role of Government. In: International Journal of Technology Management, Vol. 9, Nos 5/6/7, pp. 629-649.

Rothwell, R. (1993):
The Fifth Generation Innovation Process. In: Oppenländer, K.-H./Popp, W. (1993): Privates und staatliches Innovationsmanagement, München.

Rothwell, R./Gardiner, P. (1985):
Invention, Innovation, Reinnovation and the Role of the User: a Case Study of British Hovercraft Development. In: Technovation, Vol. 3, No. 3, pp. 167-186.

Rothwell, R./Gardiner, P. (1988):
Re-Innovation and Robust Designs: Producer and User Benefits. In: Journal of Marketing Management, Vol. 3, pp. 372-387.

Rothwell,R./Dodgson,M. (1992):
European Technology Policy Evolution: Convergence towards SMEs and Regional Technology Transfer. In: Technovation, Vol. 12, No. 4, pp. 223-238.

Roussel, P.A./Saad, K.N./Erickson, T.J. (1991):
Third Generation R&D. Managing the Link to Corporate Strategy, Boston (Massachusetts).

Roy, R./Cross, N. (1983):
Bicycles: Invention and Innovation (T263 Units 5-7), London.

Rubenstein, A.H. (1989):
Managing Technology in the Decentralized Firm, New York/Chichester /Brisbane/ Toronto/Singapore.

Rumelt, R. (1984):
Towards a Strategic Theory of the Firm. In: Lamb, R.D. (ed.): Competitive Strategic Management, Englewood Cliffs.

Sahal, D. (1985):
Technological Guideposts and Innovation Avenues. In: Research Policy, Vol. 14 No. 2, pp. 61-82.

Samuelson, P.A. (1967):
Economics, 7th edn., New York.

Saunders, D. W./Hampshire, M. J. (1986):
Teaching Company Scheme: Ein einzigartiges Modell der Zusammenarbeit zwischen Hochschule und Industrie. In: Bundesminister für Bildung und Wisssenschaft (ed.): Wissens- und Technologietransfer aus deutschen und britischen Hochschulen, Bonn.

Schaffers, J.W.M./Kuijper, J./van der Meijden, R./Prakke, F. et al. (1992):
Technologieverkenning signal processing, Report TNO-STB.

Schmidt, R. (1992):
Modelle der Informationsvermittlung. Analyse und Bewertung eines experimentellen Programms, Heidelberg.

Schmidt-Tiedeman, K.J. (1982):
A New Model of the Innovation Process. In: Research Management, Vol. 25, No. 2, March, pp. 18-21.

Schmoch, U. (1993):
Tracing the Knowledge Transfer from Science to Technology as Reflected in Patent Indicators. In: Scientometrics, Vol. 26, No. 1, pp. 193-211.

Schmoch, U./Grupp, H./Mannsbart, W./Schwitalla, B. (1988):
Technikprognosen mit Patentindikatoren. Zur Einschätzung zukünftiger industrieller Entwicklungen bei Industrierobotern, Lasern, Solargeneratoren und immobilisierten Enzymen, Köln.

Schmoch, U./Hinze, S./Kirsch, N. (1993a):
Analysis of the Dynamic Relationship between Technical and Economic Performances in Information and Telecommunications Sectors, Vol. 2, Company and Technology Case Studies, Report to the CEC, Karlsruhe.

Schmoch, U./Hinze, S./Jäckel, G./Kirsch, N./Meyer-Krahmer, F./Münt, G. (1993b):
Constraints and Opportunities for the Dissemination and Exploitation of R&D
Activities: the R&D Environment, edited by the European Commision,
Brussels/Luxembourg.

Schmoch, U./Strauss, E./Grupp, H./Reiss, T (1993c):
Indicators of the Scientific Base of European Patents, edited by the European
Commission (EUR 15330), Brussels/Luxembourg.

Schmoch, U./Breiner, S./Cuhls, K./Hinze, S./Münt, G. (1994):
Interdisciplinary Co-operation of Research Teams in Science-intensive Areas of
Technology, edited by the European Commission, Brussels/Luxembourg.

Schmookler, J. (1966):
Invention and Economic Growth, Cambridge, MA.

Schneider, D./Zieringer, C. (1991):
Make-or-Buy-Strategien für F&E. Transaktionskostenorientierte Überlegungen,
Wiesbaden.

Schneider, M. (1991):
Zyklizität von Wissenschaft und Ökonomie. Zur Dialektik von Theorieentwicklung,
Innovationsdynamik und ökonomischer Reproduktion, Frankfurt/M., New York.

Schroeder, K./Fuhrmann, F. U./Heering, W. (1991):
Wissens- und Technologietransfer, Berlin.

Schumpeter, J.A. (1912):
Theorie der wirtschaftlichen Entwicklung, Leipzig.

Schumpeter, J.A. (1942):
Capitalism, Socialism and Democracy, New York.

Seaton, R. A. F./Cordey-Hayes, M., (1993):
The Development and Application of Interactive Models of Industrial Technology
Transfer. In: Technovation, Vol. 13, No. 1, pp. 45-53.

SERC (1992):
Government review of science and technology, Submission from the Science and
Engineering Research Council, SERC, November.

Servatius, H.-G. (1992):
Sicherung der technologischen Wettbewerbsfähigkeit Europas - Von der Techno-
logie-Frühaufklärung zur visionären Erschließung von Innovationspotentialen. In:
VDI-Technologiezentrum (ed.): Technologiefrühaufklärung: Identifikation und Bewertung von Ansätzen zukünftiger Technologien, Stuttgart, pp. 17-40.

423

Servatius, H.-G./Peiffer, S. (1992):
Ganzheitliche und Evolutionäre Technologiebewertung. In: VDI-Technologiezentrum (ed.), Technologiefrühaufklärung: Identifikation und Bewertung von Ansätzen zukünftiger Technologien, Stuttgart, pp. 73-92.

Sherwin, C.W./Isenson, R.S. (1966):
First Interim Report on Project HINDSIGHT (Summary), Office of the Director of
Defense Research and Engineering, Washington, D.C.

Sirilli, G. (1992):
Measuring Science and technology activities and policies. In: Okamura, S./Salzauchi,
F./Nonaka, I. (eds.): New perspectives on global science and technology policy,
Tokyo, pp. 65-80.

Smekal, C. (1993):
Umfassendes Umweltmanagement. In: Hammer, R.M./Hinterhuber, H.H./Kutis.

Smith, K. (1990):
New Innovation Indicators: Conceptual Basis and Practical Problems. Paper
presented at the OECD conference on "Consequences of the Technology Economy
Programme for the Development of Indicators", 2nd - 5th July, Paris.

Smits, R.E.H.M. (1990):
State of the Art of Technology Assessment in Europe. Report to the Second
European Congress of Technology Assessment, Milan 14-16 November.

Soete, L. (1993):
Die Herausforderung des "Techno-Globalismus": Auf dem Weg zu neuen Spiel-
regeln. In: Meyer-Krahmer, F. (ed.): Innovationsökonomie und Technologiepolitik,
Forschungsansätze und politische Konsequenzen, Heidelberg.

Spiegel-Rösing, I. D. /de Solla Price (eds.) (1977):
Science, Technology and Society, A Cross-Disciplinary Perspective, London/Beverly
Hills.

Spinner, H. F. (1994):
Die Wissensordnung. Ein Leitkonzept für die dritte Grundordnung des
Informationszeitalter, Opladen

Stankiewicz, R. (1986):
Academics and Entrepreneurs. Developing University-Industry Relations, London.

Stankiewicz, R. (1990):
Basic Technologies and the Innovation Process. In: Sigurdson, J. (ed.): Measuring
the Dynamics of Technological Change, London/New York, pp. 13-38.

Stankiewicz, R. (1992):
Technology as an Autonomous Socio-Cognitive System. In: Grupp, H. (ed.):
Dynamics of Science-Based Innovation, Berlin/Heidelberg/New York, pp. 19-44.

Staudt, E./Kriegesmann, B./Fischer, A. (1992):
Umweltschutz und Innovationsmanagement. In: Steger, U. (ed.): Handbuch des
Umweltmanagements, München.

Steger, U. (1993):
Unternehmenskultur aus forschungstheoretischer und praktischer Sicht - Ergebnisse
eines Delphi-Prozesses. In: Dierkes, M./Rosenstiel, L. von/Steger, U. (ed.):
Unternehmenskultur in Theorie und Praxis, Frankfurt/New York.

Stifterverband (1993):
Forschung u. Entwicklung in der Wirtschaft, Ergebnisse und Schätzungen 1991-
1992, SV-Gemeinnützige Gesellschaft für Wissenschaftsstatistik mbH im
Stifterverband für die Deutsche Wissenschaft, Essen, Januar.

Tassey, G. (1992):
Technology Infrastructure and Competitive Position, Norwell.

Teece, D.J. (1986):
Profiting from Technological Innovation: Implications for Integration, Collaboration,
Licensing and Public Policy. In: Research Policy, Vol. 15, pp. 285-305.

Teece, D.J./Pisano, G./Shuen, A. (1990):
Firm Capabilities, Resources and the Concept of Strategy. Consortium of
Competitiveness and Cooperation. Working paper 90-9, University of California at
Berkeley.

Töpfer, A./Mehdorn, H. (1993):
Total Quality Management, Neuwied/Kriftel/Berlin.

Townsend, J. et al. (1981):
Science and Technology Indicators for the UK. Innovations in Britain since 1945,
SPRU Occasional Paper Series No. 16.

Traill, I. E./Miège, R. (eds., CEC) (1989):
Contract Research Organizations in the EEC, Brussels/Luxembourg.

Tsipouri, L./Gonard, T./Kuhlmann, S./Morandini, C. (1992):
Analysis of the Value Added due to Multinational University-Industry Partnerships
in EC Research Projects. Report to the CEC.

Utterback, J.M. (1977):
Dynamics of Product and Process Change. In: Stroetmann, K.A. (ed.): Innovation,
Economic Change and Technology Policies, Basel/Stuttgart, pp. 8-20.

Utterback, J.M./Abernathy, W.J. (1975):
A Dynamic Model of Process and Product Innovation. In: OMEGA, Vol.3, No. 6, pp. 639-656.

Van Vianen, B.G./Moed, H.F./Van Raan, A.F.J. (1990):
An exploration of the science base of recent technology. In: Research Policy, Vol. 19, pp. 61-81.

VDI (ed.) (1991):
Technikbewertung - Begriffe und Grundlagen, Düsseldorf.

Walter, G. H. (1992):
Integration einheimischer Hochschulen in die industrielle Modernisierung der Dritten Welt, Bollschweil.

Warnecke, H.-J. (1992):
Die Fraktale Fabrik. Revolution der Unternehmenskultur, Berlin/Heidelberg.

Weingart, P. (1976):
Das Verhältnis von Wissenschaft und Technik im Wandel ihrer Institutionen; in: Stehr, N., König, R. (eds.): Wissenschaftssoziologie, Opladen.

Weizsäcker, C.F.v. (1978):
Der Garten des Menschlichen, Munich.

Wicke, L./Haasis, H.-D./Schafhausen, F./Schulz, W. (1992):
Betriebliche Umweltökonomie. Eine praxisorientierte Einführung, München.

Wiegand, R.T./ Frankwick, G. L. (1989):
Inter-Organizational Communication and Technology Transfer: Industry-Government-University Linkages. In: Int. J. Techn. Man., Vol. 4, pp. 63-76.

Williamson, O.E. (1979):
Transaction-cost economics: The governance of contractual relations. In: The Journal of Law and Economics, 22 (2), pp. 232-262.

Wissenschaftsrat (1993):
Drittmittel der Hochschulen 1970 bis 1990, Geschäftsstelle des Wissenschaftsrates, Köln, 24.3.1993, Drs. 1069/93.

Wolff, H./Becher, G./Delpho, H./Kuhlmann, S./Kuntze, U./Stock, J. (1994):
FuE-Kooperation von kleinen und mittleren Unternehmen, Heidelberg.

Wolfrum, B. (1991):
Strategisches Technologiemanagement, Wiesbaden.

Womack, J. P./Jones, D. T./Roos, D. (1990):
The Machine that Changed the World, New York.

Wortmann, M. (1991):
Globalisation of Economy and Technology. Country Study on the Federal Republic of Germany. MONITOR/FAST Programme, Prospective Dossier No 2, Vol.17, Brussels/ Luxembourg.

Zahn, E./Braun, F. (1992):
Identifikation und Bewertung zukünftiger Techniktrends - Erkenntnisstand im Rahmen der strategischen Unternehmensführung. In: VDI-Technologiezentrum (ed.): Technologiefrühaufklärung: Identifikation und Bewertung von Ansätzen zukünftiger Technologien, Stuttgart, pp. 3-15.

TECHNOLOGY, INNOVATION, and POLICY

Series of the Fraunhofer Institute
for Systems and Innovation Research (ISI)

Volume 1:
Kerstin Cuhls, Terutaka Kuwahara
**Outlook for Japanese and German
Future Technology**
1994. XVI, 238 pages.
ISBN 3-7908-0800-8

Volume 2:
Guido Reger, Stefan Kuhlmann
**European Technology Policy
in Germany**
1995. XII, 194 pages.
ISBN 3-7908-0826-1

Springer-Verlag
and the Environment

We at Springer-Verlag firmly believe that an international science publisher has a special obligation to the environment, and our corporate policies consistently reflect this conviction.

We also expect our business partners – paper mills, printers, packaging manufacturers, etc. – to commit themselves to using environmentally friendly materials and production processes.

The paper in this book is made from low- or no-chlorine pulp and is acid free, in conformance with international standards for paper permanency.